LIVING
ON
DEATH
ROW

D1518335

LIVING
ON
DEATH
ROW

The Psychology of
Waiting to Die

Edited by
**HANS TOCH, JAMES R. ACKER, and
VINCENT MARTIN BONVENTRE**

AMERICAN PSYCHOLOGICAL ASSOCIATION
Washington, DC

Published by
American Psychological Association
750 First Street, NE
Washington, DC 20002
www.apa.org

APA Order Department
P.O. Box 92984
Washington, DC 20090-2984
Phone: (800) 374-2721; Direct: (202) 336-5510
Fax: (202) 336-5502; TDD/TTY: (202) 336-6123
Online: http://www.apa.org/pubs/books
E-mail: order@apa.org

In the U.K., Europe, Africa, and the Middle East, copies may be ordered from
Eurospan Group
c/o Turpin Distribution
Pegasus Drive
Stratton Business Park
Biggleswade Bedfordshire
SG18 8TQ United Kingdom
Phone: +44 (0) 1767 604972
Fax: +44 (0) 1767 601640
Online: https://www.eurospanbookstore.com/apa
E-mail: eurospan@turpin-distribution.com

Typeset in Minion by Circle Graphics, Inc., Columbia, MD

Printer: Sheridan Books, Chelsea, MI
Cover Designer: Naylor Design, Washington, DC

Library of Congress Cataloging-in-Publication Data

Names: Toch, Hans, editor. | Acker, James R., 1951- editor. | Bonventre, Vincent Martin, editor.
Title: Living on death row : the psychology of waiting to die / edited by Hans Toch, James R. Acker, and Vincent Martin Bonventre.
Description: Washington, DC : American Psychological Association, [2018] | Includes bibliographical references and index.
Identifiers: LCCN 2017049014| ISBN 9781433829000 (softcover) | ISBN 1433829002 (softcover)
Subjects: LCSH: Death row—United States. | Death row inmates—United States. | Criminal psychology—United States. | Criminal justice, Administration of—United States.
Classification: LCC HV8699.U5 L58 2018 | DDC 364.6601/9—dc23 LC record available at https://lccn.loc.gov/2017049014

British Library Cataloguing-in-Publication Data
A CIP record is available from the British Library.

Printed in the United States of America
First Edition

http://dx.doi.org/10.1037/0000084-000
10 9 8 7 6 5 4 3 2 1

Contents

Contributors

Ruth Armstrong, PhD, is a senior research associate at the Institute of Criminology, University of Cambridge. She studied law at the University of Nottingham and the University of Texas before completing her PhD in criminology at Cambridge. Dr. Armstrong codirects an educational initiative called Learning Together. This initiative builds learning communities that span prison and university walls.

Diane Christian, SUNY Distinguished Teaching Professor, has been a member of the University at Buffalo English Department since 1970. She and Bruce Jackson have collaborated on five documentary films and four books, among which are *Death Row* (film, 1979), *Death Row* (book, 1980), and *"In This Timeless Time": Living and Dying on Death Row in America* (2012).

Fred Cohen is a graduate of Yale Law School and a professor emeritus at the State University of New York at Albany, School of Criminal Justice, where he is one of the original founders. He is the executive editor of the *Correctional Law Reporter* and the *Correctional Mental Health Report*, and author of *A Practical Guide to Correctional Mental Health and the Law* (2011). Mr. Cohen served as a reporter to the American Bar Association (ABA)–Institute of Judicial Administration's Juvenile Justice Standards Project and assisted in drafting the current ABA Standards for Corrections. He has provided testimony on solitary confinement at U.S. Senate hearings and before other federal commissions. Mr. Cohen works with the Jesuit Social Research Institute on bringing human rights norms and training to private correction facilities.

Kimberly J. Cook, PhD, completed her doctorate in sociology at the University of New Hampshire, and is a professor of sociology and criminology at the University of North Carolina Wilmington. With Saundra Westervelt, she coauthored *Life After Death Row: Exonerees' Search for Community and Identity* (2012). Her earlier work includes *Divided Passions: Public Opinions on Abortion and the Death Penalty* (1998). Dr. Cook is also a restorative justice practitioner and serves on the Board of Directors of the nonprofit organization, Healing Justice, founded by Jennifer Thompson.

Mark D. Cunningham, PhD, ABPP, is a board-certified clinical and forensic psychologist. He has published extensively on capital offenders, rates and correlates of prison violence, violence risk assessment at capital sentencing, and capital sentencing considerations. Dr. Cunningham received the 2012 National Register of Health Service Psychologists A. M. Welner, PhD Distinguished Career Award.

Joe D'Ambrosio was convicted and sentenced to death in 1989. In 1998 he asked Fr. Neil Kookoothe to read his trial transcript and help bring his case to the attention of the public and the courts. He was released in 2009 after a federal judge ruled that key evidence was withheld that would have refuted the State's witnesses and pointed to other individuals as perpetrators of the crime. After a lengthy and prolonged appellate process, Mr. D'Ambrosio was exonerated on January 23, 2012, when the U.S. Supreme Court denied the State's appeal of the Sixth Circuit Court of Appeals' opinion upholding the bar to his re-prosecution. Mr. D'Ambrosio is the 140th exoneree from death row in the United States and the sixth in Ohio.

Gareth Evans is currently studying criminology at Anglia Ruskin University. Mr. Evans has wide-ranging interests in criminal justice and, specifically, prison reform, inspired in part by his involvement in a Learning Together criminology program with Amy Ludlow and Ruth Armstrong. He is a member of the editorial board of the *Prison Service Journal*.

Jamie Fellner, JD, spent more than 20 years with the U.S. Program of Human Rights Watch, serving as its first director and as senior counsel. Her work focused on how the United States has failed to protect the human rights of people in the criminal justice system. She has written numerous reports documenting such abuses and has advocated extensively for changed policies and practices to bring the United States into compliance with its international human rights obligations.

Bruce Jackson, SUNY Distinguished Professor and James Agee Professor of American Culture, has been a member of the University at Buffalo (UB) English Department since 1967. He is also an affiliate professor in the UB School of Law and departments of Art and Media Studies. He is a Guggenheim Fellow and Chevalier in France's Order of Arts and Letters and National Order of Merit, and the author or editor of 35 books, including *Inside the Wire: Photographs From Texas and Arkansas Prisons* (2013).

Robert Johnson, PhD, is a professor of justice, law, and criminology at American University in Washington, DC, editor and publisher of BleakHouse Publishing, and an award-winning author of works on crime and punishment, most notably, his books *Condemned to Die: Life Under Sentence of Death* (1981) and *Death Work: A Study of the Modern Execution Process* (1998). He has testified or provided expert affidavits in capital and other criminal cases in many venues, including U.S. state and federal courts, the U.S. Congress, and the European Commission of Human Rights.

Rev. Neil Kookoothe is a native of Toledo and Catholic Priest ordained for service in the Roman Catholic Diocese of Cleveland, Ohio. Fr. Kookoothe is currently pastor of Saint Clarence Church in North Olmsted and has passionately advocated for the abolition of the death penalty. Fr. Kookoothe met Joe D'Ambrosio in 1998 while serving as spiritual advisor to several men on death row in Ohio. His experience in theology, nursing, and law drew his interest to Mr. D'Ambrosio's case, bringing attention to unresolved issues never before addressed by the legal system or the courts.

Terry A. Kupers, MD, MSP, is Professor Emeritus at The Wright Institute and Distinguished Life Fellow of the American Psychiatric Association. He provides expert testimony in class action litigation regarding the psychological effects of prison conditions. He is the author of *Solitary: The*

Inside Story of Supermax Isolation and How We Can Abolish It (2017), and is a contributing editor of *Correctional Mental Health Report*. Dr. Kupers received the 2005 Exemplary Psychiatrist Award from the National Alliance on Mental Illness.

Charles S. Lanier is a part-time lecturer at the School of Criminal Justice, University at Albany, and president of Lanier Consulting and Research, Inc. He has conducted mitigation investigations in death penalty cases for over 20 years and also worked as a corrections/reentry and sentencing consultant. He has written numerous articles about incarcerated fathers and developed parenting programs for prisoners. He is coeditor of *America's Experiment With Capital Punishment: Reflections on the Past, Present, and Future of the Ultimate Penal Sanction* (3rd ed., 2014).

Amy Ludlow, PhD, is a senior research associate at the Institute of Criminology at the University of Cambridge. She has an MA in law from the University of Cambridge, an LLM from the Kathoelike Universiteit in Leuven, Belgium, and a PhD from the University of Cambridge. Dr. Ludlow has conducted research in prisons, focusing especially on organizational reforms. Her current major project is Learning Together with Ruth Armstrong, an initiative that builds learning communities bridging prison and university walls and is yielding new insights into the role of dialogic communal learning in preventing crime.

Shadd Maruna, PhD, is a professor of criminology at the University of Manchester and has previously taught at Rutgers University, the University of Cambridge, and the University at Albany, State University of New York. His book *Making Good: How Ex-Convicts Reform and Rebuild Their Lives* (2001) was named the Outstanding Contribution to Criminology by the American Society of Criminology in 2001.

Ian O'Donnell, PhD, LLD, is a professor of criminology at University College Dublin and a Fellow of the British Psychological Society. His most recent book is *Justice, Mercy, and Caprice: Clemency and the Death Penalty in Ireland* (2017).

Eleanor Price, BA (Hons), studied politics, psychology, and sociology at the University of Cambridge. She coauthored a paper on rapport-building in investigative interviews, which was published in the *Journal of Applied Cognitive Psychology*. Following graduation, she was an intern with the Texas Defender Service in Austin and managed the digital content of The Exceptionals, an online campaign that aims to inspire employers to hire people with convictions. Ms. Price is now completing her teacher training through the Teach First program, and she hopes to work with young people in the criminal justice system.

Jonathan Reed is a writer, dominoes champion, godfather, son, brother, and friend (to Ruth Armstrong, among others). In 1978, he was convicted of murder and spent over 30 years on death row in Texas. His conviction was overturned twice, and in 2011, despite exclusionary DNA evidence, he was once again convicted on the basis of eyewitness testimony alone. Mr. Reed is currently serving a life sentence and continues to protest his innocence of this offense while working toward the hope of parole.

Thomas J. Reidy, PhD, ABPP, is a clinical and forensic psychologist in Monterey, California. He has published numerous articles, most related to violence risk assessment, particularly in homicide and capital homicide cases. Dr. Reidy provides forensic evaluations for federal and state courts on a variety of topics, primarily involving violence risk and homicide. He also consults worldwide with the U.S. military.

Meredith Martin Rountree, JD, PhD, is a senior lecturer at Northwestern Pritzker School of Law. Her research focuses on how people with mental illness intersect with the law and legal institutions. Her work has been published in the *Law and Society Review* and the *Journal of Criminal Law and Criminology*. Before academic research, she represented people facing the death penalty. She graduated from Yale College, earned a law degree from Georgetown University Law Center, and a doctorate in sociology from the University of Texas at Austin.

Jonathan R. Sorensen, PhD, is a professor of criminal justice at East Carolina University. He also works as a trial consultant and expert witness. His research focuses on prison violence and capital punishment.

Saundra D. Westervelt, PhD, earned her doctorate in sociology from the University of Virginia and is a professor of sociology at the University of North Carolina Greensboro. Her research and teaching areas include criminology, law and society, and family violence, with a particular focus on the wrongful conviction of the innocent. Most recently, her work, with colleague Kim Cook, examines life after exoneration, including the book *Life After Death Row: Exonerees' Search for Community and Identity* (2012). Dr. Westervelt served for many years on the board of Witness to Innocence, the nation's only organization composed of death row exonerees and their families.

Gabe Whitbread, MA, is a doctoral student in justice, law, and criminology at American University in Washington, DC. Her primary research interests are prison reform and the ethics of punishment. Specifically, her work centers on cognitive behavioral therapy programming and restorative justice as alternative approaches to addressing crime. Before starting her graduate studies, she worked with Legal Aid on prisoner's rights issues.

Jeanne Woodford began her career at San Quentin State Prison in 1978, following graduation from Sonoma State University with a BA in criminal justice. She was appointed warden of San Quentin in 1999 and remained in that position until 2004, when she was named the director of the California Department of Corrections and Rehabilitation (CDCR), the largest correctional system in the United States. The following year she became the undersecretary of the CDCR. Ms. Woodford retired as the chief of the San Francisco Adult Probation Department in 2008 and later served, through 2013, as executive director of Death Penalty Focus, a national organization committed to ending the death penalty.

Foreword

Jamie Fellner

Years ago, I interviewed a man on Oklahoma's death row who was scheduled to be executed in a few weeks. I didn't know what to say at the end of our meeting—the usual goodbye platitudes were woefully incommensurate with his reality. So I silently embraced him. Correctional officers rushed into the room where we were meeting because no one was permitted physical contact with a condemned inmate. Prison policies even prohibited his mother from hugging him on the eve of execution. The cruel callousness of denying mother and son a final loving embrace was my introduction to death row—the plethora of rules and regimes ostensibly imposed on the condemned to protect prison security, but in reality imposed to express opprobrium and maybe just plain vindictiveness beyond that inherent in the death sentence itself.

The criminal justice system in the United States is dominated by misguided policies rooted in prejudice, anger, fear, and scant regard for the humanity of those accused or convicted of breaking the law. The death penalty and its concomitant, death row, exemplify the cruelty and disregard for human dignity and human rights that pass for justice. Because I am an optimist, I despair but nonetheless have hope. The willingness of advocates, academics, and people who have been or are still in the system to document and speak out against abuse undergirds my belief that time is on our side. Someday the country will have a criminal justice system it can be proud of: one that honors the dignity and respects the human rights of every person.

But meanwhile, at mid-year 2016, the United States had 2,905 persons condemned to death in state and federal prisons. The average length of time they will spend on death row is over 10 years, and for many, it will be 2 decades or more. *Living on Death Row* illuminates their struggle to remain human in inhumane circumstances. The authors, including individuals who formerly were consigned to death row, shed light on a hidden world of solitary confinement, daily deprivations, senseless and degrading security rules and protocols, abuse, and mistreatment.

The physical and psychological torments of solitary confinement—often further aggravated by appalling conditions—in today's U.S. prisons have been extensively documented. Less attention has been paid, however, to the way those torments are exacerbated when those who are isolated await execution. Condemned prisoners are treated as though they are highly dangerous—even though the evidence suggests they pose less of a security risk than other prisoners. Because of the uniquely dehumanizing treatment officials often inflict on them, those incarcerated with a death sentence experience "death before dying." For some, the treatment culminates in being a "dead man walking" to the execution chamber.

The anguish of awaiting death and the uncertainty of when the execution might take place also heighten the risk of mental harm from solitary confinement. Psychologists and lawyers have argued that protracted time on death row can make inmates suicidal, delusional, and insane, labeling the unique psychological results a "death row syndrome." The psychological, emotional, and spiritual pain can be so intense that some prisoners end their legal appeals so they can be executed sooner rather than later, preferring death to the cruelty and suffering of life on death row.

Historically, the time on death row in the United States was brief: Execution followed swiftly after the trial court announced the sentence. But in the last 3 decades, the length of time between trial court judgment and execution has tripled as postsentencing appeals challenging flawed death penalty laws and criminal procedures make their way through the courts. In thousands of death cases, the lengthy appeals process has uncovered crucial mistakes and errors that invalidated the sentence. Indeed, researchers have shown that about 40% of the death sentences imposed between 1973 and 2013 were overturned on appeal. Less than one quarter of those originally condemned to die were executed.

The most likely outcome of a death sentence today is the eventual reversal and a new sentence that will keep the inmate in prison. But although most condemned inmates will avoid the cruelty of execution, they will endure excruciatingly painful years on death row before their sentence is reduced or their conviction overturned. Unfortunately, many who will remain in prison will be serving sentences of life without the possibility of parole—itself a sentence that cannot be squared with human dignity.

Under current constitutional jurisprudence in the United States, the death penalty is permitted, as is prolonged solitary confinement—including on death row. In contrast, international human rights law favors abolition of the death penalty and recognizes that prolonged solitary—including on death row—can be impermissibly cruel, inhuman, and degrading. Indeed, it may even constitute torture.

Almost 3 decades ago in *Soering v. The United Kingdom*, the European Court of Human Rights considered the human rights implications of the extradition of a person from the United Kingdom to Virginia, where he would be tried for murder and might be sentenced to death. Although the death penalty was not deemed a per se violation of human rights, the court ruled that the extradition would present a real risk of prohibited cruel treatment given "the very long period of time spent on death row in such extreme conditions, with the ever present and mounting anguish of awaiting execution and the death penalty" ("Conclusion," para. 2).[1]

After reviewing human rights jurisprudence and commentary regarding death row, Juan Méndez, the former United Nations Special Rapporteur on Torture and Other Cruel, Inhuman or Degrading Treatment or Punishment, concluded in 2012 that

> individuals held in solitary confinement suffer extreme forms of sensory deprivation, anxiety, and exclusion, clearly surpassing lawful conditions of deprivation of liberty. Solitary confinement used

[1] Soering v. The United Kingdom, 1/1989/161/217, Council of Europe: European Court of Human Rights (1989). Retrieved from http://www.refworld.org/cases,ECHR,3ae6b6fec.html

on death row is by definition prolonged and indefinite, and thus constitutes cruel, inhuman or degrading treatment or punishment, or even torture. (p. 12)[2]

Death row will remain a feature of U.S. criminal justice for the foreseeable future because the demise of capital punishment in the United States is not imminent. Not only does it remain on the books in 31 states and the federal government, but in the November 2016 elections, voters in three states (California, Nebraska, and Oklahoma) approved pro–death penalty measures. Many Americans still believe that those who kill should be killed as a matter of morality and justice for the victims. President Donald Trump is a death penalty supporter and has pledged to add strong conservatives to the United States Supreme Court, making a Supreme Court ruling that the death penalty is unconstitutional highly unlikely in the foreseeable future.

Nevertheless, there is evidence that the death penalty is slowly releasing its tenacious grip on the nation. Governors have imposed moratoriums in four death penalty states, polls mark the decline in public support nationwide, the number of new capital sentences is minuscule (30 in 2016), the number of people executed in a year now barely reaches two digits (20 in 2016), and prosecutors and judges are less likely to lose their positions for anything less than full-throated embrace of state-sponsored executions.

The long-term trend against capital punishment almost certainly reflects many factors: the decrease in violent crime as a significant political issue, the financial cost to the state of prolonged litigation in capital cases, concern about the execution of innocent defendants, the availability of life without parole as an alternative sentence, the growing realization that the death penalty does not deter violent crime, and mounting evidence that the likelihood of the death penalty being imposed in a case is determined less by the "heinousness" of the crime and more by such factors as the county in which the crime is prosecuted, the predilections of individual prosecutors, inadequate public defenders, and the race of the defendants and victims.

---

[2]United Nations General Assembly. (2012). *Interim report of the Special Rapporteur on torture and other cruel, inhuman or degrading treatment or punishment*. Retrieved from https://digitallibrary. un.org/record/733853/files/A_67_279-EN.pdf

Americans may also be increasingly discomfited by the reality of killings in cold blood: handcuffed men and women led into an execution chamber, strapped to a gurney, and injected with lethal chemicals in a choreographed ritual involving guards, medical technicians, wardens, and witnesses. A growing number of religious leaders argue that the death penalty contradicts core religious principles of mercy, redemption, and the right to life—and even that the Old Testament injunction of an "eye for an eye" often cited by death penalty supporters does not, in fact, require a killing to punish a killing.

As a human rights advocate, I would like to believe that ever more Americans also realize that human dignity—the cornerstone of internationally recognized human rights—cannot be squared with executions and that the death penalty is inherently cruel, inhuman, and degrading, in violation of human rights law. The death penalty should also be condemned because of the prolonged period of life on death row and the horror of uncertainty while awaiting execution. Because of the countless flaws in capital cases, a careful—and inevitably lengthy—review process is indispensable to uncover mistakes and attempt to ensure justice.

Conditions for the condemned can certainly be ameliorated. I hope that *Living on Death Row* will at least prompt public elected officials and corrections officials to reconsider the bleak, cruel prison regimes of isolation and deprivation they needlessly impose on individuals sentenced to death. Indeed, they should reconsider the necessity or wisdom of separating those individuals from other prisoners, absent special factors in individual cases that suggest a need for extra security precautions.

I believe *Living on Death Row* will also prompt a serious rethinking of the death penalty. Even if those condemned to die have the same conditions of confinement as other prisoners (conditions that can be appalling in any event) or even if they are confined in "kinder, gentler" death rows, the cruelty of awaiting execution would remain. I see no way around the conundrum—being condemned by a court to die means being condemned to a painful period of waiting. From a human rights perspective, both are intolerable.

As those who have read them know, international human rights treaties are written in dry, legalistic language. But they express the inspired—and inspiring—affirmation of the dignity of every human being, even those who have committed heinous crimes. Within a human rights paradigm, a criminal conviction is not license for whatever sentence legislators choose to authorize, nor does it justify whatever wretched prison conditions some corrections officials might favor.

The United States has ratified several core human rights treaties, but with the proviso that they cannot be enforced in U.S. courts. Those treaties nonetheless offer a vision of justice grounded in human dignity that should guide all public officials. Human rights law insists on accountability for crime but also insists that the rights and dignity of victims are not vindicated by trampling the rights and dignity of those who have victimized them.

I am an optimist because I choose to believe that sooner or later the United States will choose a system of justice of which it can be proud. It will be a system without the death penalty, without prolonged solitary confinement, and without death row. It will be a system that rejects cruelty, pursues mercy and redemption, and affirms the dignity and humanity of each and every one of us.

Acknowledgments

The editors gratefully acknowledge many helpful suggestions and sound guidance offered by David Becker, who has made our volume stronger and our association with APA Books all the more rewarding.

LIVING
ON
DEATH
ROW

Introduction

Hans Toch, James R. Acker, and Vincent Martin Bonventre

Death row. This bleak sobriquet evokes correspondingly foreboding imagery: adjoining cells made of bars of cold steel, ensconced deep within prison walls, inhabited by an assemblage of doomed offenders who mark the relentless passage of time that alone separates them from death by execution. As of April 1, 2017, there were 2,843 prisoners under sentence of death in the United States. The 2,790 men and 53 women awaited execution in 32 states and pursuant to U.S. Military and federal authority. Racially and ethnically diverse (42% White, non-Hispanic; 42% Black; 13% Hispanic; 3% of another race), the condemned are unevenly distributed throughout the country's death penalty jurisdictions. California houses more than one-quarter of the nation's death-sentenced prisoners (744), followed in size by Florida (386), Texas (247), and Alabama (193). In contrast, three or fewer inmates await execution in six states, including New Hampshire and Wyoming, which each house a single condemned prisoner (NAACP Legal Defense and Educational Fund, Inc., 2017).

http://dx.doi.org/10.1037/0000084-001

Living on Death Row: The Psychology of Waiting to Die, H. Toch, J. R. Acker, and V. M. Bonventre (Editors)

The United States Supreme Court's ruling in *Furman v. Georgia* emptied the country's death rows in 1972 when five justices concluded that the capital sentencing laws then in effect could not be squared with the Eighth Amendment's prohibition against cruel and unusual punishments. New death sentences began accumulating the following year, as capital murder prosecutions resumed under revised death penalty laws that would later meet with the Court's approval (*Gregg v. Georgia*, 1976; *Jurek v. Texas*, 1976; *Proffitt v. Florida*, 1976). In the ensuing 4 decades, 8,466 persons were sentenced to death, yet only a minority (16.1%) within that time span had been executed. More than one third (37.7%) had their murder conviction or death sentence vacated between 1973 and 2013, including more than 150 (1.8%) who were exonerated. Nearly 5% saw their capital sentence commuted to a lesser punishment, whereas 6% died of natural causes. The rest remained under sentence of death (Death Penalty Information Center, 2017b; Snell, 2014; Williams & Murry, 2016).

Nearly half the inmates currently awaiting execution have been confined for at least 15 years, including more than 200 who have been incarcerated for more than 3 decades. The 20 prisoners executed in 2016 remained under sentence of death an average of 18½ years, including two from Georgia who were incarcerated for 34 and 36 years before dying by lethal injection (Christopher, 2016, p. 855; Death Penalty Information Center, 2017a; *Glossip v. Gross*, 2015, pp. 2764–2765, Breyer, J., dissenting; Snell, 2014). The prisoners who endure such prolonged incarceration in anticipation of execution routinely do so under conditions of extreme privation. In almost all jurisdictions, death-sentenced inmates are subjected to highly restrictive regimes of isolation, minimal out-of-cell time, and exclusion from programming and other amenities available to most other inmates (American Civil Liberties Union, 2013; Arthur Liman Public Interest Program, Yale Law School, 2016; Human Rights Clinic, University of Texas School of Law, 2017; Robles, 2017). Although death-sentenced inmates, with a few notable exceptions, are routinely required to subsist for years under conditions more severely restrictive than the normal incidents of incarceration, they do so in all but a handful of jurisdictions because of internal prison regulations rather than by legislative or judicial command (McLeod, 2016).

Putting to one side the issue of their legality, it is fair to question the necessity, wisdom, and also the fundamental decency of perpetuating the traditional attributes of death row confinement. These premises explain the impetus for this volume. In the chapters that follow, the book's contributors offer distinctive and overlapping perspectives about issues of psychology, law, corrections policy, and essential human dignity implicated in connection with rationales for death row confinement and the consequences of experiencing life under sentence of death.

HISTORY AND LEGALITY OF DEATH ROW IN THE UNITED STATES

Although marking the days until a date with the executioner would be debilitating for most people under any circumstances, both the duration and conditions of contemporary death row confinement raise issues of a different order of magnitude than prevailed earlier in this country's history. Capital punishment was practiced throughout colonial America and in all of the original states, but neither death rows nor extended preexecution delays were a feature of early death penalty regimes. Neither the facilities nor the need for the congregate confinement of condemned offenders existed at the time of the nation's founding.

The first state prisons were constructed in the 1790s, but prisons did not proliferate in the United States until after the turn of the 19th century (Rothman, 1971, pp. 60–61). Offenders, including those sentenced to death, were necessarily housed in county jails. Hangings occurred in the county where the offense was committed, in town squares, or another public venue, commonly attracting large and raucous audiences (Bannon, 2002, pp. 144–168; Linders, 2002; Masur, 1989). Executions gradually receded from public view, yet the states did not begin conducting executions centrally until after the close of the Civil War. Executions continued to be carried out locally in parts of the country, sometimes publicly, well into the 20th century (Bannon, 2002, p. 143; Bedau, 1982, pp. 12–13; Bowers, 1984, pp. 13–14). With capital offenders thus originally confined in county jails and executed in local venues, death rows simply were not needed to house the condemned.

Protracted confinement under sentence of death was similarly unheard of historically. During colonial times, executions might follow as soon as 2 to 4 days after sentencing (Aarons, 1998; Mackey, 1982). In keeping with common law tradition (Foucault, 1977; Gatrell, 1994), enough delay was typically indulged to afford offenders an opportunity to acknowledge their transgressions and offer public penitence (Bannon, 2002; Masur, 1989). Appeals were unavailable or were resolved expeditiously by courts throughout early statehood, including in capital cases. Executions thus generally occurred within a year of sentencing into the early 20th century. The average delay between the imposition of a death sentence and execution grew to approximately three years between 1930 and the mid-1960s (Aarons, 1998). The country's last pre-*Furman* execution occurred in 1967. Luis Jose Monge had remained under sentence of death for roughly 3½ years before dying in Colorado's gas chamber (Bowers, 1984; *Monge v. People*, 1965).

The U.S. Supreme Court's rulings in the wake of *Furman*, in *Gregg v. Georgia* (1976) and companion cases, spawned a vastly more demanding jurisprudence that was designed to harness capital sentencing discretion while still allowing consideration of relevant individual case circumstances. The new era ushered in a mandate for heightened reliability and corresponding layers of judicial review in death penalty cases. The rounds of appeals detected numerous serious errors. Roughly two thirds of capital convictions or sentences imposed between 1973 and 1995 were vacated by later court action (Liebman, Fagan, & West, 2000). The time required for the multiple levels of judicial scrutiny resulted in ever-increasing delays in cases that ended in execution. Inmates executed in 1984 spent just over 6 years under sentence of death. By 2004, the average gap between sentence and execution nearly doubled, to 11 years (Christopher, 2016; Death Penalty Information Center, 2017a; Snell, 2014). As noted earlier, significantly longer delays, now often measured in decades, are currently the norm.

The Supreme Court first expressed concerns about exposing prisoners awaiting execution to solitary confinement well over a century ago, in *In re Medley* (1890), a case in which a Colorado prisoner challenged (on ex post facto grounds) his being consigned to an isolation cell for 4 weeks before his scheduled hanging. Ruling in the prisoner's favor, the justices deemed the month-long stay in solitary confinement "an additional punishment of the most important and painful character" (*In re Medley*, 1890, p. 171). More recently, various Supreme Court justices have registered their views that prolonged death row confinement can support a claimed violation of the Eighth Amendment's cruel and unusual punishments clause.

Justice Brennan's concurring opinion in *Furman v. Georgia* (1972) noted that "the prospect of pending execution exacts a frightful toll during the inevitable long wait between the imposition of sentence and the actual infliction of death" (p. 288). As increasingly lengthy delays between death sentences and executions became normative in the post-*Furman* era, Justice Stevens began urging the Court to take up the question of whether executing a prisoner who has already spent years of confinement on death row violates the Eighth Amendment (*Lackey v. Texas*, 1995, dissenting from denial of certiorari). He persisted in insisting that such "*Lackey* claims" (Newton, 2012) merited the Court's attention in later cases (e.g., *Gomez v. Fierro*, 1996; *Johnson v. Bredesen*, 2009; *Thompson v. McNeil*, 2009). Justice Stevens's position came to be echoed by Justice Breyer (e.g., *Glossip v. Gross*, 2015, dissenting; *Knight v. Florida*, 1999; *Ruiz v. Texas*, 2017). The full Supreme Court nevertheless has declined to address the issue (see Sharkey, 2013), although condemned prisoners continue to urge the justices to consider it (e.g., Petition for a Writ of Certiorari, *Moore v. Texas*, 2015). Justice Kennedy recently weighed in on the issue in *Davis v. Ayala* (2015, pp. 2208–2209, concurring):

> Since being sentenced to death in 1989, Ayala has served the great majority of his more than 25 years in custody in . . . solitary confinement. . . . It is likely [he] has been held . . . in a windowless cell no larger than a typical parking spot for 23 hours a day. . . . One hundred and twenty-five years ago, this Court recognized that, even for prisoners sentenced to death, solitary confinement bears "a further terror and peculiar mark of infamy," *In re Medley*, 134 U.S. 160, 170 (1890). . . . Too often, discussion in the legal academy and among practitioners and policymakers concentrates simply on the adjudication of guilt or innocence. Too easily ignored is the question of what comes next.

Lower court rulings involving death rows in Louisiana (*Ball v. LeBlanc*, 2015) and Mississippi (*Gates v. Cook*, 2004) have declared that specific aspects of prisoners' confinement, including exposure to excessive heat, lack of sanitation, inadequate mental health care, and inadequate lighting, subjected the incarcerated to cruel and unusual punishment. The Fourth Circuit Court of Appeals recently revived a challenge to the conditions of confinement on Virginia's death row, rejecting the district court's conclusion that the case had become moot after prison officials altered several preexisting policies (*Porter v. Clarke*, 2017). Courts have rejected broad-based challenges to death row conditions in other states (e.g., *Chandler v. Crosby*, 2004 [Florida]; *Peterkin v. Jeffes*, 1988 [Pennsylvania]), and many have ruled that prolonged stays on death row in combination with the restrictive conditions of confinement do not violate prisoners' Eighth Amendment rights (e.g., *Allen v. Ornoski*, 2006; *Johns v. Bowersox*, 2000; *Moore v. State*, 2002; *Pardo v. State*, 2012; *State v. Moore*, 1999; *State v. Schackart*, 1997; *Thompson v. Secretary Dept. Corrections*, 2008).

In contrast, prisoners awaiting execution in other countries have gained judicial recognition that lengthy incarceration under sentence of death is inhumane and denies fundamental human rights (Brief of International Law and Human Rights Institutes, Societies, Practitioners and Scholars, *Moore v. Texas*, 2016; Christopher, 2015, pp. 23–28; *Knight v. Florida*, 1999, pp. 462–463, Breyer, J., dissenting from denial of certiorari; Sadoff, 2008; Tongue, 2015). And while invalidating early death penalty laws pursuant to their respective state constitutions, the Supreme Court of California (*People v. Anderson*, 1972) and members of the Massachusetts Supreme Judicial Court (*Suffolk County District Attorney v. Watson*, 1980, p. 1287, Braucher, J., concurring; pp. 1289–1295, Liacos, J., concurring) recognized prolonged death row confinement as contributing to the cruelty of capital punishment.

SURVIVING ON DEATH ROW

Living conditions on death row have tended to be purposefully inhospitable on the basis of the presumption that those who end up subjected to these custodial settings are not only the most serious possible offenders but are also extra-tough and predatory individuals who pose a continuing danger to others. As we shall be able to show, this widely advertised concern about the danger posed by death row prisoners is unsupported by evidence. However, the evidence does show us that a disproportionate number of terminally confined individuals experience serious mental health problems, and that their disabilities are predictably aggravated by the onerous conditions of confinement to which we have subjected them. In other words, we have gone on to respond to those we deem the worst of the worst by transmuting them into the worst-off.

Though dead men tell no tales, those who believe they are about to die or have spent years threatened with death and been narrowly reprieved can not only tell us a great deal about their experience but, if they are given the opportunity, can also eloquently write about it. This capability not only provides us with an invaluable source of vivid and persuasive information but also introduces us to exciting new options for collaborative inquiry.

As a side benefit, participation in such a retrospect is obviously helpful to a prisoner who is faced with the task of digesting his traumatic experiences in the course of recovering from them. This particularly mattered for contributors to our book who had spent years on death row proclaiming their innocence before they were finally exonerated and could begin to envisage the possibility of escaping from confinement. These were persons who had to endure the deprivations of their marginal existence on death row with the added pain and bitterness of knowing themselves unjustly sequestered, with minuscule hopes of redress.

And yet these are among the favored few among the denizens of death row, not only because they had been able to consistently conceive of the possibility of being released but also because they had somehow acquired or retained a group of supporters in the outside world who had reinforced and supported their beliefs. On the other extreme of the death row spectrum are the prisoners described in Chapter 6 who have testified to their lack of resources, hopelessness, and despair by "volunteering" for execution.

We are learning, however, that inhospitable conditions that demonstrably do a great deal of harm also occasionally offer surprising opportunities by providing challenges that the more resilient among death row prisoners have tackled and very often met, thus displaying surprising skill and resourcefulness and demonstrating an impressive capacity to adapt to adverse circumstances. We shall see, by reviewing daily routines that are painfully eked out on death row, evidence of the ingenuity that has to be continuously exercised on death row in evolving the approaches and strategies that enable some of the prisoners to survive an existence of incredible boredom and hopelessness.

There are reputedly gradations in hell. Prisons may be the secular equivalent, and they also offer gradations. The standard classification process deployed in every prison sorts inmates into categories that are based on the danger the prisoners are presumed to pose, and these categories determine the prisoners' placement under custodial regimens of varying severity and degrees of onerousness of living conditions. As the prisoners continue to serve their sentence, they (and presumably, the denizens of hell) then become eligible for gradual reclassification and consequent promotion to settings that are increasingly less depriving.

Death row prisoners fall at the bottom end of these prison classification schemes and always stay there, no matter how long the prisoners remain on death row. Careers on death row are consequently invariably endlessly static and hope depriving. The physical death row settings have also remained static over time, and they have continued to replicate an outdated medieval modality of prison design that has heartlessly imposed unmitigated solitary confinement.

It has become increasingly obvious that this situation has been inimical to psychological survival, and this realization has been the impetus for incipient reform. Newly ameliorated death rows are thus beginning to offer a few requisites and conditions for long-term existence and coexistence, such as means and opportunities to communicate among the prisoners.[1] As these modest changes have unfolded, it has become obvious that they have not only redounded to the benefit of the prisoners but have also appreciably improved the quality of life for the staff who work with them. Moreover, none of the risks or dangers of presumptive initial concern in the classification of death row prisoners have been observed, nor have any safety or security concerns arisen for death row prisoners who are increasingly being released into the general prison population.

---

[1] For example, death-sentenced prisoners in North Carolina have formed competitive basketball teams and play games against one another within Central Prison (May, 2017).

As prisoners spend increasing amounts of time on death rows awaiting executions that do not eventuate—or that eventuate much less frequently—we must face the reality that death rows have become transmuted into indefinite long-term storage depots. The prisoners who live in such enclaves are bound to sense that they have been relegated to serving life sentences without the possibility of parole but that they must continue to be stigmatized by the system as capital offenders. They will know they have to continue living with the ambiguity and uncertainty of their precarious situation.

The increasing number of prisoners whose sentences are bound to be vacated or commuted will concurrently have to work through the more or less nominal change of status to ex-capital offender and death row alumnus. There will be some challenges in this transition not only for the prisoners themselves but also for fellow prisoners, staff, administrators, and the public.

OVERVIEW OF THE BOOK

By dint of their remarkably diverse experiences and qualifications, the contributors to this volume are exceptionally well positioned to provide insights into the multiple and layered dimensions of death row confinement. The chapter authors include the former warden of San Quentin Prison, home to the nation's largest complement of death-sentenced prisoners; psychiatrists and psychologists, some of whom have evaluated inmates who have endured years of death row confinement and others who have systematically studied how such long-term confinement affects the incarcerated; social scientists whose research sheds light on assumptions made about the dangerousness of prisoners under sentence of death and the related issues of institutional security and the safety of correctional staff charged with their supervision; legal scholars who address constitutional questions associated with extended death row confinement; and individuals who experienced imprisonment for years in anticipation of execution and offer their unique perspectives about subsistence under a sentence of death and its consequences.

Multiple audiences will find something of value in the varied chapter offerings. Mental health professionals will gain greater familiarity with the conditions confronting prisoners under sentence of death. They may consider working in a clinical capacity with individuals so confined, helping with the risk assessment and classification of death-sentenced offenders where used, evaluating the effects of institutional policies on death-sentenced inmates' mental health, and conducting related research. Corrections officials will learn more about research that has focused on the institutional behavior of prisoners under sentence of death; the profound psychological consequences of prolonged confinement on death row; and the different strategies available for housing death-sentenced prisoners, including their possible benefits and drawbacks. They will also gain a fuller understanding of governing legal doctrine. Members of the legal community—lawyers and judges—and policy advocates will benefit from the insights provided by mental health professionals, corrections personnel, and other chapter authors, particularly with respect to matters important to the enforcement of constitutional norms and correctional management. And any reader who has not visited a death row, let alone experienced confinement under sentence of death, will gain a much deeper appreciation of what life on death row entails, especially through those chapters whose authors have existed under those conditions.

The first three chapters of this volume (Part I) provide an introductory survey of the physical environment and the political and legal landscape of death row, as well as of the treatment of death row inmates. In Chapter 1, Jeanne Woodford addresses the lengthy delays in carrying out executions of death-sentenced inmates. Having served as the warden and head of a prison system, her observations are particularly compelling. As she notes, the law has evolved to generate issues on the demands of due process and the restrictions on cruelty. And yet, this very allowance of increasingly varied appeals and collateral challenges means increased time on death row, sometimes extending through decades.

In Chapter 2, Terry A. Kupers provides damning insight on life in solitary confinement. Kupers, an experienced psychiatrist, describes the "incredibly cruel punishment" to which death-sentenced inmates are condemned in supermaximum security units. Having toured numerous isolative confinement units over the years, Kupers recounts the pain, despair, physical and mental trauma, and the pathological behaviors he has witnessed. Ultimately, he questions any penological purpose as well as the basic morality of such "immense and unnecessary suffering."

In the third and final chapter of Part I, Robert Johnson and Gabe Whitbread review the literature on life on death row and the effects on the lives of the inmates. The authors identify recurring themes in the descriptions of death row existence: dreadful conditions, abusive treatment, lack of basic medical services, mental and emotional deterioration, and deprivation of adequate physical activity or even minimal sensory stimulation—in short, "living death."

Part II explores constitutional questions that arise in challenges to death row and to the treatment of death-sentenced inmates, as well as the legitimacy and wisdom of the policies that segregate those inmates from others and subject them to long-term solitary confinement. In Chapter 4, Fred Cohen provides a veritable primer on the constitutional case law having a bearing on the extended isolation of death row inmates, and he outlines the basics of a legal blueprint for further advances in the amelioration of the cruelty those inmates are made to endure. As Cohen explains, although the federal constitution explicitly prohibits "cruel and unusual punishments," current Supreme Court interpretation distinguishes cruel conditions from the prohibited "punishment" or sentence itself. Moreover, despite the Court's repeated incorporation of "evolving standards of decency" into its death penalty jurisprudence, it has nevertheless been hesitant to prohibit any form of punishment other than that which involves the deliberate infliction of entirely gratuitous and wanton pain.

Chapter 5 examines and challenges the traditional justifications proffered for the isolated confinement of death-sentenced inmates. Mark D. Cunningham, Thomas J. Reidy, and Jonathan R. Sorensen identify the various rationales customarily asserted for the segregated, extremely restrictive conditions that characterize death row in most American jurisdictions. Inmates condemned to execution, the arguments go, are especially violent, desperate, more likely to attempt escape, and much less responsive to conduct-corrective measures. A critical flaw with such claims, the authors assert, is that the restrictive and isolating conditions of death row solitary confinement actually produce the psychological distress and disorders that lead to or aggravate the feared behavioral dysfunctions.

In Chapter 6, Meredith Martin Rountree examines the phenomenon of death-sentenced inmates choosing to abandon legal recourses and proceed to execution. Approximately one in 10 executions in this country involve inmates who had decided against contesting their convictions or sentences. Among the questions the author probes is whether mental illness, hopelessness, and psychological deterioration—effectuated either by an inmate's adverse life experiences, the conditions and treatment on death row, or a combination of these and other factors—actually belie any truly knowing, voluntary, and intelligent decision by the inmate to relinquish legal rights and surrender to execution.

The chapters in Part III address the question, How can a person who has been locked away for extended periods of time under the most adverse possible conditions go about mitigating the pain, ameliorating the stress, and transcending the limited opportunity structure of his stultifying environment? The conventional way of dealing with this question is to refuse to ask it. Ian O'Donnell, the prominent Irish criminologist, thus points out in Chapter 7 that by limiting attention, as we habitually do, to "destructive consequences," readers are invited to "ignore the heroic efforts that some of the most marginalized among us have made . . . to bear potentially unbearable circumstances" (p. 194). The "heroic efforts" that O'Donnell alludes to are subsumed by the authors of Chapters 7 to 9 under the rubric of "doing time," which is the enterprise in which we assume all prisoners to be engaging. In his chapter, O'Donnell describes the difficulty facing the prisoners over time by recalling the relationship between experienced events and memory delineated by the pioneering psychologist William James (1961)—a phenomenon O'Donnell calls *time's paradox*. James had pointed out that a period in which nothing noteworthy occurs tends to come across as lasting a long time but that the same period will appear in retrospect to have been fleeting and insignificant. O'Donnell notes that this situation does not redound to the benefit of prisoners—particularly, prisoners sequestered in death rows. He describes courses of action that serve to facilitate the doing of time, such as the inmate associating himself with a meaningful cause or keeping himself constructively occupied and retaining his focus on the present, as opposed to a past that he cannot change and a future that features the uninviting prospect of his eventual execution.

Prison systems have traditionally exercised considerable ingenuity in setting up situations that were designed to obstruct the few coping strategies that had remained available to the most resilient and enterprising prisoners. By far the most popular of these vehicles for interfering with psychological survival among inmates has been to increase their isolation. In Chapter 8, Bruce Jackson and Diane Christian provide heartrending testimonials to the success of this approach, as exercised in the Texas state prison system. Jackson and Christian document how the closing off of modest avenues of psychological survival can appreciably impair mental health among the relocated prisoners, driving several over the brink.

Chapter 9 is based on an analysis of correspondence with a long-term inmate (Jonathan Reed) who lived under both "old" and "new" versions of death row in the Texas system and who managed to survive both of them during decades of confinement. In letters to his sponsors, the inmate (Jon) provides many particulars designed to document his observation that even under the most restrictive conditions, dedicated and motivated prisoners find ways of circumventing an onerous prison regime by communicating with each other and by eking out some semblance of a marginal existence. In a personal vein, Jon describes his approach to prison adjustment with a focus on living in the immediate present, highlighting the emphasis on a superordinate goal, which in his case includes work on his appeals and a continued claim to his innocence. The authors of Chapter 9 conclude by asserting that their study exemplifies a collaborative approach to doing prison research, which in the case of their research yielded "powerful lessons in Jon's life for understanding human adaptations to extreme situations of routine trauma, loss, and isolation" (p. 251).

The chapters in Part IV feature the perspectives of individuals who spent years in prison under sentence of death before justice system officials acknowledged their wrongful conviction for capital murder and released them from custody to reenter free society. They are survivors in the sense that they escaped death row without being executed. However, they did not escape without suffering. We get glimpses from these chapters into what life is like under sentence of death and how individuals who have spent time on death row continue to be affected by what they have experienced. In Chapter 10, Joe D'Ambrosio in collaboration with Rev. Neil Kookoothe, his friend and a Catholic priest (as well as an attorney and licensed nurse), provide a vividly moving account of the dehumanizing privations that characterized his 22 years of incarceration on Ohio's death row. He describes the indignities, isolation, and fractured external relationships that not only marked those years but also robbed him of countless irreplaceable life experiences and opportunities and left scars that remain 5 years after his exoneration and release from prison. Still, D'Ambrosio disavows bitterness. He demonstrates a defiant resilience and a determination to reclaim and live a fulfilling life rather than lose more of it to the oppressive weight of his years spent on death row.

The title of Charles S. Lanier's Chapter 11, "'Dreaming That I'm Swimming in the Beautiful Caribbean Sea': One Man's Story on Surviving Death Row," is drawn from Lanier's extensive interview with Juan Meléndez-Colón, who was wrongfully convicted of murder in Florida and spent "17 years, 8 months, and 1 day" on that state's death row before being exonerated and released from prison in 2002. Meléndez-Colón's dream while under sentence of death evoked memories of his childhood in Puerto Rico and served as an important lifeline to the world beyond the bars of Florida's Raiford Prison, where he contemplated suicide, was taken under the wing and taught English by fellow death row inmates—several of whom died in the electric chair during his stay there, and where he witnessed acts of both extraordinary cruelty and compassion. The transcribed conversation between Lanier and Meléndez-Colón captures the latter's reflections, more than 14 years after regaining his freedom, about his life on death row and the adaptations he made from his arrival through his release. This rich account is contextualized by Lanier's interspersed descriptions of broader legal and policy issues surrounding death row confinement.

In Chapter 12, sociologists Saundra D. Westervelt and Kimberly J. Cook report lessons learned about the lingering effects of confinement under sentence of death from their lengthy life-history interviews with 17 men and one woman who were wrongfully convicted of murder and who spent an average of 5 years (and as long as 17.5 years) on death row in 10 different states before being exonerated. Although they eventually gained their freedom, these former prisoners did not leave death row unscathed. Relying largely on the voices of the interviewees, this chapter exposes the enduring physical, emotional, and psychological trauma caused by their confinement. The exonerees discuss confronting additional postrelease difficulties, including unjust stigmatization, a lack of monetary resources and assistance in finding housing or jobs, problems coping with technological and other societal changes, and many others.

The book concludes with an appendix that contains a report by the Yale Law School's Arthur Liman Public Interest Program, recently renamed The Arthur Liman Center for Public Interest Law. The report identifies the statutes, rules, and several interpretive judicial decisions that govern the incarceration of death-sentenced prisoners nationwide, provides an overview of related social science research, and describes and gives more detailed consideration to the programs adopted in North Carolina, Missouri, and Colorado, which are presented as alternatives to the traditional death row model for housing condemned prisoners. The report thus integrates a host of issues broached in this volume's chapters and offers a wealth of topics for further contemplation and action.

REFERENCES

Aarons, D. (1998). Can inordinate delay between a death sentence and execution constitute cruel and unusual punishment? *Seton Hall Law Review, 29*, 147–212.

Allen v. Ornoski, 435 F.3d 946 (9th Cir.), *cert. denied*, 546 U.S. 1136 (2006).

American Civil Liberties Union. (2013). *A death before dying: Solitary confinement on death row*. Retrieved from https://www.aclu.org/files/assets/deathbeforedying-report.pdf

Arthur Liman Public Interest Program Yale Law School. (2016). *Rethinking death row: Variations in the housing of individuals sentenced to death*. Retrieved from https://www.law.yale.edu/system/files/documents/pdf/Liman/deathrow_reportfinal.pdf

Ball v. LeBlanc, 792 F.3d 584 (5th Cir. 2015).

Bannon, S. (2002). *The death penalty: An American history*. Cambridge, MA: Harvard University Press.

Bedau, H. A. (1982). *The death penalty in America* (3rd ed.). New York, NY: Oxford University Press.

Bowers, W. J. (1984). *Legal homicide: Death as punishment in America, 1864–1982*. Boston, MA: Northeastern University Press.

Brief of International Law and Human Rights Institutes, Societies, Practitioners and Scholars, *Moore v. Texas*, 2016 WL 324311.

Chandler v. Crosby, 379 F.3d 1278 (11th Cir. 2004).

Christopher, R. L. (2015). The irrelevance of prisoner fault for excessively delayed executions. *Washington and Lee Law Review, 72*, 3–74.

Christopher, R. L. (2016). Absurdity and excessively delayed executions. *U.C. Davis Law Review, 49*, 843–898.

Davis v. Ayala, 135 S.Ct. 2187 (2015).

Death Penalty Information Center. (2017a). *Execution list 2016*. Retrieved from http://www.deathpenaltyinfo.org/execution-list-2016

Death Penalty Information Center. (2017b). *Innocence and the death penalty*. Retrieved from http://www.deathpenaltyinfo.org/innocence-and-death-penalty

Foucault, M. (1977). *Discipline and punish: The birth of the prison* (A. Sheridan, Trans.). New York, NY: Pantheon Books.

Furman v. Georgia, 408 U.S. 238 (1972).

Gates v. Cook, 376 F.3d 323 (5th Cir. 2004).

Gatrell, V. A. C. (1994). *The hanging tree: Execution and the English people 1770–1868*. New York, NY: Oxford University Press.

Glossip v. Gross, 135 S.Ct. 2726 (2015).

Gomez v. Fierro, 519 U.S. 918 (1996).

Gregg v. Georgia, 428 U.S. 153 (1976).

Human Rights Clinic, University of Texas School of Law. (2017). *Designed to break you: Human rights violations on Texas' death row*. Retrieved from https://law.utexas.edu/wp-content/uploads/sites/11/2017/04/2017-HRC-DesignedToBreakYou-Report.pdf

In re Medley, 134 U.S. 160 (1890).

James, W. (1961). *Psychology: The briefer course*. New York, NY: Harper & Row.

Johns v. Bowersox, 203 F.3d 538 (8th Cir.), *cert. denied*, 531 U.S. 1038 (2000).

Johnson v. Bredesen, 558 U.S. 1067 (2009).

Jurek v. Texas, 428 U.S. 262 (1976).

Knight v. Florida, 528 U.S. 990 (1999).

Lackey v. Texas, 514 U.S. 1045 (1995).

Liebman, J. S., Fagan, J., & West, V. (2000). *A broken system: Error rates in capital cases, 1973–1995*. Retrieved from https://papers.ssrn.com/sol3/papers.cfm?abstract_id=232712

Linders, A. (2002). The execution spectacle and state legitimacy: The changing nature of the American execution audience, 1833–1937. *Law & Society Review, 36*, 607–648. http://dx.doi.org/10.2307/1512164

Mackey, P. E. (1982). *Hanging in the balance: The anti-capital punishment movement in New York State, 1776–1861*. New York, NY: Garland.

Masur, L. P. (1989). *Rites of execution: Capital punishment and the transformation of American culture, 1778–1865*. New York, NY: Oxford University Press.

May, L. (2017). *The death row basketball league: Always playing against the clock*. Retrieved from https://www.themarshallproject.org/2017/03/16/the-death-row-basketball-league#.qI5O8WjAJ

McLeod, M. S. (2016). Does the death penalty require death row? The harm of legislative silence. *Ohio State Law Journal, 79*, 525–592.

Monge v. People, 406 P.2d 674 (Colo. 1965).

Moore v. State, 771 N.E.2d 46 (Ind. 2002).

NAACP Legal Defense and Educational Fund, Inc. (2017). *Death row U.S.A.: Spring 2017*. Retrieved from http://www.naacpldf.org/files/about-us/DRUSASpring2017.pdf

Newton, B. E. (2012). The slow wheels of *Furman's* machinery of death. *The Journal of Appellate Practice and Process, 13*, 41–73.

Pardo v. State, 108 So.3d 558 (Fla. 2012).

People v. Anderson, 493 P.2d 880 (Cal. 1972).

Peterkin v. Jeffes, 853 F.2d 1021 (3d Cir. 1988).

Petition for a Writ of Certiorari, *Moore v. Texas*, 2015 WL 9252271 (2015).

Porter v. Clarke, 852 F.3d 358 (4th Cir. 2017).

Proffitt v. Florida, 428 U.S. 242 (1976).

Robles, G. (2017). *Condemned to death—and solitary confinement*. Retrieved from https://www.themarshallproject.org/2017/07/23/condemned-to-death-and-solitary-confinement#.td5PfDzKF

Rothman, D. J. (1971). *The discovery of the asylum: Social order and disorder in the new republic*. Boston, MA: Little, Brown & Company.

Ruiz v. Texas, 137 S.Ct. 1246 (2017).

Sadoff, D. A. (2008). International law and the mortal precipice: A legal policy critique of the death row phenomenon. *Tulane Journal of International & Comparative Law, 17*, 77–111.

Sharkey, K. (2013). Delay in considering the constitutionality of inordinate delay: The death row phenomenon and the eighth amendment. *University of Pennsylvania Law Review, 161*, 861–896.

Snell, T. (2014). *Capital punishment, 2013—Statistical tables*. Washington, DC: U.S. Department of Justice, Bureau of Justice Statistics. Retrieved from https://www.bjs.gov/content/pub/pdf/cp13st.pdf

State v. Moore, 591 N.W.2d 86 (Neb. 1999).

State v. Schackart, 947 P.2d 315 (Ariz. 1997).

Suffolk County District Attorney v. Watson, 411 N.E.2d 1274 (Mass. 1980).

Thompson v. McNeil, 556 U.S. 1114 (2009).

Thompson v. Secretary Dept. Corrections, 517 F.3d 1279 (11th Cir. 2008), *cert. denied*, 556 U.S. 1114 (2009).

Tongue, M. E. (2015). *Omnes vulnerant, postuma necat*: All the hours wound, the last one kills: The lengthy stay on death row in America. *Missouri Law Review, 80*, 897–921.

Williams, J. J., & Murry, C. L. (2016). Dying on death row (other than by execution). *Corrections Today, 78*(4), 40–44.

OVERVIEW OF DEATH ROW CONDITIONS

1

Rethinking Classification, Programming, and Housing for Death Row Inmates

Jeanne Woodford

The management of prisons is a topic that does not often receive a great deal of attention, despite the fact that between 1980 and 2016, prison populations grew at a staggering rate. The U.S. general population grew by 37% during that interval, whereas the jail and prison population grew by 371% (Krisberg, Marchionna, & Hartney, 2015, p. 7). Similarly, death row populations increased sharply as states authorized the use of the death penalty for an ever-longer list of crimes (Death Penalty Information Center, 2017a; see Figure 1.1). The number of people sentenced to death reached an average of 300 per year through most of the 1990s. The number of people on death rows across the nation reached its highest point in 2000 with 3,593 inmates (Death Penalty Information Center, 2017c).

The author gratefully acknowledges the assistance of Susan Marchionna, who helped edit this chapter and constructed Figure 1.1 for it.

http://dx.doi.org/10.1037/0000084-002
Living on Death Row: The Psychology of Waiting to Die, H. Toch, J. R. Acker, and V. M. Bonventre (Editors)

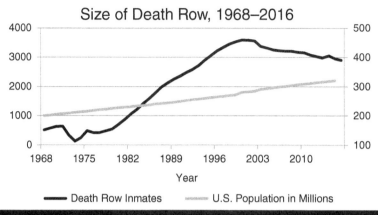

Figure 1.1

Death row growth versus U.S. population growth. Compiled from NAACP Legal Defense and Educational Fund, Inc. (2014, 2015, 2016); Snell (2014); United States Census Bureau (2016).

PRISON WITHIN A PRISON

It is difficult to make generalizations about prison management, but some prison policies and practices relating to security are virtually universal. For example, prisons have a secure perimeter, and prison staff complete scheduled inmate counts daily; they conduct searches of inmates and their living and program areas on a routine basis.

The conditions and regulations under which prisoners live vary between state and federal prison systems and even among prisons within a single correctional system. The variation, which can be significant, has mostly to do with the programs and services prisons offer to inmates. Some systems are more progressive than others. Some prisons offer a menu of programs and activities, whereas others limit prisoner activity to brief periods of out-of-cell time and not much more. Many focus primarily on punishment through incarceration and offer little more than the most basic requirements of housing and feeding inmates.

A DEATH SENTENCE FOR LIFE

Although the management of U.S. prisons has been evolving in general, one aspect of prison management has changed little, if at all, until recently: the management of death row. The death penalty is complicated and is unlike most other prison sentences. The length of a death sentence is indefinite. A person sentenced to death never knows how long the wait will be. In fact, the execution may never happen.

Litigation strategies and standards have evolved, adding to the uncertainty of the sentence. Capital cases are delayed for years as appeals work their way through the judicial process. This lengthy appeals process has increased the number of inmates sitting on death rows across the country. These long stays on death row have led to litigation and court intervention regarding the conditions of confinement for death row inmates. Further, the expansion of capital-eligible crimes has changed the profile of inmates on death row. What has changed little is how death row is managed.

It is time to rethink traditional death row management practices. Highly secure prisons with modern technology have opened the door for this kind of change. Our knowledge about inmates and their behavior has also evolved and helped to bring about evidence-based practices, which encompass the best available strategies for managing death row and death row inmates.

During its early history in this country, the death penalty was carried out relatively soon after sentencing, sometimes within weeks or a few months. Appeals from capital convictions and sentences were not uniformly taken, and executions often proceeded with little, if any, court intervention (Aarons, 1998, pp. 179–182; Acker, 2014, p. 268). Prison wardens gave death row inmates little consideration because these were individuals whose death was a fait accompli—thus the phrase "dead man walking."

During the late 1980s and early 1990s, in most states, roughly six to 10 criminal circumstances could typically render a murder eligible for the death penalty (Acker & Lanier, 1993). In the era of "get tough" sentencing, the list of capital crimes grew in several jurisdictions. For example, the California Penal Code (2016, § 190.2) currently lists 35 special circumstances that allow a sentence of life imprisonment without the possibility of parole or the death penalty.

The law has evolved to allow for more and varied appeals, which means that executions are increasingly delayed for many years, and those delays have gotten even longer, sometimes lasting decades. But death row inmates are still treated as if their stays will be short, which is to say that they are a low priority when it comes to treatment and services. Furthermore, they are unsympathetic in the eyes of the public, in the opinions of legislators, and often in the view of prison officials.

There have been successful challenges over the past several years to the execution of juveniles, people with developmental disabilities, and people who had not been convicted of homicide. As legal challenges gained traction, the length of time people were spending on death row began to grow. In contrast to early historical practices, when executions were carried out within months or a few years after a death sentence was imposed, in states such as California, inmates were spending decades on death row. Some of California's death row inmates have been there for more than 30 years. Nationally, the average time spent on death row from sentence to execution increased from 74 months in 1984 to 186 months (15½ years) in 2013 (Snell, 2014, p. 14).

As a result of these and other changes, the profile of the death row inmate also changed. The increased use of the death penalty in some counties across the nation contributed to this new profile, which included younger people and individuals with varying special needs, including the mentally ill and individuals with developmental disabilities. In some states, the death penalty was expanded to include gang-involved homicides and crimes that do not include homicide. Texas, Oklahoma, South Carolina, Montana, Louisiana, and Georgia passed various laws to apply the death penalty for specific crimes, such as repeat offenses involving rape and sex crimes against children. In *Kennedy v. Louisiana* (2008), however, the Supreme Court declared that punishing such crimes with death is unconstitutional.

Even though inmates now live a long time on death row, the conditions of their imprisonment have not changed significantly since they were dead men walking. They are still treated as though their time is short and the conditions under which they live do not matter.

A BRIEF HISTORY OF DEATH ROW IN CALIFORNIA

In *Furman v. Georgia* (1972), the United States Supreme Court struck down capital punishment in the states, finding its application "arbitrary and capricious," in violation of the Eighth Amendment. Four years later, the Court ruled in *Gregg v. Georgia* (1976) and companion cases to allow states to reinstate the death penalty, introducing a constitutional framework for states to redeploy this method of punishment. The decision of whether to carry out the death penalty thus returned to the states.

In 1977, the California state legislature voted to override a veto by then-Governor Jerry Brown and reinstated the death penalty. To ensure the death penalty would not be overturned by future legislatures, the voters of California passed the Briggs Initiative in 1978, adding additional crimes eligible to receive a sentence of death. Since that time, more than 950 men and women have been sentenced to die in the state of California.

San Quentin's death row is now the largest in the nation. The growing population of death row inmates is now housed in several housing units at San Quentin. Death Row was originally designed for the express purpose of housing death row inmates. The original death row consisted of 68 cells and was isolated from the general population, six floors above a housing unit known as North Block. The outside recreation yard is on the roof of this building, further isolating death row inmates from staff and other prison programs. Living conditions within this housing unit have changed little, and the unit typifies the kind of segregated housing still used for death row inmates across the country. Death Row inmates in California do have more out of cell time and a few more privileges than death row inmates in most states.

CONDITIONS ON DEATH ROW

For many years, conditions of confinement on death row were harsher than those in the general population or segregation units. Death row inmates were rarely allowed out of their cell. Visiting was infrequent, and contact was not allowed. There was no outdoor exercise or, for that matter, routine out-of-cell time of any kind. Inmates had no access to a library, much less a law library, making research and access to the courts extremely difficult. Phone calls were allowed only at the discretion of staff, who rarely gave such permission. Showers were allowed only three times a week. There were no group religious services and only infrequent visits by staff clergy. Formal education programs did not exist, nor did art, music, or other leisure-time activities. Televisions were not allowed.

Sanitation conditions were poor, making it difficult for inmates to practice proper hygiene. General mail and legal mail procedures were not being followed. Mental health care was lacking, and the suicide rate was high. These issues would later become a focus of civil rights litigation, forcing significant changes in treatment and programming in prisons.

Over the years, some states have attempted to implement changes to improve conditions on death row. In 1968, Arkansas placed death row inmates in the general population. The program lasted 10 months, ending with a decision by the Board of Corrections to return Arkansas death row inmates to segregated conditions. The Texas Department of Corrections implemented changes to death row in 1985, classifying death row inmates as either "work capable" or as "death row segregated." This differentiating program also came to an end, and Texas began returning all death row inmates to segregated conditions. As discussed later in this chapter and in Chapter 5 (this volume), Missouri has largely succeeded in integrating death-sentenced prisoners into the general prison population.

AMERICAN CIVIL LIBERTIES UNION REPORT

A 2013 American Civil Liberties Union report, *A Death Before Dying: Solitary Confinement on Death Row*, concluded the following:

- Cell size. The most common cell size is 8 by 10 feet (for 27% of prisoners), just a bit bigger than the size of an average bathroom.
- Basic comfort. From the survey responses received, of the beds provided in death row cells, 60% are made out of steel, 13% are concrete,

9% are steel with a mattress, 6% are concrete with a pad, and 6% are metal.

- "Enforced idleness." States that allow death row inmates to exercise for 1 hour or less: 81%.
- Social isolation. States with mandated no-contact visits for death row inmates: 67%.
- Religious services. States that fail to offer religious services to death row prisoners: 62%.

> "Inmates go crazy, become clinically mentally ill, in solitary conditions there. We end up with more staff assaults and greater instances of crisis management in a harsh and hostile environment for officers," said Lance Lowry, president of the union representing the approximately 450 guards on death row, the American Federation of State, County and Municipal Employees. (Walters, 2014, para. 6)

The concerns about conditions on death row in other states are being expressed by individuals who have been exonerated of their alleged capital crimes. Solitary Watch pointed to the testimony of Louisiana exoneree Damon Thibodeaux at a Senate Judiciary Subcommittee hearing to highlight the conditions on death row in Louisiana:

> I spent my years at Angola, while my lawyers fought to prove my innocence, in a cell that measured about 8 feet by 10 feet. It had three solid walls all painted white, a cell door, a sink, a toilet, a desk and seat attached to a wall, and an iron bunk with a thin mattress. These four walls are your life. Being in that environment for 23 hours a day will slowly kill you. Mentally, you have to find some way to live as if you were not there. If you cannot do that, you will die a slow mental death and may actually wish for your physical death, so that you do not have to continue that existence. More than anything, solitary confinement is an existence without hope. (Stahl, 2014, para. 4)

Thibodeaux was exonerated after spending 15 years on death row at Angola State Penitentiary in Louisiana.

PRISONER CLASSIFICATION

Safety

The public thinks of prisons as places secured with electric fences, barbed wire, and tall walls and towers with armed staff. In truth, the most important part of prison security is its classification system. The goal of most prison classification systems is to classify the inmate to the lowest security possible while protecting the safety of the public, staff, and the prisoner population. In the last 40 years, the classification process has evolved. Prison systems have adopted well-researched, objective classification instruments that identify key factors to help predict the safety risk the prisoner posed. These instruments rely heavily on the sentence of the inmate for the initial classification. Subsequently, they allow for a reduced classification level as prisoners show they can adjust to prison and conform, or an increase in security for prisoners who become violent or continue criminal behavior within the prison setting. This kind of system provides incentives for good behavior and is designed to protect the public, staff, and all prisoners.

General population prisoners can improve their situation by following the rules and remaining free of disciplinary problems. This is not the case for those on death row in most states. Prisoners are motivated to engage in positive programming to include work, education, and leisure time activities. Without these incentives, inmates can be difficult to manage, and security is jeopardized. The lack of classification incentives for death row inmates is a key reason for the safety and security problems on death row.

In 2014, correctional staff in Texas requested changes in how death row inmates were being treated. An article by Joanna Walters (2014) printed in *The Telegraph* stated, "Corrections officers patrolling the tough death row prison in Texas are pleading with the state to make conditions more humane for inmates and prevent 'daily' threats to staff safety" (para. 1).

Segregation

In most states, death row prisoners are housed separately (segregated) from the general prison population; prisoner behavior and case factors have little impact on housing decisions. As previously mentioned, death row policies are often more severe than those for other segregated prisoners.

Most death row inmates understand that they face a years-long state and federal appeals process. Death row inmates usually arrive in prison before they have been assigned an appellate attorney; they are often fearful of prison officials because they do not want to do or say anything that will jeopardize their case. Their trial attorney will typically caution the prisoner not to cooperate with testing of any kind. They arrive in prison facing the most severe and consequential sentence available in the United States. It is understandable that newly arrived death row prisoners are confused and fearful of the correctional system and the people who work in it. This fear can interfere with the reception center process. Death row inmates might refuse to participate in an assessment that would reveal a developmental disability if they think the results could be used against them in court. The same is true for psychological exams and other classification assessments. In some states, such as California, it may be several years before an appellate attorney is appointed to assist the inmate. Staff members are also cautious in their assessments, realizing death row prisoners have serious and consequential legal battles ahead of them. Classifying a death row prisoner can be a complicated process.

THE CASE FOR CLASSIFICATION
AND PROGRAMMING AT SAN QUENTIN,
THOMPSON v. ENOMOTO

At San Quentin, all death row classification and programming practices were at the discretion of the warden. The Central Office did not get involved in the management practices of death row in any way. This situation changed quickly as the result of the 1979 case of *Thompson v. Enomoto* (1987, 1990). Maurice Thompson and other death row inmates housed at San Quentin filed this civil rights action, complaining of prison conditions and treatment and alleging violations of the Eighth and Fourteenth Amendments to the U.S. Constitution. The parties entered into a consent decree to improve conditions and establish rights for condemned prisoners at San Quentin. This consent decree was in effect from 1980 to 2009.

For the first time, the California Department of Corrections was forced to take a hard look at the housing and programming for death row inmates. The resulting consent decree detailed every aspect of housing and confinement for death row inmates. It maintained that they continue to be housed separately from general population inmates but required program and privileges on the basis of inmate behavior, thus establishing incentives for good behavior among death row prisoners.

Instead of uniform treatment for all death row inmates, the consent decree established three classification levels for them:

- *Grade A.* Inmates were to be treated as much like general population inmates as possible, including out-of-cell time equivalent to 6 hours a day.
- *Grade B.* Conditions of confinement for these inmates were to equal those in Security Housing Units.
- *Walk Alone.* This classification was established for inmates with serious enemy problems who could not engage in programs with other inmates. They were to be given as many privileges as possible, but out-of-cell time was limited to 10 hours per week.

Under the consent decree, conditions for death row inmates with Grade A status improved. These inmates were allowed contact visits, routine telephone calls, canteen, quarterly packages, daily outdoor exercise, on-tier exercise, typewriters, access to law libraries, education, hobby craft, daily showers, and recreational equipment. Following years of ongoing litigation, the consent decree was terminated in 2009.

Despite the improvements that *Thompson v. Enomoto* (1987, 1990) brought, problems such as access to mental health treatment, appropriate recreation, and general housing conditions persist. Today, conditions on California's death row unit remain about the same as they were in the original death row. Conditions in overflow death row housing units offer less out-of-cell and recreation time due to the lack of space. Limited resources have affected the addition of education and program staff, which has not kept up with the growth of the death row population.

There are long waiting lists for education and recreational programs, less access to law libraries, and curtailed visiting.

CHALLENGES OF PROVIDING ADEQUATE SERVICES ON DEATH ROW

Mental Health Treatment

All inmates are entitled to appropriate living conditions during confinement that are, for the most part, outlined in regulation and law. Meeting both regulatory and legal requirements is more complicated than it appears and is often affected by resources and politics. For example, prison officials are responsible for providing a constitutionally adequate mental health program for all inmates—including those on death row. In general, such a program must

- provide screening and evaluation of inmates to identify those in need of mental health treatment;
- provide a treatment program that involves more than segregation and close supervision;
- employ a sufficient number of trained mental health professionals to provide treatment of mentally ill inmates;
- maintain accurate, complete, and confidential mental health records;
- provide a medication management program, including provisions for psychotropic medication with appropriate supervision; and
- provide a basic program to identify, treat, and supervise inmates at risk of suicide.

Few prison systems comply with the requirements for an adequate mental health program for non–death row inmates. As already stated, providing these services for death row inmates is especially complicated because of the typically segregated housing policies under which they live. For example, segregation offers few, if any, opportunities for death row inmates to participate in programs or social activities, group exercise, or religious services. Researchers have shown that prisoners in long-term segregation have a higher prevalence of mental health problems.

In many states, the inmate's mental health evaluation is not much more than an assessment of suicide risk. Mental health problems, if identified, are treated with medication and little else. Inmates on death row who have severe mental illness are often treated as management problems. This is typically a function of inappropriate staff, inadequate resources to monitor mental health issues, and/or inappropriate facilities for treatment services.

Wherever compliance with mental health requirements is occurring, it is often the result of litigation. Lawsuits around the country have resulted in court orders or settlement agreements the intent of which is to reduce the use of segregation. The *Coleman v. Brown* (2014) mental health lawsuit in California is one such case. It is likely that litigation will continue and will force changes in the management and treatment of death row prisoners who require mental health treatment.

Complex Prisoner Needs

Mental health care is just one of many legally mandated services that prisons must provide. Prison managers must also have policies and devote resources to address a growing list of other needs within the death row population—disabilities (including wheelchair-bound inmates) and the concerns of elder prisoners. Aging inmates on death row require significant medical monitoring and treatment for illnesses, including diabetes, high blood pressure, heart disease, arthritis, and more. This is particularly true in California, where capital punishment is effectively a life sentence.

It is difficult to even monitor the health of inmates who spend most of their time in segregation. Prisoners on death row have less ability to communicate with other inmates and staff. Psychiatric health problems are often difficult to identify until the inmate's condition is severe or critical. Medical conditions may also go unnoticed or untreated due to lack of access to the appropriate medical staff. Treatment protocols including diet and exercise are rarely followed. In some states, preventive medical practices are lacking; inmates are denied routine physicals and other prescribed medical tests and treatments.

Further, even though they may adhere to the space requirements of standard-setting agencies, such as the American Correctional Association, most prisons were not designed or built to accommodate the full range of needs and services that long-term prisoners on death row need. Thus, the very infrastructure poses limitations to addressing prisoner needs.

A lack of services can lead to an increase in violence and mental health problems and an inability to hire and retain appropriate staff. Medical and mental health providers, teachers, and other professional staff want to be effective, but these are difficult jobs. Staff turnover has been well documented in many court cases, including lawsuits in California such as *Plata v. Brown* (see *Brown v. Plata*, 2011; *Coleman v. Brown*, 2014).

For all these reasons, it is necessary to develop more appropriate medical protocols and practice for long-term inmates, including those on death row.

Resource Allocation

Providing adequate services is further affected by budget allocations and prison overcrowding. In general, providing health care services to inmates is expensive, but it is even more so in states that continue to isolate death row populations. When inmates are isolated in segregation with limited out-of-cell time, treatment and services are staff intensive. Inmates on death row are usually only removed from their cells with handcuffs and custody escort staff.

Without national standards for medical treatment, state correctional administrators are often left helpless to obtain sufficient resources to identify and treat prisoners as the Constitution requires.

INFLUENCES ON DEATH ROW

Death row and the death penalty, being largely out of the public view and the public consciousness, may be highly resistant to meaningful change. However, death row does not exist in a vacuum, and many tensions exert pressure on this singular system—social, moral, religious, economic, and legal, among others.

In recent years, there has been an increased focus on the cost of prisons and the conditions inside them. Leading the call to rethink the purpose of prisons and our criminal justice system is the growing attention to incarceration as a routine response to many social problems, including drug addiction and mental illness. Science and research have called into question the effectiveness of punishment and the lack of treatment and services for people involved in the criminal justice system. Data have shown that the increased use of prisons in the last 4 decades has led to prison overcrowding, limited resources, and worsening prison conditions across the nation. Litigation in both state and federal courts has increasingly involved incarceration practices of prisons and jails and the criminal justice system in general. More and more, policymakers and advocates for change are relying on cost versus benefit fact analysis in deciding whether criminal justice policy should include the use of the death penalty. Setting aside religious and moral arguments, the more practical questions—Does the death penalty make us safer? Is the death penalty cost effective?—are being given greater consideration as death penalty costs continue to grow.

Litigation

It took many years, but litigation has led the way for change. Court decisions have clarified the role of prisons and the reality that incarcerating people requires more than merely providing a cell. In states in which death row inmates have successfully sued, prison managers have been forced to think about the needs of death row inmates and accept that incarceration requires adequate physical and mental health care. Judicial intervention has required prison conditions to change and has even provided political cover for prison administrations to obtain resources to improve conditions on death row.

Brown v. Plata

One of the most important court decisions affecting prisons and jails nationally is a federal civil rights lawsuit filed in California that ultimately reached the United States Supreme Court: *Brown v. Plata* (2011). After years of litigation, the California Department of Corrections and Rehabilitation (CDCR) had still failed to meet court mandates to improve both medical and mental health care. A panel of three federal judges concluded that overcrowding was the primary reason the CDCR could not provide adequate medical and mental health treatment for inmates. In May 2011, the U.S. Supreme Court ruled that overcrowding in California's prisons resulted in cruel and unusual punishment in violation of the Eighth Amendment to the U.S. Constitution. The Court affirmed a January 2010 order made by a three-judge federal court directing California officials to reduce the state's severe prison overcrowding down to 137.5% of design capacity. The order was issued after the judges found that overcrowding is the primary cause of unconstitutional conditions in California's prisons, such as the system's inability to provide competent and timely medical and mental health care for prisoners. As of spring 2014, the three-judge court granted California's request for a 2-year extension of time to fully reduce prison overcrowding to the 137.5% level required by the U.S. Supreme Court.

The ruling in *Brown v. Plata* (2011) is a landmark that affirms the responsibility of states to provide appropriate physical and mental health care to incarcerated individuals. In addition, and most important, the Supreme Court also established its willingness to enter into prison management issues when states fail to remedy unconstitutional conditions of confinement. In *Brown v. Plata*, the federal courts appointed a receiver to oversee the management of health care in all California state prisons. The receiver was given the power to bring on the necessary physical and mental health staff and to order the physical plant modifications necessary to achieve compliance with court-ordered mandates.

Science and Research

Litigation has served to inspire scientific research and bring forth much-needed data and information. The use of research in litigation strategy has helped to educate judges, policymakers, criminal justice practitioners, and—to some degree—the public.

The use of research and science has had an additional impact on the death penalty. DNA evidence irrefutably demonstrated that innocent people have been sentenced to death. Kirk Bloodsworth—who was originally sentenced to death—was the first inmate to prove his innocence with this technology (Junkin, 2004). Mr. Bloodsworth—an honorably discharged Marine—was convicted in 1985 of rape and murder and sentenced to death. He was exonerated by DNA evidence in 1993. The execution of Cameron Todd Willingham in Texas was followed by scientific evidence that seriously called into question whether he was innocent of the crime for which he died; the fire scene investigation evidence used against him was found to be "junk science" (Grann, 2009). The California Commission on the Fair Administration of Justice (2008) also discussed the problems with forensic evidence. This same report documented the research as well as cases of exonerees, who—when exposed to harsh police interrogation tactics—confessed to crimes they had not committed. Further, the report discussed the use of jailhouse informants and exposed the prevalence of jailhouse informants providing false testimony for receiving leniency in their own cases.

Legislation

The awareness of policy makers, specifically state and federal legislators, has led to some criminal justice reforms. Other federal laws such as the Civil Rights of Institutionalized Persons Act (1980), the Americans With Disabilities Act (1990), and the Prison Rape Elimination Act (2003) and its accompanying standards (Prison Rape Elimination Act Prisons and Jail Standards, 2012), established rights for prisoners and applied legal compliance mandates for jails and prisons.

Politics and Economics

Securing the funds for increasing budgets for inmate services has always been a challenge for correctional agencies. The debate during legislative budget cycles tends to center on which interests deserve services most— for example, prisons, schools, veterans, or the disabled. It is even more difficult to advocate for services for violent felons and virtually impossible to advocate for death row inmates.

This political reality, coupled with the increased cost of housing a growing number of inmates, has often resulted in reduced budgets for health care, rehabilitation programs, and other prisoner services. And given that these concerns have been neglected for so long, the costs of rectifying the situation are even higher.

Still, there is political pressure to analyze resource allocation and infuse systems with greater efficiency. Interestingly, both sides of the political spectrum favor reforms, though for different reasons. Liberal and progressive reformers want more racial equity and more proportionality—the punishment fitting the crime. Conservatives want more fiscal efficiency; they have been convinced that overreliance on incarceration is simply too expensive. The watchwords have changed from "tough on crime" to "smart on crime."

The Media and Public Opinion

The media have always influenced the public perception of individuals in our prison system, including inmates on death row. In the 1980s, as crime took center stage in newspapers across the country, the political environment—coupled with sensational news reporting—had a direct impact on the ability of correctional administrators to advocate for policy changes or resources for essential services, not to mention capital improvements in jails and prisons. Capital crimes elicit strong, emotional reactions, which is the opposite of a measured and thoughtful response about justice and morality. Moreover, media exploitation of the public's emotions leads to little more than a surface knowledge of the case and the issues.

Victims' rights groups present the tragic circumstances of the families of loved ones lost to the worst kinds of crimes. These deeply moving circumstances appeal to the emotions of regular citizens and lawmakers alike. With the help of the media, the public is swayed by the apparently simple equation of an "eye for an eye."

Advocacy

Along with litigation and court intervention, the role of advocates for criminal justice change should not be overlooked. Anti–death penalty advocates expanded their challenges to the use of the death penalty on the basis of the quality of legal representation for defendants. Advocates also funded research and used the results as evidence in their efforts nation-wide to seek reforms. The work of advocacy groups has aided legislative and regulatory reforms through the use of research and litigation. Advo-cacy groups have also used education and outreach to build coalitions across political lines and further the movement to address incarceration growth, criminal justice policies, and the death penalty itself.

DEATH PENALTY LITIGATION
ACROSS THE UNITED STATES

We have seen that people on death row live out long-term sentences, and this situation should have led correctional agencies to rethink the clas-sification, programming, and housing of these individuals. Reforms to date have largely been inadequate to meet the changing needs of the death row population. As we have seen, prison managers have thought of those on death row as somehow beyond reach, and therefore undeserving—in effect, already dead.

From 1979 to 1985, death row litigation resulted in judicial inter-vention to address conditions of confinement in Alabama, Florida, Georgia, Virginia, and Mississippi. Litigation in these states primarily addressed minimum recreation periods for death row inmates, so the changes have not been as far reaching as in some states, such as California and Texas (Lombardi, Sluder, & Wallace, 1996).

Arizona

A federal class action lawsuit was filed in 2012 against the Arizona Depart-ment of Corrections (ADC) regarding inadequate physical, mental, and dental health care provided to prisoners. The lawsuit also included condi-tions of confinement in the prison's maximum-custody units to include death row inmates (*Parsons v. Ryan*, 2015).

In February 2015, a federal judge approved a settlement agree-ment requiring the ADC to provide an adequate health care system. The settlement agreement is very specific that the department meet more than 100 health care outcome measures addressing medical, mental health, and dental treatment. The ADC must also review and revise policies and procedures for their Security Housing Units (Prison Law Office, n.d.).

Texas

During the late 1970s and early 1980s, the Texas Department of Corrections was litigating *Ruiz v. Estelle* (1982, 1980), a lawsuit over numerous conditions of confinement. The *Ruiz* case affected all inmates, including those on death row. The Texas Department of Corrections thus began to increase out-of-cell time for death row inmates and began to implement a death row work program.

The judgment of the court in *Ruiz* covered staffing, support services for inmates, discipline, administrative segregation, work, health and safety, use of force, access to the courts, maintenance of facilities, programming and recreational activities, visitation, overcrowding, health services, psychiatric services, death row conditions, and enforcement procedures. The *Ruiz* case concluded in 2012 when the court entered its final judgment, dismissing the case with prejudice. The Prison Litigation Reform Act affected the court's ruling to end this case. Today, conditions on death row in Texas are harsher than ever; inmates are confined to their cell 23 hours a day (Mann, 2010).

Missouri

In 1986, death row inmates in Missouri filed a federal class-action lawsuit (*McDonald v. Armontrout*, 1988) based on a claim of unconstitutional conditions on death row. In 1990, the state of Missouri entered into a consent decree, resulting in changed conditions and management of death-sentenced prisoners. Classification for death row inmates was revised to become a behavioral- and privilege-based system with three levels: regular custody, close custody, and no-contact custody. Privileges were expanded to include religious services, more out-of-cell time, library access, more visitation, commissary, medical access, and increased telephone access.

Within a short time, prison administrators and staff began to realize that there was little difference, if any, in the behavior of death row inmates compared with those with a life sentence without the possibility of parole or those sentenced to serve 50 years to life. They also concluded that providing greater resources to segregated inmates was staff intensive, difficult, and costly.

The Missouri system began the process of integrating death row into the general population. Missouri abandoned the use of the term *death row inmate* and opted to use *capital punishment inmate* instead. We know language is important and powerful; the word *inmate* conjures up feelings of fear in many people's minds. It is easy to understand why *death row inmate* would affect staff attitude and concerns. The use of *capital punishment inmate* seemed to remove preconceived fears about inmates sentenced to death. In January 1991, capital punishment inmates were fully integrated into the general population.

The benefits to Missouri included staff cost savings, a reduction in litigation expenses, and greater flexibility in housing capital punishment inmates. The benefits to those inmates included more out-of-cell time and greater privileges for work and recreation. The benefits for line custody staff were a reduction in disciplinary behavior and violence (see Chapter 5, this volume; Lombardi et al., 1996).

North Carolina

North Carolina separates death row inmates from the general population but allows everyone similar access to resources and program opportunities. Death row inmates are able to spend 16 hours each day out of their cells, either in a day room or on exercise yards. North Carolina allows death row inmates group dining. Deputy Director Lassiter has expressed unequivocal support for North Carolina's death row policies, explaining that prisoner-on-officer violence was nearly nonexistent on death row, and prisoner-on-prisoner violence was extremely rare (The Arthur Liman Public Interest Program, Yale Law School, 2016).

Colorado

Colorado has a small death row population consisting of three inmates as of July 2016 (Death Penalty Information Center, 2017b). The state made changes to its death row housing policies in 2015. Those inmates are now housed in a housing unit designated as in need of increased supervision. Death row inmates are allowed out of their cell at least 4 hours a day and afforded most of the privileges offered other non–death row inmates in the increased supervision-housing unit. The Colorado Director of Corrections views the changes as "having a positive effect on the demeanor and personalities of the inmates" (The Arthur Liman Public Interest Program, Yale Law School, 2016, p 17). Director Rick Raemisch and his top administrative staff "believe that in the long run this policy will lead to a safer facility. . . . All the evidence is pointing to that direction" (p. 17).

MANAGING THE FUTURE OF DEATH ROW

We have in many ways arrived at a long overdue rethinking of who we lock up and for how long and what we must do with and for people while they are locked up. We are in an era of redefining incarceration and punishment. Policy makers around the country are researching and implementing new criminal justice policies in an effort to improve public safety through evidence-based practices. This era of change in philosophy and practice is affecting every aspect of the criminal justice system, from sentencing to punishment, even including an end to the death penalty in seven states since 2007, with another four states implementing a gubernatorial moratorium (Death Penalty Information Center, 2017d).

Not every state is implementing reforms; many continue death row policies and practices of the past. The time has come for all states to rethink the management of death row. The get-tough era is slowly receding into the past. Giving inmates something to hope for, even if it is as simple as a contact visit with a family member, is a way to improve conditions for not only the inmate but also for the staff who work on death row. Greater privileges and programs also provide something to lose and are powerful incentives for following the rules. This basic correctional strategy is effective in improving safety for staff and inmates. As prison managers implement required treatment, the benefits are becoming clear. Prisons are becoming safer for both staff and inmates. The new mantra of "smart on crime" is providing an opportunity for correctional departments to implement criminal justice policies and procedures that are evidence based and that lead to greater public safety and lowered criminal justice costs.

The reduction of overcrowding and the implementation of rehabilitation programs and treatment in California prisons are improving recidivism rates for the first time in several decades. This is what criminal justice should be about. Safety considerations should include the public, prison staff, and inmates alike. They are not independent issues. As a society, we must concern ourselves with how many years prisoners live on death row, whether they have incentives for good behavior, and whether their conditions of confinement are humane.

If the death penalty continues as a punishment at the state and the federal levels, change in the management of death row will be voluntarily instituted by enlightened correctional professionals and will be forced on others through costly and time-consuming litigation. The question is, Will policy makers lead the effort, or will they wait for change to be forced on them? Time will tell.

REFERENCES

Aarons, D. (1998). Can inordinate delay between a death sentence and execution constitute cruel and unusual punishment? *Seton Hall Law Review, 29,* 147–212.

Acker, J. R. (2014). *Questioning capital punishment: Law, policy, and practice.* New York, NY: Routledge.

Acker, J. R., & Lanier, C. S. (1993). Aggravating circumstances in capital punishment law: Rhetoric or meaningful reforms? *Criminal Law Bulletin, 29,* 467–501.

American Civil Liberties Union. (2013). *A death before dying: Solitary confinement on death row.* Retrieved from https://www.aclu.org/files/assets/deathbeforedying-report.pdf

Americans With Disabilities Act of 1990, 42 U.S.C.A. § 12131-34 (West 1993).

The Arthur Liman Public Interest Program, Yale Law School. (2016). *Rethinking death row: Variations in the housing of individuals sentenced to death.* Retrieved from https://law.yale.edu/system/files/documents/pdf/Liman/deathrow_reportfinal.pdf

Brown v. Plata, 563 U.S. 493 (2011).

California Commission on the Fair Administration of Justice. (2008). *California Commission on the Fair Administration of Justice final report.* Retrieved from http://digitalcommons.law.scu.edu/cgi/viewcontent.cgi?article=1000&context=ncippubs

California Penal Code, §190.2 (2016).

Civil Rights of Institutionalized Persons Act, 42 U.S.C. § 1997 *et seq.* (1980).

Coleman v. Brown, 28 F.Supp.3d 1068 (E.D. Cal. 2014).

Death Penalty Information Center. (2017a). *Crimes punishable by the death penalty.* Retrieved from http://www.deathpenaltyinfo.org/crimes-punishable-death-penalty

Death Penalty Information Center. (2017b). *Death row prisoners by state.* Retrieved from http://www.deathpenaltyinfo.org/death-row-inmates-state-and-size-death-row-year?scid=9&did=188#state

Death Penalty Information Center. (2017c). *Size of death row by year (1968–present).* Retrieved from http://www.deathpenaltyinfo.org/death-row-inmates-state-and-size-death-row-year?scid=9&did=188#year

Death Penalty Information Center. (2017d). *States with and without the death penalty.* Retrieved from http://www.deathpenaltyinfo.org/states-and-without-death-penalty

Furman v. Georgia, 408 U.S. 238 (1972).

Grann, D. (2009, September 7). Trial by fire: Did Texas execute an innocent man? *The New Yorker.* Retrieved from http://www.newyorker.com/magazine/2009/09/07/trial-by-fire

Gregg v. Georgia, 428 U.S. 153 (1976).

Junkin, T. (2004). *Bloodsworth: The true story of the first death row inmate exonerated by DNA.* Chapel Hill, NC: Algonquin Books of Chapel Hill.

Kennedy v. Louisiana, 554 U.S. 407 (2008).

Krisberg, B., Marchionna, S., & Hartney, C. (2015). *American corrections: Concepts and controversies.* Thousand Oaks, CA: Sage.

Lombardi, G., Sluder, R. D., & Wallace, D. (1996, March). *The management of death-sentenced inmates: Issues, realities, and innovative strategies.* Paper presented at the meeting of the Academy of Criminal Justice Sciences, Las Vegas, NV. Retrieved from https://doc.mo.gov/Documents/DeathSentencedInmates.pdf

Mann, D. (2010, November 10). Solitary men: Does prolonged isolation drive death row prisoners insane? *Texas Observer*. Retrieved from https://www.texasobserver.org/solitary-men/

McDonald v. Armontrout, 860 F. 2d 1456 (8th Cir. 1988).

NAACP Legal Defense and Educational Fund, Inc. (2014, Fall). *Death row U.S.A.* Retrieved from http://www.naacpldf.org/files/publications/DRUSA_Fall_2014.pdf

NAACP Legal Defense and Educational Fund, Inc. (2015, Fall). *Death row U.S.A.* Retrieved from http://www.naacpldf.org/files/our-work/DRUSA_Fall_2015.pdf

NAACP Legal Defense and Educational Fund, Inc. (2016, Summer). *Death row U.S.A.* Retrieved from http://www.naacpldf.org/files/publications/DRUSA_Summer_2016.pdf

Parsons v. Ryan, 784 F.3d 571 (9th Cir. 2015).

Prison Law Office. (n.d.). *Major cases: Medical and mental health care.* Retrieved from http://prisonlaw.com/major-cases/

Prison Rape Elimination Act. (2003). Pub. L. 108-79, 34 U.S.C. § 30301 *et seq.*

Prison Rape Elimination Act Prisons and Jail Standards United States Department of Justice Final Rule National Standards to Prevent, Detect, and Respond to Prison Rape Under the Prison Rape Elimination Act, 28 C.F.R., Pat 115 Docket No. OAG-131, Rin 1105-AB34 (2012).

Ruiz v. Estelle, 503 F.Supp. 1265. (S.D. Tex. 1980).

Ruiz v. Estelle, 679 F.2d 1115 (5th Cir. 1982).

Snell, T. (2014). *Capital punishment, 2013—Statistical tables.* Washington, DC: U.S. Department of Justice, Bureau of Justice Statistics. Retrieved from https://www.bjs.gov/content/pub/pdf/cp13st.pdf

Stahl, A. (2014). *Torture on death row: Court rules against automatic use of solitary confinement for the condemned.* Retrieved from http://solitarywatch.com/2014/03/17/may-emerging-national-trend-court-rules-automatic-placement-solitary-confinement-sentenced-execution/

Thompson v. Enomoto, 815 F.2d 1323 (9th Cir. 1987).

Thompson v. Enomoto, 915 F.2d 1383 (9th Cir. 1990).

United States Census Bureau. (2016). *Population and housing units estimates.* Retrieved from http://www.census.gov/programs-surveys/popest/data/tables.All.html

Walters, J. (2014, February 18). Prison guards working on Texas death row call for softer conditions for condemned inmates. *The Telegraph*. Retrieved from http://www.telegraph.co.uk/news/worldnews/northamerica/10647442/Prison-guards-working-on-Texas-Death-Row-call-for-softer-conditions-for-condemned-inmates.html

2

Waiting Alone to Die

Terry A. Kupers

The turning point in the argument on the death penalty is whether we believe there are crimes of such horror that their perpetrators deserve incredibly cruel punishment at the hands of the state. Execution is the ultimate cruel punishment. But then there is solitary confinement. Adding a long stint in solitary confinement before execution certainly makes life significantly more miserable for the condemned. There are levels of the logic of death penalty abolition: A significant number of those on death row will eventually be proven innocent, as then-Governor Ryan pointed out in commuting death sentences in Illinois; there is blatant racial discrimination at all steps along the way in meting out the death penalty, as Justice Blackmun argued repeatedly; and ultimately, execution is simply wrong on religious and moral grounds. The same arguments apply to the solitary confinement of those awaiting their execution on death row.

http://dx.doi.org/10.1037/0000084-003
Living on Death Row: The Psychology of Waiting to Die, H. Toch, J. R. Acker, and V. M. Bonventre (Editors)
Copyright © 2018 by the American Psychological Association. All rights reserved.

I believe, and it is my purpose in writing this piece to prove to readers, that no matter how awful a person's crimes, he or she deserves to be treated as a human being and accorded all the rights and privileges spelled out in our Constitution as well as in human rights accords. It is not acceptable to torture people just because they committed awful deeds. The multiple murderer, even if he evidences no remorse and threatens to kill again, has the right to be confined in decent surroundings and be permitted meaningful social contacts and activities. In fact, solitary confinement is not a sentence meted out by any court. It is a management strategy. The death-sentenced prisoner does not even have a prison sentence; he is merely consigned to prison to await the enactment of his sentence, execution.[1]

THE ARCHITECTURE OF DEATH ROW
INSIDE THE SUPERMAX

The architecture of the supermaximum security unit, Special Management Unit II (SMU II; subsequently renamed the Browning Unit), in Florence, Arizona (Arizona Department of Corrections), was quite familiar to me because it is strikingly similar to the Security Housing Unit (SHU) at Pelican Bay State Prison in California, a facility I toured in preparation for expert psychiatric testimony in *Coleman v. Wilson* (1993) and later in *Ashker v. Brown* (2014).[2] Death row occupied two clusters of cells within SMU II/the Browning Unit. Death-sentenced prisoners were confined alone in a cell nearly 24 hours per day, (relatively rare) exceptions being for visits, showers, medical appointments, and time alone in the small recreation area down the tier from their cells. Cells measured approximately 11½ feet deep by less than 7 feet across the front. There were no windows in the cells, no view of the sky or outdoors. There were Lexan- (indestructible Plexiglas) covered skylights high up on the wall opposite the two stacks of cells on each pod, but because there was a second Lexan cover external to the first on that wall, there was still no clear view of the sky. All cells

---

[1] Many thanks to Hank Skinner for this insight. See Skinner (2007).

[2] For a more detailed description of the Pelican Bay SHU, see my redacted report in *Ashker v. Brown*, available at https://ccrjustice.org/sites/default/files/attach/2015/07/Redacted_Kupers%20Expert%20Report.pdf

faced in the same direction, so inhabitants of cells could not see another human being except when an officer came to deliver a food tray or another prisoner from the pod passed by on the way to recreation. There were three blank walls within the cell, plus a metal grid over the door that permitted a somewhat distorted view of the blank outer wall. Then, in quite a few cells, an additional thick Lexan plate had been affixed on the hallway side of the metal grid cell covering, enhancing the stark isolation.

As I toured Arizona's death row in 2002 in preparation for testimony in federal court about Mr. Robert Comer's competency to waive his appeals and be executed, I asked to be locked into an empty, Lexan-covered cell. I was taken aback by how quickly the temperature and humidity rose in the cell, which gave me some sense of Mr. Comer's complaint that he often felt like he could not breathe in his cell. He told me he tried to work out all day to stay sane and fit—mostly he walked or ran in his cell—but difficulty catching his breath inside his cell hampered that project. Mr. Comer had not shaken a hand for many years. He was permitted one book from the library every 2 weeks, and when the book arrived, he would read it while pacing in his cell.

The quality of my writing is not adequate to fully describe the severity of the isolation and starkness of the cells and pod where Mr. Comer was confined. Many death-sentenced prisoners spend 10 or even 20 years in approximately these circumstances, even though up to 40% of them will eventually either be determined innocent, be exonerated of their capital crime, or have their death sentence commuted to a prison term or be pardoned. Thirty-two states and the U.S. Government have death rows in their prisons, and the majority of death rows involve solitary confinement within supermax prison facilities.

Death row in Texas has been located in the Polunsky Unit of the Texas Department of Criminal Justice since 1999 (for a description of conditions on Texas's death row, see Chapters 8 and 9, and Kupers, 2007). The 246 prisoners on death row (as of June 2016) are strip-searched, cuffed with their hands behind their backs and accompanied by two (or more) officers any time they leave their area. There are narrow horizontal windows high on the outside wall of the cells that cannot be opened. The windows are smaller than the width of a fist, and inmates must stand atop their bunks just to see through them. Unless the prisoner is fortunate enough to have a view of the parking lot, his view will be limited to an adjoining section of building. Often, prisoners' sole connection with the outside world is through personal radios that are only obtained if they are fortunate enough to be able to afford one. Sleep cycles are interrupted at 3:30 every morning, when officers turn on all lights to serve breakfast. The architecture of the units has been described to me by prisoners as "cavernous"; every noise or scream reverberates throughout the unit. When officers conduct counts during the night hours, they bang loudly on metal cell doors demanding the prisoner call out his number. The noise is piercing, causing most prisoners to wake instantly.

A recent declaration (part of a legal appeal) written by Juan (not his real name), a prisoner on Texas's death row, illustrates many of the phenomena that are almost universally reported by individuals in isolative confinement. It is my understanding he does not have a history of serious mental illness, and he certainly is a coherent narrator. He declared,

> The isolation is really hard for me. Sometimes I feel desperate just to see or talk to another person. . . . Although I can talk through the cell walls to other inmates on death row, I might go weeks without seeing another person's face or eyes, except for the guards who walk by my cell and slide a tray of food through my door. . . . At times, I feel trapped in a state of hyperawareness. During these times, I feel incredibly sensitive to the slightest sounds. . . . I find it impossible to relax—I feel tense and anxious from being in my tiny cell all the time, with no one to keep me company and nothing to distract me from my own thoughts. When I have gone a long period of time without a visit, I notice that I start ruminating. I spend a lot of time thinking about the violent or cruel things I've seen guards do to other inmates, and fearing that they will do the same things to me. . . . Sometimes my mind races so much that I can't focus on what I'm reading or writing and need to stop. . . . I also get extremely depressed; when this happens, I spend all my time sleeping and don't want to read, write, or take recreation. I just stare at the walls. I'm usually social

and outgoing, but then I become withdrawn and detached. Years ago, I wanted to commit suicide by waiving my appeals. I felt it wasn't worth living anymore. . . . In the past few years, something strange has started to happen to me: I sometimes see or hear things that aren't there. . . . I no longer know what is real or if I'm real. I try my best to shake these episodes and feelings off because I know too well from watching other inmates that once a person loses his sense of reality entirely, it's a slippery slope to hitting a breaking point, medication, and sedation. Men who go that route become living zombies. . . . I also have noticed that my memory seems to be slipping. . . . I used to be a big reader. . . . Reading helped keep me sane by helping me focus on the outside world and on positive things. But lately I can't concentrate on reading anymore. . . . I can almost never sleep at night and can't seem to keep a normal sleep cycle. The light fixture in my cell gives off a really bright, jarring light. They first turn the light on extremely early, around 3 or 4 a.m. . . . The sound of inmates who have lost their minds from the isolation also fills the air with scream-ing or incoherent yelling.

In other words, this man remains sane, but he is plagued by a large num-ber of serious symptoms and disabilities, and they are strikingly similar to the symptoms and disabilities that are reported by a large number of prisoners in solitary confinement throughout the country.

Robert Charles Comer had been living on Arizona's death row for 16 years when I met him. He had killed a man he encountered at a camp-site, and he had kidnapped and raped a woman from the same camp-ground. He was convicted in 1988 and given a death sentence. In prison, he exhibited a penchant for manufacturing shanks (prison-manufactured knives), and he had a knack for defeating the lock on his cell door. He would make a shank by grinding a piece of metal from the ventilation out-let in his cell against the concrete floor or cell wall. Next, he would secrete the blade by chipping away at the concrete to form a cubbyhole. Then he would mix the concrete powder he had chipped away with water to create a sufficiently realistic cover for the hiding place so that officers conducting cell searches would not find the shanks.

Mr. Comer's shank-manufacturing activities were not the reason he spent 16 years in solitary confinement. Arizona's entire death row was contained within SMU II (now the Browning Unit). And that brings us to the first question I want to address here: What is the rationale, and the morality, of situating entire death rows inside supermax isolation units? I do not believe there is solid evidence that placing death row inside a supermax unit makes the prison safer and easier to manage. Actually, on average, death-sentenced prisoners are not difficult to manage and are not especially prone to violence. Of course, there are some outliers, murderers who would murder again in the prison if left to their own devices. These dangerous men are a small proportion of the denizens of death rows.

Most prisoners on death row are older than the average prisoner; they are more interested in finding time to work on their appeals and stay in touch with loved ones than they are in getting into fights, and they long ago stopped seeking vengeance against other groups who they once felt were out to get them. In the early 1990s, in preparation for expert testimony in a previously filed class action lawsuit about the harm of double-celling prisoners in solitary confinement units in the California prisons (*Toussaint v. McCarthy*, 1984; *Wright v. Enomoto*, 1976), I visited California's death row. It was not a solitary confinement unit, and it still is not today (see Hunter, 2007). There I found prisoners of all races sitting around in a common area, sharing cigarettes and chatting across racial lines. This contrasted with all the other maximum security units in California, in which there was strict segregation of prisoners by race, presumably to minimize the risk of interracial violence.

SOLITARY CAUSES GREAT HARM

The warehousing of death-sentenced prisoners in solitary confinement causes great harm, the same harm that isolation causes in other prisoners forced to endure long-term solitary confinement (Grassian, 1983; Haney, 2003; Kupers, 2013; Scharff-Smith, 2006). It has been known for as long as solitary confinement has been practiced that human beings experience a great deal of pain and mental deterioration when they remain in solitary confinement for a significant length of time. Human beings require at least some social interaction and productive activities to establish and sustain a sense of identity and to maintain a grasp on reality. In the absence of social interactions, unrealistic ruminations and beliefs cannot be tested in conversation with others, so they build up inside and are transformed into unfocused and irrational thoughts, including paranoia. Disorganized behaviors emerge. Internal impulses linked with anger, fear, despair, and other strong emotions grow to overwhelming proportions.

Prisoners do what they can to cope. Many pace relentlessly or clean their cells repetitively, as if this nonproductive action will relieve the emotional tension. Those who can, read books and write letters. We know from much research that the social isolation and idleness, as well as the near absolute lack of control over almost all aspects of daily life, often lead to serious psychiatric symptoms and breakdown. Isolated prisoners develop massive free-floating anxiety that can trigger panic. Their thinking becomes increasingly disorganized and includes paranoid ideas. They become angry and then fearful that their anger will lead to more disciplinary problems and worse punishments.

Another symptom I hear from prisoners in isolation units around the country is that they cannot concentrate and they experience memory problems. If one is in an isolation cell, the most important activity that supports sanity is reading. But many prisoners in isolation who can read tell me they quit reading. I ask why, and they explain they cannot remember what they read three pages back. (Just imagine how difficult this symptom alone makes life for a condemned man or woman who would like to work on legal appeals.)

There are other symptoms widely reported by the denizens of solitary confinement units, including hypersensitivity to external stimuli, perceptual distortions and hallucinations, fears of persecution, lack of impulse control, severe and chronic depression, appetite loss and weight loss, heart palpitations, social withdrawal, apathy and blunting of affect, talking to oneself, headaches, severe problems sleeping, confused thought processes, nightmares, dizziness, self-mutilation, and lower levels of brain function, including a decline in electroencephalogram (EEG) activity (Grassian, 1983; Haney, 2003; Kupers, 2013; Scharff-Smith, 2006). All these symptoms and disabilities occur in prisoners who have been in solitary confinement for weeks or months. When they are consigned to solitary confinement for longer periods, decades even, as are many inhabitants of death row, even more chronic and lasting damage is likely. Prisoners who have been in solitary confinement for more than a decade report that they have become severely cut off from their feelings and have turned inward. They hardly engage in any social activity at all, even considering their limited options within the isolation unit. The damage is cumulative and often severe and in many cases can bode poorly for adjustment after release from solitary into a general population prison setting or the community.[3]

A significant proportion of prisoners on death row will never be executed, and quite a few will be exonerated and released to the community. In the United States in recent decades through July 2017, there have been 159 prisoners exonerated and released from death row, including 13 in Texas (Death Penalty Information Center, 2017). There can be other reasons why individuals exit death row. Their sentence can be commuted, they can be granted compassionate release, and so forth. But because of the years in solitary confinement, they usually have psychological damage that causes dysfunction and requires mental health treatment. There is a great risk that they will not be able to function without counseling or other therapeutic help, either in a general population prison setting or the community if they are released. I have reported on a "SHU post-release syndrome," which includes a need to retreat into a cell or a room or stay in a home without going out, an inability to relate to others, a massive fear of being in places where there are strangers, and a number of other disabling symptoms (Kupers, 2016; see also Kupers, 2017).

---

[3] See my redacted report in *Ashker v. Brown*, Footnote 2.

MENTALLY ILL PRISONERS
IN SOLITARY CONFINEMENT

So far, I have been talking about the effects of solitary confinement on prisoners who are relatively stable from a psychiatric perspective. But when there is serious mental illness, the isolation and idleness exacerbate the psychiatric disorder—for example, causing a psychotic episode or suicide attempt. In long-term isolation (or segregation) units, especially on death row inside a supermax prison, there are a disproportionate number of prisoners experiencing severe mental illness (Hodgins & Cote, 1991; Human Rights Watch, 2003). I have toured supermax isolative confinement units in over 15 states, including many death rows within supermax facilities. In the process, I have encountered the most severely decompensated and disabled individuals with serious mental illness that I have encountered anywhere else in my 40-year career as a clinical psychiatrist (including state, county, and private psychiatric hospitals).

There are quite a few very disturbed prisoners on death row. Other prisoners tell me that their incessant screaming and noisemaking, especially at night, make life on "The Row" that much more awful. There have been class action lawsuits challenging unconstitutional prison conditions and, in many corrections departments, there is a serious effort to remove prisoners with mental illness from solitary confinement (Raemisch, 2014; Raemisch & Wasko, 2016). But that is often not possible with death-sentenced prisoners. They usually are mandated to stay on death row until they are executed. And that means that prisoners with serious mental illness are forced to endure conditions well known to exacerbate mental illness and suicidal inclinations, which makes miserable the lives of others on death row.

Prisoners in long-term isolation experience despair about their plight, and some resort to suicide or nonsuicidal self-harm. Suicide is approximately twice as prevalent in prison as it is in the community. Of all successful suicides that occur in a correctional system, approximately 50% involve the 5% to 10% of prisoners who are in some form of isolated confinement at any given time (Kaba et al., 2014). This is a stunning statistic, meaning that isolative confinement is one big cause of prison suicide. By nonsuicidal self-harm I mean, for example, "cutting," when the prisoner cuts himself. I know that cutting is not typically suicidal. Someone who is suicidal and cuts himself will blame himself afterward, if he survives, that he failed even in the act of self-destruction. By contrast, someone who cuts himself for other reasons will say something such as, "I felt better after I saw the blood (or felt the pain); it reassured me that I am still alive." There is an epidemic of nonsuicidal self-harm in prison isolation units, including death rows situated inside isolation units. Staff tends to think that the prisoners committing nonsuicidal self-harm are manipulating them to get out of isolation. But the tragic truth is that the acts are compelled to a great extent and not voluntary; they are a symptomatic response to the high anxiety induced by the harsh conditions of solitary confinement.

A disproportionate number of prisoners on death row experience serious mental illness. There is a consensus in corrections today that prisoners with serious mental illness must not be consigned to solitary confinement. Litigation abounds on this issue (e.g., *Jones 'El v. Berge*, 2001; *Madrid v. Gomez*, 1995; *Presley v. Epps*, 2010). But on death row, prisoners with serious mental illness must remain right where they are. This creates the untenable situation in which federal courts keep ruling that prisoners with serious mental illness are not to be consigned to solitary confinement, but because death-sentenced prisoners are required to be housed on death row, there are many prisoners with serious mental illness in isolative confinement there. Their psychiatric disorders, as well as their prognoses and disabilities, are very much worsened by the stint in solitary confinement. In other words, prisoners with serious mental illness are excluded from supermax isolative confinement in many jurisdictions, but death-sentenced prisoners with serious mental illness are not granted that exclusion. They remain on death row, and that usually means isolative confinement in a supermax unit or facility.

The presence of a large number of prisoners with serious mental illness on death row creates hardships for the other prisoners. They are forced to endure a neighbor who hallucinates, is paranoid, and screams that he is being persecuted—at all hours of day and night. That is one more reason so many prisoners complain about not being able to sleep. An exoneree who had spent years on Texas's death row testified in a declaration he provided for another prisoner's legal appeal:

> I watched a lot of other men in solitary confinement develop serious mental illness and become suicidal. They would come in at the age of nineteen and by twenty-one they would appear to have completely lost touch with reality. I think this is because the isolation may have broken their will to live. The monotony can be so loud. Silence can be really loud. Men would drop appeals; men would commit suicide. Juan and I witnessed people slit their throats, overdose on their medication and hang themselves with their sheets. We experienced men being gassed and beaten up by guards. I remember one man screaming inside his cell. Others were replying, encouraging him and telling him to stay strong. Suddenly he went silent. We knew something bad had happened. We were banging on the side of our cells trying to get the guards' attention. They did not come. We could hear them laughing. They were eating a meal and didn't want to be disturbed. Then they were annoyed and threatened to write us up for bad behavior. Finally they came, to find that the man in question had slit his throat. This kind of thing happened frequently. The mental anguish was so intense. We were desperate just to be able to shake someone's hand, or to hug our mothers when they came to visit.

REPREHENSIBLE CONDITIONS OF CONFINEMENT

I testified as an expert in a class action lawsuit about horrid and unconstitutional conditions on death row in Mississippi in *Russell v. Epps* (2003) and *Russell v. Johnson* (2003). Death row contained between 90 and 100 cells inside the 1,000-cell supermaximum Unit 32 of the Mississippi State Penitentiary at Parchman. Beginning in the early 1990s, prisoners in Unit 32 complained of a harsh environment: severe isolation, stench and filth, unrelieved idleness and monotony, little access to exercise. The toilet in each cell had a "ping-pong" mechanism: Whenever the toilet was flushed, it pushed the waste in the bowl into the bowl in the adjoining cell. Infestations of mosquitoes and other stinging insects forced prisoners to keep their windows closed and their bodies completely covered, even in the hottest weather—and the temperatures in the cells during the long Delta summers were extreme. The light was too dim for reading and writing. Medical, dental, and mental health care was inadequate, especially on death row. Psychotic prisoners started fires, flooded the tiers, smeared feces, and screamed, often all night. Prisoners were moved into cells that had been smeared from floor to ceiling with excrement from previous, psychotic tenants. Takedown teams extracted prisoners from their cells and subdued them with pepper spray, adding to the toxic environment caused by fire and flooding. In January 2002, the prisoners on Mississippi's death row went on a hunger strike to protest the conditions of their confinement. The plaintiffs on death row, represented by Margaret Winter and the National Prison Project of the American Civil Liberties Union (ACLU), were successful in court. The resulting order requiring that the unit be brought up to constitutional muster was upheld by the Fifth Circuit Court of Appeals (see Kupers et al., 2009).

In this type of high-security unit, there evolves a vicious cycle of worsening hostility and misunderstanding between staff and prisoners. This is not to downplay the reality that rule violations do occur in such units, and an appropriate and fair disciplinary system must be maintained. But when human beings are subjected to extremes of isolation and idleness and deprived of every vestige of control over their environment, in addition to being denied social contact and all means to express themselves in a constructive manner, the consequence is entirely predictable. They (or almost any human being) will resort to increasingly desperate acts to achieve some degree of control of their situation and to restore some modicum of self-respect. The prisoners are driven to small acts of resistance, which in turn are likely to be perceived by officers as disrespectful or rule breaking. The officers, in turn, become increasingly insensitive, punitive, or even abusive toward the identified troublemakers.

THE HARM MULTIPLIES IN
THE DEATH-SENTENCED PRISONER

It is entirely disingenuous to theoretically grant the death-sentenced individual due process in the form of automatic as well as elective legal appeals and then to confine him or her in harsh isolative conditions that greatly diminish his or her capacity to participate in legal proceedings. At core, competency in court requires an understanding of the legal process and an ability to collaborate with counsel in fighting for one's rights. But solitary confinement disables these capacities. I am not arguing that the death-sentenced prisoner in solitary confinement is necessarily incompetent to proceed. To their credit, many inhabitants of death row inside solitary confinement units sustain their sanity and do manage to advance their legal appeals. But that is an extraordinary accomplishment. Too many other inhabitants of death row are driven to mental illness, despair, and incompetence. How is the death-sentenced prisoner to participate in appeals if he is so anxious he feels a need to pace in his cell relentlessly? How can he read legal documents and think through the appeals process when his concentration and memory are impaired from the isolation? How can he collaborate with his appeals attorney when the enforced isolation has caused him to forget how to relate to another human being? I do not apply the word *disingenuous* lightly.

Then there is the *death row phenomenon* (Harrison & Tamony, 2010). The term emerged in the legal discussion of the death penalty, not the psychiatric literature. It refers, for example, to the psychological experience of condemned prisoners who repeatedly get their hopes up that an appeal will be granted and then have the rug pulled out from under them when their appeal is denied and their hopes are dashed. Or, on most death rows, prisoners who are within 24 hours of being executed are moved to a special cell where they will have no contact with other prisoners—the "death watch," an especially isolating experience (and therefore more cruel), just as the prisoner is closest to death. But if he then wins a last-minute reprieve, he is moved back to a regular cell on death row. Prisoners tell me it is like a roller-coaster. First they prepare for imminent death, then they put their hopes in an appeal, then their hopes are dashed. The death row phenomenon also includes the reality that the only human beings in their lives, besides correction officers and an attorney who visits infrequently, are their neighbors on death row, and often their neighbors precede them to execution. So they repeatedly lose the only people with whom they have a relationship.

The death row phenomenon includes living for years with the knowledge that one is going to be executed, living among prisoners who will likewise be executed, and watching one after another of one's neighbors on death row undergo execution. Mr. Comer was given a date of execution in November 1991, and that date was postponed at the last minute. By 2002, Mr. Comer had been on death row for 13 years. There had been quite a few executions during that time, and he experienced a great deal of emotional pain with each one. This was especially true with regard to the execution of his best friend, Bonzai (Robert Vickers), on May 5, 1999, a loss from which Mr. Comer told me he never recovered.

The death row phenomenon is real and much discussed in the literature on capital punishment. But how much worse does the death row phenomenon become when the person facing the death penalty is forced to live in harsh circumstances replete with near-total isolation and idleness? An individual with schizophrenia is likely to have a psychotic episode triggered by the conditions of supermax isolation, and a person prone to despair and depression will likely be driven to suicide or self-harm. Similarly, the person on death row who is vulnerable to thought impairment and despair is almost certain to have that condition exacerbated by stark isolation and idleness. This is one additional reason we find so much mental illness and hear of so many suicides on death row.

Prisoners on death row are exquisitely vulnerable to the harm of solitary confinement. They are vulnerable because they are automatically prisoners in solitary confinement and there is nothing they can do to improve their situation. They experience a significant number of the symptoms and disabilities typical of prisoners in long-term solitary confinement. Beyond that, they have some additional vulnerabilities common to death-sentenced individuals. On average, death row prisoners have experienced numerous severe traumas. These may begin with physical and sexual abuse during childhood and then include witnessing "drive-by" murders on their street or being victimized by domestic violence (Hannaford, 2015). Typically, the traumas have multiplied over a lifetime before their capital sentence. The harshness and callousness of life in solitary confinement tends to trigger old traumatic memories—for example, the officer who beats the prisoner in the next cell may remind a man of the father who beat the son mercilessly. The extremities of life in prison, the violent fights and rapes on the yard, the endless hours of solitude in the segregation unit, serve as reenactments of prior traumas. In other words, the prisoner is retraumatized (Kupers, 2005).

Touring prisons and death rows in many states in preparation for testimony in class action litigation, I have witnessed a great deal of serious psychopathology, including prisoners smearing feces on walls, setting fires to their cells, and cutting themselves mercilessly. I believe that many of the most severe pathological behaviors—cutting oneself for other than suicidal purposes, for example—in fact involve reenactments of prior trauma. Because prisoners on death row, on average, have experienced more traumas in their lives than almost any other subgroup of citizens, we should make every effort to make certain that their experiences in prison do not mirror their traumatic past.

This list of symptoms and disabilities would almost certainly obstruct a death-sentenced prisoner from participating in the legal process, especially his appeals. Juan's experience also illustrated the ups and downs of hope on death row:

> I experienced a tremendous sense of relief and gratitude to God when my execution was stayed, which I didn't learn until the night of my scheduled execution. But the experience caused so much turmoil for me—not only because I had to personally come to terms with what I thought would be my death, but also because I watched what my family and friends went through. It was difficult to work through my own fear and feelings about dying, and it took a lot of time and prayer. But it was even more devastating to watch how painful my execution date was for all of the people I love. I felt so overwhelmed

as I watched my mother going through the pain of losing her one and only child. Now that I have a new execution date, we're having to go through it all over again.

Prisoners on death row are simply less able to participate in the legal process. Research findings on the human costs of solitary confinement include cognitive and memory problems. We know there are changes in the EEG when human beings are consigned to solitary. Prisoners almost universally complain they cannot concentrate and their memory is impaired by the experience of isolation. They also report that they are anxious, angry, paranoid, or despairing. They have great difficulty sleeping. Their emotional problems, including any mental illness or suicidal inclination, are exacerbated. All of this makes it much more difficult for them to participate in the legal process, to do the research on their case or the law that is needed if they are to be successful, and to collaborate peacefully and effectively with counsel.

AND THEN MANY VOLUNTEER TO DIE

Prisoners in unprecedented numbers are driven by the harsh conditions to "volunteer" or waive their appeals. According to the ACLU (2013), "to date, more than 10 percent of the 1,323 executions since 1976 were of those who dropped their appeals and sought execution. Death-row suicides are also common. Texas has seen 10, including six since 2004" (p. 8; see also Chapter 6, this volume).

"Volunteering" is the informal term for prisoners who waive their automatic appeals and all rights to appeal, which means they will be promptly executed (Blume, 2005). As I mentioned, since the 1980s, death rows in many states, including Arizona and Texas, have been moved into supermax isolation units. In the same period, the number of condemned prisoners seeking to waive their appeals has risen (Blume, 2005). In other words, they are consigned to supermax isolation, where they are condemned to live for the rest of their lives or until their death sentence is commuted, and then they volunteer in unprecedented numbers to be executed. One would hope that if such a trend were identified by experts in corrections—for example, a growing proportion of condemned prisoners being subjected to long-term solitary confinement on death row and, at the same time, more condemned men choosing to waive their appeals—that should be sufficient reason to remove death row from supermax isolation.

According to Robert Johnson (2016), professor of justice, law, and criminality at American University, who has considerable experience investigating conditions on death rows,

> Human beings cannot be stored like so many commodities without violating their human dignity. . . . We as a society are left with a punishment that, in its present and likely future form, is an instance of torture that is cruel as that term is understood in an Eighth Amendment context. (p. 1242)

John Blume (2005) provided a rigorous review of legal precedents and a well-reasoned approach to distinguishing between prisoners who waive their appeals "knowingly and intelligently," on the one hand, and "state-assisted suicide" on the other. According to Blume,

> Conditions of confinement are frequently referred to as contributing to volunteerism. . . . There is some force to this contention. Most death row prisoners are housed under conditions designed for inmates who are disciplinary problems, and not intended to be used for long term incarceration. For example, most death row inmates are typically confined to their cells for 23 hours a day in very small cells. Sanitation and eating conditions can be very poor. . . . Death-sentenced inmates are, with few exceptions, ineligible for prison jobs or correctional programs or even the usual forms of prison recreation, such as sports and movies. Generally, death row inmates are not permitted "contact" visits with their family members, or if they are, the visits must occur under the close observation of numerous correctional officers. (p. 950)

Thus, there is an additional symptom of solitary confinement on death row: volunteering. As death rows are moved into supermax prisons, more prisoners are volunteering to die at the state's hands. Although volunteers must be deemed mentally competent to abandon their appeals

(*Godinez v. Moran*, 1993), it is "not a high bar to cross . . . permit[ing] even severely mentally ill defendants to be found competent to waive trial rights" (Rountree, 2014, pp. 299–300). Hopelessness plays a significant role in one's willingness to volunteer, and hopelessness is created by a lack of belief that one can create a meaningful life in prison (Rountree, 2014, pp. 304–305). According to the Texas exoneree I quoted earlier,

> I saw guys who dropped their appeals because of the intolerable conditions. Before his execution, one inmate told me he would rather die than continue existing under these inhumane conditions. I saw guys come to prison sane and leave this world insane, talking nonsense on the execution gurney. One guy suffered some of his last days smearing feces, lying naked in the recreation yard, and urinating on himself. (ACLU, 2013, p. 3)

THE PENOLOGICAL OBJECTIVE? THE MORALITY?

What exactly is the penological objective for placing death row inside a supermax? Research on supermaximum security prisons shows that the isolation of a significant proportion of prisoners does not decrease violence in the prisons, nor does it make a dent in gang activity (Briggs, Sundt, & Castellano, 2003). It does cause immense and unnecessary suffering, as well as severe mental illness, psychological dysfunction, and suicide. In Mississippi, as the result of the *Presley v. Epps* (2010) class action lawsuit brought by the National Prison Project of the ACLU on behalf of prisoners, supermax Unit 32 at the Mississippi State Penitentiary at Parchman was downsized and then dismantled. Death row was moved to a much less restrictive facility, and the result was actually a decrease in the violence rate as well as in the number of disciplinary infractions throughout the Mississippi Department of Corrections (Kupers et al., 2009). There is no sound penological objective for placing death row within a supermaximum security prison.

Then why should death-sentenced prisoners be subjected to long-term isolation while waiting to die? The public seems obsessed with the image of the heinous murderer set on murdering again, the murderer himself demonstrating the potential for future violence in the way he grits his teeth as the television camera passes through his pod on death row. The image of the killer in an isolation cell on death row serves to rationalize the massive expansion of prison budgets. Those guys on death row are so mean they have to be isolated for everyone's safety. With more cells to isolate "the worst of the worst," the prisons and the streets would be safer! The imprisonment binge of recent decades proves profitable for some—the politicians who win votes by showing how tough they are on crime, the construction companies that build the new prisons, and the contractors who supply the rapidly growing prison population with food, medical supplies, telephone access, and even gifts from home. President Eisenhower warned of an expanding military–industrial complex. The prison–industrial complex is a contemporary reincarnation of Eisenhower's worst fears.

Public relations plays a big part in the expansion of the prison–industrial complex as well as in the placement of death rows inside supermaximum isolation prisons. Think of the news coverage when someone goes to death row and then when he is executed. There is a strong message in the public spectacle of an execution. Part of it is a stern warning to all others who might even contemplate committing a capital crime: "If you commit that crime, if you kill someone, you will be put to death." French historian Michel Foucault (1977) and sociologists of deviance in the United States (Goffman, 1962) arrived at that interpretation.

But there is another side to this development. The powers that be, including the commissioners and wardens, want to give the message that they are responsible for guarding the most dangerous of human beings, heinous murderers who truly deserve to be consigned to solitary for the rest of their lives. The execution of monsters props up the whole image of our police and correction officers as heroes. They guard the most dangerous, so they should be paid more and given more political influence in state governance. Pursuing this logic, there is the myth that the murderers on death row cannot be safely incarcerated anywhere but in solitary confinement for the remainder of their lives. Knowing this to be untrue gives us reason to explore further possible reasons for the foolhardy placement of death row within supermax security.

There is a deeper level to the morality of it all. What if, hypothetically, in a state with the death penalty, we knew for a fact that every single one of the death-sentenced prisoners would be dangerous were he or she to be mixed with other prisoners? And what if, again hypothetically, we believed that solitary confinement was a viable and ethical consignment for very dangerous criminals? (This is a huge hypothetical because, like the majority of readers, I strongly disbelieve that solitary is effective or constitutionally acceptable.) But assuming, hypothetically, that we knew a group of prisoners created a high risk of violence if mixed with other prisoners, and assuming that we believed that solitary confinement is an appropriate choice for the management of very dangerous prisoners, then we would still be confronted by this important question: Is it acceptable, in our democratic and humane society, to impose on a subgroup of prisoners that we deem to be mean and incorrigible, punishment so harsh that it is regularly deemed unconstitutional by federal courts—punishment that violates just about all standards of decency and, according to the Special Rapporteur on Torture of the United Nations, constitutes torture?

I was assigned to perform a psychiatric examination of Robert Comer to help the court determine whether he was competent to waive his appeals. The federal Court of Appeals for the Ninth Circuit had already remanded his case to a federal trial judge for determination of Mr. Comer's competence to waive his appeals. The court noted that he had been in an isolation cell with metal and Lexan covers over the doors for many years and that the conditions were harsh and known to cause human damage. The court wanted to be certain Mr. Comer was not simply in the dilemma imposed by Hobson, the 16th-century British stable owner who offered customers the choice of riding a certain less-than-healthy and less-than-appealing horse or riding no horse at all. The other horses in the stable were not available to the customer, so he would have to choose to take the one horse offered or choose to have no horse at all. Like Mr. Hobson's customer, Mr. Comer had two choices: fight his appeals while living under horrid conditions of isolation and suffocation or halt the appeals process and have his life ended. Was this simply a case of Hobson's choice? Was Mr. Comer capable of giving "knowing, intelligent, and voluntary" consent for the discontinuation of all appeals on his behalf?

I offered my opinion that, although Mr. Comer did not have a serious mental illness other than depression with some signs of posttraumatic stress disorder, the fact that he was forced to endure 16 years in an isolation cell—and for many of those years with an additional Lexan cover across the front of his cell—made his "knowing, intelligent, and voluntary" consent to waive problematic. The court found that he was competent to make a knowing, intelligent, and voluntary decision to waive all further appeals, and he was executed in 2007.

Why do we accord the death-sentenced prisoner a series of appeals and then place him in conditions that preclude his participating competently in his own defense? And why do we then accept his decision, presumably "knowing, intelligent, and voluntary," when he is in no condition to know what his legal chances are and cannot make a voluntary choice? What is the difference between placing a death-sentenced prisoner in solitary confinement, where his concentration and memory are so impaired that he cannot effectively assist his attorney in the pursuit of an appeal, and simply torturing that individual until he "hollers uncle" and begs to be killed?

REFERENCES

American Civil Liberties Union. (2013). *A death before dying.* Retrieved from https://www.aclu.org/files/assets/deathbeforedying-report.pdf

Ashker v. Brown, 4:09-cv-05796-CW (N.D. Cal. 2014).

Blume, J. H. (2005). Killing the willing: "Volunteers," suicide and competency. *Michigan Law Review, 103,* 939–1009.

Briggs, C., Sundt, J., & Castellano, T. (2003). The effect of supermaximum security prisons on aggregate levels of institutional violence. *Criminology, 41,* 1341–1376. http://dx.doi.org/10.1111/j.1745-9125.2003.tb01022.x

Coleman v. Wilson, 912 F.Supp. 1282 (E.D. Cal. 1993).

Death Penalty Information Center. (2017). *Innocence and the death penalty.* Retrieved from https://deathpenaltyinfo.org/innocence-and-death-penalty#inn-st

Foucault, M. (1977). *Discipline and punish: The birth of the prison* (2nd ed.; A. Sheridan, Trans.). New York, NY: Vintage Books.

Godinez v. Moran, 509 U.S. 389 (1993).

Goffman, E. (1962). *Asylums: Essays on the social situation of mental patients and other inmates.* Chicago, IL: Aldine.

Grassian, S. (1983). Psychopathological effects of solitary confinement. *The American Journal of Psychiatry, 140*, 1450–1454. http://dx.doi.org/10.1176/ajp.140.11.1450

Haney, C. (2003). Mental health issues in long-term solitary and "Supermax" confinement. *Crime and Delinquency, 49*, 124–156. http://dx.doi.org/10.1177/0011128702239239

Hannaford, A. (2015, June 22). Letters from death row: The biology of trauma. *The Texas Observer*. Retrieved from http://www.texasobserver.org/letters-from-death-row-childhood-trauma/

Harrison, K., & Tamony, A. (2010). Death row phenomenon, death row syndrome and their effect on capital cases in the U.S. *Internet Journal of Criminology*. Retrieved from https://docs.wixstatic.com/ugd/b93dd4_0af562fdf3e44a8789 6b5e6366c484e9.pdf

Hodgins, S., & Cote, G. (1991). The mental health of penitentiary inmates in isolation. *Canadian Journal of Criminology, 33*, 177–182.

Human Rights Watch. (2003). *Ill-equipped: U.S. prisons and offenders with mental illness.* New York, NY: Author.

Hunter, M. W. (2007). California's death row. In M. Mulvey-Roberts (Ed.), *Writing for their lives: Death Row USA* (pp. 78–90). Urbana: University of Illinois Press.

Johnson, R. (2016). Solitary confinement until death by state-sponsored homicide: An Eighth Amendment assessment of the modern execution process. *Washington and Lee Law Review, 73*, 1213–1242.

Jones 'El v. Berge, 164 F. Supp. 2d 1096 (W.D. Wis. 2001).

Kaba, F., Lewis, A., Glowa-Kollisch, S., Hadler, J., Lee, D., Alper, H., . . . Venters, H. (2014). Solitary confinement and risk of self-harm among jail inmates. *American Journal of Public Health, 104*, 442–447. http://dx.doi.org/10.2105/AJPH.2013.301742

Kupers, T. (2005). Posttraumatic stress disorder (PTSD) in prisoners. In S. Stojkovic (Ed.), *Managing special populations in jails and prisons* (pp. 10–21). Kingston, NJ: Civic Research Institute.

Kupers, T. (2007). Conditions on Terrell Unit, Texas. In M. Mulvey-Roberts (Ed.), *Writing for their lives: Death Row USA* (pp. 69–77). Urbana: University of Illinois Press.

Kupers, T. (2013). Isolated confinement: Effective method for behavior change or punishment for punishment's sake? In B. Arrigo & H. Bersot (Eds.), *The Routledge handbook of international crime and justice studies* (pp. 213–232). Oxford, England: Routledge.

Kupers, T. (2016). The SHU post-release syndrome. *Correctional Mental Health Report, 17*, 81–95.

Kupers, T. (2017). *Solitary: The inside story of supermax isolation and how we can abolish it*. Berkeley: University of California Press.

Kupers, T., Dronet, T., Winter, M., Austin, J., Kelly, L., Cartier, W., . . . McBride, J. (2009). Beyond supermax administrative segregation: Mississippi's experience rethinking prison classification and creating alternative mental health programs. *Criminal Justice and Behavior, 36*, 1037–1050. http://dx.doi.org/10.1177/0093854809341938

Madrid v. Gomez, 889 F Supp. 1146 (N.D. Cal. 1995).

Presley v. Epps, No. 4:05CV148-JAD (N.D. Miss. 2010).

Raemisch, R. (2014, February 20). My night in solitary. *The New York Times*. Retrieved from https://www.nytimes.com/2014/02/21/opinion/my-night-in-solitary.html

Raemisch, R., & Wasko, K. (2016). Open the door—Segregation reforms in Colorado. *Corrections.com*. Retrieved from http://www.corrections.com/news/article/42045

Rountree, M. (2014). Volunteers for execution: Directions for further research into grief, culpability, and legal structures. *University at Missouri Kansas City Law Review, 82*, 295–333.

Russell v. Epps, Civ. No. 1:02CV261-D-D (N.D. Miss. 2003).

Russell v. Johnson, Civil No. 1:02CV261-D-D (N.D. Miss. 2003), consolidated with Gates v. Cook, Civil No. 4:71CV6-JAD (N.D. Miss. 2003).

Scharff-Smith, P. (2006). The effects of solitary confinement on prison inmates: A brief history and review of the literature. In M. Tonry (Ed.), *Crime and justice, 34* (pp. 441–528). Chicago, IL: University of Chicago Press.

Skinner, H. (2007). Running in: Cell extraction. In M. Mulvey-Roberts (Ed.), *Writing for their lives: Death Row USA* (pp. 65–68). Urbana: University of Illinois Press.

Toussaint v. McCarthy, 597 F. Supp. 1388 (N.D. Cal. 1984), *reversed in part*, 801 F.2d 1080 (9th Cir. 1986).

Wright v. Enomoto, 462 F. Supp. 397 (N.D. Cal. 1976).

3

Lessons in Living and Dying in the Shadow of the Death House: A Review of Ethnographic Research on Death Row Confinement

Robert Johnson and Gabe Whitbread

Don't tell me about the Valley of the Shadow of Death. I live there.
—Mumia Abu-Jamal, *Live From Death Row*

My job, I knew, was to explore life in what was later described for me as a "mausoleum for the living."
—Robert Johnson, *Condemned to Die*

The place was a dungeon, full of men who were as good as dead.
—Michael Lesy, *The Forbidden Zone*

I think this will be my last calendar. Tell you the truth, after 24 years [on death row], I'm not too sad about the dreamless peace of the grave.
—Donald J. Wallace, Jr., quoted in *Death Row Letters*

http://dx.doi.org/10.1037/0000084-004
Living on Death Row: The Psychology of Waiting to Die, H. Toch, J. R. Acker, and V. M. Bonventre (Editors)

In this chapter we examine the main dimensions of life on death row, drawing on the words and insights of death row prisoners and academic ethnographers who have studied death row confinement. The great majority of condemned prisoners live under conditions of individual solitary confinement for 22 or more hours a day (American Civil Liberties Union, 2013, p. 5). Some condemned prisoners live under conditions of congregate solitary confinement in which they "are allowed out of their cells, sometimes for many hours during the day, but are contained in small groups in dayrooms on the pod or tier in which they are housed, in complete isolation from the larger prison" (Johnson, 2016, p. 1216). Death rows, whether they offer individual or congregate solitary confinement, are human warehouses (Johnson, 2016).

We conducted a thorough review of the literature on life and adjustment on death rows, looking for recurring themes as well as evocative language that might best communicate those themes in a concise and compelling manner. We categorized themes into several topics to illustrate how the condemned perceive and respond to the pressures and constraints under which they live on death row. The topics we identified include dismal conditions, institutionalized abuse, isolation, and mental anguish, which break down further into subcategories of powerlessness, fear, emotional emptiness, and the ever-present threat of deterioration and despair, culminating in dehumanization.

DISMAL CONDITIONS

The physical conditions of death row are emblematic of its advertised mission. Tellingly, several prisoners have explicitly described death row as a tomb for prisoners who feel more dead than alive (Johnson, 1981, 1990; see also Johnson, 2016). Paradoxically, death row is a noisy tomb. Rossi (2004), a condemned prisoner, described death row as a cacophony of haunting and invasive noises that threaten one's sanity:

> Steel doors slamming all day and night. Alarms sounding, two-way radios blasting, and intercoms blaring. With 60 prisoners in a cluster, one hears as many as 60 different conversations going on at a

time. Men call out to friends in different pods to check on their welfare.... Angry men cuss at each other for hours.... The constant roar becomes a living, breathing entity of its own. It is not hard to go crazy from the din. (p. 33)

This "living, breathing" tidal wave of noise, we learn, "invades and pollutes our minds. We become desensitized to everything around us. We decay and rot like unpicked fruit" (Rossi, 2004, p. 33). Spiritual decay seemingly merges with the distinctive odor of death that Rossi (2004) reported is a unique and demoralizing feature of the death row environment:

All cell blocks smell, but they do not come close to death row. We all die a little bit each day on the row, and the odor accumulates and builds to an unbelievable level. There are 60 men in this cluster, and we cannot escape the stink of fear, anger, rancid sweat, blood, stale urine, wasted semen, feces, and flatulence. (p. 32)

In the free world, food is often a comfort and a distraction from stress. Unfortunately for condemned prisoners, who need that distraction more than most, food is but another dispiriting facet of the bleak existence of death row. Food on death row is reportedly so lacking in both flavor and nourishment that it is difficult to know whether it can, in fact, be called food.

We only get five to seven minutes to eat our meals, sometimes the officers don't give us even that much. The food is half cooked, it has no taste whatsoever. We get no fruit or milk. We are all so lacking in vitamins till it's not funny any more. (Lezin, 1999, p. 125)

From the prisoner's point of view, food may well be "the single most basic thing in a prisoner's life. When they mess with our food it is cruel and unusual punishment" (Rossi, 2004, p. 29).

Existence on death row is devoid of care, including responsive medical and mental health care. There are long waiting lists to see dentists and doctors; procedures are palliative, at best. In some instances, the absence of care is purposeful negligence, as if condemned prisoners are as good as dead and hence ineligible for meaningful medical treatment. "I have seen at least six men die of cancer or other major illnesses because they were not [seen and] diagnosed early enough," reported Rossi (2004, p. 41). "You're on death row," one dentist reportedly told a prisoner missing his front teeth. "You're going to die so you don't need no teeth" (Jackson & Christian, 2012, p. 105). Even desperate bids for care may be brutally rebuffed.

> He said, "I want my medication." He talked to doctors. He talked to guards. They wouldn't do nothing about it. He cut himself. They took him to the clinic, put stitches in him, brought him back. The next day, they put him in another cell, and on the edge of the bunk, he hit himself on the forehead. And it cracked the skull. For one hour, he hit his head on the bunk, on the edge of the bunk. After one hour, doctor finally came down here while the boss, the young boss they had, he stand in front of the cell and just look at him and laugh. Laughed at him. (Jackson & Christian, 2012, p. 65)

Death rows are a species of special housing unit, sometimes called simply a SHU (security housing unit; pronounced "shoe") or supermax or control unit. Whatever the name, the theme is not special care or even minimal care but rather total or near-total control of the captives, who are deemed beyond care and correction. "Control units," Rossi (2004) stated, "are the scourge of the American prison system" (p. 81). These settings are steeped in a laundry list of hurt and loss including "pain and suffering," "isolation," "fear," "sensory deprivation," "lack of human touch," "lack of stimulus," "anger," "psychological warfare," "torture," "the smell of death all around," "disrespect," "lack of competent medical services," "paranoia and mental illness," and finally, "the guards' belligerent macho attitude accompanied by sadism" (Rossi, p. 81). Remarkably, Rossi ended this catalog of abuse and neglect with this disclaimer: "None of this is an exaggeration. If anything, I am understating what goes on in here" (p. 81).

INSTITUTIONALIZED ABUSE AND VIOLENCE

In prison, and especially on death row, officers have near complete control over the inmates, whereas inmates have virtually no power whatsoever. Such a stark division of power creates a profound split between the guards and offenders; as a general matter, there is little hope of connection or understanding between these groups. Indifference is the norm; antagonism and abuse often ensue. Inmates feel they are routinely treated as inferior beings who must endure neglect, humiliation, pain, and degradation. Cruelty and debasement, they report, are routine and often are more damaging than physical abuse. "We're treated just like animals put in a cage. You know, like sometimes they come by with their sticks and they poke at you like you're an animal or something" (Johnson, 1981, p. 56). "I wonder how many times in 24 plus years I've had guards tear my cell apart and seize anything that made life a little better? Hundreds, at least. You always feel like it's an act of hatred against you" (Leslie, 2008, p. 198).

Abuse of this sort—taunting, invasive cell searches—is part of a process of "psychological warfare" in which "things are done intentionally to unnerve us" (Rossi, 2004, p. 86; see also Poyck, 2013). Though the inmates imply that these mind games are more demoralizing and painful than physical abuse, beatings are said to be common. Here again, the damage from beatings is described as more than skin deep—for offenders, the physical assault is just another tactic used to make them feel less than human, unworthy of civilized treatment. They dread these incidents out of fear for their safety but, even more urgently, out of fear for their compromised dignity.

> [An inmate was] placed in a straightjacket [sic] that was left open at the back to secure him to a bare mattress on the bunk. In addition, handcuffs were placed on his wrists. A crash helmet much like a motorcyclist would wear was placed on his head, and there he lay for weeks, helpless, alone, and drugged. The care and feeding he received was from the inmate porters. At times, he'd call for assistance for over an hour before a guard would open the door and untie him so he could urinate. (Brasfield, 1983, pp. 91–92)

> Prisoners are often stripped and made to stand around naked, sometimes for hours, sometimes while in handcuffs, often in front of female officers or under surveillance cameras. We're made to bend over and spread our cheeks often. If you refuse or resist, you'll be shocked or maced or beaten into submission. Here at MCC they have a device called "the chair." It half seats and half lays you into a

rack-like position, and you're bound to it at the wrists, ankles, waist and chest. The usual dose is 4 hours. (Leslie, 2008, p. 206)

Some officers are seen by inmates to take an exaggerated pleasure in flaunting their authority in ways that demean and violate.

They're saying, "I've got you, you know, and I'm going to get my respect. And if I don't, I'll just write you up for insubordination or beat your ass, and anything I say is going to go." So your morale is just shot, because you know that they've got you and there's not a whole lot you can do about it. (Johnson, 1981, p. 68)

They're tryin' to carry things back into what the prison was in the 50s and 40s and things like that. They tryin' to go back to the inmate ain't got no rights. He had no privileges. He had nothin'. He had a cell, and he said, "yes sir, boss," "no sir, boss," "yes sir, captain," and all this. He done whatever ya said, whatever the officer said was right, and whatever he told ya to do, ya did. If he told ya to jump, ya jumped, and on the way up ya asked him "how high." If they come to you, they look at you and say "I don't like the way you look." And you say, "Boss, I'd change it if I could." That's the way they wanta get it back to bein'. (Johnson, 1981, p. 67)

As if the condescending attitude and various manifestations of abuse were not enough to endure, those living on death row report feeling a special sort of neglect in connection with their death sentence: "The night before they executed Byrd, they showed *The Green Mile* [on the prison movie channel]. Real sense of humor; they like to mess with us" (Lose, 2014, p. 41). Pointed exchanges may be used to remind prisoners that they will soon be put to death, that their position is hopeless.

Prisoner: They ask me, "Am I ready."

Interviewer: What? They ask you, "Are you ready?"

Prisoner: Yes, for the chair.

Interviewer: So, they come up to your cell, and they say, "Are you ready to go?" and that kind of thing. And then what do you say?

Prisoner: I stay back in the corner and say "no."

Interviewer: You say "no." And . . .

Prisoner: And I start to crying and get nervous.

Interviewer: Well, I don't blame you. What do they do next?

Prisoner: Hit the lock and walk on. They laugh about it.

Interviewer: So, in other words, the guards are just sort of having fun, kind of—come down the cell, give you a hard time, and then move on?

Prisoner: Yes.

Interviewer: Is this most of the guards, or just some of them, or just one guy, or what?

Prisoner: It's most of them.

Interviewer: This happens a lot, does it?

Prisoner: Yes. (Johnson, 1981, p. 68)

Psychological abuses, like the exchange reported by this prisoner, are seen by inmates as the most damaging. "They leave no marks that anyone can see, but your soul is scarred . . . and never heals" (Leslie, 2008, p. 206).

ISOLATION

Death row prisoners spend most of the day in their solitary cells, described by one prisoner as "a 7′ by 10′ cell with no color, sound, or sunshine. It's a nightmare of total boredom" (Lose, 2014, p. 33). Many speak as if their cells are the sum total of their world, as revealed in an excerpt from a death row prisoner's correspondence:

> Every week. Every month. Every year. Every decade. Nothing changes . . . I just sit in a cell and sit in a cell and sit in a cell and sit in a cell and sit in a cell. And then, I sit in a cell some more after that. Sometimes, early in the morning, I sit in a cell. Occasionally, I sit in a cell. Eat, breathe, shit, sleep, sit in a cell. When I can't stand it anymore and feel as if my ears are bells of ringing madness. I sit in a cell.

Sit in a cell

Sit in a cell

Sit in a cell

Sit in a cell

Well, I must go now. I have to sit in a cell. Hope you never have to
sit in a cell. (Leslie, 2008, p. 182)

For some condemned prisoners—perhaps many, given what we know
about the effects of extended solitary confinement in other prison populations (cf. Ferguson, 2014; Haney, 2003; Toch, 1992)—the cell becomes a
mental pressure cooker, threatening their sanity on a daily basis, as seen in
the haunting commentary of this prisoner:

> I sit in that cell, you know, and it seems like I'm just ready to scream
> or go crazy or something. And you know, the pressure, it builds up,
> and it feels like everything is—you're sitting there and things start,
> you know, not hearing things, things start to coming in your mind.
> You start to remember certain events that happened, bad things.
> It just gets to a person. I sit up at night, you know. You just sit
> there, and it seems like you're going to go crazy. You've got three
> walls around you and bars in front of you, and you start looking
> around, you know, and it seems like things are closing in on you.
> Like last night, when I sit in there and everything's real quiet, things,
> just a buzzing noise gets to going in my ears. And I sit there, and I
> consciously think, "Am I going to go crazy?" And the buzzing gets
> louder; and you sit there and you want to scream and tell somebody
> to stop it. And most of the time you get up—if I start making some
> noise in my cell, it will slack off. And it sounds stupid, I know, but it
> happens. . . . sometimes I wonder if I don't get it stopped, I'm going
> crazy or something. And you know, maybe tonight when I lay down
> it's not going to break when I get up and try to make some noise.
> (Johnson, 1981, p. 49)

The stultifying routine of life in the cell may be broken by brief
showers or short stints in the yard or exercise cage, though some prisoners
limit or even decline these seeming respites from their regimented lives

because they are either afraid to leave their cells or simply do not want to interact with officers and others.

> You have to more or less watch what you say to these guys because if they want to get you back, they could easily do that. You're on your way out to the yard, the guy could say as soon as you get out of the center—around that little bend—where the rest of the guys couldn't see you, they could easily claim "well, he turned around and hit me," "he turned around and I thought he was attacking me," or "he pushed me." And one whack with one of those axe handles up against your head, if you're not going to be dead, you're going to be insane for the rest of your life. And then you're not going to be able to help no one. That's what happened to one of the fellows over there. I understand he got beat in the head so much, he doesn't even know which way is up now. (Johnson, 1981, p. 72)

> They come around and they say "come on, let's go such and such place," you know. And you get kind of paranoid, cause you don't know whether to go or whether to just say "well, whoever it is, just tell 'em to go ahead on, I don't want to see nobody," you know? . . . They handcuff the handcuffs behind your back. You're rendered in a helpless position when you got your hands behind your back. It kind of throws you off balance, so you can't do nothin' else but be open to whatever kind of attack they want to make on you. (Johnson, 1981, p. 73)

In one prisoner's words, "I've started to become so apprehensive and anxiety-stressed that I rarely go to recreation." He showers only on occasion. Outside the cell, there is nothing of value to do "but there is constant observation." If and when you leave the cell, "You feel like an exhibit at the zoo" (Mulvey-Roberts, 2007, p. 71).

Visits, for those lucky enough to have visitors, offer another break in the solitary routine. Visits provide a welcome distraction from the pains and deprivations of life on death row, offering a rare opportunity to escape isolation and feel connected to others. But for death row inmates, visits are accompanied by invasive strip searches, which can be deeply alienating.

The rage and frustration in reports of visits ruined by strip searches are palpable.

> Your people come to this place. You go down and you sit down for an hour or whatever you stayed and you get your mind away from this place. And just as soon as you come in after having enjoyed yourself for a little bit, just as soon as you get up from out there and walk in here, they strip you, look up your asshole and in your mouth and strip search you and handcuff you behind your back and drag you back up that hall. Well, you see, they just broke your whole fucking visit. You would have been better off, in a way, if you'd just stayed in your cell and if you could have slept through that hour. . . . I mean that's the kind of attitude that leaves you with after they fuck with you. Knowing your people drove and went through all this trouble to come see you, to give you an hour or something. Then they have taken the fucking time to figure out a way to fuck it up for you. (Johnson, 1981, p. 54)

> Last night, when I was coming back from my visit, they started something new. They used a set of cuffs that had what I can only describe as an anchor attached to it. I had the shackles as usual, but the cuffs had a heavy chain on them that was approximately 4 inches long. At the end of it was a metal structure about a foot tall that the sergeant carried. It's stupid and insulting and infuriating. I'M NOT A DOG TO BE PUT ON A LEASH! (Towery, 2012, p. 33; emphasis in original)

The loneliness bred on death row seems beyond remediation for many prisoners, even for those with occasional visits, perhaps because the isolated nature of the setting makes feelings of loss impossible to communicate to those from the real world who may care but simply cannot comprehend the world in which the prisoners live. In one prisoner's words, "No one really knows what loneliness is until they come to the row. . . . On the row a person feels lost in deep despair. You feel no one will ever be able to help you. All is lost" (Arriens, 1997, p. 44).

MENTAL ANGUISH

As described earlier, mental anguish can be broken down into four subcategories: powerlessness, fear, emotional emptiness, and deterioration and despair.

Powerlessness

The looming threat of death by execution, paired with the lack of meaningful control over the details of daily existence, leads to an overwhelming sense of powerlessness. Condemned prisoners have little choice but to accept whatever insults, invasions, or abuses they encounter in their daily lives. Prisoners look for any aspect of life that they can claim for themselves, anything that might grant them a shred of autonomy, but there is little room for such independence. Resistance brings on more repressive control from officers. Several inmates have reported orchestrating mental escapes into vivid flights of fancy—"tripping," in the parlance of the prisoners—which, liberating while they last, always end in the vacuum of the solitary prison cell (McGunigall-Smith & Johnson, 2008).

Waiting helplessly for death by execution is perhaps the chief reason for the overwhelming sense of powerlessness that rules death row, and yet many prisoners report that they think of execution as a relief insofar as it offers a real, physical, and irreversible escape from the sheer, crushing weight of dead time that rules their lives.

> Well, for me personally, when you go through life out there, time is like air to you. You breathe it in, and you breathe it out; it passes through you, and you sort of pass through time. But when you're here and it's final . . . time doesn't go anywhere. It comes and it stops. It builds up inside, and it's actually like a weight after a while. Ten years weighs an awful lot. It just builds up, and there's time in the morning when . . . you almost literally feel it crushing you when you wake up and you have to look around and see the same things in here and you're in the same cell and doing the same things that you did years ago, and nothing's going to change. (Light & Donovan, 1997, p. 14)

In one man's words, "This supermax segregation has done me in. Sad, though, when death looks brighter than a prison" (Leslie, 2008, p. 197).

Fear

On death row, offenders fear for their sanity, safety, and everything in between. They feel there are myriad ways they can be harmed, and that they cannot turn anywhere for help or protection. They fear the staff, their fellow prisoners, and the emotional turmoil building within themselves, which can lead them to threaten destructive or self-destructive violence. Furthermore, the environment itself is surreal in its desolation; anything and everything can seem suspect and nightmarish, "a living hell" in which fear, fed by threat and uncertainty, bleeds into hate (Lezin, 1999, p. 63).

Prisoners on death row are in a constant, exhausting state of high alert that starts when they arrive in this threatening setting and continues on into their daily lives in the cell, where feelings of vulnerability can reach great heights.

> The biggest fear is when you walk onto this place. I've seen one man walk out there and he stood right there and he broke down and cried. I've seen more come in here and live three days and start praying. I've seen them come in here and cuss the day they was born because of fear. I've seen grown men come in here and get down and pray like kids. And cry. (Jackson & Christian, 1980, p. 78)

> When you're on death row and you're laying down in your cell and you hear a door cracking, you'll think of where it comes from. When you hear it crack. And when you hear the keys and everything, when something like this happens, the keys come through there: I'm up. I'm up, because you don't know when it's going to take place. The courts give you an execution date, that's true. But you don't know what's going to take place between then and when your execution date arrives. You don't know when you're going to be moved around to the silent cell over here. That's right down the hall, what they call a waiting cell. Up there, you don't know when you're going to be moved

down there. And this keeps you jumpy, and it keeps you nervous, and it keeps you scared. (Johnson, 1981, p. 74)

Given the nature of death row confinement, it is almost certainly true that, as Lezin (1999, p. 151) maintained, "every death row inmate lives each day wondering how much longer he has to live." Changes in the rigid routines that constrain life on death row threaten life as the prisoners have been conditioned to know it and can readily be seen as portents of disaster, including imminent execution.

> It is amazing to observe how conditioned we become after being treated like this for years on end. Occasionally, when the meals are delayed by as little as a few minutes, our bodies and minds go through changes. We start worrying if we are to be fed at all, or if our entire world is coming to an end. Perhaps World War III has started and orders have been given to kill the prisoners. Maybe the death squads are coming. (Rossi, 2004, p. 27)

Emotional Emptiness

Death row robs lives of meaning because it so thoroughly isolates its inhabitants from the larger social world from which most of us, if not all us, draw meaning (cf. Dewey, 1922, p. 9). Though human beings are resilient and seek to create their own meaning even in the most barren and isolated circumstances, the research we reviewed suggests that few succeed on death row (cf. Johnson, 2014). Years, even decades, are spent in a barren cell that offers nothing to ground one's sanity and sense of place in the world. It is a feat to survive in this environment for any length of time without experiencing emotional atrophy. Alongside the pain wrought by the emotional vacuum of death row, there is a profound numbness (Lezin, 1999, p. 160). "You need love and it just ain't there," said one prisoner. "It leaves you empty inside, dead inside" (Johnson, 1981, p. 112). "I fear that death row means a gradual killing of my humanity," said another, "which is more painful than any execution can ever be" (Johnson, 1998, p. 62). It is one thing to say that to live is to suffer. On death row, suffering is one's life. "There is no reality to my life except continual mental agony. . . . That is all forever and ever, year upon year" (Leslie, 2008, p. 181).

Deterioration and Despair

Many death row inmates describe a process of mortification or death of the self in anticipation of death by execution. There is no relief from the knowledge that whatever remains of life is to be spent awaiting execution. "You know, day by day, regardless of what you do, it's always there in the back of your mind: 'Hey, you on death row. You could be executed. They could kill you'" (Jackson & Christian, 2012, p. 74). Simply being sent to death row is arguably like "suffering a small death" in the face of "the awesome omnipresence" of cold-blooded executions (Johnson, 1998, p. 10). To live under the threat of death by execution is more painful to many than death itself.

> It's the unending, uninterrupted immersion in death that wears on you so much. It's the parade of friends and acquaintances who leave for the death house and never come back, while your own desperate and lonely time drains away. It's the boring routine of claustrophobic confinement, punctuated by eye-opening dates with death that you helplessly hope will be averted. It's watching yourself die over the years in the eyes of family and friends, who, with every lost appeal, add to the emotional scar tissue that protects them . . . from your death, long before you're gone. (*Turner v. Jabe*, 1995, para. 22)

This "unending, uninterrupted immersion in death" means that every day on death row is a nightmare version of the day before and the day to come. Each day is a "redundant experience of failure and rejection—of being powerless to effect change, cut off from supportive human contact, vulnerable to others in a world where people want you dead." As a result, "each day the condemned are a little more dead—more like passive objects and less like autonomous beings—than the day before" (Johnson, 1998, p. 96).

Surrounded by death, it is perhaps unsurprising that many prisoners are vividly aware of those who turn to suicide or drop their appeals and submit to execution (cf. Johnson, McGunigall-Smith, Miller, & Rose, 2014). In one prisoner's experience,

> After roughly 10 years in the death row environment, it appears that coping mechanisms fail, hope dies, and inmates develop a death wish. Their desire to die is intense, strong enough that most resort to suicide attempts with dull home-made knives. (Lose, 2014, p. 177)

Another prisoner reported that he was not resigned to execution but rather was eager to be put to death: "I yearn for it with all my heart. . . . Death is my only escape from this hell" (Leslie, 2008, p. 210).

CONCLUSION

The evidence provided by firsthand accounts of condemned prisoners themselves and the ethnographic accounts provided by researchers suggests that "nobody fully adapts to the pressures of death row confinement" (Johnson, 1998, p. 85). Examining his experience as a long-term death row prisoner, Willie Lloyd Turner concluded,

> Nothing could have prepared me for the despair and the frustration, for the loneliness and the abuse, for the shame and the sorrow, for the hopes raised and dashed, for the dreams and nightmares of my death that my seventeen years facing my own advancing demise have served up to me. (*Turner v. Jabe*, 1995, para. 22)

Several studies of death row invoke the image of "living death" to capture the essential or cumulative experience of the condemned prisoner. As understood in this body of work, the notion of living death is "intended to convey the zombie-like, mechanical existence of an isolated physical organism—a fragile twilight creature that emerges when men are systematically denied their humanity" (Johnson, 1981, p. 17). It is important to note that this image has been spontaneously and forcefully rendered by the prisoners themselves to convey that they are alive as bodies but dehumanized and hence dead as persons. The image of living death on death row "serves as a dramatic summary statement of the death row experience, encompassing its central psychological features of power-lessness, fear, and emotional emptiness," culminating in dehumanization (Johnson, 1981, p. 17).

In this chapter, we have sought to recreate the degrading and often brutal experience of confinement on death row. Through powerful language compiled from numerous accounts, we have seen that every element of daily life contributes to profound suffering. For most condemned prisoners, death itself is not the worst part of the sentence—it is the relentless anticipation of death, played out daily in countless degradations big and small, that wears down their sanity and their will to live, rendering them docile objects of execution.

Reforms of death row are of course possible, but the prospects for major reforms are limited. There are examples of instances in which death row prisoners have been integrated into the general prison population, at least until their execution dates draw near, after which they are confined under conditions of solitary confinement (see Chapter 5, this volume). Short of this radical reform, which has much to recommend it in principle but has proven difficult to implement in practice, attempts could be made to diminish the suffering that occurs on death row. For instance, offering more nutritious and palatable food, attending to pest control, and addressing the miserable conditions described at the beginning of this chapter would go a long way toward making death row more fit for human habitation. Systematic mistreatment, described in detail earlier, could be reduced by promoting a less rigid prison protocol and providing better training to officers to assist them in the management of more responsive custodial procedures. For example, "rest and recuperation assignments might help staff to better handle the pressures of their job," pressures that are now too often translated in neglect or abuse of prisoners (Johnson, 1981, p. 122).

Isolation, profoundly tied to the sense of impending death as experienced by condemned prisoners, could be reduced in several ways. Special programs of study or work in the cells, for example, would reduce the loneliness and boredom of life on death row. One example would be in-cell hobby work, which would offer a pastime to break up the day. Another possibility is self-help. Said one condemned prisoner,

> The aspect of us helping each other could be a big asset, because I believe that when men are thrown together with one prime purpose in mind, which is to survive, they could more or less come up with some method or some way to help themselves. (Johnson, 1981, p. 124)

Though condemned prisoners spend most of their time in their solitary cells, opportunities for recreation when prisoners are out of their cells could be expanded to include small-group activities, including organized sports.

Visits, and especially contact visits, could be made more readily available, facilitating the efforts of prisoners to sustain ties to family and friends. Finally, modern communications technology, ubiquitous in the free world today, might be made available on death row in small, controlled doses, opening up solitary cells to virtual engagement with the larger world by e-mail, for example, and making it easier for families to visit loved ones on death row by offering video visits as an option for those who find it difficult to visit the prisoner in person (Jewkes & Johnston, 2009; Johnson, 2005; Johnson & Hail-Jares, 2016). The bottom line is this: "Solitary confinement need not, and should not, comprise the extent of the correctional effort on death row" (Johnson, 1981, p. 123). Solitary confinement may be a necessary evil on many death rows, but it is an evil that can be greatly mitigated when the human experience of life under sentence of death is taken into account.

REFERENCES

Abu-Jamal, M. (1995). *Live from death row.* Reading, MA: Addison-Wesley.

American Civil Liberties Union. (2013). *A death before dying: Solitary confinement on death row.* Retrieved from https://www.aclu.org/files/assets/deathbeforedying-report.pdf

Arriens, J. (1997). *Welcome to hell: Letters and writings from death row.* Boston, MA: Northeastern University Press.

Brasfield, P. (1983). *Deathman pass me by: Two years on death row.* San Bernardino, CA: Borgo Press.

Dewey, J. (1922). *Human nature and conduct: An introduction to social psychology.* New York, NY: Modern Library.

Ferguson, R. A. (2014). *Inferno: An anatomy of American punishment.* Cambridge, MA: Harvard University Press.

Haney, C. (2003). Mental health issues in long-term solitary and "supermax" confinement. *Crime & Delinquency, 49,* 124–156. http://dx.doi.org/10.1177/0011128702239239

Jackson, B., & Christian, D. (1980). *Death row.* Boston, MA: Beacon Press.

Jackson, B., & Christian, D. (2012). *In this timeless time: Living and dying on death row in America.* Chapel Hill: University of North Carolina Press.

Jewkes, Y., & Johnston, H. (2009). "Cavemen in an era of speed-of-light technology": Historical and contemporary perspectives on communication within prisons. *Howard Journal of Criminal Justice, 48,* 132–143. http://dx.doi.org/10.1111/j.1468-2311.2009.00559.x

Johnson, R. (1981). *Condemned to die: Life under sentence of death.* New York, NY: Elsevier.

Johnson, R. (1990). *Death work: A study of the modern execution process.* Belmont, CA: Brooks-Cole.

Johnson, R. (1998). *Death work: A study of the modern execution process* (2nd ed.). Boston, MA: Cengage.

Johnson, R. (2005). Brave new prisons: The growing social isolation of modern penal institutions. In A. Liebling & S. Maruna (Eds.), *The effects of imprisonment* (pp. 255–284). London, England: Willan.

Johnson, R. (2014). Reflections on the death penalty: Human rights, human dignity, and dehumanization in the death house. *Seattle Journal for Social Justice, 13,* 583–598.

Johnson, R. (2016). Solitary confinement until death by state-sponsored homicide: An Eighth Amendment assessment of the modern execution process. *Washington and Lee Law Review, 73,* 1213–1242.

Johnson, R., & Hail-Jares, K. (2016). Prisons and technology: General lessons from the American context. In Y. Jewkes, B. Crewe, & J. Bennett (Eds.), *Handbook on prisons* (pp. 284–306). London, England: Routledge.

Johnson, R., McGunigall-Smith, S., Miller, C., & Rose, A. (2014). Autonomy in extremis: An intelligent waiver of appeals on death row. *American Journal of Criminal Justice, 39,* 787–807. http://dx.doi.org/10.1007/s12103-014-9260-8

Leslie, C. M. (2008). *Death row letters: Correspondence with Donald Ray Wallace, Jr.* Newark: University of Delaware Press.

Lesy, M. (1987). *The forbidden zone.* New York, NY: Farrar Straus & Giroux.

Lezin, K. (1999). *Finding life on death row: Profiles of six death row inmates.* Boston, MA: Northeastern University Press.

Light, K., & Donovan, S. (1997). *Texas death row.* Jackson: University of Mississippi Press.

Lose, E. (2014). *Living on death row.* El Paso, TX: LFB Scholarly Publishing LLC.

McGunigall-Smith, S., & Johnson, R. (2008). Escape from death row: A study of "tripping" as an individual adjustment strategy among death row prisoners. *Pierce Law Review, 6,* 533–545.

Mulvey-Roberts, M. (Ed.). (2007). *Writing for their lives: Death row USA.* Urbana: University of Illinois Press.

Poyck, W. V. (2013). *Death row diary.* Retrieved from http://deathrowdiary. blogspot.com

Rossi, R. M. (2004). *Waiting to die: Life on death row.* London, England: Vision.

Toch, H. (1992). *Living in prison: The ecology of survival.* Washington, DC: American Psychological Association. http://dx.doi.org/10.1037/10137-000

Towery, R. (2012). *Death watch diary: The last days of a death row prisoner.* Retrieved from https://www.amazon.com/Death-Watch-Diary-Robert-Towery-ebook/dp/B007JD3LUM

Turner v. Jabe, Declaration of Willie Lloyd Turner, pursuant to petition for writ of habeas corpus, April 27, 1995.

TWO

LEGAL AND POLICY ISSUES

Death Row Solitary Confinement and Constitutional Considerations

Fred Cohen

This chapter focuses on the use of solitary confinement for prison inmates who have been sentenced to death. This unites two independent criminal justice reform issues, each with singular vitality and with basic reform concentrated on abolition.

The extensive history of death penalty litigation and the efforts to use the Eighth Amendment ultimately to condemn its imposition will not be reviewed. Along the way, of course, there have been constitutional limits placed on who may be executed, for what crimes, and by what methods. There has been so much "special law" developed by the United States Supreme Court on the death penalty that it is fair to say we have a "jurisprudence of death." The particular emphasis here is on the extended solitary confinement of the death-sentenced inmate.

This chapter was written with the extremely valuable assistance of Joseph M. Radochonski, third-year student, University of Arizona James E. Rogers College of Law.

http://dx.doi.org/10.1037/0000084-005
Living on Death Row: The Psychology of Waiting to Die, H. Toch, J. R. Acker, and V. M. Bonventre (Editors)

If capital punishment suddenly disappeared, reform of extended solitary confinement would retain its vitality. If extended solitary confinement were banished, efforts to ban the death penalty would continue apace. In combining state-authorized killing with state-authorized extended social isolation of prisoners, we examine government's most severe criminal sanction along with its most onerous condition of prison confinement.

The more extreme forms of solitary confinement combined with almost unimaginably extended terms—10, 20, even 43 years—are under concerted pressure in the federal courts. Although there is not yet a federal court decision prohibiting extreme and extended penal isolation, juveniles and prisoners with, or particularly vulnerable to, serious mental illness, have had success in achieving categorical exemption due to their enhanced vulnerability to isolation. Solitary confinement, or penal isolation, is not without variations. The cells may look very different, and procedures for gaining entrance and release will vary. "Solitary" may actually include double-celling, there may be more visits or recreational time, and so on. At its core is the loss of social interaction. That is the principal and profoundly harmful loss imposed by extended penal isolation; the concept is developed more fully later in the chapter.

Are prisoners with a death sentence entitled to less constitutional consideration regarding severe and extended terms of solitary confinement? Does the death sentence somehow identify a group of particularly dangerous inmates, thus justifying these extreme measures of security? Is it possible that a sentence of death puts such inmates in a unique category of disadvantaged inmates? Does impending death coupled with claims of innocence or trial errors and the hope of executive clemency aggravate the grievous harm of extended social isolation?

If it is ultimately unconstitutional to confine any inmate under extreme conditions of isolation for an extended period, is there any reason death-sentenced inmates would not be entitled to the same protection? Ultimately, I answer the final question in the negative. Death-sentenced inmates appear to be no more dangerous as a class than others. Accordingly, the conditions of their confinement should be dictated by their reception classification and subsequent conduct, subject to generally applicable constitutional limits on procedure, conditions, and duration. Extended penal isolation for any inmate should be proscribed as cruel and unusual punishment, and there is no valid basis for framing an exception for those inmates sentenced to death.

Inmates under sentence of death should be subject to all the lawful rules of prison management, certainly including security concerns and the imposition of proportionate punishment for prison rule infraction.

Criminal justice reform inches forward in many venues: academic research and advocacy, legislation, executive orders, advocacy organizations, and the courts. In the areas of our concern, it is the federal courts that are the fulcrum of reform, and it is the Eighth Amendment to the U.S. Constitution that is the doctrinal foundation.[1]

CONSTITUTIONAL FRAMEWORK

The Eighth Amendment, adopted in 1791 and strongly influenced by the English Bill of Rights of 1689, addresses excessive bail and fines and concludes with "nor cruel and unusual punishments inflicted." Over time, judicial concern for the "unusual" has virtually disappeared, leaving "cruel" and "punishment" as the operative prohibitory terms.

The U.S. Supreme Court is the ultimate arbiter of what these terms mean. It has produced a large body of case law involving the Eighth Amendment, much of it arising from lawsuits challenging the death penalty itself, as well as jail and prison conditions. Other cases are as disparate as challenges to loss of citizenship and proportionality in criminal sentencing. The Constitution does not provide courts with a decisional formula or a philosophical perspective for interpreting and applying such crucial terms as *cruel* or *punishment*. A judicial perspective with basic philosophical issues at its jurisprudential core has emerged, but it is not without dissent. The decisional dichotomy here ranges from the Justice Scalia and Justice Thomas view that the meaning of cruel punishment should be fixed as of the time of constitutional enactment to one more

---

[1] For a comprehensive review of reform issues in "restricted housing," see National Institute of Justice (2016), and for the overview of legal issues on point, see Cohen (2016).

generally adopted by the Court that tracks evolving notions of civilized decency and current views on what constitutes the essence of human dignity. What is judicially regarded as cruel takes its ultimate view on what it means to identify and then respect more current views on the inherent human dignity.

Before reviewing the specific legal developments on solitary confinement, it will be useful to refine further the Supreme Court's Eighth Amendment philosophy and the decisional criteria it uses to make decisions on prison conditions. The Court has repeatedly made clear that the Eighth Amendment is not a constitutional repository for what may be regarded as best prison practices. On the contrary, prison conditions that are harsh and restrictive are considered part of the price rightly extracted from prisoners for their crimes. Conditions are not violations of cruel and unusual punishment proscriptions unless they constitute the unnecessary and wanton infliction of needless suffering (see *Rhodes v. Chapman*, 1981).

In the context of living conditions, generally, prisoners must show unquestioned and serious deprivations of basic human needs or deprivations of the minimal civilized measure of life's necessities. The basic human needs identified thus far by the Supreme Court are food, clothing, shelter, medical care, and reasonable safety.

Notably absent from this listing is a right to visitations or some form of minimal human interaction. In *Overton v. Bazzetta* (2003), the Court upheld severe restrictions on outside visiting while opining that there may be some as yet undiscovered inmate right to intimate association.

The First Amendment to the U.S. Constitution has been construed as providing for a right of association, but it is a right that is judicially viewed as the least compatible with lawful incarceration. The right of association by inmates with persons in the free world, whether family, friends, mentors, or strangers, is to be distinguished from claims made by inmates held in solitary confinement to interaction with fellow inmates. Fellow inmates represent the primary human community in this context, with persons in the free world more of a suburban but important reference group. As we shall see, the core grievance of those held in extended solitary confinement is the psychologically destructive force of involuntary solitude—the absence of human interaction.

Professor Matthew Lieberman (2013), in his notable first book, wrote that we are profoundly social beings, and the importance of social connection is so strong that when rejected we feel pain in the same way as we feel physical pain. Psychiatrist Terry Kupers (2017) identified a "SHU [Special Housing Unit; pronounced "shoe"] post-release syndrome" associated with extended solitary confinement and the deprivation of human contact. If we accept socialization as a basic human need, then its enforced deprivation should take its place in the Court's panoply of previously listed enforceable human needs. Professor Sharon Dolovich (2009) referred to providing those human needs as the state's carceral burden, a duty to protect prisoners from serious physical and psychological harm.

By linking the dimensions of cruel punishment to inmates' essential needs, basic to physical and to some extent psychological survival, the Supreme Court has also operationalized its decisional philosophy. The Court, in its Eighth Amendment, fundamentalist jurisprudence, has elected to patrol the outer limits of civilized decency. This is not to say that the specific challenges to conditions of confinement that the Court does agree to review are all challenges of that fundamental dimension. It is to say, however, that how the Court resolves such inmate challenges as cell temperatures, overcrowding, furnishings, ventilation, lighting, noise, sanitation, food, clothing, and solitary confinement reflects its view that judicial prohibitions on cruel punishment operate as a prisoner survival mechanism. For example, it is not a question of comfortable cell temperatures; it is whether it is so hot or cold that the inmate's very survival is at stake. Where the Scalia–Thomas originalist position is static and shackled to its history, the Supreme Court clearly has adopted a dynamic, evolving view of cruelty, but the cruelty it condemns violates our most deeply held beliefs on the autonomy and essential dignity of man.

In *Farmer v. Brennan* (1994), the Court dealt with a prisoner's claim that prison officials were deliberately indifferent to her right to be reasonably protected from assaults by other inmates. Earlier, in *Estelle v. Gamble* (1976), the Court had decided that prisoners had an Eighth Amendment right to medical care but only for their serious medical conditions, and prison officials could not be deliberately indifferent either in their omission of care or how the care was extended. The Court, however, failed to define deliberate indifference. Justice Thurgood Marshall stated only that it was a standard of care less than that required of medical professionals in malpractice cases.

Estelle, as to prisoners' medical care, and *Farmer*, as to prisoners' right to reasonable protection from the assaults of other inmates, were both decided under the Eighth Amendment. Neither dealt with claims to mere amenities. Each dealt with the preservation of life and limb, with avoiding needless pain and suffering, and ultimately with human survival. The Court's approach to extended solitary confinement also involves whether the inmate's psychological survival is at stake.

The withholding of responsive medical care when an inmate has a serious medical condition is viewed as cruel punishment because of the needless suffering, even death, that this omission causes. It is awkward to extrude an affirmative right to care from a negative injunction regarding punishment. With extended penal isolation we confront the imposition of draconian living conditions, often for very long terms, and frequently either the aggravation of an existing mental condition or the triggering of such a condition. There is the simultaneous degradation of the inherent dignity of the person and the demonstrable pain and suffering regularly leading to prolonged harm. Whereas a medical care claim often is phrased as a denial of some vital aspect of care, an isolation claim is the imposition of a condition so harsh that the person's psychological, or even physical, survival is at stake.

The Court in *Farmer* attempted to breathe definitional life into the meaning of that enigmatic term *deliberate indifference*. However we may ultimately evaluate that effort, deliberate indifference is what governs the analysis of extended solitary confinement for any prison inmate—the death-sentenced included.

DELIBERATE INDIFFERENCE AS FAULT

The *Farmer* decision adopted *recklessness* as the closest analogue to what is meant by deliberate indifference. Recklessness, in effect, is a type of risk creation followed by ignoring that risk. The actor may create the risk or simply become aware of a risk he has a duty to ameliorate or eliminate. In the world of jails and prisons, the custodian has the duty to provide a safe environment and to not knowingly cause otherwise avoidable deleterious mental or physical health conditions. Just below recklessness in culpability is *negligence*—that is, acting carelessly or imprudently and causing harm.

Just above recklessness in culpability is *intent*, when a person consciously acts in a manner to achieve a forbidden result. A person acts with intent when he holds a loaded pistol to the head of another and pulls the trigger. He acts negligently when he leaves the loaded pistol on the kitchen table and an unexpected visiting neighbor picks it up out of curiosity and it goes off unexpectedly, with the discharged bullet ricocheting into his thigh.

We move into the territory of recklessness when prison officials elect to double-cell an inmate known to have severe asthma with a chain smoker, when an adult pedophile is housed with a young offender, and when a claustrophobic, paranoid inmate is placed in extreme solitary confinement, even for a relatively brief duration.

The standard adopted by the Court in *Farmer* is a particularly virulent form of recklessness. That is, a corrections official must be shown to have had actual knowledge of the risk. That an official should have known or might have known with a little curiosity is not enough. This, of course, means that corrections staff does not have a clear duty to investigate or to act in a preventive fashion.

Farmer's conservative position on deliberate indifference did not come as a total surprise. Justice Antonin Scalia had influentially reasoned that the Eighth Amendment does not outlaw cruel conditions. It only outlaws cruel punishment. *Punishment*, by definition, is the intentional infliction of pain as a penalty. Intentionality means acting voluntarily to achieve a particular end. It is the legal equivalent of the Greek philosophical concept of teleology (see *Wilson v. Seiter*, 1991). The Scalia literalist and rights conservative view exerted considerable influence on the Court.

To this point, we have established that if extended solitary confinement is to be judicially challenged and found unconstitutional, it will be under the Eighth Amendment's proscription of cruel punishment. The semantics of the Eighth Amendment—cruel punishment—certainly invite the Court's conservative posture, but do not require it. Although the Court's decisions "patrol the outer edge of civilized decency," they have also adopted something of a dynamic approach, one that "draws its meaning from evolving standards of decency that mark the progress of a maturing society" (see *Rhodes v. Chapman*, 1981). In my view, extended application of the more extreme forms of solitary confinement deprives recipients of the fundamental right to association and human interaction and thus may be unconstitutional punishment even within the Court's conservative jurisprudence. The boundaries of civilized decency will have to be expanded, but just a bit. For those thousands of inmates in extended solitary confinement, including those 3,000 death-sentenced inmates, it changes the world.

WHAT DO WE MEAN BY SOLITARY CONFINEMENT?

There is no single meaning or rationale for imposing solitary confinement. Indeed, what is termed *solitary* or *restricted housing* at times perversely includes the double-celling of inmates. Christie Thompson of The Marshall Project recently described the lethal consequences of housing two men in a 4'8" by 10'8" space in the Illinois Menard Prison (Thompson & Shapiro, 2016). With a toilet, sink, shelf, and two beds and 24-hour-a-day lockdown, this is hardly an antidote to solitary, as in alone. Thompson described how two inmates fought and one lay dead, killed by a cellmate who earlier pleaded to be alone.

I have visited this crumbling, post–Civil War prison on the banks of the Mississippi, investigating the prison's (virtually nonexistent) mental health program. The cells used for isolated confinement were unfit for even a moment's human habitation.

The social isolation that is at the heart of solitary confinement may be imposed for a variety of reasons ranging from a disciplinary measure to protective custody, from confinement for medical observation or to prevent the spread of contagion to administrative segregation (AdSeg). It is typically imposed without a shred of due process and based on a unilateral administrative decision that the inmate is in some fashion dangerous to staff or other inmates.

AdSeg is the most pernicious form of social isolation in terms of duration (open-ended), the arbitrariness with which it is imposed, and the inherent difficulties of predicting dangerousness. When an inmate is assigned to solitary (or special housing) exclusively because of the nature of the offense and the sentence of death, we encounter a unique category of why it is imposed. That is, it is imposed not as discipline and not on the basis of an individualized prediction of dangerousness or even for the safety of the inmate. It is the offense and the sentence alone on which extended penal isolation is based. There may be a hunch about the death-sentenced inmates' potential for violence but, as we shall see, this is not a well-grounded hunch.

In the last decade, the average time between sentencing and execution has grown from 11 years to nearly 18 years. In Florida, the last 10 prisoners executed spent an average of nearly 25 years on death row before execution (see *Glossip v. Gross*, 2015, Breyer, J. dissenting).

Analysis of the constitutionality of solitary confinement always includes its duration and the precise conditions of the confinement, followed by a description of the adverse consequences. Labeling something as solitary confinement or an equivalent will not transform it into solitary for legal purposes. More to the point, using an antiseptic or utterly misleading label will not convert a segregation cell or unit into something more acceptable. A *Special Housing Unit*, *Special Treatment Unit*, *Restricted Housing Unit*, or *Special Management Unit* is quite likely to be a verbally decorated, soul-deadening solitary confinement unit. *Death row* is not so nicely decorated, but it will almost always be de facto solitary confinement.

A recent American Civil Liberties Union (ACLU; 2013) report aptly described death row solitary confinement:

> Death row prisoners are housed alone in tiny cells, ranging from just 36 square feet to little more than 100 square feet. Most are the size of an average bathroom. Most cells generally contain a steel bed or concrete slab, steel toilet, and small utility table. The majority of death row prisoners eat alone in their cell, fed on trays inserted through a slot in the door. They also receive the majority of their medical

and mental health care through these slots. Face-to-face contact with another human being is rare. (ACLU, 2013, p. 4)

The report went on to note that 93% of states lock up their death row prisoners for 22 hours or more a day, and they impose extreme restrictions on exercise, showers, and visits, as well as access to religious services (ACLU, 2013, pp. 15–16).

Thomas Silverstein is a notorious prisoner serving a life term in the Federal Bureau of Prisons under the nation's most extreme conditions of solitary confinement. Silverstein killed three people at various times early in his federal confinement and, as a result, has now served over 30 years in extreme conditions of solitary, which he describes as

> [a] cell so small that I could stand in one place and touch both walls simultaneously. The ceiling was so low I could reach up and touch the hot light fixture. My bed took up the length of the cell, and there was no other furniture. . . . The walls were solid steel and painted all white. I was permitted to wear underwear but I was given no other clothing. I was completely isolated from the outside world and had no way to occupy my time. I was not allowed to have any social visits, telephone privileges, or reading materials except a bible. I was not allowed to have a television, radio or tape player. I could speak to no one and there was virtually nothing on which to focus my attention. (Cohen, 2016, p. 368)

Neither his offense of conviction nor his sentence is relevant to the question of what conditions may be imposed on him for his prison brutality. Silverstein's unprecedented prison violence clearly served as a reasonable basis for the infliction of some form of effective insulation from other inmates and staff. Whether the conditions had to be so severe or imposed for so long are separate questions. The death-sentenced inmate, as noted, is not isolated as punishment for prison misconduct or even a current finding of dangerousness.

If one may raise legal and ethical questions about the duration and the conditions of confinement for a Silverstein, and I believe they may reasonably be raised, how much more compelling are the same questions for the death-sentenced inmate whose conduct is irrelevant to the constitutional decision?

The American Bar Association (ABA), Criminal Justice Standards Committee (2011) *Standards for Criminal Justice: Treatment of Prisoners* approach recommends the ban of what is termed *extreme isolation*. Extreme isolation includes sensory deprivation, lack of contact with other persons, enforced idleness, minimal out-of-cell time, and lack of outdoor recreation.

The commentary to Standard 23-3.8 takes a progressive stance, noting that even extremely dangerous prisoners need mental, physical, and social stimulation. Avoiding the most damaging conditions for them is not only more humane but also contributes to prison and public safety as well as rehabilitation of the inmate. For inmates awaiting execution, public safety and rehabilitation may be illusory goals, but respecting their human dignity has a leavening effect on staff and the dehumanization process that sucks the soul out of the inmate as execution nears (see Johnson, 2016).

Over the years, multiple U.S. Supreme Court Justices have stated their view that dignitarian values reside at the core of the Eighth Amendment. Put simply, this means that every person, whether convicted and imprisoned or not, retains certain human and dignitarian attributes that may not be taken by even the most seemingly lawful measures.

In the prison setting, that includes the avoidance of gratuitous pain and suffering. The constitutional right to conditions that allow for human survival is, of course, the most fundamental of constitutional, carceral burdens. The coincident right to be free of gratuitous, prolonged pain and suffering is inextricably tied to the dignitarian values supportive of the constitutional ban on cruel punishments. Punishment is permissible and linked to conviction as part of our constitutional heritage expressed in the Thirteenth Amendment to the Constitution. That a
hibits slavery and involuntary servitude "except as a punis
whereof the party shall have been duly convicted."

EARLY SOLITARY

Solitary confinement in America's prisons may be traced to the opening of Philadelphia's Eastern State Penitentiary in 1829. Under the influence of Quaker philosophy, which sought reformative penitence for criminal offenders, Eastern's key innovation was solitary confinement (see Cohen, 2016).

Prisoners were confined alone in 16-foot cells but could perform in-cell work. The prison's solitude and work norm reflected the penal philosophy that crime itself was a result of the noisome, morally tempting industrial revolution then underway. The quiet of solitude and the rectitude of work were believed to combine and create a humane and reformative atmosphere.

Today's use of solitary confinement reflects no theory of crime causation. The absence of industry, recreation, treatment, and reformative programs reflects no valid theory of reformation. Today, extended isolation is either a management tool that coincidentally inflicts enormous suffering, or it is a disciplinary measure whose overt purpose is to inflict punishment. The extraordinary allowable duration of solitary confinement and the crushing conditions of confinement invite application of the term *torture* to this process. For death row inmates, the years in solitary will average 18 years, or 6,570 days.

NOTHING TO LOSE

The rationale for imposing solitary confinement on condemned prisoners is difficult to isolate. One prison official, when recently asked by the author, stated the most commonly proffered justification: the "nothing to lose" predicate. With a death sentence already imposed, what other punishment might be imposed? On examination of multiple social science studies on the "nothing left to lose" assertion, it appears to be just that: an assertion, a belief.

Sorensen and Cunningham (2009) summarized those studies as showing that former death-sentenced inmates were neither likely nor proportionately more likely than the comparison groups to engage in serious violence in prison. The Arizona study conducted by Sorensen and Cunningham involved a retrospective review of 80 former death-sentenced inmates. Only 3.8% of former death-sentenced inmates committed an assault including great bodily injury over the 13-plus years studied. Only 1.3% (one inmate) killed again in prison.

There are caveats to this and the other studies mentioned earlier, including the operation of the prison culture itself that may inhibit serious, violent offenses. The Arizona study had a relatively small database. There does appear to be enough acceptable data available to seriously question a jury finding of extreme dangerousness and/or that the death-sentenced inmate is the "worst of the worst." The data similarly suggest that automatic placement on death row is extremely dubious on the "what do they have to lose" assumption.

I have visited the death rows in Alabama, Pennsylvania, and Ohio. In each case, these were the cleanest, most orderly, and quietest units in the prison system. Inmates pored over law books, were at pains to be well groomed, and behaved with an eerie politeness toward me.

In Ohio's death row, which I last visited in 2014, cell doors are open all day, and inmates mingle with each other virtually at will. A few were locked in their cell as punishment for rule infractions, but the cells were not the solid "boxcar" variety, and even those locked down were not totally sensorily isolated.

To the extent that a death-sentenced inmate misbehaves in prison, of course, that inmate should be subject to the same disciplinary rules as any inmate. If a death-sentenced inmate is found to be conducting illegal business from or within the prison system (e.g., arranging outside drug deals, ordering a "hit" on another prisoner), effective restrictive measures aimed at prison discipline and security may be imposed by the requisite procedures and imposed well within the limits of Eighth Amendment prohibition of cruel and unusual punishments.

The prison official referenced earlier added that some death-sentenced inmates have committed notorious crimes and, like Jeffrey Dahmer, who was killed by a fellow inmate, need the protection of solitary confinement. Notorious offenders, whether or not sentenced to death, may be placed in a form of protective custody (PC). By its own terms, PC need not, and should not, impose the harshness of AdSeg or disciplinary segregation. Restricted access by and to such an inmate need not mean that the one being protected should be deprived of safe access to recreation and certain congregate activities with carefully chosen and monitored fellow inmates.[2]

In the *ABA Standards* (2011), Standard 23-5.5(g) represents an excellent guide for PC. They provide that

> (g) If correctional authorities assign a prisoner to protective custody, such a prisoner should be:
> (i) Housed in the least restrictive environment practicable, in segregated housing only if necessary, and in no case in a setting that is used for disciplinary housing;
> (ii) Allowed all of the items usually authorized for general population prisoners;
> (iii) Provided opportunities to participate in programming and work as described in Standards 23-8.2 and 8.4; and
> (iv) Provided the greatest practicable opportunities for out-of-cell time.

There is no specific reference to death-sentenced inmates, but there is nothing inherent in this standard that should preclude PC on these terms for such inmates.

Federal District Court Judge Leonie Brinkema, in *Prieto v. Clarke* (2013), dealt with a Virginia prisoner sentenced to death and automatically housed on death row under particularly onerous conditions. After 8 years, Prieto challenged his confinement on the basis of its automatic imposition, arguing, inter alia, that he had been denied his due process rights under *Sandin v. Conner* (1995).

Judge Brinkema noted that Prieto had been a model prisoner, and she convincingly rebutted the "nothing to lose" rationale. She noted that death row inmates have obvious incentives to behave well and take rehabilitation seriously, including the possibility that new forensic evidence might

---

[2] PC may be extended grudgingly as a filter to separate those actually in jeopardy from those seeking PC as a friendly respite from the rigors of prison.

undercut a conviction or habeas corpus might be granted or even that good behavior might improve the prospects for an executive commutation. With life there is hope, and with hope, there is something left to lose.

We return to *Prieto* later, but here I simply note that Prieto ultimately argued that the conditions were sufficiently harsh that he should have received due process safeguards. That claim must be distinguished from the fundamental Eighth Amendment claim that if a punishment is constitutionally cruel, it cannot be imposed regardless of the procedure used. That latter issue had been dismissed earlier in the case.

REFORM IS IN THE AIR

Reforming solitary confinement as imposed on death-sentenced inmates is not high on the present advocacy-reform agenda. Federal litigation has produced the most advances in reforming extended penal isolation but with little focus on the death-sentenced inmate. Federal legislation, the Solitary Confinement Reform Act (S.3432), was introduced in November 2016, and its enactment would affect the approximately 10,000 inmates held in solitary confinement in federal prisons. Solitary, for example, would be available only for the "briefest term" and "least restrictive conditions practicable," with at least 4 hours of daily out-of-cell time, programming, and interactions with others "as much as practicable."

An ombudsman would be created to provide oversight, deal with inmate complaints, and identify areas in need of improvement. Juveniles and the mentally ill would have special consideration in line with the judicially stimulated requirements. Passage in the post-Obama administration is not likely, but the mere existence of the comprehensive bill and multiple sponsorship is a step forward in reform and, of course, importantly outside the realm of the judiciary.

No decision of the U.S. Supreme Court has ever determined that extended solitary confinement per se is unconstitutional. The lower courts have been most receptive to the claims of individuals who belong to groups that are determined to be particularly vulnerable to the psychological and physical impact of isolation. That has not included death-sentenced inmates.

In re Medley (1890) involved death-sentenced Colorado inmate James Medley, who brought a writ of habeas corpus to the Court and actually prevailed. Medley was being held under a Colorado law that became effective after the commission of his offense of conviction and, inter alia, it newly required that the condemned prisoner be held in solitary confinement while awaiting execution.

Medley argued that this requirement constituted an ex post facto law, viewing the solitary confinement requirement as punishment. Justice Miller reviewed the early history of solitary confinement, concluding that solitary caused persons to become violently insane or fatuous, from which they could not be aroused.

Medley was to be kept alone and with scarcely any visits permitted. The newly enacted law, then, did impose what was considered a severe punishment—solitary confinement—and represented post-sentence punishment that was not available at the time of Medley's offense. He was ordered released.

The *Medley* Court did not outlaw solitary confinement. Rather, it found solitary to be a severe punishment and thus invalid as within the scope of an ex post facto law. Thus, *Medley* should not be read as a decision even addressing solitary confinement as in need of reform going forward. It does, however, characterize the Colorado law on solitary as extremely rigorous.

Juveniles came first, and fairly early, in the current reform movement. In *Lollis v. New York State Department of Social Services* (1971), the Federal District Court voided the 2-week room confinement of a 16-year-old girl in a stripped room with no recreational outlets or reading material. The same court also found it legally impermissible to use shackles on a young male inmate held in isolation for periods of 40 minutes to 2 hours.

The experts of that time argued that juveniles experienced time differently than adults. Adolescents might internalize 2 weeks in social isolation as years. What exactly should follow from the "youth experience time differently" formula was never fully clarified. Its mere utterance was deemed evidence of (proscribed) harm.

Today, developmental psychology teaches that the brain development of adolescents is incomplete and vulnerable during this time of plasticity. Their heightened vulnerability to the psychological rigors of prolonged isolation may lead to anger, physical resistance to educational and reformative efforts, and a type of posttraumatic stress disorder syndrome.

Long-term isolation in terms of a Silverstein or the 18-year average served for death-sentenced inmates was never an issue in juvenile justice. However, youthful status, the fact that an adjudication of delinquency is not the equivalent of a criminal conviction, and that juvenile justice itself rests on a reformative premise not found in criminal justice all contribute to the early successful reformative efforts in this area.

MENTAL ILLNESS

Prisoners with serious mental illness or who are especially psychologically vulnerable have had even more impact on reform than juveniles. Prisons and jails have become "the new asylums." Inmates with serious mental illness (SMI) have an Eighth Amendment constitutional right to responsive mental health care that is not deliberately indifferent in its provision. They also have an Eighth Amendment right to reasonable protection and physical conditions not inconsistent with the illness and treatment regimen. All too often, peculiar or threatening behavior of an inmate with SMI evokes verbal and physical reactions from staff and inmates from which he or she needs protection. More likely, locking down a troublesome inmate with SMI simply puts the problem out of sight but not always out of hearing. Inmates in solitary either produce an eerie silence because of their medication or deafening outbursts from the lack thereof. A death sentence does not convert such a prisoner to a nonperson, to a captive so lacking in the attributes of human dignity as to be deprived of the fundamental constitutional right to mental health treatment and the special concerns for safety that are associated with being seriously ill.

Deliberate indifference sets a very low bar by which to legally evaluate mental health care either in an individual case or a class action when there are structural and systemic challenges. It is, of course, the class action that is the essential vehicle for reform that will at least be institution wide or, more often, system wide.

Two somewhat separate pathways for such challenges have emerged. First, there are those inmates with SMI who mount an empirical challenge that emphasizes the additional harm to them in the form of needless suffering from extended solitary confinement. Again, the duration and actual conditions in a given setting or system are vital.

The second pathway focuses on long-term solitary confinement for those inmates who are particularly vulnerable to needless suffering and when the risk is high that a serious mental illness will emerge. This is the more difficult category to develop. Litigation often will bog down over whether courts should recognize such a class and, if so, what it takes to establish membership in it.

Helling v. McKinney (1993) is the key supportive Supreme Court decision in this area. *Helling* determined that exposure to second-hand smoke in a prison setting is subject to analysis as a condition that may constitute cruel and unusual punishment. This, in effect, supports a predictive and preventive approach to the actual harm requirement imposed by the Eighth Amendment.

As Justice White put it, you do not have to make inmates drink polluted water and acquire dysentery to foreclose the drinking of such water. An inmate with asthma cannot be celled with a chain-smoking cellmate. Why? The risk of more serious harm or death is so great and the harm so profound that it is a cruel punishment that must be prevented. The emotionally fragile inmate facing solitary confinement is the precise counterpart of the asthmatic inmate confronted with a heavy smoker.

Psychiatrist Terry Kupers (2016; see also Chapter 2, this volume), with extensive academic and on-the-ground experience with prisoners with mental illness, began with the premise that time in solitary breaks the prisoner. When the prisoner has a mental illness, the "breaking" is even worse. An existing psychotic state is prolonged and the SMI more intractable.

Life skills are damaged over time, and the longer a person suffers with schizophrenia, replete with hallucinations, delusions, and bizarre thinking, the worse the prognosis.

Kupers wrote that the isolation cell becomes a petri dish for the germination of more severe and chronic illnesses. Patterns of neural activity in the brain often become more established. They also become more fixed, and after, say, 6 months in isolation, remission is more and more difficult (Kupers, 2016).

Psychologist Craig Haney (2003) wrote

> To summarize, there is not a single published study of solitary or supermax-like confinement in which nonvoluntary confinement for longer than 10 days, where participants were unable to terminate their isolation at will, failed to result in negative psychological effects. The damaging effect ranged in severity and included such clinically significant symptoms as hypertension, uncontrollable anger, hallucinations, emotional breakdowns, chronic depression, and suicidal thoughts and behavior. (p. 132)

The ACLU study (2013, p. 16) suggested that empirical research consistently demonstrates that prisoners subjected to isolation experience many of the same symptoms caused by physical torture, including hypersensitivity to external stimuli. Thus, we have juveniles and adolescents, along with those who have SMI and those whose emotional fragility puts them at risk of SMI from extended isolation, as groups (or classes) that I shall simply label as *vulnerables*. That is, there is something in their makeup or development as persons that renders them the equivalent of the asthmatic who cannot cell with a smoker.

There is no judicial decision of which I am aware in which a court has ruled even extended solitary confinement unconstitutional when there is not some heightened vulnerability, some membership in a vulnerable class. There are a few cases when pregnant inmates were found to be immune from the rigors of solitary confinement, but I am not aware of any general principle that has emerged to encompass this group (see *Nelson v. CMS*, 2009, prohibiting shackling in labor).

Ashker v. Governor (2015) initially offered the promise of a broad-based ruling on extended solitary confinement for inmates regardless of their youth or mental or emotional impairment. The case, however, was settled and stopped well short of forbidding extended isolation for inmates not in a vulnerable category. A death-sentenced inmate, of course, would be included in any such broad-based injunction.

In one sense, virtually everything to this point in this chapter is a legal–policy framework for closer consideration of extended penal isolation of the death-sentenced inmate. This category, or class, of inmates does not possess the vulnerability, transient as it may be, of adolescents or the emotional and psychological vulnerability of those with mental illness.

Death row inmates come in all colors, ages, genders, and with all degrees of intellectual and emotional strengths and weaknesses. They are united only in the seriousness of their crime and in their sentence: death. The argument here, of course, is that these two factors cannot continue to serve as a basis for imposing solitary confinement.

As noted earlier, time spent on death row now averages about 18 years. Thus, this may be viewed as another common feature. As we shall see, the infliction of the death penalty itself is under scrutiny because of the extensive time between sentence and execution. That issue, however, is not dependent on the conditions of confinement, although the more onerous the conditions, the more aggravated the durational issue.

In *Moore v. Texas* (2016), the Supreme Court was asked to decide whether the execution of a Texas inmate 3½ decades after sentence was imposed is itself constitutionally cruel punishment. The durational question was underscored in Moore's petition for certiorari (p. 30) by the assertion that the prolonged duration claim is particularly aggravated when the condemned inmate is isolated in his cell for virtually the entire day. The Court ultimately agreed to review Moore's death sentence on an unrelated issue, but it did not take up questions relating to the length or conditions of his death row confinement.

Justice Anthony Kennedy's condemnation of the "dual death sentence" in *Davis v. Ayala* (2015) has attracted attention for his condemnation of placing death-sentenced inmates in solitary whether or not it is done automatically.

The Death Sentenced Inmate

> *"FRIDAY, OCTOBER 2, 2015*
> *SUPREME COURT OF THE UNITED STATES*
> *ORDER IN PENDING CASE*
> *15A343 PRIETO, ALFREDO R. V. CLARKE, DIRECTOR, VA*
> *DOC, ET AL.*

> *The application for stay of execution of sentence of death presented to The Chief Justice and by him referred to the Court is dismissed as moot."*
> (*Prieto v. Clarke*, 2015a)

Alfredo Prieto was executed the night before the order was issued. A case is moot when the relief sought is no longer needed or available. Here, Prieto's lawyers had frantically sought a stay of execution from our highest court. Earlier, this case seemed to be a good vehicle for the Court to examine the question, May states automatically put all death row inmates in solitary confinement? It is the type of issue in a controversial area that the Justices usually like.

The automatic feature in Virginia (and elsewhere) invites the Court to condemn the automatic and prolonged solitary confinement of death-sentenced inmates and then open a debate about what findings, if any, in individual cases might support the prolonged isolation. Ultimately, prolonged isolation under *Prieto*-like conditions should constitutionally be faced and prohibited. There are no strong arguments that place death-sentenced prisoners in a dangerous class, the only plausible reason for imposing isolation, and empirical evidence appears to undermine it. Stripped of the makeweight rationales, the solitary confinement of a death-sentenced inmate is imposed as punishment. It is an additional punishment imposed by administration and is highly vulnerable to legal attack.

Virginia's attorney general argued in opposition to the challenge that his state and *Prieto* were the wrong vehicles for a Supreme Court decision because Virginia was extraordinarily efficient in executing the condemned inmates in 7 to 10 years (see Liptak, 2015).

A closer examination of the *Prieto* case in the Federal District Court and the Fourth Circuit Court of Appeals provides a vehicle to introduce and more closely examine the constitutional issues particularly relevant to this chapter (see *Prieto v. Clarke*, 2015b). Prieto was automatically and permanently placed in the highly restrictive death row at Sussex I State Prison (SISP), a maximum-security prison. Judge Brinkema noted that SISP itself is a form of solitary confinement. On average, Prieto had to remain in his single cell for all but 1 hour of the day. That cell measured 71 square feet and featured only a narrow mesh-covered window for natural light. It was otherwise illuminated by a main light mounted on the wall. In the evening hours, when the main light was turned off, a nightlight remained on in the cell, as did the pod lights immediately outside it, ensuring that his cell was never completely dark.

He was allowed to leave his cell for just 1 hour of outdoor recreation approximately 5 days per week. During that time, however, he was limited to a similarly sized outdoor cell with a concrete floor and no exercise equipment. He was not allowed to use the gymnasium or prison yard nor given an opportunity for in-pod recreation. He could leave his cell for a 10-minute shower 3 days per week and could also purchase a television and compact disc player for use in his cell, as well as request delivery of certain books from the law library.

Typically, inmates are subjected to a highly intrusive search when they leave the cell and return. Inmates elsewhere have told me that alone causes them to refuse the meager offering of out-of-cell exercise. As one inmate put it, "I don't need those guys regularly looking at parts of my body I have never seen."

District Court Judge Brinkema astutely noted that the most significant restrictions involved the deprivation of human contact. As described earlier, this is the significant human right (or emerging liberty interest) that is at stake in extended solitary confinement.

Prieto had to spend almost all his time alone. Although death row then housed seven other inmates, they were separated by at least two (and often many more) empty cells within the 44-unit pod. Solid metal doors with no openings apart from small slits substantially impeded any communication among death row inmates. In addition, Prieto took all three daily meals in his cell. Visitation opportunities were limited to noncontact visits from immediate family members on weekends in a room with a glass partition, though in actuality no one ever came. Prieto's only regular source of human contact was prison officials, including those who administered medical and mental health services in his cell. He was not allowed to join general population inmates for vocational, educational, or behavioral programming nor to attend group religious services.

This is yet another extreme example of solitary confinement and, again, it is imposed without any process or any findings related to the need for such an intense level of security. A nominal classification for computer purposes only is assigned by the prison but is never again reviewed. The inmate is frozen in place until he dies or there is some unlikely form of executive clemency.

It would seem, then, that I have just described conditions that might reasonably be described as cruel and unusual punishment, as being on the fringe of (if not beyond) evolving standards of civilized decency and thus impermissible regardless of the inmate's offense of conviction.

Judge Brinkema had earlier dismissed the unadorned Eighth Amendment challenge. Unfortunately, then, *Prieto* would not be resolved even at trial on that substantive basis. The automatic feature remained the only viable legal issue for decision. *Prieto* had morphed from a substantive challenge into a procedural due process case that was reviewed under the cryptic holding in *Sandin v. Conner* (1995). *Sandin* dealt with the question of when prison conditions were sufficiently onerous to warrant a modicum of procedural due process before its imposition.

The Supreme Court in *Sandin* invented the decisional formula that a prisoner's due process liberty interest is at stake when prison conditions constituted an atypical and significant hardship in relation to the ordinary incidents of prison life. Without such a determination, even the nominal procedures required in a disciplinary proceeding (*Wolff v. McDonnell*, 1974) were deemed unnecessary. One wonders where to draw the line between an atypical and significant hardship that could be imposed after due process and a cruel and unusual punishment that may never be imposed or allowed to continue.

Judge Brinkema compared death row conditions with those in SISP's general population and found the duration and conditions for Prieto were significantly harsher. There are no legitimate penological goals advanced, she found, and nothing to support a "nothing to lose" dangerousness assumption about death-sentenced inmates.

Having found a protected liberty interest and its impairment, the question was what process is due. The answer: not very much—only notice and a fair opportunity to respond in an informal, non-adversary process. Here there was no notice of the factual basis for solitary confinement and no opportunity to review or contest it.

The state argued that a classification review for death row inmates would be futile because death-sentenced inmates would invariably be assigned to the highest level of security. And there you have it as to the futility of accepting a modest procedural solution to solve a substantive problem: an admission of futility. The defendants well understood that any evidentiary burden on them was so slight as to afford them de facto total discretion.

A *Sandin* hearing is not actually a hearing if by *hearing* is meant notice and a fair opportunity before an impartial tribunal to affect the outcome. The accepted process more closely resembles an interview.[3] Virginia, however, was not content to merely add a brief ceremonial event. Virginia appealed to the Fourth Circuit Court of Appeals, and in *Prieto v. Clarke* (2015b) it prevailed.

Circuit Judge Diana Gribbon Motz, writing for a divided 2-to-1 panel, bordered on incoherence when she wrote that Prieto's apparent belief that just because conditions for him are as harsh as the conditions in Ohio's

---

[3] The specifics of a *Sandin*-generated hearing derive from *Wolff v. McDonnell* (1974) where the Court decided that a loss of good time in a prison disciplinary proceeding called for notice, a written statement of the evidence supportive of the decision and the punishment, a limited right to call witnesses and present evidence, and a very narrow right to some assistance.

supermax (OSP), he too must have a protected liberty interest. The U.S. Supreme Court, some years earlier, had found OSP to be sufficiently severe that inmates were deprived of a liberty interest when confined there. That is, Judge Motz believed that severity alone was not enough to require even the nominal *Sandin* hearing.

First, conditions on Virginia's death row were far harsher than those at OSP, a prison I have visited many times as a federal monitor for health care services. Second, harshness in the comparative sense is exactly what *Sandin* formulated: atypical and significant hardship in relation to the ordinary incidents of prison life. What else could comparative hardship mean except relative harshness?

The majority simply misunderstood and then misapplied *Sandin*. Judge James Wynn, in dissent, correctly asserted that the Supreme Court made an analysis of the actual conditions of confinement as the touch-stone for finding a *Sandin* liberty interest and need for nominal due process. He agreed that Prieto's conditions were far more severe than those imposed at OSP. However, whether the Fourth Circuit majority panel was right or wrong in result does not affect the constitutionality of the conditions imposed or their duration. A hurried "show-and-tell hearing" before a prison official or officials, even with a little annual review, would not alter the incidence of use or harshness of such confinement. A fictional scenario: "After review of the file and a hearing with the death-sentenced inmate, we find that prison security, the always present danger of escape, and staff safety support retention (or placement) of inmate [XY] in solitary confinement. . . . Next case."

In *Incumaa v. Stirling* (2015), decided just weeks after *Prieto*, another Fourth Circuit panel that included Judge Motz determined that a Virginia prisoner serving a life without parole term did have a protected liberty interest calling for procedural safeguards. The inmate-plaintiff had served 20 years in solitary confinement but had once been in general population, as Prieto had not. Once again, the fundamental issue of the Eighth Amendment and severe conditions of confinement over a long period was eluded.

DIGGING DEEPER

A legal challenge to how extended solitary confinement is imposed can lead only to a procedural solution. The *Sandin* solution is, in effect, a mock hearing before a prison official with no assistance, no clarity on what is to be proved or by what standard, and no fair review process.

There is some high-level support for the proposition that execution after an inordinate delay alone is cruel punishment. Justice John Paul Stevens in *Lackey v. Texas* (1995) referred to conclusions by English jurists that execution after inordinate delay would have infringed the prohibition of cruel and unusual punishments found in Section 10 of the English Bill of Rights of 1689. In *Sireci v. Florida* (2016), Justice Stephen Breyer dissented from the Court's denial of certiorari to a Florida inmate whose death sentence was imposed some 40 years earlier. Breyer has used dissents in these cases as a platform to try to move the Court to overturn the death penalty. When a 40-year wait is spent in solitary confinement, the case for nullifying the death sentence is more powerful.

A prisoner assigned to death row has, in effect, been classified for housing purposes. As a general legal principle, classification decisions are normally left to prison officials. There is no right to any particular classification, although inmates have a right to reasonable protection, and classification will likely be the vehicle by which to secure such safety. Classification decisions and prison and cell-block placements that are based on retaliation, racial discrimination, or political views may be voided. A classification decision that negatively affects a release date also may be subjected to a procedural due process challenge.

Is it in some fashion unconstitutional to classify inmates for housing solely on the basis of their crime and sentence? Using a rational basis test approach, the best answer is it quite probably is legal but not good policy. For example, one could end up with rival gang members as close neighbors, a victim's brother in the same cell, and so forth.

In support of a conviction-crime–based housing classification (or grouping), it may be asserted that death penalty inmates and staff have shared concerns based on the sentence of death, that relevant services may be more easily delivered to a shared cell block, and that group mental health services may be more easily delivered. As long as there is some plausible or logical relationship between the decision and a legitimate governmental interest, the rational basis test is satisfied.

In our case, the question is refined by using the crime and sentence as a basis to house inmates in the most severe conditions imaginable and for periods of time that may average some 18 years. It is when the duration and conditions approximate those experienced by a Prieto or Silverstein that we encounter either the *Sandin* procedural issue or the more basic Eighth Amendment prohibitive issue. Thus, instead of the "automatic imposition" question, we now have the question, Is it constitutional to classify and then impose extended extreme solitary confinement based solely on a conviction of aggravated murder and a sentence of death?

A sentence of death, with its precarious facial constitutionality, may be meted out only for the most aggravated of murders. Prieto, indeed, was convicted of two gruesome murders. Although the ultimate penalty is now justified on a proportionality basis and its constitutional reference in the Fifth Amendment,[4] the conditions of incarceration until the execution may not serve as additional punishment.

As previously noted, the duration and conditions of confinement are the key factors in a constitutional cruel punishment analysis. Twenty days in the type of deep-end solitary described earlier in this chapter may be considered the point at which the term *extended* or *prolonged* may be attached.

Using the conditions described earlier by Silverstein as well as in *Prieto* as a touchstone for conditions that should be found to violate the Eighth Amendment, I continue to develop the legal analysis. There are two analytical pathways to finding extended solitary confinement unconstitutional. The first is empirical and depends primarily on the amount of anticipated harm and the amount of gratuitous suffering endured, along with the mounting evidence of permanence or at least long-lasting damage.[5]

---

[4] The Fifth Amendment, *inter alia*, requires a presentment or indictment for a "capital" crime.

[5] Some inmates do survive incredibly long periods of deep-end solitary confinement. Some persons survived the atomic bombing of Hiroshima and Nagasaki. One person happened to survive both bombings. The atypical survivor hardly supports extended solitary confinement or the use of atomic weapons.

The second is a human rights, ethical pathway which does not depend on specific evidence of physical or psychological harm.

Professor Robert Johnson (2016) wrote passionately and eloquently on this subject. The death-sentenced inmate, he wrote, dies twice. The dehumanization process of prolonged and profound solitary confinement is a form of extended torture that should be constitutionally condemned.

Johnson's (2016) research on the experience of death row prisoners supports his assertion that death row prisoners die psychologically before they are killed. He went further and asserted,

> Our understanding of what it means to be a human being—to appreciate our own humanity and that of others—creates a bright line distinction: while punishments can legitimately deprive persons of their liberty, they cannot degrade them by ignoring or violating their essential human dignity. (Johnson, 2016, p. 5)

Fundamental notions of privacy and autonomy are bound up in the more fundamental notion of human dignity. In *Hope v. Pelzer* (2002), Justice Stevens's opinion for the majority characterized the Eighth Amendment as a repository for rights associated with human dignity.

Stevens wrote that the nonemergency use of a hitching post, as used by Alabama prison officials, violated the basic concept underlying the Eighth Amendment, which is nothing less than human dignity: the gratuitous infliction of wanton and unnecessary pain. I argue, how much more so, then, to take death-sentenced inmates and house them for 10, 15, or 20 years in utter social isolation and with only the bare necessities required for physical survival.

It is important to continue to emphasize that the duration and conditions of confinement described throughout this chapter are not putatively unconstitutional for only the death-sentenced inmate. Those serving life terms or extremely long sentences have not forfeited their basic human dignity either. Because the death-sentenced inmate ordinarily has been convicted of a horrendous crime and sentenced to the most extreme punishment, he or she may then appear to be eligible for the longest isolate terms in the most onerous conditions imaginable.[6] That is true only if it can be shown that the offense and sentence have somehow stripped the inmate of personhood, of the basic human dignity of the person. That cannot be done, and there is much law and dicta at the U.S. Supreme Court level to support that proposition.

Hope v. Pelzer (2002), as noted, and a host of other decisions by the Supreme Court support this assertion. Inmates retain a constitutional right to marry, a right to mental health care that preserves their individual identity and autonomy, a right to practice their religion, a right of access to the courts, and so on. Each of those rights, and more, are predicated on the survival of the inmate as a person. They are not distributed on the basis of an inmate's offense or sentence. They are based on the premise of an inmate-as-a-person. By definition, confinement limits one's freedom, but it does not limit one's status as a person. Human dignity, then, is at the core of the Eighth Amendment and at the core of simply being alive as a person. A sentence of death does not extinguish this core right. Those sentenced to death retain their right to medical care, to life-sustaining food and shelter, to not be assaulted by staff or inmates. It is but a short step to recognize the right of association, the right to be maintained under conditions of psychological survival.

In *Baze v. Rees* (2008), the U.S. Supreme Court held that the risk of improper administration of a state's three-drug lethal injection protocol did not violate the Eighth Amendment. In analyzing the issue, the Court looked at *In re Kemmler* (1890), which explained,

> Punishments are cruel when they involve torture or a lingering death; but the punishment of death is not cruel, within the meaning of that word as used in the constitution. It implies there something inhuman and barbarous, something more than the mere extinguishment of life. (*Baze v. Rees*, 2008, p. 49, quoting *In re Kemmler*, 1890)

Petitioners had claimed that there was a substantial risk that the procedure would not be performed correctly. The Court found, however, that the

---

[6] See Cohen (2008) for more comprehensive views on banning such conditions.

mere possibility of an accident was not enough to show that the Eighth Amendment was violated.

Justice Kennedy, concurring in *Baze*, explained the Court's understanding of torture and what determined whether a punishment was torture under the Eighth Amendment.

> Quite plainly, what defined these punishments was that they were *designed* to inflict torture as a way of enhancing a death sentence; they were *intended* to produce a penalty worse than death, to accomplish something "more than the mere extinguishment of life." (*Baze v. Rees*, 2008, p. 102, original emphasis)

PERSONHOOD AND PRIVACY AND ITS VIOLATION THROUGH SOLITARY CONFINEMENT

The U.S. Supreme Court has long held that liberty or *personhood* is a right in and of itself and deserves the protection of the courts. This right was emphasized in *Planned Parenthood of Southeastern Pennsylvania v. Casey* (1992):

> These matters, involving the most intimate and personal choices a person may make in a lifetime, choices central to personal dignity and autonomy, are central to the liberty protected by the Fourteenth Amendment. At the heart of liberty is the right to define one's own concept of existence, of meaning, of the universe, and of the mystery of human life. Beliefs about these matters could not define the attributes of personhood were they formed under compulsion of the State. (p. 851)

Other cases allude to this right of personhood. In *Washington v. Glucksberg* (1997), the Court mentioned that some rights come from the "zone of conscience and belief" (p. 727). In *Kallstrom v. City of Columbus* (1998), the Sixth Circuit explained that

> individuals have "a clearly established right under the substantive component of the Due Process Clause to personal security and to bodily integrity," and that this right is fundamental where "the

magnitude of the liberty deprivation that [the] abuse inflicts upon the victim ... strips the very essence of personhood." (pp. 1062–1063)

This protected right is better understood when compared with the Court's protection of one's right to privacy. In *Griswold v. Connecticut* (1965), the Court explained "that specific guarantees in the Bill of Rights have penumbras, formed by emanations from those guarantees that help give them life and substance" (p. 484).

Various constitutional guarantees combine to create zones of privacy. The right of association contained in the penumbra of the First Amendment is one, as we have seen. The Third Amendment in its prohibition against the quartering of soldiers "in any house" in time of peace without the consent of the owner is another facet of that privacy. The Fourth Amendment explicitly affirms the "right of the people to be secure in their persons, houses, papers, and effects, against unreasonable searches and seizures." The Fifth Amendment in its Self-Incrimination Clause enables the citizen to create a zone of privacy that government may not force him to surrender to his detriment. The Ninth Amendment provides, "The enumeration in the Constitution, of certain rights, shall not be construed to deny or disparage others retained by the people" (p. 484).

The concurrences in *Griswold* also believed that a right to privacy existed in other ways—for example, through the Ninth Amendment, or was "implicit in the concept of ordered liberty" (p. 500). Furthermore, in *Lawrence v. Texas* (2003), the Court explained that there is "a promise [in] the Constitution that there is a realm of personal liberty which the government may not enter" (p. 578).

All these decisions, as well as the constitutional text itself, create an internal zone of privacy that is an inherent aspect of human autonomy. The foundation for this right relates to reproductive activity, but its self-generating power easily reaches the concept of personhood and protects our existential journey.

In a recent article, Robert Johnson explained how death row strips away personhood. The fundamental traits of a "human being—awareness of self, reason, choice, connection to others—are part and parcel of what it means to be a member of the human species" and are destroyed through the use of death row (Johnson, 2014, p. 586). "Prisoners on [solitary confinement versions] of death row are relegated to a kind of existential limbo, existing as entities in cold storage rather than living as human beings with even a modicum of self-determination" (p. 589). Furthermore, Johnson (2016) explained that at its core, the essential characteristic of self-determination is accomplished only through social interaction.

> It has been my contention that self-determination, in whatever degree and form it exists in a given environment, is achieved in the world of other human beings through a process of self-defining social interactions. These interactions, in my assessment, require some degree of autonomy, security, and relatedness to others.
>
> In making these assertions, I understand autonomy to mean the capacity to influence one's environment and hence exert some modicum of control over the conditions of one's existence. I understand security to mean shelter from harm, which entails some element of social stability; secure and safe, one is defined in some measure by one's choices rather than by the vagaries of one's environment. Relatedness or connectedness to others entails the ability to feel for oneself and others and hence to have caring and constructive relationships in which other human beings are seen as persons in their own right. Autonomy, security, and relatedness to others develop in interaction with one another as individuals become persons. The process of becoming a person is never fully finished, however, as "man's nature is a self-surpassing and a self-transcending one." We are, then, emergent persons. The element of growth is thus a part of our nature and must be respected, even in the context of punishment. (pp. 1224–1225)

Johnson and court decisions point to a person's right to be a self-determining being. This self-determination is what makes a human a human being. It is the mental growth and self-determination, the "existential journey" persons pursue that separate us from every other being. Personhood and the right to mental privacy secures a person's ability to entertain choices and possibilities. It is the freedom of the mind that no government has the right to intrude on. Although the First Amendment right to association is limited, the right to social interaction, as discussed earlier, remains intact. This penumbra right is essential to personhood and mental privacy. Because extended solitary confinement strips away the essential characteristics of a person, risking an inmate's psychological survival, such a punishment is "*designed* to inflict torture as a way of enhancing a death sentence," violating the Eighth Amendment (*Baze v. Rees*, 2008, p. 102, Kennedy, J., concurring, original emphasis).

It would not be a giant step for the Supreme Court to outlaw extended solitary confinement as cruel and unusual punishment and sweep within such a decision those inmates with a death sentence. The most conservative view of the Court's enforcement of the Eighth Amendment refers to enforcing practices at the outer limits of civilized society, of incorporating evolving standards of decency and not remaining anchored to prohibiting punishments such as drawing and quartering or the use of the iron maiden to enclose and pierce the vital parts of the victim and in a way to assure a slow death.

The Court need not free itself from the history of a constitutional provision, but there is a crucial difference between being tethered and retaining a reference point. The deadly combination of the death penalty and extended terms of solitary confinement—torture in its own right—is a worthy candidate for a ringing decision condemning and outlawing the practice.

CLOSING

Years from now, observers may look back at our practice of killing fellow human beings for their crimes after an extended period of confining them in a small, secure enclosure devoid of any meaningful interaction with others as barbaric, as prolonged torture. Even the most efficient and timely of executions do not satisfy those who are fundamentally opposed to capital punishment. And those opposed to extended periods of solitary confinement do not limit their opposition to those awaiting execution.

Neither do they exclude such prisoners. Criminal law and procedure factor into a sentence the seriousness of the offense (based on a combination of the harm inflicted and the offender's culpability) and relevant mitigating and aggravating considerations. Prison authorities are to execute the court's lawful sentence. They do not have the authority to enhance the punishment, to determine who is more or less deserving among their inmates.

They do have the authority—indeed, the obligation—to house inmates in accordance with security, health-related, associational, and similar custodial-inmate factors. When there is a legislative mandate to create a death row that is, in fact, also a solitary confinement unit, the challenge must be directed to the legislation. When there is simply a practice or an administrative regulation to the same effect, the cruel and unusual punishment challenge must be aimed at the practice or regulation.

Inmates with a death sentence must, of course, be kept secure and must be regulated as to their harmful conduct or rule infractions. I spent long days at Ohio's death row. I moved easily among the inmates, who moved about freely on the unit and who interacted with each other, and I entered and exited their cells during the day at will. There was a semblance of life in that unit. Nothing was lost, much was gained. As an interim reform measure, such practices cry out for implementation. Albert Woodfox spent 43 years in solitary confinement in Louisiana's notorious Angola for a crime he steadfastly denied. Rachel Aviv (2017) described his heroic measures to survive while isolated and then the new battle to discover a self after his release to a world he hardly knew. Earlier, fellow inmates at Angola told him, "Thanks for not letting them break you." It was the first time he had grasped that in staying sane he had done something unusual.

REFERENCES

American Bar Association, Criminal Justice Standards Committee. (2011). *ABA standards for criminal justice: Treatment of prisoners* (3rd ed.). Washington, DC: American Bar Association.

American Civil Liberties Union. (2013). *A death before dying: Solitary confinement on death row*. Retrieved from https://www.aclu.org/files/assets/deathbeforedying-report.pdf

Ashker v. Governor, C-09-05796 Civ., N.D.Cal. (2015).

Aviv, R. (2017, January 16). How Albert Woodfox survived solitary. *The New Yorker*. Retrieved from http://www.newyorker.com/magazine/2017/01/16/how-albert-woodfox-survived-solitary

Baze v. Rees, 553 U.S. 35 (2008).

Cohen, F. (2008). Penal isolation: Beyond the seriously mentally ill. *Criminal Justice and Behavior, 35*, 1017–1047. http://dx.doi.org/10.1177/0093854808317569

Cohen, F. (2016). Restricted housing and legal issues. In National Institute of Justice, *Restrictive housing in the U.S.: Issues, challenges, and future directions* (pp. 367–400). Washington, DC: National Institute of Justice. Retrieved from https://www.ncjrs.gov/pdffiles1/nij/250325.pdf

Davis v. Ayala, 135 S.Ct. 2187 (2015).

Dolovich, S. (2009). Cruelty, prison conditions, and the Eighth Amendment. *New York University Law Review, 84*, 881–979.

Estelle v. Gamble, 429 U.S. 97 (1976).

Farmer v. Brennan, 511 U.S. 825 (1994).

Glossip v. Gross, 135 S.Ct. 2726, 2764 (2015).

Griswold v. Connecticut, 381 U.S. 479, 484 (1965).

Haney, C. (2003). Mental health issues in long-term solitary and "supermax" confinement. *Crime & Delinquency, 49*, 124–156. http://dx.doi.org/10.1177/0011128702239239

Helling v. McKinney, 509 U.S. 25 (1993).

Hope v. Pelzer, 536 U.S. 730 (2002).

Incumaa v. Stirling, 791 F.3d 517 (4th Cir. 2015).

In re Kemmler, 136 U.S. 436 (1890).

In re Medley, 134 U.S. 160 (1890).

Johnson, R. (2014). Reflections on the death penalty: Human rights human dignity, and dehumanization in the death house. *Seattle Journal for Social Justice, 13*, 583–598.

Johnson, R. (2016). Solitary confinement until death by state-sponsored homicide: An Eighth Amendment assessment of the modern execution process. *Washington and Lee Law Review, 73*, 1213–1242.

Kallstrom v. City of Columbus, 136 F.3d 1055 (6th Cir. 1998).

Kupers, T. (2016). Alternatives to long-term solitary confinement. *Correctional Law Reporter, 28*(3), 33, 38, 45–46.

Kupers, T. (2017). *Solitary: The inside story of supermax isolation: How we can abolish it.* Oakland: University of California Press.

Lackey v. Texas, 514 U.S. 1045, 1046-47 (1995).

Lawrence v. Texas, 539 U.S. 558, 578 (2003).

Lieberman, M. (2013). *Social: Why our brains are wired to connect.* New York, NY: Crown.

Liptak, A. (2015, September 14). Virginia has solitary confinement case, if justices want it. *The New York Times.* Retrieved from https://www.nytimes.com/2015/09/15/us/virginia-has-solitary-confinement-case-if-justices-want-it.html

Lollis v. New York State Department of Social Services, 328 F.Supp. 1115 (S.D. N.Y. 1971).

Moore v. Texas, 136 S.Ct. 2407 (2016).

National Institute of Justice. (2016). *Restrictive housing in the U.S.: Issues, challenges, and future directions.* Retrieved from https://www.ncjrs.gov/pdffiles1/nij/250315.pdf

Nelson v. CMS, 583 F.3d 522 (8th Cir. 2009).

Overton v. Bazzetta, 539 U.S. 126 (2003).

Planned Parenthood of Southeastern Pennsylvania v. Casey, 505 U.S. 833, 851 (1992).

Prieto v. Clarke, 2013 WL 6019215 (E.D.Va.).

Prieto v. Clarke, 136 S.Ct. 29 (2015a).

Prieto v. Clarke, 780 F.3d 245 (4th Cir. 2015b).

Rhodes v. Chapman, 452 U.S. 337 (1981).

Sandin v. Conner, 515 U.S. 472 (1995).

Sireci v. Florida, 137 S.Ct. 470 (2016).

Sorensen, J., & Cunningham, M. (2009). Once a killer, always a killer? Prison misconduct of former death-sentenced inmates in Arizona. *Journal of Psychiatry & Law, 37,* 237–263. http://dx.doi.org/10.1177/009318530903700205

Thompson, C., & Shapiro, J. (2016, March 24). The deadly consequences of solitary with a cellmate. *The Marshall Project.* Retrieved from https://www.themarshallproject.org/2016/03/24/the-deadly-consequences-of-solitary-with-a-cellmate#.dubHk7hzx

Washington v. Glucksberg, 521 U.S. 702 (1997).

Wilson v. Seiter, 501 U.S. 294 (1991).

Wolff v. McDonnell, 418 U.S. 539 (1974).

5

The Failure of a Security Rationale for Death Row

Mark D. Cunningham, Thomas J. Reidy, and Jonathan R. Sorensen

A merican correctional policy toward capital punishment inmates is broadly characterized by solitary confinement and security-driven procedures embodied in "death row." These segregated (death sentence only), highly restrictive units house condemned inmates in federal and virtually every state jurisdiction holding offenders under a sentence of death, Missouri notably excepted. Various rationales appear to support

The authors have made equal contributions to this chapter and thus are listed alphabetically. The authors acknowledge and thank the Missouri Department of Corrections and particularly David Oldfield for providing assistance in data collection. We also wish to acknowledge the invaluable contributions of Director George Lombardi and his staff and Warden Cindy Griffith and her staff at the Potosi Correctional Center. The views expressed in this chapter are not necessarily those of the Missouri Department of Corrections.

Disclosure: The authors derive income from evaluations and testimony at capital sentencing specifying varying levels of improbability of future prison violence and/or describing prison conditions of confinement. Funding for travel expenses and data analysis was provided by the Missouri State Public Defender. Dr. Cunningham has been retained by death row plaintiffs regarding their conditions of confinement.

Adapted from "Wasted Resources and Gratuitous Suffering: The Failure of a Security Rationale for Death Row," by M. D. Cunningham, T. J. Reidy, and J. R. Sorensen, 2016, *Psychology, Public Policy, and Law, 22*, pp. 185–199. Copyright 2016 by the American Psychological Association.

http://dx.doi.org/10.1037/0000084-006

the near ubiquitous use of death row. The most obvious and overtly expressed rationale for death row is that condemned inmates are particularly incorrigible, violence-prone, disposed to escape, and desperate (see Johnson, 1990; Lombardi, Sluder, & Wallace, 1997; Salinas, 2002). This is a critically important consideration: Are death-sentence inmates, as a class, more likely to commit acts of serious violence in prison than other high-security inmates, requiring correspondingly more intensive security measures? If the institutional violence risk from death-sentenced inmates is not greater than non–capital punishment high-security inmates, supermaximum conditions on death row would not be justified by an authentic security rationale.

A view that death-sentenced inmates are particularly violence-prone prisoners is likely to be driven, in part, by the depravity of the capital murder(s) that resulted in a sentence of death, the revulsion toward those who have committed such misdeeds, and the expectation that this offending and its underlying personality pathology predict serious violence in prison. Expectations of future prison violence are strengthened by an intuitive hypothesis that, already under a sentence of death, condemned inmates have nothing to lose in engaging in desperate acts (see McShane, 1996; Salinas, 2002).[1] Though the security rationales undergirding segregated, highly restrictive death row housing of capital punishment inmates are intuitively appealing and apparently widely accepted by corrections administrators and public policymakers, a growing body of data demonstrate these supermaximum procedures to be unwarranted as a violence risk intervention.

That is not to say intensive security procedures have no impact on rates of serious prison violence. It is inarguable that supermaximum conditions of confinement almost entirely negate the potential for prison assaults resulting in serious injury for inmates and prison staff. Despite this effectiveness, only a small minority of prisoners are held at this custody level. The staffing, expense, and deprivations and suffering associated

---

[1] In federal litigation regarding death row conditions in Virginia, a corrections expert retained by the Commonwealth asserted these rationales for highly restrictive death row security as self-evident and widely accepted.

with supermaximum security make this level of security impractical and injurious, and therefore it is not universally applied. Instead, corrections departments tolerate a certain level of violence among inmates as an unavoidable reality, applying supermaximum conditions only as punishment for violent behavior or to immobilize those inmates who are a disproportionate risk of serious violence (e.g., by virtue of prior serious prison violence or security threat group membership).

DEATH ROW CONDITIONS OF CONFINEMENT

Death row conditions nationwide are characterized by solitary confinement, little social interaction, and sharply restricted activities. Both the American Civil Liberties Union (ACLU; 2013, regarding death rows in 26 states) survey and the Death Penalty Information Center (n.d., regarding death rows in 31 states) survey found that out-of-cell recreation is typically limited to 1 to 3 hours daily (93%; ACLU, 2013) or even to an hour daily or less (81%). Half provide only a cage, pen, or cell in which to exercise, and the provision of exercise equipment or even a simple ball to bounce is rare (ACLU, 2013). Recreation on death row is most often solitary (ACLU, 2013; Death Penalty Information Center, n.d.). Most jurisdictions have no provision for educational or work programming (Death Penalty Information Center, n.d.). The activity restrictions on death row are particularly notable: Cell sizes range from 4 feet by 9 feet (36 sq. ft.) to 9 feet by 12 feet (108 sq. ft.). When moved, death row inmates are generally chained and cuffed and require special security procedures involving two or three guard escorts. Two thirds of states do not allow contact visitation between death row inmates and loved ones.

"COSTS" OF DEATH ROW

Fiscal and Staffing Costs

The supermaximum conditions of confinement characterizing death rows are resource intensive. For example, Alarcón and Mitchell (2012) reported, on the basis of current mortality rates of death row inmates in California, that the state will pay an estimated $1,134,800,000 more to house inmates on death row between 2013 and 2050 compared with the cost of housing the same number of inmates with life-without-parole status. In addition, the availability of staff to provide greater supervision to the general prison population is reduced by the supervising, escorting, and cell-front feeding of capital punishment inmates.

The interpersonal isolation and activity deprivations of supermaximum confinement on death row may further add to staffing burdens by provoking or exacerbating psychological disorders. Research has consistently shown that inmates displaying impairment in psychological functioning engage in more institutional misconduct and present unique challenges for prison systems (Felson, Silver, & Remster, 2012; Lovell, Allen, Johnson, & Jemelka, 2001; O'Keefe & Schnell, 2007; Walters & Crawford, 2014).

Psychological Costs

Because supermaximum solitary confinement in prisons nationwide has not historically and is not currently restricted to death row inmates, a broader literature is available on the psychological impacts of this isolation (see Arrigo & Bullock, 2008; Cohen, 2006; Grassian, 2006; Haney, 2003, 2006, 2008; Haney & Lynch, 1997; Lovell, 2008; McLeod, 2009; Pizarro & Stenius, 2004; Smith, 2009, 2011; Toch, 2001, 2003). Although a comprehensive review is beyond the scope of this chapter, the scholarly literature supports a conclusion that sustained supermaximum conditions of confinement are both psychologically painful and deleterious (but see Metzner & Dvoskin, 2006; O'Keefe et al., 2013; the latter was criticized for mischaracterized literature and methodological weaknesses by Smith, 2011).

An application of research on solitary confinement to the deprivations of supermaximum security on death row and their psychological impacts has been detailed (see Bohm, 2008; Harrison & Tamony, 2010; Lyon & Cunningham, 2006; Yuzon, 1996). Lyon and Cunningham (2006) summarized that psychological health and equilibrium depend on routine social interaction, as well as meaningful activity and varied stimulation; capital punishment inmates are not "somehow immune to the impact of fundamental psychological deprivations" (p. 19).

Limitations of Capital Punishment Inmates

Because they are denied the array of physical, social, work, and recreational activities and stimulation afforded other inmates, prisoners in supermaximum custody are more reliant on the ability of their minds to provide stimulation and a sense of purpose. In other words, their coping strategies, by necessity, are almost entirely internal and self-generated. Assessments of death row inmates,[2] however, have demonstrated that a substantial minority lack sufficient intelligence and/or literacy to successfully occupy themselves in supermaximum custody by reading or engaging in solitary intellectual pursuits. Meanwhile, they are denied the more concrete activities allowed other inmates, such as inmate work roles, group recreation or sports, and routine social exchange. The intellectual limitations of many capital punishment inmates are compounded by marginal literacy capabilities; they demonstrate mean educational achievement abilities ranging from fifth to eighth grade, and a minority exhibit particularly compromised literacy skills (see Cunningham, Sorensen, Vigen, & Woods, 2011; Cunningham & Vigen, 1999; Gallemore & Panton, 1972). Frequently observed neurological abnormalities and neuropsychological deficits among these inmates (see Cunningham, 2013; Cunningham & Vigen, 1999) serve to reduce psychological resilience to sustain the deprivations and stresses of supermaximum confinement, as well as reduce the likelihood of the successful application of solitary intellectual pursuits.

Further, capital punishment inmates nationwide can anticipate long tenures on death row. Offenders executed nationwide in 2013 had averaged

---

[2] Fourteen clinical studies (involving direct assessment or individual file review) of death row inmates were identified: Bluestone and McGahee (1962); Cunningham, Sorensen, Vigen, and Woods (2011); Cunningham and Vigen (1999); Evans (1997); Freedman and Hemenway (2000); Frierson, Schwartz-Watts, Morgan, and Malone (1998); Gallemore and Panton (1972); Johnson (1979); P. W. Lewis (1979); D. O. Lewis, Pincus, Feldman, Jackson, and Bard (1986); Lisak and Beszterczey (2007); Panton (1976, 1978); Smith and Felix (1986). See also Cunningham (2013). For a discussion of pre-2002 studies, see Cunningham and Vigen (2002).

186 months under a sentence of death (Snell, 2014), with the range of death row tenure extending to over 30 years. Such an extended period under potential solitary or supermaximum conditions of confinement serves to exacerbate the impacts of the associated deprivations (Pizarro & Stenius, 2004). Unlike almost all other inmates held in supermaximum custody, death row inmates can do nothing short of being exonerated, securing a reduction of their sentence, or dying to curtail the duration of the deprivations. This engendered helplessness can be expected to induce even greater passivity and exacerbate the deleterious effects.

Psychological Distress and Disorders on Death Row

Consistent with these perspectives, capital punishment inmates have been described as vulnerable to *death row syndrome*, a term used to describe the psychologically harmful effects of the segregating death row conditions of confinement while an inmate is awaiting a death sentence (Harrison & Tamony, 2010; see also Johnson, 1979). This concept is similar to what came to be known as the *SHU* [Secure Housing Unit] *syndrome* following research by Grassian (1983). Johnson (1979) concluded from in-depth interviews with death row inmates in Alabama that "the stresses of death row confinement are enormous. Adjustment proves, at best, precarious and fragile" (p. 179). Similarly, Cunningham and Vigen (1999) described Mississippi death row inmates as reporting a high frequency of psychological symptoms during clinical interviews, as well as exhibiting pathologically elevated personality testing profiles.

Of course, the prevalence of psychological disorders among death-sentenced inmates may reflect preexisting psychological disorders (i.e., importation factors) and/or the stress of a pending death sentence, as opposed to being solely a function of death row deprivations. Regardless, however, the psychological stresses of supermaximum confinement would be expected to exacerbate such vulnerabilities.

The psychological hazards of death row are also demonstrated in elevated suicide rates. Lester and Tartaro (2002) reported a suicide rate among death row inmates from 1976–1999 as 113 per 100,000 inmates—10 times the national suicide rate and 6 times the rate of suicide for general population inmates (see also Blume, 2004). Acknowledging that capital punishment inmates may have other agendas and preexisting risks for suicide, these ratios nevertheless are startling. The number of suicides on California death row from 1978 to the present ($n = 24$) is nearly double the number of executions ($n = 13$; California Department of Corrections and Rehabilitation, 2015a, 2015b). Still other capital punishment inmates forgo further appeals and "volunteer" for execution. Nationwide, 145 inmates made this decision since 1976 when the death penalty was reinstated (Death Penalty Information Center, 2017a; see also Chapter 6, this volume), but only two capital punishment inmates from Missouri have made such a decision since Potosi Correctional Center (PCC) integrated these inmates with the general population (Death Penalty Information Center, 2017b; PCC Warden Cindy Griffith, personal communication, July 28, 2015). Rountree (2014) found some support for the hypothesis that supermaximum conditions of confinement on death row increased the proportion of inmates seeking to hasten their executions but cautioned that confounding factors were present.

Implications of Costs

The fiscal and staffing costs of segregated, supermaximum conditions for capital punishment inmates, whether or not warranted by security, only trigger considerations of budgetary allocation of limited tax revenues, responsible stewardship of the public trust, and political accountability. These costs, however, have no constitutional implications. Wasting resources may reflect poor governance but is not unconstitutional.

The psychological costs of a segregated, supermaximum death row are more constitutionally complex, primarily involving Eighth Amendment considerations of whether this treatment represents cruel and unusual punishment. An Eighth Amendment analysis of retributive rationales for the deprivations of death row is beyond the scope of this paper. Rather, the current analysis limits itself to testing the security-driven justification for the perpetual supermaximum confinement of capital punishment inmates. In applying an Eighth Amendment analysis of this security-driven rationale, an initial consideration is whether such a punishment is "unusual."

By an "objective" standard (see *Rhodes v. Chapman*, 1981, citing *Rummel v. Estelle*, 1980; *Coker v. Georgia*, 1977), supermaximum confinement per se would not be considered "unusual" for risk management. Virtually every correctional jurisdiction has such units. Indeed, as of August 31, 2014, there were 6,565 inmates in administrative segregation in the Texas Department of Criminal Justice (2014). Although widely used, supermaximum custody may still have constitutional implications. Collins (2004) observed that the restrictions accompanying supermaximum units "mean that, even under the best of circumstances, these facilities operate very close to the edge of what the Constitution allows" (p. 2).

What is not just "unusual" but unique to capital punishment inmates, though, is the arbitrary assignment to indefinite supermaximum custody on the basis of sentence alone, independent of an individualized assessment of risk. By contrast, Collins (2004) described the multifaceted procedures, arguably necessitated by constitutional protections, that are applied to the extended placement of other inmates in supermaximum confinement, limiting assignment to such units to "the highest security risks in a state's prison system . . . the 'worst of the worst'" (p. 6).

Also "unusual" is a potential tenure of supermaximum conditions that may extend for decades. Cohen (2006) cited *Mitchell v. Maynard* (1996) in articulating how the duration of isolated confinement may affect its constitutionality: "Indeed, assuming that the conditions of isolated confinement are in some fashion onerous but marginally constitutionally acceptable, the harsher the conditions, the shorter the period of duration legally available for the use of such isolated confinement" (p. 323).

Both the arbitrary assignment of capital punishment inmates to segregated, supermaximum units and the indefinite duration of confinement under such conditions call for objective scrutiny of the penological rationale for this convention. Security, the assertion that capital punishment inmates are particularly likely to perpetrate serious prison violence, is the ostensible primary "penological purpose" justifying the psychological suffering of capital punishment inmates in segregated, supermaximum custody. A crucial determination is whether this security is "pain with a penological purpose" (see *Estelle v. Gamble*, 1976; *Hutto v. Finney*, 1978; *Turner v. Safley*, 1987) or alternatively reflects the unnecessary and wanton infliction of pain, without penological justification (see *Rhodes v. Chapman*, 1981; and cited precedents, e.g., *Coker v. Georgia*, 1977; *Estelle v. Gamble*, 1976; *Gregg v. Georgia*, 1976; *Trop v. Dulles*, 1958; *Weems v. United States*, 1910; see also Chapter 4, this volume). The security aspects of this determination are objectively tested by the comparative violence rates of capital punishment inmates as opposed to other high-security inmates.

ARE CAPITAL PUNISHMENT INMATES INHERENTLY MORE VIOLENT?

An assertion could be made that offenders who have been sentenced to death are a distinct class of inmates—the "worst of the worst." Under this theory, their inherent depravity renders them at particular risk of serious violence in prison. Consistent with this theory, a substantial proportion of condemned inmates were sentenced with a jury finding of a likelihood of future violence (i.e., whether there is a "probability the defendant would commit criminal acts of violence that would constitute a continuing threat to society"; see *Jurek v. Texas*, 1976). This "probability of future violence" is a capital sentencing "special issue" (in Texas and Oregon) or a statutory/nonstatutory aggravating factor in many state jurisdictions, as well as in federal capital sentencing. To illustrate the prevalence of this consideration, Shapiro (2009) reported that the threat of future violence was the sole aggravating factor in a quarter of Virginia's 103 executions and was one of the aggravating factors in 50 other cases.

Supermaximum confinement seems to be an intuitively sound response to offenders determined to be the worst of the worst, particularly when their proclivity for future violence has been jury determined as a death-sentencing factor. Despite the intuitive appeal of this logic, empirical findings have revealed that neither the assertion of future dangerousness by the prosecution nor a finding of future dangerousness by a capital jury is predictive of serious prison violence or escape. This has been a consistent finding among federal capital offenders alleged pretrial by the Government to be a "future danger" but subsequently sentenced to life without parole (Cunningham, Sorensen, & Reidy, 2009), Texas inmates sentenced to death under a "future dangerousness" special issue and subsequently gaining relief from these sentences (Cunningham, Sorensen, Vigen, & Woods, 2010; Edens, Buffington-Vollum, Keilen, Roskamp, & Anthony, 2005; Marquart, Ekland-Olson, & Sorensen, 1989), and capital punishment inmates in Oregon who had been prosecuted under this special issue and subsequently sentenced to death or life without parole (Reidy, Sorensen, & Cunningham, 2013). In all these studies, only a small and not disproportionate minority of inmates who had faced capital charges committed assaults with the potential for serious injury. Although conceivably contemplating contexts beyond prison, neither prosecutors nor capital jurors demonstrated an ability to predict serious prison violence in their probability determinations (i.e., no improvement over the base rates of violence in their probability findings in either direction). Thus, neither could identify those inmates who required preemptive supermaximum conditions of confinement and those who did not.

The low prevalence and not disproportionate rate of serious violence among these violence-predicted offenders when in the general prison population (postrelief) have significant implications for the assumptions of inherent violence proclivity in all contexts that ostensibly served to underlie their prosecutions and capital jury death sentencing. The abhorrent violence of their capital offenses was context dependent, at least in terms of not crossing the community-to-prison barrier. Serious assaults were a rarity among former capital punishment inmates.

These findings demonstrate that an inherent and irrepressible violence proclivity cannot be assumed from a capital murder offense, at least not a violence proclivity that finds expression in serious prison assaults occurring in spite of standard institutional controls (e.g., classification, disciplinary sanctions, supermaximum security applied as individually indicated). These institutional controls had an incapacitating effect on the most serious prison violence, even though over half of the offenders in the Cunningham et al. (2011) sample had histories of a prior violent crime arrest in the community and half had served a prison sentence before their capital offense.

Supermaximum confinement was among the institutional controls brought to bear on a case-by-case basis on a minority of former death row inmates (see Cunningham et al., 2010). This selective application illustrates the appropriate security role of supermaximum confinement: to incapacitate a small minority of offenders who have been demonstrated through their history of prison violence and/or membership in prison gangs to represent a disproportionate risk to safety and security.

Intuitive rationales of future prison violence based on the depravity or violence proclivity of condemned prisoners as a class are belied by empirical data. Further, prosecution assertions and jury probability determinations of future violence are not a sound basis for determining which inmates require segregation and/or supermaximum security measures.

DOES BEING UNDER A SENTENCE OF DEATH RESULT IN A HIGH RISK OF VIOLENCE?

An alternative intuitive argument could be posed that it is not an inherent personality feature or related violence proclivity that renders capital punishment inmates at high risk of serious prison violence but rather that, already being under a death sentence, they are both desperate and have nothing to lose (see McShane, 1996; Salinas, 2002). More simply, this rationale posits that the nature of the sentence rather than the character of the inmate drives a high risk of prison violence or escape. Objectively testing this appealing hypothesis is relatively straightforward: Examine the comparative violence rates of capital punishment prisoners as opposed to other high-security inmates held under the same or equivalent conditions of confinement (i.e., controlling for factors other than the sentence). Three correctional jurisdictions, Arkansas, Texas, and Missouri, offer such comparative perspectives. These studies provide strong evidence that capital punishment inmates are not disproportionately likely to perpetrate serious violence when confined in the general prison population or an equivalent context.

The Arkansas Experience of Integrating Capital Punishment Inmates in General Population Programming

The most far-reaching early effort to reform death row conditions occurred at the Tucker Prison Farm in Arkansas in 1968 under the leadership of a reform warden appointed by a progressive governor (see Murton, 1969). As part of a "demonstration project" to foster a more humane environment, the harsh restrictions and deprivations used at the time were gradually eased, with capital punishment inmates being integrated into general population programs, except for separate housing, and permitted similar privileges. The changes resulted in beneficial effects for inmates and staff, with none of the anticipated violence or disruption. In fact, just the opposite was the case. As Murton (1969) commented, "They [the capital punishment inmates] became the model prisoners of the institution" (p. 109). Although the changes proved successful, the state's Board of Correction was unsupportive of the reform warden's innovative efforts. The integration program was ended after a little more than a year, reinstituting conditions of confinement more compatible with the prevailing correctional practice of heightened security, isolation, and marked restrictions of death row.

The Texas Experience of a Death Row Approximating General Population Conditions

The conditions on the Texas death row were fundamentally altered by a 1985 consent decree signed in conjunction with *Ruiz v. Estelle* (1980). Before the consent decree, the daily activity of inmates on death row reflected the dominance of security, characterized by 20 plus hours daily of cell confinement, meals in cells, strict custody procedures, and restraints in out-of-cell movement. Following the consent decree, these procedures were only applied to death row "segregation" inmates. Approximately one third of death row inmates were classified as work capable, placed in two-man cells, and programmed with out-of-cell work and recreation activities much of the day. A portion of these work-capable inmates worked as orderlies and janitors on the cellblock, but most worked in a self-contained garment factory on death row.

Inmates in the work-capable program had ample occasion and means to commit serious assaults, but few serious violent incidents occurred in the living or work areas. Of 421 inmates who passed through Texas death row between 1974 and 1988, 10.7% committed an assault, equivalent to the rate of aggravated or weapons assaults of life-sentenced murderers and rapists followed across an 11-year period in the Texas general prison population (Marquart et al., 1994).

In response to two escape attempts from the Texas death row, other isolated serious misconduct, and the expiration of the consent decree, the death row work-capable program on Texas's death row was terminated in 1998, and an administrative segregation (supermaximum) protocol was reimposed for virtually all death row inmates. By contrast, escapes, prison homicides, and serious prison assaults perpetrated by convicted armed robbers or noncapital murderers in Texas prisons have not resulted in the supermaximum confinement of whole classes of similarly convicted inmates. This differential in security response raises serious questions about whether Texas's decision to reimpose supermaximum confinement on capital punishment inmates was authentically security driven or instead a reflection of a punishment enhancement agenda or political repercussions.[3]

The Missouri Experience of "Mainstreaming" Capital Punishment Inmates

In 1986, the Missouri Department of Corrections (MDOC) entered into a consent decree to reform the austere and "dungeon-like" conditions of its death row (Lombardi et al., 1997). During the next 5 years, death row

---

[3] While the Texas death row work-capable program was in effect, offenders in the program would be returned to segregated status when Texas Department of Criminal Justice (TDCJ) administration was notified that the setting of an execution date was imminent. Typically, this notice was received approximately five weeks before the execution date. The day before the execution, the inmate would be moved from Ellis I to a segregated holding cell in the Huntsville Unit. A meal of the inmate's choosing would be served at dinner that evening. Noncontact visitation with family, friends, and counsel would be available. The following day, at 6:00 p.m., the execution would occur (S. O. Woods, TDCJ retired, personal communication, March 1, 2017).

remained a segregated unit, but progressive modifications were made in housing and management of capital punishment inmates, especially after the relocation of death row in 1989 to the newly opened Potosi Correctional Center, a C-5-level maximum-security facility for men in MDOC. As prison administrators began considering alternatives for managing capital offenders, they recognized the "irony" that capital punishment and noncapital murderers had been convicted of similar offenses but were segregated from each other (Lombardi et al., 1997). Incremental liberalization of the conditions of death row followed.

In January 1991, capital punishment inmates were fully integrated or "mainstreamed" into the general inmate population of PCC (Lombardi et al., 1997). During this tenure and continuing to date (2017), capital punishment inmates have been eligible for the same housing, programming, activities, and sanctions as the life-without-parole and term-sentenced inmates also incarcerated at PCC. Thus, they share cells, work details, recreation, interaction, privileges, and sanctions with other maximum security inmates—on the basis of their institutional behavior rather than a pending death sentence. For the first time, an "apples to apples" comparison of the institutional violence rates of capital punishment and noncapital punishment inmates, jointly housed over an extended period in the modern era, became possible.[4]

2005 Study

During the 11-year period spanning January 1991 to January 2002, 3,402 inmates were confined for various periods at PCC. This population included 149 "mainstreamed" inmates sentenced to death, 1,054 inmates sentenced to life without parole (LWOP) for first-degree murder,[5] and 2,199 inmates sentenced to parole-eligible terms.

Cunningham, Reidy, and Sorensen (2005) undertook a comparative examination of the prevalence and frequency rates of violent institutional

---

[4] Sorensen and Wrinkle (1996) examined the comparative misconduct of capital punishment, life-without-parole, and life-with-parole inmates from 1977 to 1992, partially overlapping the mainstreaming era.

[5] Life-without-parole inmates were all housed at Potosi Correctional Center during the time of this study, but subsequently were dispersed throughout Missouri Department of Corrections (Director George Lombardi, personal communication, July 8, 2015).

misconduct among the capital punishment, LWOP, and term-sentenced inmates who had been confined in PCC between 1991 and 2002. The results of this comparison confirmed the subjective observations of the MDOC regarding the success of this policy of mainstreaming capital punishment inmates. During 11 years of mainstreaming, the capital punishment inmates committed no institutional homicides or attempted homicides. Their annualized rate of violent misconduct (3.1/100) was comparable to that of inmates serving LWOP sentences (5.1/100) and only one sixth that of parole-eligible inmates (19.4/100). Only the prevalence rate of violence was higher among the capital punishment group. Regression analysis supported an interpretation that this increased prevalence was an artifact of having significantly more years at risk (the capital punishment group had been confined at PCC 50% longer than the LWOP inmates and 400% longer than the parole-eligible inmates).

2016 Replication and Extension

Cunningham, Reidy, and Sorensen (2016) conceptually replicated the 2005 retrospective analysis, extending the comparison of violence rates through February 2015, a follow-up of nearly 25 years. The sample ($n = 3,787$) in the 2016 study consisted of inmates confined at PCC on August 1, 2006, or included at some time thereafter up through the end point of the initial data collection, February 27, 2015. This population included inmates sentenced to death (CP[6]; $n = 85$),[7] LWOP for first-degree murder ($n = 702$), and a term-sentenced group (TS; $n = 3,000$). As was the case with the 2005 study, the custody level an inmate is assigned in MDOC is based on the length of the offender's sentence, as well as his institutional behavior. At the time of the 2016 study, all inmates with more than 12 years remaining on their sentence were classified to C-5 facilities (currently five institutions),

---

[6] When Missouri Department of Corrections integrated death-sentenced inmates with the general population, they were designated "capital punishment" inmates in an effort to reduce the stigma attached to their sentence. This convention has been adopted throughout this chapter.

[7] The reduction in capital punishment inmate population from 149 in the earlier study to 85 in the current study results in large part from executions; 32 have occurred since January 2002, the last date of data collection in the prior study. It has also resulted from deaths due to natural causes and the removal of inmates from a death sentence due to case reversals. Perhaps more important, far fewer defendants have been sentenced to death in Missouri in recent years, a trend which has resulted in the nationwide drop in the number of persons under a sentence of death for more than a decade (Snell, 2014).

as were those considered institutional and custody risks by virtue of their prison classification scores. The CP inmates were mainstreamed into the PCC population and participated in any of the extensive and innovative incentive programs available to other inmates housed in this facility. Depending on conduct, the CP, LWOP, and TS inmates may be placed in one of nine specific PCC housing units.

The yearly rate of violent misconduct per 100 inmates is a standardized measure allowing for direct comparison of groups. As illustrated in Table 5.1, CP and LWOP inmates were significantly less likely than TS inmates to be involved in violent misconduct. Because they had served longer times, CP inmates had a higher prevalence of involvement in violent misconduct. However, once time at risk was controlled for through the calculation of yearly rates of offending, CP inmates were found to have the lowest rate of violent misconduct among the three groups. During the total of 1,168 inmate years served by the group of CP inmates, 41 violent acts were perpetrated, an average of 3.5 per 100 inmates annually. More than half the assaults were classified as minor, and none of the CP inmates in this sample were involved in a murder or manslaughter or attempted murder or manslaughter, a hostage situation, or a forcible sexual assault. From the data presented in Table 5.1, it appears that CP and LWOP inmates were involved in violent misconduct at a far lower rate than TS inmates. However, when demographic factors such as race and age at intake were controlled through logistic regression analysis, these differences largely disappeared.

To answer the question about the long-term efficacy of mainstreaming, Figure 5.1 presents violent misconduct data by sentence from various eras (Cunningham et al., 2005; Sorensen & Wrinkle, 1996). The comparison is not an exact one. Although the outcome measures are similar, including murder or manslaughter, attempted murder or manslaughter, forcible sexual assault, major assault, and minor assault, the samples and prison contexts vary. With that caution, what is most obvious from Figure 5.1 is that the rate of violent misconduct among CP inmates has actually decreased from the previous two eras. In other words, the

Table 5.1

Violent Misconduct Committed by Capital Punishment, LWOP, and Term-Sentenced Inmates Confined in PCC

	Capital punishment			LWOP			
							Yearly rate per 100 inmates
Violation	Rate	Stat. test	Effect size	Rate	Stat. test	Effect size	TS[a] Rate
Murder/manslaughter	0.0(0)	—[b]	—	0.04(2)	—	—	0.01(1)
Attempted murder/manslaughter	0.0(0)	—	—	0.1(7)	—	—	0.1(10)
Hostage/restraint	0.0(0)	—	—	0.0(0)	—	—	0.01(1)
Forcible sexual misconduct	0.0(0)	—	—	0.1(7)	—	—	0.03(3)
Major assaults	1.6*(19)	$t = -5.1$	$\eta = -.02$	2.9*(144)	$t = -2.2$	$\eta = -.02$	5.7(522)
Minor assaults	1.9*(22)	$t = -6.1$	$\eta = -.03$	2.7*(135)	$t = -6.6$	$\eta = -.07$	6.5(591)
Total violent misconduct	3.5*(41)	$t = -7.5$	$\eta = -.03$	6.0*(295)	$t = -5.4$	$\eta = -.05$	12.3(1,129)
Prevalence (% of inmates involved)	27.1*	$\chi^2 = 9.8$	$\phi = .06$	17.9*	$\chi^2 = 4.5$	$\phi = .04$	14.7
Average years at risk in Potosi	13.7*	$t = 16.0$	$\eta = .46$	7.0*	$t = 18.9$	$\eta = .39$	3.1
Group sum of years spent in Potosi	1,168	N/A	N/A	4,947	N/A	N/A	9,150

Note. LWOP = life without parole; PCC = Potosi Correctional Center; TS = term sentenced. Adapted from "Wasted Resources and Gratuitous Suffering: The Failure of a Security Rationale for Death Row," by M. D. Cunningham, T. J. Reidy, and J. R. Sorensen, 2016, *Psychology, Public Policy, and Law, 22,* p. 193. Copyright 2016 by the American Psychological Association.

[a]The TS group serves as the reference category for statistical comparisons. [b]"—" indicates that group incidence or rates were too small to calculate statistical tests.

* $p < .05$.

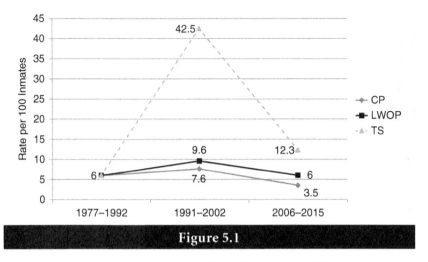

Figure 5.1

Annual rate of violent misconduct among Missouri Department of Corrections capital punishment (CP), life-without-parole (LWOP), and term-sentenced (TS) prisoners. From "Wasted Resources and Gratuitous Suffering: The Failure of a Security Rationale for Death Row," by M. D. Cunningham, T. J. Reidy, and J. R. Sorensen, 2016, *Psychology, Public Policy, and Law, 22*, p. 194. Copyright 2016 by the American Psychological Association.

mainstreaming of CP inmates has not increased the level of threat to the institution from violence committed by this group of inmates. The pattern among LWOP inmates was similarly flat, with a slight uptick during the early PCC 1991–2002 era. The huge discrepancy in the TS comparison group at PCC during that same period lies mainly in how they were selected. General population inmates, especially in the early era, migrated to PCC for bad behavior, so the worst TS inmates in the system were being compared with the CP and LWOP inmates during the spike in violent misconduct apparent in the early operation at PCC. Although the same was true in 2015, the availability of additional high-security units and institutional controls on the TS inmates' behavior had led to levels of violence well below that of the early PCC era.

As of February 2015, 32% of CP inmates were housed in the "honor dorm," a further indication of positive adaptation and a progressive improvement from the 21% who were in the honor dorm in the prior study of Missouri CP inmates (Cunningham et al., 2005).[8] At the time of 2015 data collection, no CP inmates were under administrative segregation for serious infractions. It was remarkable that no CP inmate in Missouri in 2015 required the security restrictions that were ubiquitously applied to CP inmates in almost all other jurisdictions.

Implications of Comparative Data From the Arkansas, Texas, and Missouri Experiences

Comparative data from Arkansas (Murton, 1969), Texas (Marquart et al., 1994), and Missouri (Cunningham et al., 2005, 2016) compellingly demonstrate that CP inmates have not been disproportionately violent when in the general prison population or confined under equivalent conditions. Rather than exhibiting a desperation fueled by having nothing to lose, these offenders as a group were equally responsive to the incentives that maintain order and engender compliance in the general prison population. Intuitive assumptions regarding the depravity of the capital offense and associated personality pathology as predictive of continuing high risk of violence in prison are not supported by the data.

APPLICATIONS

Corrections Applications

Classification

The redundant experience of low and not disproportionate serious violence in these "demonstration projects" of normalized or mainstreamed procedures for the management of CP inmates illustrates, again, that neither a conviction for murder or capital murder nor the associated sentence (death or LWOP) is a useful metric of classification within the

---

[8] Inmates at Potosi Correctional Center have the opportunity to progress through four levels of general population classification, each with greater privileges: baseline, basic general population, semiprivileged general population, and honor dorm. All are allowed participation in core programs, but higher levels have more out-of-cell time, access to premium pay jobs, and other incentives.

confines of a high-security prison. A growing body of research indicates that the majority of individuals convicted of capital murder are not cited for serious violent misconduct in prison. In some studies, capital offenders represent better institutional assault risks than inmates serving shorter sentences. Associated research includes retrospective examinations of the records of former CP inmates in Arizona (Sorensen & Cunningham, 2009) and Texas (Cunningham et al., 2010, 2011; Marquart et al., 1989), federal capital offenders serving LWOP sentences in the Bureau of Prisons (Cunningham, Reidy, & Sorensen, 2008), mainstreamed CP inmates in Missouri (Cunningham et al., 2005), and aggravated murderers sentenced to death or serving life sentences in Oregon (Reidy et al., 2013).

Incentives

The amenability of CP inmates to incentives has important lessons for corrections administrators as well. First, the success of Missouri in mainstreaming CP inmates did not simply reflect a relaxation in security. Rather, the "web of incentives" (Lombardi et al., 1997) at PCC for CP and other high-security inmates has been progressively augmented. The responsiveness of CP inmates to the expanded social interactions and activities of being in a general prison population, as well as access to the innovative incentives and programming described earlier, reflects a motivation shared with other long-sentence inmates to do the "easiest time possible" (see Cunningham & Sorensen, 2007; Flanagan, 1980, 1995; Morris, Longmire, Buffington-Vollum, & Vollum, 2010). Such incentives may be even more powerful for an offender with a pending death sentence. Because the CP inmate has a limited life expectancy, he is arguably particularly motivated to make those remaining days as positive for himself as possible. Rather than having "nothing to lose," the CP inmate may pragmatically recognize he has more at stake in each day and thus more to gain or lose by misconduct.

Of course, inmate management at PCC does not rely on incentives alone. Highly restrictive security measures are brought to bear on a case-by-case basis. They are simply not applied as a matter of course by sentence type.

Because Missouri did more than simply relax security regarding CP inmates, by implementing extensive incentives and programming, it is anticipated that other jurisdictions seeking to adopt this model would be faced with augmenting their incentive procedures, and perhaps modifying their administrative and correctional staff cultures as well. Such transitions may meet resistance, even when well conceived. Generalization of the level of success demonstrated by Missouri mainstreaming to other jurisdictions may thus require more than simply individualized classification or security designation.

Efficiencies

Lombardi et al. (1997) detailed a number of advantages of mainstreaming Missouri's CP inmates. These efficiencies have continued to be observed throughout the 25-year tenure of mainstreaming and include cost savings, more efficient staff utilization, expanded commissary hours for all inmates, improved access of CP inmates to legal materials and assistance, improved access of CP inmates to health care and psychological services, integration of CP inmates into prison work activities and programs, increased visitation, more recreational opportunities, and reduced stigmatization of CP inmates who are not identified in any visible manner from other inmates.

Public Policy Implications

There is now compelling, multidecade evidence that CP inmates can be mainstreamed in the general prison population without disproportionate violence. These findings are strengthened by collateral evidence from Texas that CP inmates have low rates of violence when their segregated confinement approximates the general prison population (see Marquart et al., 1994). Quite simply, CP inmates, as a class, do not require segregated, solitary, highly restrictive confinement to prevent serious prison violence. This well-established finding is an indictment of wasted fiscal and staff resources in an era of correctional budget crises. This finding also robs assumptions of high-violence risk for condemned inmates of scientific validity and deprives the institution of "death row" of a legitimate security rationale (i.e., legitimate penological interest).

The legitimacy of any public policy rests on the accuracy of its assumptions and the quality of its reasoning. Public policy regarding death row is not an exception to this principle. Historical legacy and reification of the timeworn, as reflected in stereotypes regarding death row, are no more a sound basis of corrections practice than bloodletting was for medicine, phrenology for psychology, flat-earth for navigation, or indentured service for creation of credit.

Generalization of Findings

There are a number of reasons to believe the Missouri experience with mainstreaming CP inmates would generalize to other states. First, the Missouri experience does not stand in isolation. Two other jurisdictions, Arkansas and Texas, had low rates of serious violence among CP inmates in the general prison population or equivalent conditions. Second, the number of CP inmates passing through Missouri's mainstreaming procedure in the past 25 years provided a wide spectrum of offender and offense features.

Third, the mainstreaming of CP inmates in Missouri is not as novel as it appears. It reflects no more than a logical extension to death-sentenced prisoners of the ubiquitous individualized classification metrics and individualized screening procedures for assignment to extended super-maximum custody. Such individualized appraisal and security assignment already exist as sound penological policy in all jurisdictions for all inmates except those sentenced to death. Thus, such individualized procedures are already widely accepted as generalizing between corrections departments, despite differences in the geographic origin, ethnicity, and gang-affiliation features of their inmate populations. Interestingly, an argument that the Missouri results would not generalize because of differences in jurisdictional context is an affirmation that CP inmates are responsive to context and are not in and of themselves more institutionally violence prone. Fourth, collateral research on former death-sentenced inmates and capital offenders sentenced to LWOP demonstrates that these offenders are not inherently more violent in prison, despite their offenses and independent of whether or not prosecutors or juries predicted them to be institutionally violent.

These data and the discussion, of course, only address the security rationale for a segregated, supermaximum death row. Other rationales for the enduring convention of death row are hypothesized as including (a) cultural stereotypes or popular "mythology" regarding CP inmates (see Lyon & Cunningham, 2006) growing out of media depictions (e.g., *The Green Mile*, 1999) and the reification of corrections history, (b) a desire to inflict punishment and suffering beyond confinement and execution (see Blecker, 2013; *In re Medley*, 1890), (c) a post hoc justification for assertions of "future dangerousness" or offender depravity as capital sentencing determinants, and/or (d) a lack of political will to tolerate a level of violence among CP inmates that is routinely accepted among other high-security inmates. Whatever their penological legitimacy or political expediency, the hypothesized agendas undergirding the convention of death row reflect social values. Unlike the security-driven rationales for death row, these alternative agendas are not empirically testable. Accordingly, we encourage their being asserted candidly in public policy discussions regarding the conditions of confinement for CP inmates, without seeking cover in security rationales that are unsupported by science.

CONCLUSION AND RECOMMENDATIONS FOR REFORM

From a violence risk-management standpoint, widespread adoption of mainstreaming CP inmates is fiscally sound, promotes the most efficient use of limited staffing resources, reflects a scientifically informed approach to classification, and reduces the substantial psychological costs of death row. The closing of death row is efficient, enlightened, and humane. To do otherwise is to perpetuate a legacy of wasted resources and gratuitous suffering.

Though this observation and the associated recommendation reflect the best application of corrections science, we recognize that the institution of death row has attitudinal and political aspects that only seek cover in security rationales. If there is a genuine commitment to match death row procedures to security requirements, rather than to promote suffering, the available reforms need not be complete to be meaningful. Whatever measures reduce isolation and increase stimulation also serve to lessen the deleterious psychological impact of solitary confinement. Among such incremental modifications are greater out-of-cell time in small group recreation and meals, double-celling for inmates who desire this, exercise equipment and recreational programming, an educational curriculum, shelter dog training, expanded craft materials, group work opportunities within death row, greater phone access at reduced cost, and contact visitation. In-cell televisions can markedly increase stimulation, as well as provide a medium for a wide range of educational and therapeutic programming. Access to computer terminals is a near untapped opportunity for work, educational, and recreational activities.

Apart from its impact on inmate mental health, the PCC experience suggests that the availability of expanded incentives serves to reduce misconduct and violence, easing demands and stresses on corrections staff. Prison administrators are encouraged to consider how greater inmate incentives may have positive impact on budgeting and staff morale.

As scientist–practitioners, psychologists are well positioned to make scientific findings understandable to corrections administrators and policymakers. Disseminating best science is a critically important first step in more enlightened public and correctional policies and procedures. Psychologists are also arguably best equipped to be innovative in developing programs and explaining the rationales for reforms that have the potential to promote psychological well-being with only modest and incremental impact on security.

REFERENCES

Alarcón, A. L., & Mitchell, P. M. (2012). Costs of capital punishment in California: Will voters choose reform this November? *Loyola of Los Angeles Law Review, 46*. Retrieved from http://digitalcommons.lmu.edu/llr/vol46/iss0/1

American Civil Liberties Union. (2013). *A death before dying: Solitary confinement on death row.* Retrieved from https://www.aclu.org/sites/default/files/field_document/deathbeforedying-report.pdf

Arrigo, B. A., & Bullock, J. L. (2008). The psychological effects of solitary confinement on prisoners in supermax units: Reviewing what we know and recommending what should change. *International Journal of Offender Therapy and Comparative Criminology, 52*, 622–640. http://dx.doi.org/10.1177/0306624X07309720

Blecker, R. (2013). *The death of punishment: Searching for justice among the worst of the worst*. New York, NY: Palgrave Macmillan.

Bluestone, H., & McGahee, C. L. (1962). Reaction to extreme stress: Impending death by execution. *The American Journal of Psychiatry, 119*, 393–396. http://dx.doi.org/10.1176/ajp.119.5.393

Blume, J. (2004). Killing the willing: "Volunteers, suicide, and competency." *Cornell Law Faculty Publications.* Retrieved from http://scholarship.law.cornell.edu/lsrp_papers/16

Bohm, R. M. (Ed.). (2008). *The death penalty today.* Boca Raton, FL: CRC Press. http://dx.doi.org/10.1201/b15785

California Department of Corrections and Rehabilitation. (2015a). *Capital punishment: Inmates executed, 1978 to present.* Retrieved from http://cdcr.ca.gov/Capital_Punishment/Inmates_Executed.html

California Department of Corrections and Rehabilitation. (2015b). *Condemned inmates who have died since 1978.* Retrieved from https://www.cdcr.ca.gov/Capital_Punishment/docs/CONDEMNED-INMATES-WHO-HAVE-DIED-SINCE-1978.pdf

Cohen, F. (2006). Prison reform: Commission on Safety and Abuse in America's Prisons: Isolation in penal settings: The isolation-restraint paradigm. *Washington University Journal of Law and Policy, 22*, 295–324.

Coker v. Georgia, 433 U.S. 584 (1977).

Collins, W. C. (2004). *Supermax prisons and the constitution: Liability concerns in the extended control unit* (NIC Accession No. 019835). Washington, DC: U.S. Department of Justice, National Institute of Corrections. Retrieved from https://s3.amazonaws.com/static.nicic.gov/Library/019835.pdf

Cunningham, M. D. (2013). Capital punishment inmates. In L. Gideon (Ed.), *Special needs offenders in correctional institutions* (pp. 377–404). Thousand Oaks, CA: Sage.

Cunningham, M. D., Reidy, T. J., & Sorensen, J. R. (2005). Is death row obsolete? A decade of mainstreaming death-sentenced inmates in Missouri. *Behavioral Sciences & the Law, 23*, 307–320. http://dx.doi.org/10.1002/bsl.608

Cunningham, M. D., Reidy, T. J., & Sorensen, J. R. (2008). Assertions of "future dangerousness" at federal capital sentencing: Rates and correlates of subsequent prison misconduct and violence. *Law and Human Behavior, 32*, 46–63. http://dx.doi.org/10.1007/s10979-007-9107-7

Cunningham, M. D., Reidy, T. J., & Sorensen, J. R. (2016). Wasted resources and gratuitous suffering: The failure of a security rationale for death row. *Psychology, Public Policy, and Law, 22*, 185–199. http://dx.doi.org/10.1037/law0000072

Cunningham, M. D., & Sorensen, J. R. (2007). Capital offenders in Texas prisons: Rates, correlates, and an actuarial analysis of violent misconduct. *Law and Human Behavior, 31*, 553–571. http://dx.doi.org/10.1007/s10979-006-9079-z

Cunningham, M. D., Sorensen, J. R., & Reidy, T. J. (2009). Capital jury decision-making: The limitations of predictions of future violence. *Psychology, Public Policy, and Law, 15*, 223–256. http://dx.doi.org/10.1037/a0017296

Cunningham, M. D., Sorensen, J. R., Vigen, M. P., & Woods, S. O. (2010). Life and death in the Lone Star State: Three decades of violence predictions by capital juries. *Behavioral Sciences and Law, 29*, 1–22. http://dx.doi.org/10.1002/bsl.963

Cunningham, M. D., Sorensen, J. R., Vigen, M. P., & Woods, S. O. (2011). Correlates and actuarial models of assaultive prison misconduct among violence-predicted capital offenders. *Criminal Justice and Behavior, 38*, 5–25. http://dx.doi.org/10.1177/0093854810384830

Cunningham, M. D., & Vigen, M. P. (1999). Without appointed counsel in capital postconviction proceedings: The self-representation competency of Mississippi death row inmates. *Criminal Justice and Behavior, 26*, 293–321. http://dx.doi.org/10.1177/0093854899026003002

Cunningham, M. D., & Vigen, M. P. (2002). Death row inmate characteristics, adjustment, and confinement: A critical review of the literature. *Behavioral Sciences & the Law, 20*(1–2), 191–210. http://dx.doi.org/10.1002/bsl.473

Darabont, F. (Producer & Director) & Valdes, D. (Producer). (1999). *The Green Mile* [Motion picture]. United States: Warner Brothers.

Death Penalty Information Center. (2017a). *Searchable execution database: Volunteers*. Retrieved from http://www.deathpenaltyinfo.org/views-executions?exec_name_1=&sex=All&sex_1=All&federal=All&foreigner=All&juvenile=All&volunteer=y

Death Penalty Information Center. (2017b). *Searchable execution database: Volunteers, Missouri*. Retrieved from http://www.deathpenaltyinfo.org/views-executions?exec_name_1=&sex=All&state%5B%5D=MO&sex_1=All&federal=All&foreigner=All&juvenile=All&volunteer=y

Death Penalty Information Center. (n.d.). *Death row conditions*. Retrieved from http://www.deathpenaltyinfo.org/time-death-row

Edens, J. F., Buffington-Vollum, J. K., Keilen, A., Roskamp, P., & Anthony, C. (2005). Predictions of future dangerousness in capital murder trials: Is it time to "disinvent the wheel"? *Law and Human Behavior, 29*, 55–86. http://dx.doi.org/10.1007/s10979-005-1399-x

Estelle v. Gamble, 429 U.S. 97 (1976).

Evans, J. R. (1997). Quantitative EEG findings in a group of death row inmates. *Archives of Clinical Neurology, 12,* 315–316.

Felson, R. B., Silver, E., & Remster, B. (2012). Mental disorder and offending in prison. *Criminal Justice and Behavior, 39,* 125–143. http://dx.doi.org/10.1177/0093854811428565

Flanagan, T. J. (1980). Time served and institutional misconduct: Patterns of involvement in disciplinary infractions among long-term and short-term inmates. *Journal of Criminal Justice, 8,* 357–367. http://dx.doi.org/10.1016/0047-2352(80)90111-7

Flanagan, T. J. (Ed.). (1995). *Long term imprisonment: Policy, science, and correctional practice.* Thousand Oaks, CA: Sage.

Freedman, D., & Hemenway, D. (2000). Precursors of lethal violence: A death row sample. *Social Science & Medicine, 50,* 1757–1770. http://dx.doi.org/10.1016/S0277-9536(99)00417-7

Frierson, R. L., Schwartz-Watts, D. M., Morgan, D. W., & Malone, T. D. (1998). Capital versus noncapital murderers. *Journal of the American Academy of Psychiatry and the Law, 26,* 403–410.

Gallemore, J. L., Jr., & Panton, J. H. (1972). Inmate responses to lengthy death row confinement. *The American Journal of Psychiatry, 129,* 167–172. http://dx.doi.org/10.1176/ajp.129.2.167

Grassian, S. (1983). Psychopathological effects of solitary confinement. *The American Journal of Psychiatry, 140,* 1450–1454. http://dx.doi.org/10.1176/ajp.140.11.1450

Grassian, S. (2006). Prison reform: Commission on Safety and Abuse in Americas Prisons: Psychiatric effects of solitary confinement. *Washington University Journal of Law and Policy, 22,* 325–383.

Gregg v. Georgia, 428 U.S. 153 (1976).

Haney, C. (2003). Mental health issues in long-term solitary and "supermax" confinement. *Crime & Delinquency, 49,* 124–156. http://dx.doi.org/10.1177/0011128702239239

Haney, C. (2006). *Reforming punishment: Psychological limits to the pains of imprisonment.* Washington, DC: American Psychological Association. http://dx.doi.org/10.1037/11382-000

Haney, C. (2008). A culture of harm: Taming the dynamics of cruelty in supermax prisons. *Criminal Justice and Behavior, 35,* 956–984. http://dx.doi.org/10.1177/0093854808318585

Haney, C., & Lynch, M. (1997). Regulating prisons of the future: A psychological analysis of supermax and solitary confinement. *New York University Review of Law and Social Change, 23,* 477–552.

Harrison, K., & Tamony, A. (2010). Death row phenomenon, death row syndrome and their effect on capital cases in the US. *Internet Journal of Criminology.* Retrieved from https://docs.wixstatic.com/ugd/b93dd4_0af562fdf3e44a87896b5e6366c484e9.pdf

Hutto v. Finney, 437 U.S. 678 (1978).

In re Medley, 134 U.S. 160 (1890).

Johnson, R. (1979). Under sentence of death: The psychology of death row confinement. *Law and Psychology Review, 5,* 141–192.

Johnson, R. (1990). *Death work: A study of modern execution process.* Pacific Grove, CA: Brooks/Cole.

Jurek v. Texas, 428 U.S. 262 (1976).

Lester, D., & Tartaro, C. (2002). Suicide on death row. *Journal of Forensic Sciences, 47,* 1–4. http://dx.doi.org/10.1520/JFS15524J

Lewis, D. O., Pincus, J. H., Feldman, M., Jackson, L., & Bard, B. (1986). Psychiatric, neurological, and psychoeducational characteristics of 15 death row inmates in the United States. *The American Journal of Psychiatry, 143,* 838–845. http://dx.doi.org/10.1176/ajp.143.7.838

Lewis, P. W. (1979). Killing the killers: A post-*Furman* profile of Florida's condemned. *Crime and Delinquency, 25,* 200–218. http://dx.doi.org/10.1177/001112877902500205

Lisak, D., & Beszterczey, S. (2007). The cycle of violence: The life histories of 43 death row inmates. *Psychology of Men & Masculinity, 8,* 118–128. http://dx.doi.org/10.1037/1524-9220.8.2.118

Lombardi, G., Sluder, R., & Wallace, D. (1997). Mainstreaming capital punishment inmates: The Missouri experience and its legal significance. *Federal Probation, 61,* 3–11.

Lovell, D. (2008). Patterns of disturbed behavior in a supermax population. *Criminal Justice and Behavior, 35,* 985–1004. http://dx.doi.org/10.1177/0093854808318584

Lovell, D., Allen, D., Johnson, C., & Jemelka, R. (2001). Evaluating the effectiveness of residential treatment for prisoners with mental illness. *Criminal Justice and Behavior, 28,* 83–104. http://dx.doi.org/10.1177/0093854801028001004

Lyon, A. D., & Cunningham, M. D. (2006). Reason not the need: Does the lack of compelling state interest in maintaining a separate death row make it unlawful? *American Journal of Criminal Law, 33*(1), 1–30.

Marquart, J. W., Ekland-Olson, S., & Sorensen, J. R. (1989). Gazing into the crystal ball: Can jurors accurately predict dangerousness in capital cases? *Law & Society Review, 23,* 449–468. http://dx.doi.org/10.2307/3053829

Marquart, J. W., Ekland-Olson, S., & Sorensen, J. R. (1994). *The rope, the chair, and the needle: Capital punishment in Texas, 1923–1990.* Austin: University of Texas Press.

McLeod, J. S. (2009). Anxiety, despair, and the maddening isolation of solitary confinement: Invoking the first amendment's protection against state action that invades the sphere of the intellect and spirit. *The University of Pittsburgh Law Review, 70,* 647–663.

McShane, M. D. (1996). Death row. In M. D. McShane & F. P. Williams, III (Eds.), *Encyclopedia of American prisons* (pp. 229–231). New York, NY: Taylor & Francis.

Metzner, J., & Dvoskin, J. (2006). An overview of correctional psychiatry. *Psychiatric Clinics of North America, 29,* 761–772. http://dx.doi.org/10.1016/j.psc.2006.04.012

Mitchell v. Maynard, 80 F.3d 1433 (10th Cir. 1996).

Morris, R. G., Longmire, D. R., Buffington-Vollum, J., & Vollum, S. (2010). Institutional misconduct and differential parole eligibility among capital inmates. *Criminal Justice and Behavior, 37,* 417–438. http://dx.doi.org/10.1177/0093854810361672

Murton, T. (1969). Treatment of condemned prisoners. *Crime and Delinquency, 15,* 94–111. http://dx.doi.org/10.1177/001112876901500108

O'Keefe, M. L., Klebe, K. J., Metzner, J., Dvoskin, J., Fellner, J., & Stucker, A. (2013). A longitudinal study of administrative segregation. *Journal of the American Academy of Psychiatry and the Law, 41,* 49–60.

O'Keefe, M. L., & Schnell, M. J. (2007). Offenders with mental illness in the correctional system. *Journal of Offender Rehabilitation, 45,* 81–104. http://dx.doi.org/10.1300/J076v45n01_08

Panton, J. H. (1976). Personality characteristics of death-row prison inmates. *Journal of Clinical Psychology, 32,* 306–309. http://dx.doi.org/10.1002/1097-4679(197604)32:2<306::AID-JCLP2270320224>3.0.CO;2-M

Panton, J. H. (1978). Pre- and post-personality test responses of prison inmates who have had their death sentences commuted to life imprisonment. *Research Communications in Psychology, Psychiatry & Behavior, 3,* 143–156.

Pizarro, J., & Stenius, V. M. K. (2004). Supermax prisons: Their rise, current practices, and effect on inmates. *The Prison Journal, 84,* 248–264. http://dx.doi.org/10.1177/0032885504265080

Reidy, T. J., Sorensen, J. R., & Cunningham, M. D. (2013). Probability of criminal acts of violence: A test of jury predictive accuracy. *Behavioral Sciences & the Law, 31,* 286–305. http://dx.doi.org/10.1002/bsl.2064

Rhodes v. Chapman, 452 U.S. 337 (1981).

Rountree, M. M. (2014). Volunteers for execution: Directions for further research into grief, culpability, and legal structures. *University of Kansas City Law Review, 82*, 295–333.

Ruiz v. Estelle, 503 F. Supp. 1265 (S.D. Tex. 1980).

Rummel v. Estelle, 445 U.S. 263 (1980).

Salinas, P. R. (2002). Death row. In D. Levinson (Ed.), *Encyclopedia of crime and punishment* (Vol. II, pp. 472–478). Thousand Oaks, CA: Sage.

Shapiro, M. (2009). An overdose of dangerousness: How "future dangerousness" catches the least culpable capital defendants and undermines the rationale for the executions it supports. *American Journal of Criminal Law, 35*, 101–156.

Smith, C. E., & Felix, R. R. (1986). Beyond deterrence: A study of defense on death row. *Federal Probation, 50*, 55–59.

Smith, P. S. (2009). Solitary confinement—History, practice, and human rights standards. *Prison Service Journal, 181*, 3–11.

Smith, P. S. (2011). The effects of solitary confinement: Commentary on one-year longitudinal study of the psychological effects of administrative segregation. *Corrections & Mental Health*, 1–11.

Snell, T. L. (2014). *Capital punishment, 2013—Statistical tables* (NCJ 24848). U.S. Department of Justice, Bureau of Justice Statistics. Retrieved from https:// www.bjs.gov/content/pub/pdf/cp13st.pdf

Sorensen, J. R., & Cunningham, M. D. (2009). Once a killer always a killer? Prison misconduct of former capital punishment inmates in Arizona. *Journal of Psychiatry & Law, 37*(2-3), 237–263. http://dx.doi.org/10.1177/ 009318530903700205

Sorensen, J. R., & Wrinkle, R. D. (1996). No hope for parole: Disciplinary infractions among capital punishment and life-without-parole inmates. *Criminal Justice and Behavior, 23*, 542–552. http://dx.doi.org/10.1177/ 0093854896023004002

Texas Department of Criminal Justice. (2014). *Statistical report: Fiscal year 2014.* Retrieved from http://www.tdcj.state.tx.us/documents/Statistical_Report_ FY2014.pdf

Toch, H. (2001). The future of supermax confinement. *The Prison Journal, 81*, 376–388. http://dx.doi.org/10.1177/0032885501081003005

Toch, H. (2003). The contemporary relevance of early experiments with supermax reform. *The Prison Journal, 83*, 221–228. http://dx.doi.org/10.1177/ 0032885503083002007

Trop v. Dulles, 356 U.S. 86 (1958).

Turner v. Safley, 482 U.S. 78 (1987).

Walters, G. D., & Crawford, G. (2014). Major mental illness and violence history as predictors of institutional misconduct and recidivism: Main and interaction effects. *Law and Human Behavior*, *38*, 238–247. http://dx.doi.org/10.1037/lhb0000058

Weems v. United States, 217 U.S. 349 (1910).

Yuzon, F. J. (1996). Conditions and circumstances of living on death row-violative of individual rights and fundamental freedoms? Divergent trends in judicial review in evaluating the "death row phenomenon." *George Washington Journal of Law and Economics*, *30*, 39–73.

6

Execution "Volunteers": Psychological and Legal Issues

Meredith Martin Rountree

Approximately 10% of those executed in the United States are death-sentenced prisoners who sought, or at some point declined to contest, their own execution. Commonly called *volunteers*, these prisoners succeed in hastening execution by waiving their right to full judicial review of their conviction and sentence. Volunteers have been executed in 28 states and by the federal government. Between 1977, marking the first execution in the modern (post–*Furman v. Georgia*, 1972) era of capital punishment, and 2016, nearly as many volunteers (145) were executed as death-sentenced prisoners were exonerated (156; Death Penalty Information Center, 2017b, 2017c).

Exonerations have prompted extensive scrutiny of the legal processes leading to the death sentences in those cases. By contrast, the fact that volunteers bypass legal procedures designed to ensure that only the "worst of the worst" are executed has attracted considerably less attention

http://dx.doi.org/10.1037/0000084-007

Living on Death Row: The Psychology of Waiting to Die, H. Toch, J. R. Acker, and V. M. Bonventre (Editors)

and effort at legal reform despite the fact that executing prisoners without this review diminishes the legitimacy of capital punishment. The muted response may stem in part from uncertainty in interpreting volunteers' actions.

Certain theories dominate. Some emphasize prisoners' desire to control their destiny and the need to respect their autonomy (see Muschert, Harrington, & Reece, 2009). Those opposed to a prisoner's efforts to waive appeals often argue that the prisoner's history of mental instability suggests the prisoner is suicidal (see Muschert et al., 2009). A related narrative contends that conditions of confinement and the limbo of legal appeals wear the prisoner down to the point that he loses the will to live; these also contribute to *death row syndrome*, an evolving (and controversial) psychiatric diagnosis describing a mental condition that some prisoners develop as a result of living under a death sentence in socially isolating and stark conditions of confinement (*Glossip v. Gross*, 2015, pp. 2765–2767, Breyer, J., dissenting; Muschert et al., 2009; A. Smith, 2008). The empirical support for these explanations remains sparse, although in this chapter I outline recent work that complicates assumptions about the impact of death row conditions. Further, I suggest that the availability of the death penalty influences many people's decisions before they are even sentenced to death, let alone set foot on death row.

In this chapter, I discuss volunteers first as a legal phenomenon—the legal steps a prisoner must take to hasten execution—and then report on research that seeks to illuminate the "suicidality versus autonomy" debate. I then situate the volunteer in a larger legal framework by examining how the law treats desires to die in other contexts.

THE LEGAL FRAMEWORK GOVERNING DECISIONS TO VOLUNTEER

A death-sentenced prisoner hastens execution by abandoning full judicial review of his or her conviction and/or sentence (referred to here as his or her *appeals*), typically by discharging counsel and electing not to file any pleadings on his or her own behalf. Prisoners have three, usually sequential, avenues of appeals.

Typical Appellate Process for Death Penalty Cases

In the first appeal, often called the *direct appeal*, the prisoner argues to the state's highest criminal court that the trial judge made erroneous legal rulings in the course of the trial. The degree to which capital cases are routinely subjected to appellate review may be overstated because of the prevalence of statutory provisions characterizing the direct appeal as "automatic." The availability of the appellate mechanism does not necessarily mean that the direct review cannot be waived. A few states prohibit waiver of direct review in capital cases, but others permit death-sentenced prisoners to forgo direct appeal at least in part (see, e.g., *Commonwealth v. McKenna*, 1978; *People v. Massie*, 1998; *Robertson v. State*, 2014; *State v. Brewer*, 1992; *State v. Ovante*, 2013). Thus, in some jurisdictions, a death-sentenced prisoner can waive his or her "personal" right to appeal the conviction, but the sentence nevertheless must undergo appellate review, albeit one restricted to certain issues. For example, in the state of Washington, a volunteer is permitted to waive a legal claim that evidence was erroneously admitted during the guilt or innocence phase of the trial. But the state supreme court is required to consider whether "there are not sufficient mitigating circumstances to merit leniency"; whether "the sentence . . . is excessive or disproportionate to the penalty imposed in similar cases"; and whether "the sentence . . . was brought about through passion or prejudice" (*State v. Dodd*, 1992, pp. 97–98; see also *Geary v. State*, 1999; *Grasso v. State*, 1993; *Newman v. State*, 2002; *Patterson v. Commonwealth*, 2001; *Pennell v. State*, 1992; *State v. Motts*, 2011).

The second appeal—variously called a *collateral attack*, *postconviction appeal*, or *state habeas proceeding*—provides the prisoner an opportunity to argue to the state court that he was deprived of a fair trial because of events not reflected in the trial record. These claims typically include ineffective assistance of counsel or prosecutorial suppression of material exculpatory

evidence. When it had the death penalty, only New Jersey prevented prisoners from waiving postconviction appeals in capital cases. The New Jersey
Supreme Court reasoned that the public's "interest in the reliability and
integrity of a death sentencing decision . . . transcend[ed] the preferences
of individual defendants" (*State v. Martini*, 1996, p. 1107; see also *Pike v.
State*, 2005).

The final avenue of appeal combines all federal constitutional claims
raised on direct appeal and in state habeas proceedings into a petition for
writ of habeas corpus filed in federal district court. An adverse adjudication
by the federal district court may, under certain circumstances, be appealed
to the federal court of appeals (28 U.S.C. §§ 2253, 2254, 2012). The Ninth
Circuit Court of Appeals suggested at one point that its interest in ensuring
the just administration of the death penalty could permit a federal court
to reject a prisoner's effort to waive appeals, but it subsequently stepped
away from that position (*Comer v. Schriro*, 2006, 2007). The federal courts
simply focus on whether a prisoner has met the legal criteria for a waiver,
as outlined next (see, e.g., *Dennis ex rel. Butko v. Budge*, 2004; *Ford v. Haley*,
1999; *Harper v. Parker*, 1999; *In re Zettlemoyer*, 1995; *Simpson v. Quarterman*, 2009; *Smith ex rel. Mo. Public Defender Comm'n v. Armontrout*, 1987;
White v. Horn, 1999).

Legal Criteria for Waiving Appeals

A court will grant a request to abandon appeals if it finds that the prisoner is mentally competent and is making a knowing, voluntary, and
intelligent waiver of his or her rights to appeal. These criteria, commonly
applied throughout the criminal justice system, are intended to ensure
that, after having been advised by counsel, the prisoner understands the
consequences of his or her decision, including that he or she is abandoning certain constitutional rights (the "knowing and intelligent" waiver),
and that he or she has not been coerced into giving up these rights (the
"voluntariness" requirement; *Godinez v. Moran*, 1993; *Johnson v. Zerbst*,
1938; *Rees v. Peyton*, 1966). The competency determination is usually the
pivotal inquiry. If prisoners are found competent, they will be able to

waive their rights and appeals. Only if the prisoner is found incompetent can others—such as a parent—move to intervene as a "next friend" to continue the appeals (*Demosthenes v. Baal*, 1990; *Gilmore v. Utah*, 1976; *Whitmore v. Arkansas*, 1990).

In the context of death-sentenced prisoners waiving appeals, courts rely on the United States Supreme Court's 1966 decision in *Rees v. Peyton*, which formulated the test to determine whether the prisoner had the

> capacity to appreciate his position and make a rational choice with respect to continuing or abandoning further litigation or on the other hand whether he is suffering from a mental disease, disorder, or defect which may substantially affect his capacity in the premises. (p. 314)

In *Rumbaugh v. Procunier* (1985), the Fifth Circuit confronted a tension inherent in this standard. Charles Rumbaugh, who had a history of self-injury and suicide attempts, sought to waive appeals. Indeed, in the middle of his competency hearing, he charged a court officer to provoke the officer into shooting him. Mental health professionals testified that Rumbaugh understood he would be executed if he waived his appeals, but his decision to hasten his execution was substantially affected by a mental disease, severe depression. The court found Rumbaugh competent because he was aware of his situation and the logical consequences of waiving further appeals. This analysis has been criticized for confusing *rational* with *logical* and for misreading *Rees* by shifting the inquiry from whether the mental impairment "may affect" to "must affect" his capacity (Cooper, 2009). The analysis nevertheless has been cited and relied on in other jurisdictions (*Comer v. Schriro*, 2007; *Lonchar v. Zant*, 1993; see also Cooper, 2009). A few courts and judges resist this analysis, however, refusing to become a "particip[ant] in a program of state-assisted suicide" (*State v. Robert*, 2012, p. 143; see also *Grasso v. State*, 1993, p. 811, Chapel, J., specially concurring).

In *Godinez v. Moran* (1993), the Supreme Court had to decide whether distinct types of waivers required different types of mental competencies. Like Rumbaugh, Moran had previously attempted suicide, was experiencing "deep depression" at the time of his waiver (p. 417, Blackmun, J., dissenting), and took psychiatric medication. At his capital trial, he sought to discharge counsel and plead guilty. Harmonious with *Rumbaugh*'s holding, the Supreme Court ruled that the Constitution requires only a single type of mental competency, namely, that the prisoner have "sufficient present ability to consult with his lawyer with a reasonable degree of rational understanding" and "a rational as well as factual understanding of the proceedings against him" (*Godinez v. Moran*, 1993, p. 396). The majority opinion noted that "requiring that a criminal defendant be competent has a modest aim: It seeks to ensure that he has the capacity to understand the proceedings and to assist counsel" (p. 402). As *Moran* and *Rumbaugh* make clear, mental competence is not a high threshold. "It is entirely possible for a clinically depressed but nonpsychotic defendant to waive his appeals and to volunteer for execution" (Oleson, 2006, p. 170; see also *Indiana v. Edwards*, 2008).

EMPIRICAL OBSERVATIONS OF VOLUNTEERS

Volunteers tend to be White: Of the 145 volunteers executed since 1977, 123 (85%) were identified as White (Death Penalty Information Center, 2017c). A few states have exclusively or primarily executed volunteers. For example, both of Oregon's executions, three out of five Washington executions, and 11 of Nevada's 12 executions were of volunteers (Death Penalty Information Center, 2017c). Few systematic examinations have been made of volunteers, but recent research has focused on the possible suicidality of volunteers.

Mental Illness and Suicidality

John Blume (2005) asked whether volunteers resembled the nonincarcerated or "free-world" American suicide population. After collecting questionnaire responses from legal team members in cases involving volunteers and attempted volunteers, Blume reviewed the literature on free-world suicide and noted important similarities between free-world suicides and death row volunteers. In addition to predominantly involving

White males, both groups had significant histories of mental illness and substance abuse. Blume also found some support for the proposition that, in common with suicide, a single execution hastening can spur others to do the same—that is, volunteering can be "contagious."

The primary limitation of Blume's (2005) study, however, is its comparison group. Because of the higher prevalence of mental illness in the death row population, substance abuse, and addiction (Cunningham & Vigen, 2002), free-world suicides may not offer the most illuminating comparison. Vandiver, Giacopassi, and Turner (2008) overcame the comparison group limitation in part by comparing all volunteers nationally with all executed nonvolunteers. Their study provided a statistical profile of volunteers and, guided by Émile Durkheim's (1897/1966) theory of suicide,[1] proposed an "exploratory typology" of volunteers based on

> reviews of academic studies, newspaper interviews of volunteers, published accounts of volunteers' backgrounds and crimes, final statements given by volunteers before their executions, discussions with defense lawyers and mitigation specialists, and the experience of one of the authors in several cases. (pp. 188, 195)

Overall, they argued that Durkheim's macrolevel theory is a poor fit for this population because of death row's extreme environment and the population's history of childhood abuse, dysfunctional families, and mental illness.

A limitation of both studies is their reliance on execution dates rather than decision-point data. Contagion effect would be better measured by the prisoner's moments of decision, for example, than by the execution date, something the prisoner does not directly control (Rountree, 2014). In addition, both studies aggregated all the volunteers executed nationally,

---

[1] Durkheim (1897/1966) theorized that suicide should be understood along two axes: social integration and social regulation. *Social integration* provides a sense of belonging that helps people during difficult times and therefore helps stem the desire for self-destruction. Too much integration could lead to *altruistic suicide*—destroying the self to benefit the whole. Too little and the individual was susceptible to *egoistic suicide*. *Social regulation*, by contrast, consists of social controls that constrain individuals and thereby protect them from the frustration of wanting what they cannot have. Too little social regulation creates a sense of normlessness that leads to *anomic suicide*; too much regulation, to *fatalistic* suicide. The question of fatalistic suicide is naturally raised in the highly regulated prison setting.

which could conceal important state-level variation. As noted earlier, some states have almost exclusively executed volunteers. Some states have conducted so few executions that prisoners might expect to live decades on death row before facing execution. Death row conditions also vary across states. If any of these factors matter, it is reasonable to believe that factors contributing to the hastening of executions could be quite different in different jurisdictions. Comparing all prisoners who hastened their executions with all prisoners who have been executed in the modern era would mask these potentially important differences.

I conducted a study of the 31 Texas prisoners who abandoned their appeals and were executed between 1976, when the death penalty was reinstated, and 2012 (the "Texas study"). I compared them with a matched sample of death-sentenced Texas prisoners who were executed after exhausting their appeals. (For more on the findings and study design, see Rountree, 2014.) According to the literature regarding suicide in prison, for both the volunteer population and the nonvolunteer sample, the study coded for prior criminal history, experience of incarceration, and characteristics of the capital crime. From that group, I derived a subgroup of 38 cases I studied more closely, noting experiences of juvenile neglect and abuse, juvenile delinquency, mental illness, and attempted suicide. This subgroup (MS2) oversampled prisoners I believed had expressed a desire to volunteer and/or had any history of depression and/or suicide (Rountree, 2014).

The Texas study confirmed that death row prisoners in Texas had a high incidence of both adverse childhood experiences and adult mental dysfunction. Within the MS2 subgroup, 47.4% had childhood experiences with adjudications of delinquency, time in juvenile detention, foster care, early drug use, and/or chaotic living environments. Among the volunteers, 43.8% had one or more of these childhood experiences. Proportionately more volunteers experienced depression, suicidal ideation, and/or attempted suicide at some point during their lives (Rountree, 2014).

Other forms of mental illness, as Blume (2005) noted, can also elevate the risk of suicide. For example, bipolar disorder increases the risk of suicide far more than does major depressive disorder. With respect to other kinds of mental illness, members of the MS2 subgroup also scored high, with 26.3% ($n = 10$) reportedly diagnosed with a mental illness or having a history of psychiatric hospitalization. This is somewhat higher than the prevalence of mental illness other than depression among the volunteers: 19.4% ($n = 6$; Rountree, 2014).

We should exercise caution in making inferences based on these differences because of the small number of cases. In addition, because volunteers have to demonstrate competence to be granted permission to waive their appeals, they may be motivated to suppress information regarding mental illness. Court records may, therefore, understate the prevalence of mental disorder. Court records are also problematic sources of information because their quality depends in large part on defense counsel's diligence in obtaining historical information about the client, on having the resources required to conduct a comprehensive investigation, and on strategic decisions about what information to elicit (Rountree, 2012). Although these data certainly support the proposition that death row prisoners, on the whole, are a psychologically vulnerable group, it is less clear that volunteers are uniquely fragile.

That said, those who committed their capital crime in the midst of a domestic crisis appear to be overrepresented in Texas executions. During the period of the study, 25.8% (eight) of the Texas volunteer population committed an offense related to a domestic dispute, whereas only 7.4% (33) of the 444 nonconsensual Texas executions of men involved similar crimes. This category of domestic-related killings includes not only those who murdered their intimate partners but also those who committed murder ostensibly because of a domestic crisis. For instance, when Eliseo Moreno's brother-in-law refused to disclose the whereabouts of Moreno's wife, Moreno murdered the brother-in-law, his sister-in-law, and four others. Robert Anderson attributed his murder of a child to an argument he had had that day with his wife over her infidelity. She had told him that he had to leave their house before she returned home. George Lott is believed to have opened fire in a courtroom because he was upset with the handling of his divorce and child custody proceedings (and perhaps his stress over an upcoming trial on charges that he had sexually abused his child; Rountree, 2014).

These findings suggest possible parallels between murder–suicides of those who take their lives after killing an intimate partner and this category of execution volunteers. This latter group's criminal experience was also less extensive than the other volunteers, whether measured by their prior convictions, crimes against persons, or time in prison. In addition, they tended to be older than volunteers who were not in the midst of a domestic crisis. In these ways, they resemble conventional murder–suicides (Anno, 1985; Liebling, 1999). Perpetrators of murder–suicides are generally male, and their victims are generally their current or estranged wives or girlfriends. They typically are White and are older than other murderers. Their offenses are usually linked to a disruption in the romantic relationship when the perpetrator fears losing the victim. They tend not to have serious criminal histories but do have a history of depression (Eliason, 2009; Liem, Hengeveld, & Koenraadt, 2009; Liem, Postulart, & Nieuwbeerta, 2009; Stack, 1997; Starzomski & Nussbaum, 2000).

Hopelessness figured throughout volunteers' accounts of their decisions. This is noteworthy because hopelessness plays a crucial role in mediating the relationship between suffering and the desire to die generally (Chapman, Specht, & Cellucci, 2005; Nissim, Gagliese, & Rodin, 2009; Nock et al., 2008; Plahuta et al., 2002). Hopelessness may play a greater role in premeditated rather than impulsive efforts to end life (Wenzel, Brown, & Beck, 2012). In light of the legal procedures required for waiving execution, volunteering for execution plainly falls on the premeditated side of the scale.

Blume (2005) reported that 39% of his respondents cited hopelessness as a factor in the volunteers' decisions to abandon appeals, and the Texas study suggested that feelings of hopelessness may be multifaceted. The Texas volunteers seldom publicly expressed hopelessness or cynicism about the legal process (Rountree, 2012). More common were expressions of hopelessness about the possibility of creating a meaningful life in prison (Rountree, 2014). Aaron Foust was typical:

> I am just ready to hurry things along, you know. Prison is not really the place to live. It's not like living out in the world, you know. It's not really a life, and that's my sentence, so I am ready to speed it up. (Rountree, 2012, p. 603)

If appeals led to release, at least some volunteers would have been more interested in contesting their cases. "But if it's just one of these, give me a new sentencing hearing and I have to stay in jail for the next however many years, forget it," said one study informant regarding the motivations of a volunteer that the person knew (Rountree, 2014, p. 305). Jerome Butler also echoed another relatively common complaint: Even if he won a life sentence, he would be too old to restart life when released: "I'm 57 now, and I'd be in my 70s when I got out. What am I supposed to do? Go live under a bridge?" (Rountree, 2014, p. 305). James Porter wrote to the Texas Court of Criminal Appeals:

> To be honest I would wrather [sic] be executed than spend my life in prison with no chance of ever getting out. (IF) I had the chance of getting out one day while still young enough to enjoy life, getting the right help to become a productive member of society, (but) I don't see and want [won't?] see this [sic] happen in the state of Texas prison system. (Rountree, 2014, pp. 305–306)

Complex Contribution of Prison Conditions to Decision to Waive Appeals

These quotations signal that incarceration matters, but how it matters is less clear. Blume (2005) found little support for the contention that prison conditions affect decisions to hasten execution. Only a few prisoners in the Texas study (16.1%) complained about the conditions of incarceration, as distinct from the fact of incarceration (51.6%; Rountree, 2015, pp. 165–166). Incarceration appears to contribute to many volunteers' indubitably complex decisions to end their lives. However, incarceration itself, rather than the conditions of incarceration, may better account for why so many sought execution before arriving on death row.

Volunteers Often Facilitated Execution at the Earliest Stages of the Legal Process

About half of the Texas volunteers took action in the trial court, including by pleading guilty to capital murder, asking the jury for the death penalty, and/or refusing to permit lawyers to present any mitigating evidence in order to get the death penalty. An even greater number expressed a desire at trial to be sentenced to death (Rountree, 2015).

In some cases, court records document the volunteers' efforts. However, responses to changes in the legal options available to death row prisoners also suggest that many volunteers reach their decisions very early. Before 1994, Texas law was understood to require an adversarial direct appeal for all death penalty cases. Courts and lawyers told defendants that the first point at which they could waive appeals was at the state habeas stage. In 1994, in a high-profile case involving an attack in a courthouse, the Texas Court of Criminal Appeals concluded that an adversarial direct appeal was not in fact necessary. Instead, the court would conduct its own review for "fundamental error" (a category of error it has never defined) and ruled that such review is sufficient (*Lott v. State*, 1994). Before that change in the law, 12 out of 14 volunteers waived further review at state habeas. After that change, seven out of 15 waived further review before state habeas, with five out of 15 waiving at state habeas (Rountree, 2014).

Although this empirical work focused on Texas, the 25 volunteers executed nationally (and who were not in the Texas study) over the past 10 years showed similar tendencies. Thirteen[2] of those 25 took some action at or before trial making the death penalty more likely (*Chapman v. Commonwealth*, 2007; Crimesider Staff, 2016; *Gleason v. Commonwealth*, 2012; *Gleason v. Pearson*, 2013; *Holton v. State*, 2006; *Johnson v. State*, 2009; *Lopez v. Stephens*, 2014; MacDonald, 2009; *State v. Barton*, 2006; *State v. Bordelon*, 2009; *State v. Downs*, 2004, 2006; *State v. Ferguson*, 2006; *State v. Robert*, 2012). For example, Christopher Johnson of Alabama represented himself at trial, pled guilty during trial, offered no mitigating evidence, and asked the judge for a death sentence. Gerald Bordelon of Louisiana contested guilt but waived his right to present mitigating evidence.

---

[2] Rocky Barton (Ohio), Gerald Bordelon (Louisiana), Marco Chapman (Kentucky), William Downs (South Carolina), Darrell Ferguson (Ohio), Robert Gleason (Virginia), Daryl Holton (Tennessee), Christopher Johnson (Alabama), Daniel Lopez (Texas), Christopher Newton (Ohio), Eric Robert (South Dakota), Steven Spears (Georgia), Jack Trawick (Alabama). Note that although Trawick wrote to the judge during trial to warn him that if he were not sentenced to death, he would kill a prison employee, he nevertheless appealed his case through federal habeas appeals.

Rocky Barton of Ohio limited the defense case in mitigation and refused to cooperate with a neuropsychiatric exam, and he asked jurors to sentence him to death. An additional two[3] volunteers waived or attempted to waive their direct appeal (*Lackey v. State*, 2010; *State v. Motts*, 2011), and another three[4] waived after their direct appeal (Bellisle, 2005; Death Penalty News, 2012; Murderpedia, 2006). Seven[5] of the 25 appear to have acted to expedite their execution for the first time after their postconviction proceedings commenced (Associated Press, 2016; Blanco, n.d.; *Comer v. Schriro*, 2006; Cotterrell, 2013; Crimesider Staff, 2012; *Dawson v. State*, 2000; *Fuller v. TDCJ-CID*, 2016; *Hill v. State*, 2008; *Lopez v. Stephens*, 2014; MacDonald & McKee, 2006). Of those, two volunteers—Hill and Martin—dropped their appeals before the postconviction claims were adjudicated (Blanco, n.d.; *Hill v. State*, 2008).

The Impact of Isolation Confinement

As discussed elsewhere in this volume, isolation confinement is associated with mental stress and deterioration. Texas presented a natural experiment on the relationship between prison conditions and volunteering. Until 1999, the men's death row was housed at the Texas Department of Criminal Justice's (TDCJ) Ellis Unit. At Ellis, many of the death row prisoners engaged in a range of activities, including working in the garment factory and at handicrafts. Most were permitted to recreate with others and to participate in congregate activities such as religious worship and Bible study (Clines, 1994; Perkinson, 2010).

After a Thanksgiving 1998 escape attempt by a small group of death row prisoners, TDCJ decided to move the men's death row to Polunsky, a newer facility in Livingston, Texas, that had a housing unit designed to control difficult or dangerous prisoners through isolation confinement. Over the course of 1999, TDCJ moved male death row prisoners into this

---

[3] Andrew Lackey (Alabama), Jeffrey Motts (South Carolina).

[4] Shannon Johnson (Delaware), Daryl Mack (Nevada), Elijah Page (South Dakota).

[5] Robert Comer (Arizona), David Dawson (Montana), Barney Fuller (Texas), William Happ (Florida), David Hill (South Carolina), Jerry Martin (Texas), Donald Moeller (South Dakota).

unit, where they were housed in single cells with solid doors. The only time prisoners leave their pods at Polunsky is to meet outside visitors in a neighboring building. Although these prisoners can communicate with prisoners in nearby cells by yelling or passing notes and small items on a string slid from cell to cell, they are otherwise isolated from other prisoners in every aspect of their lives. They eat alone, recreate alone, and worship alone. Depending on their disciplinary record, they are permitted from 3 to 12 hours per week of solitary out-of-cell time in a larger recreation cell, and they can have from 2 to 8 hours per month of noncontact social visits with visitors from outside the prison. They have no access to television, and only the best-behaved prisoners can own a radio. They participate in no educational, work, or other structured activities of any kind (Mann, 2010; Perkinson, 2010).

The proportion of volunteers indeed increased in the Polunsky period. Comparing two 17-year periods—from 1983 to 1999 and from 2000 to 2016—the proportion of volunteers went from 2.9% of the population received on death row to 4.5%. In the first period, 18 condemned prisoners sought execution out of the 611 added to death row during that time (Texas Execution Information Center, 2017). In the second period, 12 men volunteered out of the 264 added to death row during that time (TDCJ, 2017; Texas Execution Information Center, 2017). The two who had previously lived on Ellis and then been moved to Polunsky, Richard Foster and David Martinez, notably volunteered late in their appeals.

A number of other changes in Texas's administration of the death penalty, however, suggest caution and further study before concluding that the conditions account for the increase. For one, as discussed earlier, volunteers tend to seek execution early in the process, often at trial, not after years of grinding prison life. It is also essential to recognize how individual prison experiences vary. Kerry Max Cook's account (2008) of the physical abuse he experienced at Ellis makes clear that relative freedom and greater social opportunities can be dangerous. Volunteers, who are often viewed as weak, are particularly vulnerable (Rountree, 2014). One volunteer who spent most of his time on death row at Ellis complained about the tedium of death row. But he also stressed "how frightful and 'hazardous' his condition is while he has been in TDC.[6] . . . He is fearful of bodily harm on a daily basis" (Rountree, 2012, pp. 602–603). Life in isolation at Polunsky could be more bearable for a prisoner afraid of victimization.

Other dynamics outside prison are also at work that could be curbing the number of volunteers. Capital defense practices have also undeniably changed since the 1980s. The 2003 American Bar Association (ABA) *Guidelines for the Appointment and Performance of Defense Counsel in Death Penalty Cases* state unequivocally that attorneys must resist their clients' efforts to get the death penalty:

> Some clients will initially insist that they want to be executed—as punishment or because they believe they would rather die than spend the rest of their lives in prison; some clients will want to contest their guilt but not present mitigation. It is ineffective assistance of counsel to simply acquiesce to such wishes. (pp. 1009–1010)

The ABA Guidelines, along with more local norms, may be making it harder for defendants to pursue the death penalty at trial, and the Polunsky conditions of confinement may make it easier for those who took initial steps toward the death penalty to change their minds and litigate what remains of their appellate issues (see, e.g., *Austin v. Stephens*, 2015; *Tabler v. Stephens*, 2014).

For anyone sentenced after 2005, the prosecution has had the option of pursuing a punishment of life without possibility of parole. This may have contributed to the state seeking the death penalty in fewer cases (McCord, 2010; R. Smith, 2012). Shrinking the pool of possible volunteers at the front end could affect the number of volunteers after 2005.

Finally, the decline in raw numbers of volunteers—from 18 to 12—suggests the possibility that the increased percentage, from 2.9 to 4.5, is merely an artifact of the rapid increase in the Texas death row population before 2004 (Texas Execution Information Center, 2017). It could be fruitful to theorize about other meaningful chronological periods, such as times of rapid growth of the death row population or increased pace

---

[6] In 1989, the Texas Department of Corrections became the "Institutional Division" of the Texas Department of Criminal Justice (Perkinson, 2010, p. 321).

of executions. Texas was particularly active in executing prisoners in the late 1990s, peaking in 2000 (Death Penalty Information Center, 2017a). Prisoners may well have believed they would be executed swiftly without discharging counsel or, conversely, assumed appeals were futile.

In all, changes in the number of volunteers over time raise theoretical questions that point to the complexity of understanding the volunteer phenomenon and the operation of the death penalty more generally.

LEGAL ISSUES

The legal issues raised by volunteers are not limited to the question of whether they competently, knowingly, intelligently, and voluntarily waive their appeals. Volunteers also expose tensions with other legal regimes. For example, legal ethical rules can constrain a full hearing on the prisoner's waiver. Less robust hearings, in turn, permit superficial forensic mental health examinations to go unchallenged. The law has also created a right to die for death row prisoners that is unusually permissive when compared with that of non–death-sentenced prisoners and people in the free world.

Conflicting Legal Ethical Responsibilities

The legal ethics of representing a volunteer are the subject of considerable debate within the legal academy, but the debate offers no clear guidance (see, e.g., Garnett, 2002; Harrington, 2000; Mello, 1999; Oleson, 2006). Although an agency role is the putative norm for the attorney–client relationship, as the ABA Guidelines quoted earlier make clear, it is not the contemporary standard of practice in death penalty cases.

The Texas study found that although lawyers expressed discomfort in enabling their clients' execution and many sought to dissuade their clients from waiving appeals, in practice lawyers saw themselves as bound by the clients' wishes. If counsel decides that her responsibility is to advocate on behalf of her client's goal—here, execution—no evidence will be tested. The client's attorney will not challenge the evidence, and attorneys for the state may be reluctant or unprepared to do so. In one Texas waiver hearing, the state's attorney was the first to stumble on an inconsistency between the volunteer's courtroom testimony about his history of anxiety and depression medications and what he had told the examining psychiatrist. This volunteer asserted on cross-examination that he had been prescribed Thorazine, a powerful antipsychotic medication, for sleep. This assertion went wholly unexplored, despite its implication that the prisoner sought to hide a psychiatric illness. The state's lawyer promptly terminated this unhelpful line of questioning the volunteer, and his lawyers declined to follow up. Without asking TDCJ physicians whether they had prescribed Thorazine for a psychotic disorder—a fact that would not be in the volunteer's interest—the lawyer may not have had actual knowledge that this contention was false (which would require counsel to report that fact to the court). The lawyer may additionally have believed that it is disloyal to the client to investigate (Rountree, 2012).

In the Texas study, the forensic mental health evaluations—if conducted—frequently fell short of what normally would be expected in an adversarial proceeding. For example, in some cases, no mental health expert was consulted. Two prisoners were simply asked by the judge whether they had a history of mental illness. When mental health evaluations were conducted, only three included use of a standardized competency assessment tool. Instead, mental health professionals relied heavily on an interview with the prisoner, even to learn about the prisoner's mental health history. Volunteers know that perceived mental competence is essential for them to waive their appeals. In his December 1997 letter to the Texas Court of Criminal Appeals, Charles Tuttle wrote, "Moreover, I am competent to make this decision, as I am sure the trial authorities will recognize" (Rountree, 2012, p. 606). Larry Hayes wrote, "I understand psychological testing will be required before this can be done and I am ready and willing for this to be done any time" (Rountree, 2012, p. 606). The prisoners, in such instances, have ample reason to understate any history of mental dysfunction.

Christopher Swift, who a court-appointed psychiatrist had previously found was insane at the time of the crime, was the sole source of information for his mental health assessment when he sought to waive his appeals. Swift acknowledged his schizophrenia but emphasized that he was much better than he was at trial, when he was beset by auditory hallucinations. The hallucinations "don't lead me to hurt myself or others" and the "voices are significantly less intense, frequent and meaningful." After his evaluation, he wrote a frantic letter to the court, explaining that he "had been manipulated into giving an interview which could potentially destroy my chances of foregoing an appeal(s)." At the subsequent hearing on his competency, he clarified:

> At the time of my examination with Dr. Martinez I believe six or more months ago, I confessed that to a small degree I still heard strange voices although these voices did not dictate my actions. Since that time and thanks be to God and my Christian friends who have encouraged me so, I have been freed completely from these voices. (Rountree, 2012, p. 606–607)

Joe Gonzales, Jr. described his previous experience with psychiatric treatment as undertaken solely to appease his fiancée, with headaches as the only lingering sequelae to a month-long coma he experienced after a car accident. These assertions were never explored beyond Gonzales's representations. Alexander Martinez forbade an examiner from contacting any of his intimates, and the examiner complied (Rountree, 2012).

Not only were mental health evaluations based primarily (and sometimes solely) on the information the prisoner sought to present during the interview, but some examiners also failed to consider readily available information from other times in the prisoner's life, including mental health evidence presented at trial. One evaluator, for example, reflected no awareness of psychological evidence presented at trial regarding a prisoner's brain impairment, history of head trauma, and serious drug abuse, as well as his history of depression, anxiety, guilt internalization, fear, and distress (Rountree, 2012).

Paradoxical Privileging on Volunteers' Desires to Die

No Comparable Right to Die for Noncapital Prisoners

Eighth Amendment guarantees of food, essentially safe and clean shelter, clothing, and medical care extend to the death-sentenced as much as they do to other prisoners. California death row prisoner Clarence Allen's attempt to refuse medical treatment laid bare the contradictions in how and when prisoners have rights to die. Allen, an elderly prisoner with significant health problems and physical disabilities, had a heart attack about three months before his scheduled execution. Allen asked that he be allowed to die if he had another heart attack before his execution. The prison refused. Instead, officials maintained that they would resuscitate and then execute him (Associated Press, 2006).

California's position was consistent with case law. Courts permit prisons to intervene forcibly when prisoners try to die, citing the state's interest in preserving life and preventing suicide. In *In re Caulk* (1984) prison officials sought to force-feed a prisoner facing life without parole in prison. The prisoner had decided to stop eating because he

> never expects to be released from prison again. He says he is tired, unhappy, disappointed with the promise that life holds, that he does not "belong on the streets." He maintains that if he cannot live freely, he does not want to live at all. . . . He testified that he has hurt a lot of people, and whenever he feels pain on his starvation diet, he believes he is paying another debt for his past misdeeds. (p. 95)

The court rejected Caulk's position, concluding that the state's interest in preserving life and preventing suicide trumped the prisoner's interests and his desire to die.

In *Laurie v. Senecal* (1995), the Rhode Island Supreme Court considered a case in which the prisoner had no physical ailment but simply "no longer desired to live because of the stigma of his conviction" (p. 807). He felt "continuous psychological pain" because of his crime (p. 807). Despite finding the prisoner was competent, that he "had made a knowing and voluntary decision to stop taking food and water for the purpose of ending his life," and that he had no dependents who would suffer from his death, the court concluded that prison officials had a "right and duty to intervene" because of the state's interest in preserving life and preventing suicide (pp. 807–808).

> In respect to an incarcerated prisoner, we believe that there is no right under either the State or the Federal Constitution to override the

compelling interest of the state in the preservation of his or her life
and the prevention of suicide. (p. 809)

In Maine, a court permitted a jail to force-feed an inmate who "refus[ed]
to take life-sustaining sustenance as a result of a sense of hopelessness" (*Ross
v. Emerson*, 2005, p. 1). The court reasoned that the sheriff of the jail had "the
obligation to take reasonable measures to maintain the wellbeing of individuals in his custody" (p. 2). The Seventh Circuit Court of Appeals limited
prisoners' right to refuse medical treatment by referring to the psychological
impact of incarceration (and the state's duty to mitigate that impact):

> Incarceration can place a person under unusual psychological strain
> and the jail or prison under a commensurate duty to prevent the pris-
> oner from giving way to the strain. The analysis is applicable when
> suicide takes the form of starving oneself to death. (*Freeman v. Berge*,
> 2006, pp. 546–547)

The remorse, hopelessness, and stress of incarceration articulated in
these cases are strikingly similar to the reasons many death row volunteers
give for wanting to die. For non–death-sentenced prisoners, courts reject
the notion that hopelessness or a desire to atone for one's crimes entitles
a prisoner to hasten death. Instead, courts impose a duty on the state to
maintain life; whether and when to die is simply not for the prisoner to
decide. In the death row context, in contrast, these reasons are accepted,
even before courts have had the full opportunity to rule whether the prisoner's conviction and sentence are legally correct.

Rights to Die for the Terminally Ill Are More Restrictive

When competent nonincarcerated individuals ask to discontinue life-
sustaining medical intervention, hospitals and courts will permit them to
do so. This is not true, however, when the patient asks a third party to take
affirmative action to hasten death. In *Vacco v. Quill* (1997) and *Washington
v. Glucksberg* (1997), the Supreme Court considered challenges to state statutes that prohibited physicians from helping patients die. Although rejecting any constitutional right to help in dying, the Supreme Court observed
that states were free to enact statutes permitting physician-assisted dying.

Montana and New Mexico courts thereafter struck down assisted suicide bans and California, Colorado, Oregon, Vermont, Washington, and the District of Columbia have passed laws allowing physicians to help people die (*Baxter v. Montana*, 2009; California End of Life Option Act, 2016; Colorado End of Life Options Act, 2016; District of Columbia Death With Dignity Act, 2016; Milford, 2014; Oregon Death With Dignity Act, 1997; Vermont Patient Choice at End of Life, 2013; Washington Death With Dignity Act, 2009).

Notably, these statutes impose limits that are not required of death-sentenced prisoners. The assisted-dying statutes passed in California (California End of Life Option Act, 2016), Oregon (Oregon Death With Dignity Act, 1997), Vermont (Vermont Patient Choice at End of Life, 2013), and Washington (Washington Death With Dignity Act, 2009) allow physicians to prescribe a lethal dose of medication, but patients must administer the medication themselves. This is more restrictive than the practice for volunteers, where execution technicians administer the lethal drugs. Indeed at least one volunteer wanted the state to execute him because suicide was contrary to his religion (Rountree, 2015).

The statutes also restrict the availability of physician-assisted suicide to individuals who have an incurable and irreversible disease that will, within reasonable medical judgment, claim the patient's life within 6 months. In the Texas study, more than 80% of the volunteers had waived appeals by the time their cases had reached state postconviction proceedings. They bypassed state postconviction proceedings, federal habeas proceedings in district court, and federal appellate litigation. This litigation would ordinarily take far longer than 6 months to conclude (Rountree, 2015).

Further, not all death-sentenced prisoners will be executed. A study of state and federal court reversal rates in capital cases between 1973 and 1995 found that courts identified "serious, reversible error" in 68% of capital cases. During this period, state courts reversed 47% of capital cases, and federal courts reversed 40% of those cases affirmed by the state courts. Of those prisoners granted a new trial, 82% were resentenced to punishments less than death. Not even Texas, which uses the death penalty vigorously, can claim that any individual death-sentenced prisoner will be executed within 6 months. Since the return of the death penalty in 1977, only 46% of persons sentenced to death in Texas have been executed, with almost 22.5% winning reversal or commutation (Liebman, Fagan, & West, 2000; Snell, 2014).

Finally, Oregon, Washington, and the District of Columbia prohibit providing assistance to any terminally ill individual who has "a psychiatric or psychological disorder or depression causing impaired judgment" (Or. Rev. Stat. 127.825 § 3.03 (2013); Wash. Rev. Code §70.245.060 (2011); DC Act 21-577 § 5(b)). California prohibits prescribing lethal drugs to those who are "suffering from impaired judgment due to a mental disorder" (Cal. Health and Safety Code §443.5(a)(1)(A)(iii)).

Vermont and Colorado impose a lower standard. The Vermont statute provides that "'impaired judgment' means that a person does not sufficiently understand or appreciate the relevant facts necessary to make an informed decision" (18 V.S.A. ch. 113 § 5281(5)). The Colorado statute resembles that applied to volunteers even more closely. Mental illness is relevant only to the extent that it prevents someone from making an informed decision. The person seeking assistance in dying must have "the ability to make and communicate an informed decision to the health care providers" (C.R.S. 25-48-102(10)). An "informed decision" is one "based on an understanding and acknowledgment of the relevant facts" (C.R.S. 25-48-102(5)(b)).

CONCLUSION

Although it is difficult to imagine tolerating a life on death row, most death row prisoners, in fact, persevere until they are executed, die of natural causes, or leave death row when their capital sentences are vacated. We still understand too little about why some prisoners hasten their execution by curtailing full judicial review of their convictions and sentences. It is clear, however, that volunteers challenge not only a fundamental premise of the death penalty—that it is a punishment reserved exclusively for the worst of the worst offenders following meticulous judicial review—but also disparities in how law regulates access to death.

Although volunteers continue to be executed, empirical research unfortunately lags. More study, particularly research that focuses on individual states' death rows, would be particularly valuable. Every death row is its own society with its own dynamics. How a volunteer engages with that society—whether participating in its friendships, alliances, exchanges—may provide insight into why he or she may or may not be able to construct a world that can help him or her survive on death row.

At the same time, a focus on the individual state can also permit a look at how law may contribute to the volunteering phenomenon. In Texas, for example, defendants are asked at sentencing whether they would like counsel to be appointed to pursue postconviction remedies (Tex. Code of Criminal Procedure §11.071(2)(b), 2015). Delaying this decision point may give the would-be volunteer a greater chance to reflect on his or her options. Whether a state permits a volunteer to waive all appeals, as opposed to only postconviction litigation, may also matter. Certainly in Texas, after death-sentenced prisoners were permitted to waive direct appeal, their time on death row decreased significantly (Rountree, 2014, pp. 318–320).

Finally, attention to an individual state can give insight into the training and culture of forensic experts called in to opine on whether the volunteer is making a knowing, intelligent, and voluntary waiver. In Texas, mental health experts relied heavily on single interviews with the volunteer and did not appear to seek out relevant medical or psychological information. They did not explore how conditions of incarceration might make life unbearable for the volunteer. In addition, they seldom articulated how depression, for example, may affect an individual's decision-making abilities (Rountree, 2012). Some of this was surely driven by legal standards and standards of local legal practice. This points, however, to the crucial role mental health experts can play in educating lawyers and judges in these complex cases.

REFERENCES

American Bar Association. (2003). Guidelines for the appointment and performance of defense counsel in death penalty cases. *Hofstra Law Review, 31,* 913–1070.

Anno, B. J. (1985). Patterns of suicide in the Texas Department of Corrections 1980–1985. *Journal of Prison & Jail Health, 5,* 82–93.

Associated Press. (2006, January 18). Senior prisoner on California's death row is executed at age 76. *Washington Post*. Retrieved from http://www.washingtonpost.com/wp-dyn/content/article/2006/01/17/AR2006011701327.html

Associated Press. (2016). Barney Fuller Jr. execution: Texas murderer asks for death. *CBS News*. Retrieved from http://www.cbsnews.com/news/barney-fuller-jr-execution-texas-murderer-asks-for-death/

Austin v. Stephens, 596 F.3d Appx. 277 (5th Cir. 2015).

Baxter v. Montana, 224 P.3d 1211 (Mont. 2009).

Bellisle, M. (2005, October 26). Death-row inmate drops appeals. *Reno Gazette-Journal*, p. 8A.

Blanco, J. I. (n.d.). *Jerry Duane Martin*. Retrieved from Murderpedia website: http://murderpedia.org/male.M/m1/martin-jerry-duane.htm

Blume, J. (2005). Killing the willing: "Volunteers," suicide and competency. *Michigan Law Review*, *103*, 939–1009.

California End of Life Option Act, Cal. Health and Safety Code §§ 443 *et seq.* (2016).

Chapman, A., Specht, M., & Cellucci, T. (2005). Factors associated with suicide attempts in female inmates: The hegemony of hopelessness. *Suicide & Life-Threatening Behavior*, *35*, 558–569. http://dx.doi.org/10.1521/suli.2005.35.5.558

Chapman v. Commonwealth, 265 S.W.3d 156 (Ky. 2007).

Clines, F. X. (1994, January 12). Self-esteem and friendship in a factory on death row. *The New York Times*. Retrieved from http://www.nytimes.com/1994/01/12/us/self-esteem-and-friendship-in-a-factory-on-death-row.html?pagewanted=all

Colorado End of Life Options Act, Colo. Health Code §§ 25-48-101 *et seq.* (2016).

Comer v. Schriro, 463 F.3d 934 (9th Cir. 2006).

Comer v. Schriro, 480 F.3d 960 (9th Cir. 2007).

Commonwealth v. McKenna, 383 A.2d 174 (Pa. 1978).

Cook, K. M. (2008). *Chasing justice: My story of freeing myself after two decades on death row for a crime I didn't commit*. New York, NY: Morrow.

Cooper, P. (2009). Competency of death row inmates to waive the right to appeal: A proposal to scrutinize the motivations of death row volunteers and to consider the impact of death row syndrome in determining competency. *Developments in Mental Health Law*, *28*, 105–125.

Cotterrell, B. (2013). Florida executes man with new lethal injection drug. *Reuters*. Retrieved from http://www.reuters.com/article/us-usa-florida-execution-idUSBRE99F00020131016

Crimesider Staff. (2012). South Dakota executes Donald Moeller for rape, murder of 9-year-old. *CBS News*. Retrieved from http://www.cbsnews.com/news/south-dakota-executes-donald-moeller-for-rape-murder-of-9-year-old-girl/

Crimesider Staff. (2016). Ga. death row inmate says he won't fight execution scheduled for Wed. *CBS News*. Retrieved from http://www.cbsnews.com/news/steven-frederick-spears-georgia-death-row-inmate-scheduled-for-execution-wednesday/

Cunningham, M., & Vigen, M. (2002). Death row inmate characteristics, adjustment, and confinement: A critical review of the literature. *Behavioral Science & Law, 20*, 191–210. http://dx.doi.org/10.1002/bsl.473

Dawson v. State, 10 P.3d 49 (Mont. 2000).

Death Penalty Information Center. (2017a). *Executions by state and year: Texas.* Retrieved from http://www.deathpenaltyinfo.org/node/5741#TX

Death Penalty Information Center. (2017b). *Innocence and the death penalty.* Retrieved from http://www.deathpenaltyinfo.org/innocence-and-death-penalty

Death Penalty Information Center. (2017c). *Searchable execution database: Volunteer.* Retrieved from http://www.deathpenaltyinfo.org/views-executions?exec_name_1=&sex=All&sex_1=All&federal=All&foreigner=All&juvenile=All&volunteer=y

Death Penalty News. (2012). *Delaware executes Shannon Johnson.* Retrieved from https://deathpenaltynews.blogspot.com/2012/04/delaware-executes-shannon-johnson.html

Demosthenes v. Baal, 495 U.S. 731 (1990).

Dennis ex rel. Butko v. Budge, 378 F.3d 880 (9th Cir. 2004).

District of Columbia Death With Dignity Act, D.C. Act 21-577 (2016).

Durkheim, É. (1966). *On suicide.* New York, NY: The Free Press. (Original work published 1897)

Eliason, S. (2009). Murder–suicide: A review of the recent literature. *The Journal of the Academy of Psychiatry and the Law, 37*, 371–376.

Ford v. Haley, 195 F.3d 603 (11th Cir. 1999).

Freeman v. Berge, 441 F.3d 543 (7th Cir. 2006).

Fuller v. TDCJ-CID, 2016 WL 3079608 (E.D. Tex. 2016).

Furman v. Georgia, 408 U.S. 238 (1972).

Garnett, R. (2002). Sectarian reflections on lawyers' ethics and death row volunteers. *Notre Dame Law Review, 77*, 795–830.

Geary v. State, 977 P.2d 344 (Nev. 1999).

Gilmore v. Utah, 429 U.S. 1012 (1976).

Gleason v. Commonwealth, 726 S.E.2d 351 (Va. 2012).

Gleason v. Pearson, 2013 WL 139478 (W.D. Va. 2013).

Glossip v. Gross, 576 U.S., 135 S. Ct. 2726 (2015).

Godinez v. Moran, 509 U.S. 389 (1993).

Grasso v. State, 857 P.2d 802 (Okla. Crim. App. 1993).

Harper v. Parker, 177 F.3d 567 (6th Cir. 1999).

Harrington, C. L. (2000). A community divided: Defense attorneys and the ethics of death row volunteering. *Law & Social Inquiry, 25,* 849–881. http://dx.doi.org/10.1111/j.1747-4469.2000.tb00163.x

Hill v. State, 661 S.E.2d 92 (S.C. 2008).

Holton v. State, No. M2005-01870-SC-S10-PD (Tenn. May 4, 2006).

In re Caulk, 480 A.2d 93 (N.H. 1984).

In re Zettlemoyer, 53 F.3d 24 (3d Cir. 1995).

Indiana v. Edwards, 554 U.S. 164 (2008).

Johnson v. State, 40 So.3d 753 (Ala. Ct. Crim. App. 2009).

Johnson v. Zerbst, 304 U.S. 458 (1938).

Lackey v. State, 104 So.3d 234 (Ala. Ct. Crim. App. 2010).

Laurie v. Senecal, 666 A.2d 806 (R.I. 1995).

Liebling, A. (1999). Prison suicide and prisoner coping. In M. Tonry & J. Petersilia (Eds.), *Prisons* (pp. 283–359). Chicago, IL: University of Chicago Press.

Liebman, J., Fagan, J., & West, V. (2000). *A broken system: Error rates in capital cases, 1973–1995.* Retrieved from https://www.fedcrimlaw.com/members/DeathPenalty/ErrorRates-DeathPenalty.pdf

Liem, M., Hengeveld, M., & Koenraadt, F. (2009). Domestic homicide followed by parasuicide: A comparison with homicide and parasuicide. *International Journal of Offender Therapy and Comparative Criminology, 53,* 497–516. http://dx.doi.org/10.1177/0306624X09334646

Liem, M., Postulart, M., & Nieuwbeerta, P. (2009). Homicide–suicide in the Netherlands: An epidemiology. *Homicide Studies, 13,* 99–123. http://dx.doi.org/10.1177/1088767908330833

Lonchar v. Zant, 978 F.2d 637 (11th Cir. 1993).

Lopez v. Stephens, No. 2:12-CV-160, 2014 WL 2981056 (S.D. Tex. July 1, 2014).

Lott v. State, 874 S.W.2d 687 (Tex. Crim. App. 1994).

MacDonald, J. (2009). Updated: Alabama executes Jack Trawick for slaying of Stephanie Gach. *The Birmingham News.* Retrieved from http://blog.al.com/spotnews/2009/06/jack_trawick.html

MacDonald, J., & McKee, J. (2006). Dawson put to death six minutes past midnight. *Independent Record.* Retrieved from http://helenair.com/news/state-and-regional/dawson-put-to-death-six-minutes-past-midnight/article_3cf14d13-80a7-5a3f-a55d-4bf6c090d8ad.html

Mann, D. (2010). Solitary men: Does prolonged isolation drive death row prisoners insane? *The Texas Observer.* Retrieved from https://www.texasobserver.org/solitary-men/

McCord, D. (2010). What's messing with Texas death sentences? *Texas Tech Law Review, 43,* 601–613.

Mello, M. (1999). *The United States of America versus Theodore John Kaczynski: Ethics, power and the invention of the Unabomber.* New York, NY: Context.

Milford, P. (2014). Right to die with doctor's help affirmed in New Mexico. *Bloomberg.* Retrieved from https://www.bloomberg.com/news/articles/2014-01-14/right-to-die-with-doctor-s-help-affirmed-in-new-mexico

Muschert, G., Harrington, C. L., & Reece, H. (2009). Elected executions in the U.S. print news media. *Criminal Justice Studies, 22,* 345–365.

Newman v. State, 84 S.W.2d 443 (Ark. 2002).

Nissim, R., Gagliese, L., & Rodin, G. (2009). The desire for hastened death in individuals with advanced cancer: A longitudinal qualitative study. *Social Science & Medicine, 69,* 165–171. http://dx.doi.org/10.1016/j.socscimed.2009.04.021

Nock, M., Borges, G., Bromet, E., Cha, C., Kessler, R., & Lee, S. (2008). Suicide and suicidal behavior. *Epidemiologic Review, 30,* 133–154. http://dx.doi.org/10.1093/epirev/mxn002

Oleson, J. C. (2006). Swilling hemlock: The legal ethics of defending a client who wishes to volunteer for execution. *Washington & Lee Law Review, 63,* 147–230.

Oregon Death With Dignity Act. (1997). Or. Rev. Stat. §§ 127.800 *et seq.* (2013).

Murderpedia. (2006). *Elijah Page.* Retrieved from http://murderpedia.org/male.P/p1/page-elijah-photos.htm

Patterson v. Commonwealth, 551 S.E.2d 332 (Va. 2001).

Pennell v. State, 604 A.2d 1368 (Del. 1992).

People v. Massie, 967 P.2d 29 (Cal. 1998).

Perkinson, R. (2010). *Texas tough: The rise of America's prison empire.* New York, NY: Metropolitan Books.

Pike v. State, 164 S.W.3d 257 (Tenn. 2005).

Plahuta, J., McCulloch, B. J., Kasarskis, E., Ross, M., Walter, R., & McDonald, E. (2002). Amyotrophic lateral sclerosis and hopelessness: Psychosocial factors. *Social Science & Medicine, 55,* 2131–2140. http://dx.doi.org/10.1016/S0277-9536(01)00356-2

Rees v. Peyton, 384 U.S. 312 (1966).

Robertson v. State, 143 So. 3d 907 (Fla. 2014).

Ross v. Emerson, No. CV-05-262, 2005 WL 3340087 (Me. Super. Nov. 3, 2005).

Rountree, M. M. (2012). "I'll make them shoot me": Accounts of death-sentenced prisoners advocating for execution. *Law & Society Review, 46,* 589–622.

Rountree, M. M. (2014). Volunteers for execution: Directions for further research into grief, culpability, and legal structures. *University of Missouri–Kansas City Law Review, 82*, 295–333.

Rountree, M. M. (2015). Criminals get all the rights: The sociolegal construction of different rights to die. *Journal of Criminal Law & Criminology, 105*, 149–202.

Rumbaugh v. Procunier, 753 F.2d 395 (5th Cir. 1985).

Simpson v. Quarterman, 341 F. App'x 68 (5th Cir. 2009).

Smith, A. (2008). Not "waiving" but drowning: The anatomy of death row syndrome and volunteering for execution. *Boston University Public Interest Law Journal, 17*, 237–254.

Smith ex rel. Mo. Public Defender Comm'n v. Armontrout, 812 F.2d 1050 (8th Cir. 1987).

Smith, R. (2012). The geography of the death penalty and its ramifications. *Boston University Law Review, 92*, 227–281.

Snell, T. (2014). *Capital punishment, 2012—Statistical tables.* Retrieved from https://www.bjs.gov/content/pub/pdf/cp12st.pdf

Stack, S. (1997). Homicide followed by suicide: An analysis of Chicago data. *Criminology, 35*, 435–453. http://dx.doi.org/10.1111/j.1745-9125.1997.tb01224.x

Starzomski, A., & Nussbaum, D. (2000). The self and the psychology of domestic homicide–suicide. *International Journal of Offender Therapy and Comparative Criminology, 44*, 468–479. http://dx.doi.org/10.1177/0306624X00444005

State v. Barton, 844 N.E.2d 307 (Ohio 2006).

State v. Bordelon, 33 So.3d 842 (La. 2009).

State v. Brewer, 826 P.2d 783 (Ariz. 1992).

State v. Dodd, 838 P.2d 86 (Wash. 1992).

State v. Downs, 604 S.E.2d 377 (S.C. 2004).

State v. Downs, 631 S.E.2d 7 (S.C. 2006).

State v. Ferguson, 844 N.E.2d 806 (Ohio 2006).

State v. Martini, 677 A.2d 1106 (N.J. 1996).

State v. Motts, 707 S.E.2d 804 (S.C. 2011).

State v. Ovante, 291 P.3d 974 (Ariz. 2013).

State v. Robert, 820 N.W.2d 136 (S.D. 2012).

Tabler v. Stephens, 588 Fed. Appx. 297 (5th Cir 2014).

Texas Code of Criminal Procedure §11.071 (West 2015).

Texas Department of Criminal Justice. (2017). *Death row information: Offenders on death row.* Retrieved from https://www.tdcj.state.tx.us/death_row/dr_offenders_on_dr.html

Texas Execution Information Center. (2017). *Death row since 1974.* Retrieved from http://www.txexecutions.org/statistics.asp

Vacco v. Quill, 521 U.S. 793 (1997).

Vandiver, M., Giacopassi, D., & Turner, K. B. (2008). "Let's do it!": An analysis of consensual executions. In R. Bohm (Ed.), *The death penalty today* (pp. 187–206). Boca Raton, FL: CRC Press.

Vermont Patient Choice At End Of Life, 18 Vt. Stat. Ann. Tit. 113 §§ 5281 *et seq.* (2013).

Washington Death With Dignity Act, Wash. Rev. Code §70.245.010 *et seq.* (2009).

Washington v. Glucksberg, 521 U.S. 702 (1997).

Wenzel, A., Brown, G., & Beck, A. (2012). Characteristics of individuals who make impulsive suicide attempts. *Journal of Affective Disorders*, *136*, 1121–1125.

White v. Horn, 54 F. Supp. 2d 457 (E.D. Pa. 1999).

Whitmore v. Arkansas, 495 U.S. 149 (1990).

THREE

CONCEPTS OF TIME ON DEATH ROW

7

Psychological Survival in Isolation: Tussling With Time on Death Row

Ian O'Donnell

A person's relationship with time is ruptured by his or her imprisonment. Time no longer has value as a scarce resource to be spent carefully in pursuit of individual goals but becomes a hyperinflated currency,
vast quantities of which must be frittered away in the face of an ever-
diminishing return. Despite its centrality to their lived experience, little is
known about how prisoners engage with an aspect of their existence that
cannot be touched, heard, smelled, seen, or tasted but that nevertheless
bombards the senses.

Solitary prisoners, with so few diversions, feel time's passage all the
more painfully; it has a smothering quality that frustrates easy passage
through the day. Koestler (1942) drew on the image of the grave to describe
how it felt awaiting execution in solitary confinement in Spain: "The cell
was like a vault enclosed in three-fold armour-plating; the three-fold wall
of silence, loneliness and fear" (p. 107). Piercing this armor plating is an

http://dx.doi.org/10.1037/0000084-008
Living on Death Row: The Psychology of Waiting to Die, H. Toch, J. R. Acker, and V. M. Bonventre (Editors)

enormous challenge. Without the distraction that company brings, temporal pressures build and threaten to overwhelm.

The lack of meaningful activity and the unvarying routine contribute to a sense of boredom—always situational, sometimes existential—on the part of men and women whose futures have been deferred and whose presents must be lived according to the dictates of others. On death row, where the "overwhelming majority" of prisoners are held in solitary confinement (American Civil Liberties Union, 2013, p. 4), there is the additional stress of knowing that while they wait—alone—the state wants them dead. Jackson and Christian (2012) characterized this as "life in the moment. It is limbo time, endlessly cyclical, endlessly repetitive" (p. 167). Molineux (1903) recalled how, when his death was scheduled by a New York court, normal relationships with time were sundered and his life was characterized by "an endless waiting without expectancy" (p. 23). This stops when the execution date is confirmed and the countdown begins; the prisoner is now back in time.

Themes that are well developed in the literature relating to solitary confinement include those of passivity, lethargy, disintegration (psychological and bodily), anger, and injustice (especially with regard to racial bias and wrongful convictions). Seldom encountered are themes of choosing, changing, coping, and overcoming. To highlight the latter is not to minimize the obvious and manifold harms of solitary confinement, a practice that should be trenchantly opposed on the grounds of its inherent inhumanity, not its purported effects. To limit attention to the destructive consequences of an objectionable practice is to ignore the heroic efforts that some of the most marginalized among us have made—and continue to make—to bear potentially unbearable circumstances. (See O'Donnell, 2014, for an account of the emergence of solitary confinement as a penal aim, its contemporary manifestations, the challenges it poses, and the responses it evokes.)

Not to accept what prisoners tell us about their capacity to adapt to environments to which they should never have been exposed is to further reduce them as thinking, feeling, striving agents. It is possible to condemn prolonged solitary confinement and also to recognize that prisoners have identified benefits that can be found among the burdens.

Suffering—however cruel, unfair, and persistent—does not efface the humanity of those on whom it is imposed. The death row environment severely restricts opportunities and choices, but it does not eliminate them completely.

THREATS TO THE SELF

What prisoners on death row describe as a fear of mental deterioration may alternatively be conceptualized as a fear of being unable to revive their pre-prison identities. They are afraid that they will lose the sense of their selves enduring over time, that the role of prisoner will come to define them so completely that their previous identity is overwritten. This is punishment as palimpsest.

If their sentence is overturned or commuted and release eventually beckons, they may emerge fortified, but different, and whether this difference will interfere with their ability to lead fully social lives is a cause of anxiety. Prisoners who withdraw worry they will be withdrawn in perpetuity. Those who become self-sufficient worry they will lose the capacity for intimacy. They are anxious about not being able to return to the core of who they were before a court decided they deserved to die. They are afraid that the identity changes wrought to play the role of death row inhabitant will acquire an irreversible quality. They yearn to remain the same despite the erosion of character caused by an unforgiving environment. (Some, of course, desire to be different and initiate a change process to distance themselves from the misdeeds and regrets of the past.)

The degree of identity transformation required to deal with lengthy isolation and the fear of being lawfully killed (and the accompanying ontological insecurity) is so far reaching that it is understandable why those who live on death row worry about the extent to which it can be undone. (Physical, as opposed to psychological, survival is further beyond their reach, depending on lawyers, judges, and other actors outside the prison walls.) When life is stripped of meaningful human interaction, it is degraded. The person treated in this way sees their emotional range reduced and fears that their capacity for full-blooded engagement will be forever limited. In the event that a prisoner makes it off death row alive, the challenge of reconstituting his or her identity is major and urgent.

SUNDERING TIES

Prisoners are sequestered from family and community and, while they continue to age, their opportunities for growth are stunted. They inhabit an arid emotional hinterland. Sapsford (1983) found that prison time was viewed as "an interruption of life, not a part of it, like a form of cryogenic suspension through which the patient remains fully conscious" (p. 76). For the man or woman in solitary confinement, this suspension is all the more profound. Prisoners who know they will never be released confront a different challenge in temporal terms. So too the prisoner who faces execution, for whom there exists an unusual degree of clarity around when time will cease to be of significance. Drawing on his personal experience of death row, Zietz (1961) observed that the conception of time for the condemned man is unique as "the scheduled date of execution becomes the known end of time" (p. 51). In a cruel irony, the solitary life ends with a death that is inflicted before spectators.

Outside distractions give life meaning but may also introduce fretfulness. Not all prisoners are willing to make space in their lives for disruption they cannot control, problems they cannot solve, and joy they cannot fully share. Some exacerbate their isolation as part of a deliberate survival strategy. Family ties are difficult to nourish from a prison cell, and the tribulations and triumphs of those outside, which the prisoner is unable to influence, can corrode even the most committed relationships.

Visits can make time harder to serve because they jolt prisoners back to an alternative reality that is often an unhappy reminder of their predicament. They are memento mori. Contacts with the outside world signal that while people they care about are moving forward in time, the prisoner's development is arrested. To avoid the inevitable frustration and distress, some prisoners sever these ties before time causes them to fray beyond repair. Toch (1992) referred to the strategy of preemptively severing connections as the "de-cathexis of relationships" (p. 386). He described it as involving the suppression of thoughts of the outside world and the minimization of contact with significant others to allow an exclusive focus on coping with the demands of imprisonment. On death row, this coping is poignantly futile if the order of the court is ultimately upheld.

Prisoners who choose to shift their gaze from outside and live the desiccated life that remains conspire with the prison authorities in paring away their own humanity; "When the view of self is restricted to what a prison setting reflects, this is life as beheld in a distorting mirror" (O'Donnell, 2014, p. 224). Others continue to engage, but over the course of a long sentence directed toward execution, this is a strategy that requires a rare degree of confidence in the sturdiness of human relationships. No ties, or the indestructible bonds enjoyed by the fortunate few, trump the vicissitudes of ordinary alliances.

TRUNCATING DURATION

The death row prisoners who fare worst are those who watch the minutes crawl past. They are saturated by an awareness of time and feel impotent to accelerate its passage. By paying such close attention to time, the prisoner extends its perceived duration. Koestler was vividly aware of this phenomenon. During a period of illness he was unable to read, write, or otherwise distract himself. The result was that he could not ignore time but became acutely aware of its slothful progress, concluding that "an inexorable law prevails: increasing awareness of time slows down its pace" (Koestler, 1942, p. 155).

Prisoners cannot avoid serving time in the sense of allowing it to pass in an environment they would rather not be in, but they struggle to avoid serving it as a slave would a master. Solitary prisoners take a variety of steps to modify the quality of their temporal experience. In the free world, such modifications can have a playful quality. On death row, this is a serious business. The secret to lightening time's burden—whatever the imposed sentence—lies in truncating its perceived duration. This is done via what I characterize as the seven Rs of survival: rescheduling, removal, reduction, reorientation, resistance, raptness, and reinterpretation. (These stratagems are more fully elaborated in my book *Prisoners, Solitude, and Time* [O'Donnell, 2014], on which this chapter is based.)

The seven Rs betoken a creative engagement with temporality. Some prisoners master none of them and their solitary time results in withdrawal, ruinous rumination, and perhaps, mental breakdown. Those who do not cope are characterized by a low level of ability to reframe time in a way that makes it seem less empty, less immense, less threatening. They find it virtually impossible to fill the large swathes of empty time with any meaningful activity. They have not learned how to counteract loneliness. They are unable to resolve the paradox that emptier time feels heavier. This leaves them vulnerable to the intrusion of unwelcome thoughts or at risk of a retreat into fantasy and passivity.

Not every prisoner can locate within themselves the resources required to carry on, and a small number decide to conquer time by ending it. The prisoner who contemplates suicide may view this as a chance to wrest back control of their fate from the authorities. For some, self-harm and the response it evokes become a survival strategy of sorts. Although it may be a temptation for many, self-destruction is not often translated into a concrete plan, especially in an environment where the opportunities for suicide are so severely limited. A key goal of death row is to prevent its occupants from determining their own date of death; this must count as the bleakest of penal aims.

THE SEVEN Rs

The challenge for prisoners held in isolation for a prolonged period is to find methods of ensuring that the weight of accumulating time does not bring them entirely to a halt. The ways they have found to do this are described next.

Rescheduling

Some shape must be imposed on a sentence if it is not to become oppressive. A span of time broken down into meaningful chunks seems more manageable. Although such an approach is common among prisoners serving fixed terms, it is not an option for men or women on death row who cannot count down toward their eventual freedom and whose date of death remains enervatingly uncertain until it is confirmed, at which point only days or hours remain. The temporal focus must be on other benchmarks such as forthcoming court hearings. If all possibilities of eventual survival have been eradicated, the prison's priorities assume even greater significance and the choice is between allowing them to become paramount (the route to institutionalization) or attempting to maintain a parallel focus on the outside world (a route fraught with difficulty). Whichever route is taken does not affect the destination, which is deliberately inflicted death.

Removal

Goffman (1961) defined *removal activities* broadly, to include a wide range of

> voluntary unserious pursuits which are sufficiently engrossing and exciting to lift the participant out of himself, making him oblivious for the time to his actual situation. If the ordinary activities in total institutions can be said to torture time, these activities mercifully kill it. (p. 63)

The term is used differently here because for prisoners whose lives are on the line these pursuits are anything but "unserious." In addition, it is unduly optimistic to think that such pursuits kill time; the best that can be hoped for is that they anesthetize the prisoner to it. Removal, in my scheme, is about busyness as an end in itself. One of the best ways of speeding the passage of time is to become absorbed in an activity such as reading, working, or keeping fit. Given the restrictions on the amount of property death row prisoners are allowed to store in their cells, and the limited opportunities for employment and recreation, removal activities are problematic.

Reduction

Another way of reducing the burden of lived time is to sleep through as much of it as possible or to deaden its impact through drug use. Prisoners on death row may take to their beds, but obtaining drugs is seldom a realistic option given the prevailing levels of security and surveillance. Watching television alone in-cell is another type of reduction, providing an effortless form of diversion. It has the added attraction of allowing prisoners to keep something in common with those outside by following the same programs, if they are allowed access to extra-institutional channels.

Reorientation

For prisoners to survive psychologically it is important that they shift their time orientation. Dwelling on the past and any associated misgivings, or fretting about a future life that is unlikely to arrive as wished for, is at odds with successful navigation of the temporal landscape. Prisoners live in an extended present. Looking backward to a nonprison past becomes increasingly difficult, even if it is still desired, as time spent in custody increases and a forward orientation is brimful of anxiety as too many of the variables required for effective planning lie outside the prisoner's direct control. Their lives have been put on hold; they cannot share in the futures of those they care about, so forward thinking is best avoided. Much of the richness of human life involves reimagining the future. This is negated by imprisonment. At a fundamental level, therefore, prisons will always be dehumanizing, no matter how good the physical conditions or the relationships between prisoners and staff, because they curtail the individual's capacity to look ahead, to plan, to wonder, to project themselves into novel scenarios.

To escape the pain associated with the dashing of dreams that might not be realized, prisoners on death row—who may have spent decades there—try to eschew thinking about the future. Stretching the present and remaining within it is an important form of adaptation. Prison life is most comfortable for the person who has managed to refocus his or her attention on the present and has found a way to allow the days to slip by, almost unnoticed.

The struggle against time is given added impetus when the death row prisoner runs out of memories. A point arrives in a long sentence when one can no longer look to the past for recollections to sustain one in the present. The outside world has become so distant that it cannot be related to, or conjured up, in a meaningful way. To sustain psychological integrity requires the topping up of intellectual reservoirs so that the internal dialogue continues to flow. If it ceases, the personality may collapse in the absence of other sources of stimulation. These are more than conversations; they are "survival soliloquies" (O'Donnell, 2014, p. 220). But they deteriorate in the retelling. Echols (2013) spent 18 years in prison in Arkansas awaiting execution for crimes he did not commit. Much of this time was spent in solitary confinement, and he recalled,

> You don't make many memories in prison—at least none you'd want to keep, or look back on fondly. . . . The ones you came in with are the only ones you'll ever have. I would revisit mine constantly, trying desperately to wring every ounce of nourishment out of them that I possibly could. I was like a vampire, sucking them dry and then sifting through the dust in hopes of finding a drop I'd overlooked the previous hundred times. (p. 298)

Canny prisoners know that the erosion of memory cannot be prevented, and they intensify their efforts to live in the present. Molineux (1903) captured this shift in temporal perspective when he wrote of his time in the hushed solitude of death row in Sing Sing, where guards and prisoners alike wore felt-soled shoes to muffle the sound of their movement, as a

> sort of noiseless purgatory in which, as the months go by, past experiences, the hopes and fears and happinesses which were, grow fainter and fainter, till, like the future, they inspire us with nothing but indifference, leaving only the present to be endured. (p. 24)

The attempt to live within a prison-present becomes a more pressing consideration when the denial of human company is protracted. A prisoner on Florida's death row captured this sentiment perfectly:

> Back home in rural Alabama, where I grew up we often use a colloquialism, "even a blind hog finds an acorn every now and then." I believe Mr. Nietzsche found just such an acorn when he wrote, *amor fati*: that one wants nothing to be different—not forward, not backward, not

in all eternity. I take this to mean that we should become so enrap-
tured in today that we haven't time to regret yesterday or hope for
a better tomorrow, but simply revel in today. I implore you to head
[sic] Nietzsche's words and do not dare hope there will be a morrow,
and don't writhe beneath the cumbersome weight of yesterday's mis-
steps. (Calhoun, 2016, p. 1)

There is a tragic irony here: To survive, prisoners have to focus on
the present, but for some, this focus threatens to devastate because they
lack the skills required to speed up or to ignore or simply to bear time's
passage.

Resistance

Some prisoners feed off the hate that solitary confinement incites, believing it to be a whetstone for character formation. But to what end if death
awaits? Constant enragement is at odds with psychological stability, and
most prisoners seem to replace explosive rage with simmering anger or
grudging acceptance. The energy needed to hate depletes an individual's
resources so that what is left for self-preservation may be inadequate. The
lengthy legal battles that occupy death row prisoners require whatever
energy they can muster. The diminution of physical strength is relevant
also, along with the obvious inequality of arms. Even the fiercest and fittest
prisoner is no match for a team of guards with batons, shields, and ready
reinforcements.

The prison system's attempts to quash resistance are never complete.
A measure of negotiation is always possible between an individual (however tightly controlled in time and space) and their environment (however
stimulus deprived and heavily guarded). Even when stripped, unarmed,
and outnumbered, prisoners can use their body products offensively. A
handful of human waste hurled from within a death row cell is a statement
of dissatisfaction that is as eloquent as it is fetid. Although contrary to the
thrower's interests, such behavior can be seen as "a pungent declaration
of autonomy" (O'Donnell, 2014, p. 245) in a setting where most routes to
self-expression have been foreclosed. Desperate situations evoke desperate
acts of resistance.

Raptness

Raptness relates to a state of focused absorption in a goal-directed activity such as creative writing, craftwork, or painting. The activity is one that is important to the individual and, if accomplished, may become a key part of their identity. Raptness is distinguished from removal because it is more specialized and purposive. Removal involves the stress-busting aspects of keeping busy. Generally speaking, this is not the kind of activity that requires mastery in the way that raptness does.

As well as speeding the passage of time, raptness results in a product that may enhance the status of the person who produced it. This distinguishes it from involvement in prison work more generally, in which the individual may invest no particular significance beyond its value as a removal activity. As well as helping time to pass, such pursuits imbue it with purpose, and this further reduces its weight. This is difficult on death row given the limited access to the necessary materials. But it is not impossible. Jackson and Christian (2012) reported the following prisoner account from death row in Texas:

> So one day I picked up a pencil and started to do a little sketching. And it turned out to be nice. So I felt that I possibly have a little talent. I started in drawing, and I've been drawing for the last two years. I make greeting cards, and I've gotten off into doing portraits and larger paintings of scenes with birds and trees and so forth. If there's anything good that's come out of receiving the death penalty, it's that I've discovered that I have a little talent in art. So I can be thankful for that. (p. 111)

Reinterpretation

Prisoners who adopt a frame of reference that puts their pain in context cope better. This can happen in a variety of ways. Some find comfort in organized religion and cast themselves as players in a drama where worldly suffering is of little consequence when compared with an afterlife in paradise. Others find shelter with those who share a political creed or have a common enemy. Seeing oneself as a valued part of a larger enterprise eases the pain of confinement. For prisoners who can reimagine and recast their predicament, the potential rewards are substantial.

Reinterpretation is the most elusive of the seven Rs. Prisoners who achieve it create a bearable psychological environment where the tight confines within which they are forced to exist can be perceived and felt differently. Some speak of maturity and growth, of inextinguishable hope, of redefining adversity so that it hurts less. As Nietzsche (1994) put it, "If we have our own why of life, we shall get along with almost any how" (p. 468). An overarching purpose lends coherence to life events that might otherwise feel disjointed. Prisoners who emerge unbroken from long periods of arduous solitude rise in their own estimation and in that of their peers. They become benchmarks for endurance.

After 5 years of solitary confinement, and having spent many more waiting for a death sentence to be overturned, Jacobs (2007) came to realize the limits of the prison:

> They might be able to keep me here, take my time and circumscribe my space, but they can't have my mind or my heart or my spirit. Those are mine and no one can take them away from me. . . . Within these walls, it is up to me what kind of a world this will be—a joyous one, or a sad one, filled with peace and calm, or misery and fear. (p. 122)

She began to meditate and introduced yoga to her daily routine: "I was no longer a prisoner. I was a monk in a cave. . . . The only way I was restricted was bodily. Except for that, I was as free, or more free, than I had ever been" (p. 124). Meditation and yoga promote orientation toward the present, and that is one reason why they are found helpful by prisoners who discover them.

Molineux (1903) described how the isolation he experienced on death row allowed him to cultivate his imagination: "No one could sentence my thoughts to imprisonment, they were free. I began to live mentally" (pp. 236–237). Despite the awfulness of his surroundings and the uncertainty about his future (he was acquitted following a retrial that took place 3 years after his original conviction), he turned the situation to his profit, concluding, "I 'found *myself*' in the Death-Chamber" (p. 240, emphasis in original).

Although the past cannot be changed, one's attitude toward it can be, and every individual can rewrite his or her personal narrative. The prisoner's life, like anyone's, is a work in progress. For prisoners on death row there is one significant difference: The final chapter has been drafted for them, and they struggle to change the ending.

THE SEARCH FOR MEANING

Prisoner accounts contrast the expeditions taken by the mind with the entrapment of the body. When the latter is immured, the former can wander, unfettered. In this way, the deprivation of liberty can never be total. If death row prisoners succeed in decoupling their mental life from their physical environment, the rewards can be great. Despite the enormous odds, some prisoners manage to turn their incarceration to their advantage and to engage in the process of remolding the self.

Not everyone manages reinterpretation. Those who do try to share a sense of what this means to them, even if easy articulation is not possible. For those who possess (or discover) a religious sensibility, suffering can be accompanied by acceptance, self-actualization, and gratitude: "God is company for prisoners who discover that they cannot go it alone" (O'Donnell, 2014, p. 266). Whatever their inclinations, prisoners are likely to come into contact with organized religion more regularly in prison than outside. If religion becomes important to them, this shapes the way that prisoners experience solitary confinement.

Death row forces a confrontation with the self that seems to open new possibilities. Abu-Jamal (1997) recounted watching a lightning storm from his cell. He believed that he had less than 1 month left to live but found himself inspired by the relative triviality of humankind and its rules and systems compared with the raw power of nature. The apprehension of universality restored his sovereignty over time. At this moment he felt he would prevail (as ultimately he did in 2011 when his death sentence was vacated in favor of a term of life imprisonment without the possibility of parole):

> I saw that there is a Power that makes man's power pale. It is the power
> of Love; the power of God; the power of Life. I felt it surging through

every pore. Nature's power prevailed over the man-made, and I felt, that night, that I would prevail. I would overcome the State's efforts to silence and kill me. (p. 31)

A cynic might suggest that the religious fervor described by some of those who have experienced extended isolation on death row is a symptom of a break with reality that is triggered by loneliness and despair. But this would be a caricature. Those who have this experience can be hesitant about acknowledging it. It seems to be a sense of something profound but indescribable, of something bigger, of an appetite for meaning that cannot be sated. It is a phenomenon that unfolds slowly, while the chances of a psychotic episode are greater during the early phase of a sentence. Given the regularity of its appearance we should be slow to dismiss this aspect of the solitary experience. Regardless of how it might appear to a neutral observer, it is invested with meaning by those exposed to it, and if we are to remain true to their accounts, this aspect should not be neglected.

Given the exigencies of life on death row, its prisoners may find little scope for rescheduling, removal, reduction, resistance, and raptness. This distinguishes them from other prisoners in solitary confinement. For the death row isolate, the way forward is through reorientation and reinterpretation, both of which are heedless of the external environment.

TIME'S PARADOX

One of the key paradoxes of time is that intervals that seem to drag as they pass, appear to have flown in retrospect. Rideau (2011), a former death row prisoner in Louisiana, recalled, "In prison, days inch along like snails, and years zoom past like rockets" (p. 238). For the solitary prisoner whose days are characterized by tedious repetition, and where there are few interesting events to recollect, the past contracts rapidly. Periods of profound boredom generate few memories, so when looked back on there is little to distinguish them from the similarly empty periods on either side. Each lonesome prison day can feel excruciatingly long. But in retrospect, even the years seem to have flown past. These are the twin terrors of solitary confinement as it is lived (grindingly slow—when will the day end?) and as it is remembered (agonizingly quick—where did the months go?). As I put it, "monotony stretches time as it passes and squeezes it on reflection" (O'Donnell, 2014, p. 186). Yarris (Riley, Rose, & Sington, 2015) described the paradoxical nature of his 21 years on death row in Pennsylvania thus:

> Time; this is the strangest one. Do you know that the worst part—and yet the best part—of being in solitary confinement is time can be a blisteringly fast thing where in the blink of an eye you can look and ten years are gone from your life, but the next week is agony. . . . I always wanted to tell somebody that.

The time that was felt to drag on account of its dreary uneventfulness was remembered as having rushed past. Echols (2013) recalled,

> Time has changed for me. I don't recall exactly when it happened, and I don't even remember if it was sudden or gradual. Somehow the change just crept up on me like a wolf on tiptoe. Hell, I don't even remember when I first started to *notice* it. What I *do* remember is how when I was a kid every single day seemed to last for an eternity. . . . Now I watch while years flip by like an exhalation, and sometimes I feel panic trying to claw its way up into my throat. . . . I truly don't understand how it happened. How it *continues* to happen. (pp. 206–207, emphasis in original)

The "wolf on tiptoe" analogy is apt. By the time one becomes aware of the danger it may be too late to take evasive action. So too is the image of years flipping by "like an exhalation," the solitary prisoner gasping in the realization that so much life has slipped by and that it cannot be recovered.

CONCLUSION

Prisoners in solitary confinement have devised a variety of ways to put their stamp on their temporal lives, particularly how they experience duration. They do this because the stakes are so high; to relinquish the belief that one can continue to engage with time is to give up hope and thereby to be diminished as a human being. Solitary prisoners endeavor to become survivors, not victims, of their environment. Given the vast scale of the institution's power, there are many aspects of temporality where any attempt to wrest back control is doomed in advance. But this is not always the case. In the stimulus-poor environment of death row, prisoners tussle with time by focusing their temporal gaze firmly on the present—reorientation—and recasting their predicament—reinterpretation.

Although difficult, the death row prisoner's plight is not hopeless. The prison timetable, resented because it is inflexible and imposed, offers a refuge of sorts. The unvarying repetition of food trays being delivered, of counts, of exercise periods, of staff changeovers, of mail deliveries, provides scaffolding for the day. Because today is the same as yesterday and tomorrow will mirror today, life can be lived according to this numbing beat. The penal metronome is restarted each morning. Rather than moving forward, the prisoner is treading water, the aim being nothing more ambitious than to stay afloat to greet the next day. Like their Victorian predecessors on the treadwheel, a great deal of effort is expended to no net effect, but too little effort will be harmful. Prisoners describe how "the unbearable is borne, the future recedes, and the lack of novelty compresses time so that the tedium of years has an amnesic quality" (O'Donnell, 2014, p. 217). Even under the most arduous of circumstances, when each minute seems unbearably attenuated, it passes and another one follows. To quote a writer appreciated by prisoners who have been forced to contemplate the nullification of their existence: "You must go on, I can't go on, I'll go on" (Beckett, 2010, p. 134). One takes the next step forward and then another; that's it.

Timetables are important because they allow prisoners to avert their gaze from the future. They offer certainty when much is uncertain and give velocity to the day. One clear advantage of routinization is that time passes more quickly; predictability, stability, and sameness speed it along, providing waymarks for the prisoner who might otherwise get lost. Timetables offer a deadening solace that is welcomed because it makes life bearable but feared at the same time because it might usher in a form of passivity and institutionalization that will be difficult to shake off.

The concentration camp taught Frankl (2004) that when everything meaningful had been removed from a person's life, the freedom to choose one's attitude remained: "Everything can be taken from a man but one thing: the last of the human freedoms—to choose one's attitude in any given set of circumstances, to choose one's own way" (p. 75). The miserable conditions, starvation, and terror of impending death could not obliterate this fundamental freedom: "Any man can, even under such circumstances, decide what shall become of him—mentally and spiritually" (p. 75). Although protecting his physical integrity and prolonging his life were almost always beyond his control, how he made sense of his suffering and with what degree of dignity it was borne, fell to each individual to determine. This freedom gave life its meaning:

> There is also purpose in that life which is almost barren of both creation and enjoyment and which admits of but one possibility of high moral behaviour: namely in man's attitude to his existence, an existence restricted by external forces. (p. 76)

It was a rare person who could remain courageous and humane among the horrors of the concentration camp, but some managed to do so, and through their attitude to suffering they embodied the human potential to make the critical decision that Frankl (2004) described. These exemplary few showed how sense could be wrought from suffering and how even a life that was almost certain to be further degraded and then extinguished had not been emptied of meaning. Not many men or women have the wherewithal to behave like this, but the fact that some do suggests that all might. It is important not to exaggerate the degree to which prisoners in a 21st-century death row cell will be able to triumph over adversity, but the message from Frankl is clear:

> This is not happenstance; those who win out have decided to do so and those who withdraw, take their own lives, prey on (or pray with)

their comrades, or conspire with the authorities have also chosen their course of action. (O'Donnell, 2014, p. 278)

Frankl's insight was that life can be meaningful as well as desperately unhappy. For the death row prisoner who conquers time, this is as good as it gets.

REFERENCES

Abu-Jamal, M. (1997). *Death blossoms: Reflections from a prisoner of conscience.* Farmington, PA: Plough.

American Civil Liberties Union. (2013). *A death before dying: Solitary confinement on death row.* Retrieved from https://www.aclu.org/files/assets/deathbefore dying-report.pdf

Beckett, S. (2010). *The unnamable.* London, England: Faber & Faber.

Calhoun, J. (2016). Revel in today. *Compassion: Written by death-row prisoners, 21*(90), 1.

Echols, D. (2013). *Life after death: Eighteen years on death row.* London, England: Atlantic Books.

Frankl, V. E. (2004). *Man's search for meaning* (I. Lasch, Trans.). London, England: Rider Books.

Goffman, E. (1961). On the characteristics of total institutions: The inmate world. In D. R. Cressey (Ed.), *The prison: Studies in institutional organization and change* (pp. 15–67). New York, NY: Holt, Rinehart & Winston.

Jackson, B., & Christian, D. (2012). *In this timeless time: Living and dying on death row in America.* Chapel Hill: University of North Carolina Press.

Jacobs, S. (2007). *Stolen time: The inspiring story of an innocent woman condemned to death.* New York, NY: Doubleday.

Koestler, A. (1942). *Dialogue with death* (T. Blewitt & P. Blewitt, Trans.). New York, NY: Macmillan.

Molineux, R. B. (1903). *The room with the little door.* New York, NY: G. W. Dillingham.

Nietzsche, F. (1994). *The portable Nietzsche* (W. Kaufmann, Trans. & Ed.). New York, NY: Penguin Classic.

O'Donnell, I. (2014). *Prisoners, solitude, and time.* Oxford, England: Oxford University Press. http://dx.doi.org/10.1093/acprof:oso/9780199684489.001.0001

Rideau, W. (2011). *In the place of justice: A story of punishment and deliverance.* London, England: Profile Books.

Riley, C. (Producer), Rose, H. (Producer), & Sington, D. (Producer & Director). (2015). *The fear of 13* [Motion picture]. England: Dogwoof Pictures.

Sapsford, R. J. (1983). *Life sentence prisoners: Reaction, response and change.* Milton Keynes, England: Open University Press.

Toch, H. (1992). *Mosaic of despair: Human breakdowns in prison.* Washington, DC: American Psychological Association. http://dx.doi.org/10.1037/10136-000

Zietz, H. (1961). Prisoners' views of time—By a lifer. *The Prison Journal, 41,* 50–52. http://dx.doi.org/10.1177/003288556104100203

8

Time on Death Row

Bruce Jackson and Diane Christian

The single most common slang expression for "serve a prison sentence" is "do time." It conjugates: I'm doing time, I did do time, I will do time. It also works as a noun: "Where have you been?" "I've been doing time."

In the penitentiary, if you ask someone, "What are you doing?" you will get as a temporal answer, even if that person is at that moment reading a magazine, writing a letter, drawing a chicken, "A nickel," "a dime," "25 to life," "I'm doing it all." The answer to "What are you doing?" is for them what the judge said at the end of the trial: the sentence being served. But there is in the penitentiary one group of inmates who are not doing time at all, who are instead outside of time: the inhabitants of death row, the condemned, those who are there not to expiate an act but merely to wait.

Many men and women are in prison for murder, and many of those are in for first-degree murder, which is murder with malice aforethought:

http://dx.doi.org/10.1037/0000084-009
Living on Death Row: The Psychology of Waiting to Die, H. Toch, J. R. Acker, and V. M. Bonventre (Editors)

Juries decide the defendants knew what they were going to do, knew it was a crime, decided to do it, and then did it. But nearly all those sentenced murderers are doing time. Seventy percent of prisoners serving life sentences are eventually released, and most violent offenders only serve about 50% of the court's sentence, so even prisoners doing life sentences are doing time; they just do not know how much time they are doing. But, like all prisoners other than the condemned, they are in the active voice.

Not so the condemned. They are "on the row" just as patients with mental disorders are "in the hospital." Time does not count for the condemned because they are not serving a sentence. If you are on death row a year or 20 years, the time you have been there matters not at all when your time there ends. The condemned, unlike all the prisoners in all the other cells in all the other cellblocks, are not there to become better persons or to be punished. Time spent on death row is not the sentence; it is collateral damage occasioned by the sentence.

If, on the row, you ask, "What are you doing?" you will get as an answer, "Reading a magazine," "Writing a letter," "Drawing a chicken," or "Use your eyes."

If you become a nice guy while on the row, if Jesus fills your heart and you are ready to tend to the lepers without wearing gloves, it matters not at all; if you turn into a brute, it matters not at all; if you go mad, it matters not at all. The row is not for improvement, and it is not for atonement, and no one except outside sentimentalists and your family care whether you do either, and their opinions do not matter to anyone who counts. The row is limbo, a place men and women wait for years between the day a judge pronounces the sentence of death and the final determination in reversal, commutation, pardon, natural death, suicide, murder, or execution.

JACK HARRY SMITH, 1937–2016, WHO DIED ON THE ROW

We met Jack Harry Smith in April 1979 when we spent 2 weeks at Ellis Unit of the Texas Department of Corrections working on a film and a book about life on death row (Jackson & Christian, 1979, 1980). He had been there since October 9, 1978, when a Harris County jury convicted him of killing Roy A. Deputter, who tried to interfere with Jack's holdup of Corky's Corner convenience store in Pasadena, Texas, on January 7 of the same year. Jack had previously received a 7-year sentence for robbery and assault (1955) and a life sentence for robbery by assault (1960; paroled 1977). He attempted to escape in 1963.

Jack died of cancer in the medical facility of Estelle Unit of the Texas Department of Criminal Justice on April 8, 2016. He had been brought to Estelle from death row, which is now located on the Polunsky Unit, 50.9 miles southeast of Estelle. He was 78 years old and in his 38th year on death row. He had been sick with cancer for several years by the time of his final move to Estelle.

Jerome Lee Hamilton, Jack's partner in the holdup, testified against Jack and, in return, received a life sentence. Jerome was paroled in February 2004. That is not uncommon in capital cases in Texas when two individuals are accused of equal responsibility for a felonious killing: One testifies against the other and after a while is set free; the other is given a death sentence and is subsequently executed, commuted to life-without-parole, dies or is murdered in prison, or in rare instances, is exonerated.

Three prisoners on Texas death row (Clarence Jordan, Harvey Earvin, Raymond Riles) were, by a few months, there longer than Jack, but he was the oldest resident of the row. When Jack was sent to death row, it was located on the Ellis Unit of what was then called the Texas Department of Corrections (the prisons are now part of the Texas Department of Criminal Justice). Ellis is 13.2 miles northeast of Huntsville, Texas, home of the administrative offices of the prison system and the Huntsville Unit, which everyone calls "The Walls." The Huntsville Unit has that name because it is the only prison in the system bounded by a wall rather than chain-link fences and concertina razor wire. The Walls was and remains the location of the death house—a row of six cells to which inmates were moved before their execution—and the killing room, with the gurney and elaborate system of tubes that delivers to the veins of condemned prisoners the drug cocktail Texas uses for executions.

Having the killing apparatus in one place and death row in another means that the prison officials putting someone to death meet that prisoner for the first time the day of the execution. It is more work to haul the condemned from another unit to be killed, but the process is far easier on the staff because the people who know the person being put down are not party to the event, and the people doing it are not familiar with the person they are killing.

In 1999, death row moved to the Allan B. Polunsky Unit, 44.8 miles east of Huntsville. The ostensible reason was that three men had, the year before, escaped death row on Ellis, but not one of the three made it off the prison grounds. The real reason was that Polunsky was the Texas prison system's supermax, and the officials in charge wanted its crown jewel to be the max within the max: death row.

The Polunsky Unit was originally to have been named the Terrell Unit, after Dallas insurance executive Charles Terrell, but when he learned that the prison would be the location of the new death row, he requested his name not be used in connection with it. So the prison system renamed Ramsey III Unit in honor of Terrell and the new unit after Allan B. Polunsky, a former chairman of the Texas Department of Criminal Justice.

From the condemned men's point of view, there are two changes resulting from the move of death row from Ellis to Polunsky. The first is the length of the drive to the death house at The Walls: With Polunsky being nearly 45 miles from Huntsville, the condemned man's last ride is a good deal longer than the 13-mile trip from Ellis (women under death sentences are kept at another prison entirely). The other is the condition of confinement: Polunsky is far more brutal and vicious.

On Ellis, the condemned were kept in regular cells on the two sides of Cellblock J. One side of the block—Row J-23—had been populated when Texas killed with the electric chair, so there were no electric outlets or lights within the cells. The theory was that because Texas killed with electricity, the condemned had to be prevented from committing suicide by electricity. All the transparent windows on J-23 (the last row in the prison, so it had a view all the way to the cyclone fence and guard picket and beyond) had been replaced with frosted glass. No one remembered why.

By the time there were enough prisoners to start populating J-21, Texas was killing by lethal injection, so those cells had electric lights and electric outlets for fans and such. And the windows were clear glass. After

J-21 began holding condemned prisoners, broken windows on J-23 were replaced by clear glass panes.

Prisoners on J-23 and J-21 were allowed out of their cells one at a time for showers and in groups of 19 for three 90-minute recreation periods a week. If the weather was good and the ground dry, they could go outside to a small exercise yard. If the weather was bad and the ground wet, they went to a dayroom with four steel tables, each of which had four welded steel seats. The dayrooms also had water fountains. In the day room they could talk and play dominoes; in the yard, they could play volleyball or sit on benches and play chess. Opposite the cells were eight television sets bolted to the walls between the windows. During the day they would play soaps; in the evening they would mostly play sports.

In their cells, they could not see people in adjoining cells directly, but they all had mirrors they could stick through the bars of their cell doors to have conversations with people on either side. They would play chess on hand-made chessboards suspended by string between the cells and dominoes on blankets on the walkways.

Jack, who was in Cell 18 of Row 1 of J-23, would work on his case with Mark Fields, who was in Cell 19. Mark was important to him because Jack could not read. He had documents about his case, but he needed Mark to tell him what they said.

Everything changed with the move to Polunsky. There is no more group recreation: Individuals are allowed out one at a time in a small walled yard. The yard has two cages, so if someone else is out, that provides a brief opportunity for conversation. It is the prisoners' only such opportunity. There is no more communication with people going by on the walkway or in the next cell: Everyone is in a single cell with a solid door, broken only for a small slot through which food trays come and go and hands are thrust to be handcuffed in case of the rare visit. There is no looking at the outside because the only window is another narrow slit high on the wall; it lets some light in, but there is no way to see anything through it. There is no television. For most prisoners, there is no radio and the few who are allowed radios only get occasional reception because of all the layers of steel and concrete surrounding them. Most prisoners are allowed no more than one book. No family pictures can go up on the walls.

Jack told the Associated Press in 2001, "I feel that the system is waiting for me to pass away of old age. I'm angry at the justice system, at the courts for wasting taxpayers' money for giving me this hospitality" (Associated Press, 2016, para. 3). The last legal action of importance in Jack's case was in 2008, when the U.S. Supreme Court rejected an appeal of his 1978 conviction. Since then, he waited to be killed or to die. His body got him before the State of Texas did.

Jack was right. There was no reason to keep a dying old man in silent solitary confinement as his body wound down. There is no reason to keep the other 216 men on death row of Polunsky prison in such hideously cruel conditions. The prison officials cite security; they always cite security. But death row murderers differ in only one regard from non–death row prisoners serving time for murder: They got the death penalty, and the others did not. The severity of the crime has nothing to do with it; the extent of their criminal career has nothing to do with it. It is entirely a function of the county where the trial was held and whether the defendant had enough money for retained counsel.

Texas and Oklahoma have accounted for nearly half (45%) of all U.S. executions between 1977 and 2016 (Death Penalty Information Center, 2017b). Death row conditions in both prisons are similar. Texas and Oklahoma prisoners wait out their days under conditions that by comparison make the daily routine of a medieval monk festive. Oklahoma death row prisoners are in their two-man cells 23 hours a day. No natural light or fresh air reaches the cells. They are allowed three showers a week and 3 to 5 hours of recreation in a closed concrete yard. All meals are eaten in the cells. Most prisoners have no work, educational, or vocational programs, though a few have correspondence studies.

Most other death rows are not much better: 93% of all condemned prisoners in the United States are in solitary confinement cells 23 to 24 hours a day (American Civil Liberties Union [ACLU], 2013). The conditions under which people are kept on death row in Texas have been described by the United Nations General Assembly (2011) as torture. The

UN is right. Texas does it to prove it is tough; it gets away with it because the Supreme Court has turned a blind eye to what goes on there.

LIFE WITHOUT PAROLE

We wrote earlier that death row prisoners are the only American penitentiary prisoners for whom time does not count. Time does not count for political prisoners at Guantanamo, and neither does it count for detainees in mental institutions. Neither of those populations is in the penitentiary system; they are another discussion. Neither does time count for pretrial detainees who could not make or were not allowed bail. If they are convicted, the pretrial detention time may be subtracted from the sentence; if they are not convicted, that pretrial detention is just time stolen from their lives. They are not so much in the criminal system as in limbo at its periphery.

But what about people doing life without parole (LWOP)? They are sentenced not to a period of time but to a change in condition: death within prison. Their condition is nonetheless qualitatively different from that of death row prisoners. They can hope for a change in the law or a reduction in their sentence. Neither is probable—more LWOP sentences have been handed down in recent years, not fewer, and the minuscule amount of legal assistance for convicted prisoners primarily goes to those facing execution. But either is always possible.

Nonetheless, the difference in the conditions of imprisonment is profound. From the outside, a prison sentence is the punishment. But once inside, there is a great spectrum of ways of doing time. Prison is a place to which someone is sentenced; once there, it is a place where people live. Most jurisdictions have a wide variety of carceral structures, some easy, some not. Some units within a prison system permit a great deal of movement and interaction; others permit little of either. A prisoner serving LWOP can, depending on the jurisdiction, do easy time or hard time. For those prisoners, behavior, performance, and relation with the guards and administrators count. In most states, LWOP prisoners serve time under exactly the same conditions as other prisoners.

A 2011 report for the Connecticut Legislature (Reinhart, 2011) compared prison conditions of condemned prisoners and prisoners serving an LWOP sentence:

1. Death row inmates are held in single cells while life without parole inmates are in double celled housing,
2. death row inmates have two hours of recreation outside of their cells six days a week and are always by themselves while life without parole inmates are usually outside their cells six to seven hours a day and can be with other inmates,
3. both types of inmates have access to the commissary but death row inmates face more restrictions on the types of property they can have,
4. death row inmates eat meals alone in their cells while life without parole inmates eat in their cells or in a chow hall or day room,
5. both types of inmates have access to programs and services but fewer programs are available at Northern [the unit housing death row] than at other prisons,
6. death row inmates may have work assignments that are restricted to the death row housing unit while life without parole inmates have more opportunities including industry jobs, and
7. death row inmates are allowed up to three non-contact visits per week that are limited to one hour each while life without parole inmates may qualify for contact visits and are usually allowed at least two visits per week of at least one hour.

In addition, the directives require death row inmates to be escorted by at least one staff person and are placed in restraints when moving outside their cell. Directives do not specify these procedures for inmates sentenced to life without parole. (para. 4)

The report expanded on that final item (Reinhart, 2011). When death row prisoners are out of their cells, they are

1. handcuffed behind the back for routine out-of-cell movement including showers, recreation, social visits, social phone calls, using dayrooms (restraints are removed once the inmate is

     secured in the area and the process is reversed to return the inmate
     to his cell);

2. fully restrained in front (handcuffs, leg irons, and tether chain) for professional visits including attorney, medical, mental health, and related visits and video conferencing which require staff being secured in an area with the inmate (restraints remain on at all times); and

3. fully restrained behind the back (handcuffs, leg irons, and tether chain) for out-of-unit movement within the facility except when a medical or dental procedure requires full restraints in the front (restraints remain on at all times). ("Movement Outside Cell," para. 1)

Connecticut is a liberal Northeastern state that repealed its death penalty in 2012. That discrepancy between the way condemned prisoners and LWOP prisoners spend time is the same, or worse, throughout the nation.

NUMBERS AND THE DEATH ROW SYNDROME

According to a Bureau of Justice Statistics report (Snell, 2014), 8,466 death sentences were meted out in the United States between 1973, the year following the Supreme Court's invalidation of capital punishment laws in *Furman v. Georgia* (1972), and the end of 2013. Those sentences resulted in 1,359 executions (16%). During that interval, 509 deaths resulted from suicide, murder, or natural causes (6%), and 3,619 prisoners were removed from sentence of death owing to a judicially invalidated sentence, conviction, or capital statute, plus a few unknown reasons (43%). Consequently, 2,979 prisoners were left on the row (35%).

A prisoner who left death row, therefore, was more than 3 times as likely to leave for reasons other than execution. With the recent decline in executions (20 in 2016, compared with 39 in 2013 and a high in the modern death penalty era of 98 in 1999; Death Penalty Information Center, 2017a), that discrepancy is now even greater.

The average elapsed time from sentence to execution in 2013 was listed as 186 months: 15.5 years (Snell, 2014). The actual average time is longer; the Bureau of Justice Statistics dates elapsed time only since the most recent death sentence, and many death row inmates are sentenced more than once.

The number also undercounts suicide: It includes only death row prisoners who kill themselves. It does not include death row prisoners who abandon their appeals. The ACLU (2013) estimated that more than 10% of the executions since 1976 were prisoners who sought execution: "Facing isolated conditions, helplessness, despair, and the anxiety and anguish of waiting to die for years on end, many death row prisoners take control in the only way they know: they drop their legal appeals and 'volunteer' for execution" (p. 8; see also Chapter 6, this volume).

Those same conditions exact a cruel price from all death row inmates—those who are executed and those who are not, those who go into population and the ones set free, the guilty and the innocent. Rates of troubling personality disorders, anxiety, paranoia, depression, delusions, and suicide are far greater among prisoners on death row than prisoners in population. The pendency of death accounts for only part of that. The greater factor is life on the row.

FOUR MEN WE KNEW AT ELLIS

One prisoner we met on death row, Kerry Max Cook, had three trials. Two resulted in death sentences; another was declared a mistrial. In 1997, before the start of a fourth trial, Kerry agreed to a deal that would let him plead no contest in exchange for release. "The lawyer told me 'We're sure to win this one,'" Kerry said to us. "I said to him, 'That's what they told me the last three times.'" In each trial, more of the prosecution's evidence was tossed out: testimony about a jailhouse confession by someone charged with a felony, whose felony charges evaporated immediately after he testified; testimony from a fingerprint "expert" who said that Kerry's fingerprint found outside the crime scene was less than 24 hours old (it is impossible to determine the age of a fingerprint; see Starr, 2014), and so on. But, after 20 years at Ellis and then at Polunsky, Kerry was not up to taking the risk one more time. Sometime after his release, DNA evidence cleared Kerry of the crime, but because he had taken that plea, Texas refused to compensate him for the lost years. While still at Ellis, frustrated because no one would listen to him, he attempted to amputate his penis. "People often ask me," he said to us, "'How did you keep from going crazy in there?' I tell them, 'I don't know that I did,'" (Kerry is one of the ex-condemned prisoners featured in the 2002 play, *The Exonerated*; Blank & Jensen, 2003).

Thelette Brandon argued every night with two people he insisted lived in the pipe chase—the service passageway between the two sides of the cellblock that houses water and sewer pipes and electrical conduits. At the back of every cell was a small air vent to the pipe chase that was supposed to help airflow in the cells. Thelette and his two antagonists would sometimes talk, sometimes shout. Everyone else on the row heard only Thelette. One day, coming back from a shower, he smashed his coffee glass—an emptied instant coffee jar—against the cell of a young inmate who was a good friend of his. That is one way you blind someone in the penitentiary: smash the glass against the bars and scores of glass shards fly toward anyone standing at the other side. When he was back in his cell, I asked him why he had tried to blind Donnie. "I don't know, Bruce, I just don't know. I was trying to blind Wolf." Wolf was an inmate in another cell. All day long, Thelette rocked back and forth in his cell: If he was standing, he rocked from foot to foot; if he was sitting on the toilet eating from the steel tray that had been slid under his cell door, he rocked from side to side. One of the porters on the row told me, "Brandon wasn't like that when he got here. It took two years for him to get like that."

We do not remember the names of the third and fourth prisoners because we never spoke. One slept almost all the time. Night and day, he would sleep. Sometimes he would get up for meals; sometimes he would not. He never made eye contact with anyone; he never watched television; he never wrote letters or read anything. He just slept, used the toilet, and ate some of the food on the trays. The other was always stark naked, sitting on the concrete floor or standing at the bars. Sometimes he was shivering; sometimes he was not.

There are more we could tell you about, but you get the idea. And that was when they were on Ellis, where they could talk, hang out a little while in the day room or exercise yard, watch television, hand things from cell to cell. We can only imagine when happened to them when they were moved to Polunsky, where there was no television, no conversation, contact with almost no one but guards, and most of that through a slot in the solid steel door.

THE QUESTION WE ARE LEFT WITH

What or whose interests does death row serve? We have never met a prison administrator or death row guard who has said death row prisoners are any more dangerous than any other murderers in a maximum-security prison. No one argues for the malign effects death row conditions have on the psyche of most people confined there. Most people confined there are not and will not be executed; they will go into general population, or they will go free. Why torture and twist them?

Death row is not a creature of law. Conditions there do not result from legislative or judicial action. Death row is an artifact of prison administration. As was true in Connecticut, prison administrators decide on differential treatments for condemned prisoners and everyone else. Perhaps it continues to exist because the courts have been so focused on cases of condemned prisoners who argue the validity of their conviction or sentence, that they have not taken time to examine the conditions under which all condemned prisoners live. The courts should take a serious look at this time that is out of time, this life that is out of life.

REFERENCES

American Civil Liberties Union. (2013). *A death before dying: Solitary confinement on death row*. Retrieved from https://www.aclu.org/files/assets/deathbeforedying-report.pdf

Associated Press. (2016, April 12). Texas's oldest death row inmate dies of natural causes after 38 years waiting to be executed. *Mail Online*. Retrieved from http://www.dailymail.co.uk/news/article-3531012/Oldest-inmate-Texas-death-row-dies-natural-causes.html

Blank, J., & Jensen, E. (2003). *The exonerated*. London, England: Faber & Faber.

Death Penalty Information Center. (2017a). *Executions by year*. Retrieved from http://www.deathpenaltyinfo.org/executions-year

Death Penalty Information Center. (2017b). *Number of executions by state and region since 1976*. Retrieved from http://www.deathpenaltyinfo.org/number-executions-state-and-region-1976

Furman v. Georgia, 408 U.S. 238 (1972).

Jackson, B. (Producer & Director), & Christian, D. (Director). (1979). *Death row* [Motion picture]. United States: Documentary Research.

Jackson, B., & Christian, D. (1980). *Death row*. Boston, MA: Beacon Press.

Reinhart, C. (2011). *Prison conditions for death row and life without parole inmates*. Retrieved from https://www.cga.ct.gov/2011/rpt/2011-R-0178.htm

Snell, T. L. (2014). *Capital punishment in the United States, 2013—Statistical tables*. Washington, DC: Bureau of Justice Statistics. Retrieved from https://www.bjs.gov/content/pub/pdf/cp13st.pdf

Starr, M. (2014, June 4). Researchers discover how to tell the age of a fingerprint. *C/NET*. Retrieved from https://www.cnet.com/news/researchers-discover-how-to-tell-the-age-of-a-fingerprint/

United Nations General Assembly. (2011). *Torture and other cruel, inhuman or degrading treatment or punishment*. Retrieved from http://solitaryconfinement.org/uploads/SpecRapTortureAug2011.pdf

9

Spending Time on Death Row: A Case Study

Gareth Evans, Eleanor Price, Amy Ludlow,
Ruth Armstrong, and Shadd Maruna,
with Jonathan Reed

In 1978, Jonathan (Jon) Bruce Reed was convicted and condemned to death for the rape and murder of flight attendant Wanda Jean Wadle, at her northeast Dallas apartment. Jon has always maintained that he did not commit this offense[1] and his conviction has been overturned twice—first in 1983 and again in 2009. In 2011, after DNA evidence excluded him from the sexual assault element of the offense, Jon was tried again and found guilty of murder, on the basis of 30-year-old eyewitness testimony. The rape charge was dropped. Having stood trial for his life three times, for different elements of the same offense, Jon is now serving a life sentence. He continues to assert his innocence. DNA testing of new evidence, found at the scene of the murder, is currently ongoing.

Jon spent over 30 years of his life on death row in Texas. During that time, Jon's main contact with the outside world was through correspondence

---

[1] Jon pled guilty to another, noncapital offense that was the genesis of the arrest that led to him being charged with the Wadle rape and murder.

http://dx.doi.org/10.1037/0000084-010
Living on Death Row: The Psychology of Waiting to Die, H. Toch, J. R. Acker, and V. M. Bonventre (Editors)
Copyright © 2018 by the American Psychological Association. All rights reserved.

with family, friends, and lawyers. It is a subset of these letters from Jon, sent between 2000 and 2009, that form the basis of this chapter. This case study of time on death row is based on our analysis of correspondence between Jon Reed and Ruth Armstrong. Jon met Ruth in 2000. Their correspondence began in August 2000 and continues to this day. In this chapter, we draw on their correspondence during Jon's final 9 years on death row, before he won his second appeal and was moved to Dallas County Jail to fight his third capital trial. Through this unique data set, we have explored how Jon experienced time on death row and, more profound, how he was able to survive. Directed by Jon's account, our core ambition has been to shed light on one man's relationship with, and through, time on death row. We consider what might be distinctive about Jon's experiences of time on death row, compared with experiences of time in prison when death is not part of a person's sentence.

Jon's account of time and survival on death row is the lifeblood of this chapter. We, Jon's coauthors, have brought quite different perspectives and life experiences to the writing of this chapter. Our interests combine the personal and sociological. They are personal because some of us know Jon as a friend, some for as long as 17 years, and others of us know, from personal experience, the pains of spending time in prison ourselves. Further, they are sociological because we all believe that Jon's account of living in and through time on death row tells us important and valuable things about the experience and effects of this form of sanction and about our capacity and motivation for life, even in the most unlikely or hostile of places. We recognize that Jon's situation and situatedness has many elements that are unique: He has maintained his innocence; he has overturned his conviction twice; and he has spent a long time on death row in Texas, a particularly proactive death penalty state. However, in terms of the routines and realities of life on death row that Jon describes in this chapter, his experiences are likely to have many similarities with the other unique individuals also struggling to survive this sentence in Texas and perhaps beyond.

We start by contextualizing Jon's experiences within the existing literature about the meaning of time, the experiences of time in prison, and what we know about how people cope with time as one of the pains of imprisonment. In our review of the literature, we pay particular attention to studies of long-term imprisonment and temporal distinctions that have been drawn to explain experiences of time and strategies for coping with time across different stages of a prison sentence. However, in the presentation of our analysis on time we move away from this focus on the stages of a sentence to understand Jon's relationship with time on death row. Instead, we draw on concepts developed in the sociological literature about time to consider Jon's actions, the ways he makes life meaningful, and his feelings in and through time. After outlining how Jon's letters were analyzed, we share some of our recent correspondence with Jon in which he reflected explicitly on his experiences of time and everyday life on death row. Our hope is that this provides some personal and institutional context for data from Jon's older letters that follow.

Our overarching argument is that serving time on death row while maintaining innocence is uniquely precarious and precious, a double-edged sword that changes the experience of time, making it simultaneously something that is treasured and torturous. We describe these differences in light of the realities of daily life on death row, and through this lens, we consider how Jon's relationship with time is both a component of, and mediated through, his relationship with others on death row and beyond. We end by admitting how working together to craft this piece has pushed us to reflect on the assumptions of time embedded in our methods and how collaborating in research with people in prison can helpfully challenge ingrained assumptions about how we produce good scholarship, as well as how we use it.

TIME AND PRISON TIME

The concept of *time* is both utterly simple and highly complex. Chronological time or *clock time*, measured in minutes and seconds, has become intrinsic to modern society as a currency of industrialization. As Barbara Adam (1990) wrote in *Time and Social Theory*, "Clock time is, after all, the one aspect of time that all scientists [social or otherwise] use" (p. 7).

However, this tangible and measurable form of chronological time is far from the only sense of time we experience. Schroeder (1976) contrasted *chronological time* with what he called *ontological time*, or what time means to individuals in the abstract. Ontological time describes our existential relationship with time as an aspect of our temporal identity and is a framework for giving meaning to the times of our life. A further distinction is *experiential time*, or how a particular unit of time feels to different people and how they engage with it. We often think of how we experience time through spatial or physical metaphors—time "drags," "stands still" or else "flies by," needs to be "found" or is "lost." These terms, which describe a physical position or an experience of time, are chronologically untrue in measurable clock time but capture something crucial about the essence of time (Adam, 1990).

In prison, time is equated with punishment. A convicted prisoner is "given time" and "does time." Although a complex interaction of personal and institutional factors cause individual experiences of imprisonment to vary (Flanagan, 1981), studies of long-term imprisonment (e.g., Flanagan, 1981; Hulley, Crewe, & Wright, 2016; B. Richards, 1978), including sentences of life without parole (Leigey & Ryder, 2015), have found considerable consistency between the experiences of time by prisoners, despite different penal contexts, climates, and locations. Time in prison is often experienced as monotonous (Cope, 2003) and featureless, with one day resembling another (Wahidin, 2006). Consequently, time is experienced as "meaningless, empty and boring" (Meisenhelder, 1985, p. 45). Unlike time in the outside world, time in prison is experienced less as a "resource to be *used, spent* or *saved*, but rather an object to be managed" (Wahidin & Tate, 2005, p. 70, italics added).

Previous studies have described the different ways in which people in prison cope with the pains of time (see especially O'Donnell, 2014). In a study of young people in prison, Cope (2003) found that for this group, resisting the control imposed on them by the prison was one way to control the passing of time. Similarly, Crewe, Hulley, and Wright (2016) found that people in the early stages of long sentences resisted prison routines they found "unbearably repetitive," although this research also found that in later stages of imprisonment, individuals created ways to customize their routines within the prison's regime. Zamble (1992) recognized that people often face specific difficulties at the beginning of their sentence but argued that "the constancy of the prison environment leads to a slow and gradual amelioration" of these pains (p. 420). This kind of adaptation to the repetitive routines of imprisonment has been described as psychologically beneficial because it makes each day predictable and therefore less anxiety inducing (Cohen & Taylor, 1972). Even for the wrongfully convicted (Grounds, 2005), and those sentenced to death or life without parole (Johnson & McGunigall-Smith, 2008), research has suggested that experiences of prison routines and regimes can improve over time, as prisoners become accustomed to coping with adversity and living in an "extended present" rather than engaging with a painful past or a longed-for future (Cohen & Taylor, 1972; Meisenhelder, 1985; O'Donnell, 2014).

Time in prison is experienced as a loss, but this loss can be felt and managed in many different ways. Time in prison can feel like it is standing still (Wahidin, 2006), and some seek to resist the drudgery of the daily regime to minimize this pain. Others engage in a process of "cryogenic suspension" (Wahidin, 2006), psychologically refusing to experience time in prison as a part of life outside, as a way to limit the pains of losing time through punishment (Cope, 2003). Suspending life outside and gradually submitting to life within the routines of the prison can serve to ameliorate not only the chronological pains of time in prison but also the ontological pains of finding meaning in life within prison. In a study of long-term patients in a residential hospital, Calkins (1970) found that patients began to disregard traditional time-markers in the outside world in favor of frequent events specific to their environment, such as "noting the flow of patients through the institution" (p. 492).

This shift of focus from time outside to time inside echoes Calkins's (1970) distinction between linear and "cyclical" time, in which "the present may be engulfing, and the future, unpredictable" (p. 490). Her analysis is reflected in O'Donnell's (2014) assertion that many long-term prisoners cope with time in prison through reimagining their temporal context in a way that accounts for the absence of an imaginable future. O'Donnell argued that long periods of enforced solitude can bring about a "reorientation," which involves "resetting temporal horizons so that the focus is on the present" because

> dwelling on the past and any associated remorse or regret, or obsessing about a future life that is unlikely to arrive in the wished-for format, introduces a degree of fretfulness that is inimical to a successful navigation of the temporal landscape. (p. 186)

This, he argued, gives "the solitary prisoner who can achieve immersion in the present . . . an important advantage over his or her environment" (O'Donnell, 2014, p. 186; see also Flanagan, 1981; Zamble, 1992).

This more inward focus can also help to mitigate against the pain of diminishing connections with the world outside as friends and family contacts outside of prison dwindle over time (Hulley et al., 2016; Johnson & McGunigall-Smith, 2008; Leigey & Ryder, 2015). Writing in a nonpenal context, Sennett (2016) drew analogies with the natural world to argue that borderlines of interaction in natural sciences are the most intense zones in which "time is productive of evolutionary change," noting that a more closed boundary "establishes closure through inactivity" ("Borders and Boundaries," para. 2), but that eventually, when evolutionary change becomes more stagnant in time, things wither and die. Life in the present within prison and withdrawal from a more connected, more "borderline" existence with people and life outside of prison can make time more manageable, but this may come at an existential cost.

The experience of time in prison is unlikely to be static and may shift throughout a sentence. For instance, in their recent study of long-term imprisonment, Crewe et al. (2016) described a shift from experiencing time as a form of "stasis" or "stagnation" in the early stages of a sentence to a sense of time as "a resource to be harnessed" (p. 529) in the mid to late stages.[2]

---

[2] The study involved people in prison with life sentences with a minimum of 15 years to serve before they could be considered for parole, who were sentenced when they were 25 years old or younger. Early-stage participants were within the first 4 years of their sentence at the time the study began and had a mean age of 22 years. Mid-stage participants were at the mid-point of their individual sentence (at least 7.5 years served) plus or minus 2 years, with a mean age of 30 years. Late-stage participants were at the end of their sentence period (at least 15 years served) plus or minus 2 years, with a mean age of 46 years. Prisoners with whole life sentences and no prospect of release were not included.

They noted the ontological basis of this shift as "a realization that effort was better spent 'thinking about what is ahead,' than on reminiscence and regret for a past that was no longer salient" (Crewe et al., 2016, p. 529). In their analysis, a tangible sense of heading toward a brighter future gave a different meaning to, and way of experiencing, present time, which meant that prisoners began to "swim with the tide," rather than "against it." Because all the participants in this study had the prospect of release, their findings are not straightforwardly applicable to the situation in which there is no "tide," but rather only the threat of an impending tsunami in the form of execution.

In an analysis of the same data, Hulley et al. (2016) found that the pains of imprisonment associated with their composite measure of time[3] were particularly acute for prisoners in the early stages of their sentence. Although studies have shown that the pains of imprisonment decrease over time, this is not because the pains of imprisonment change or diminish but because people in prison develop strategies to cope with the deprivations, separations, and frustrations of incarceration (Leigey & Ryder, 2015). Whereas Crewe and colleagues (2016) highlighted some of the more positive facets of coping, such as turning to faith or spiritual practices to manage a sense of powerlessness (p. 12) and eschewing "sentiments of bitterness and desperation" to psychologically survive (p. 22), in a subsequent analysis the authors also described the more sinister underbelly of inward-looking "emotional numbing" (Liem & Kunst, 2013, p. 335) as a feature of coping with a long prison sentence (Hulley et al., 2016, p. 787).

Whether the strategy to cope with time in prison is to resist or embrace internal institutional regimes and time zones, the driving motivation seems similar, namely, the desire to invest one's energies in occupying a temporal zone within which one can meaningfully exist. The luxury of psychologically buffering the pain of lost time by suspending time until release is arguably less available to long-term prisoners, who fear deterioration, as well as the loss of friends, family, and self-identity, while in prison (Cohen & Taylor, 1972), and by extension, is less affordable still to people who are under sentence of death.

---

[3] These were made up of three dimensions: feeling that you are losing the best years of your life, feeling that the length of your sentence is unfair, and thinking about the amount of time that you might have to serve.

In the following analysis, we explore Jon's experience of time on death row and the forms of coping that living in these circumstances of extreme incapacitation have demanded. We describe his actions (his chronological experience of time), his efforts to find meaning (his ontological experience of time), and how he negotiated his feelings (his emotional experiences of time). Before this, we outline the methods we used in this study and use Jon's account to contextualize the day-to-day realities of life on death row in Texas to situate his experiences in their context.

METHODS

We recognize that our data set is unique. Not only do the letters that form the data underpinning our analysis describe Jon's experiences of time on death row, but they also describe those experiences as they are unfolding. This is especially valuable because most existing literature about experiences of time in prison involves retrospective interviewing whereby individuals are asked to reflect back on how they have felt at certain points in their incarceration, as opposed to chronicling these experiences as they occur. Also, the correspondence that forms our "data set" was not written with any academic analysis in mind. The correspondence consists of letters written between two friends. Unquestionably, Jon omits some aspects of his experiences from his letters, particularly perhaps some of the more profound pains of his existence. It also seems probable that what Jon corresponded about with Ruth in 2000 when they first met had developed by 2009 due to the deepening of their friendship as well as the passing of time.

Vannier (2016) used testimonies in letter form to understand the experiences of women serving life without parole in California. Reflecting on her data set, she wrote, "Doing research using prisoners' letters makes it difficult to rectify misunderstandings and misinterpretation. . . . Letters can also prompt different, at times irreconcilable, accounts of experiences of punishment, none of which produce an absolute or generalizable 'truth'" (p. 330). Despite these limitations, she argued that "letters have the propensity to include authentic and rich details that only those who experience a phenomenon can relate" (p. 330).

The task of analyzing and writing together has not been straightforward, not least because we were a geographically disparately located group, and two of the research team were serving time in prisons on different sides of the Atlantic Ocean at the point of analysis. Much of our work was conducted within a prison in England, with all the technological, security, and logistical constraints of that environment.[4] Collectively, harnessing our varied strengths and experiences, we hope to have represented, at least to some extent, one man's experiences of being on death row.

There were approximately 400 letters from Jon in our data set. To analyze the letters, the correspondence was organized into batches that were, as closely as possible, chronologically ordered. We worked independently to generate themes from our analysis of the data (see Birks & Mills, 2015; Vannier, 2016), then tested these themes for interrater consistency across the different coders. We corresponded with Jon about emerging themes to include his reflections on this analysis, and in November 2016, we asked Jon to share with us some more detailed and focused reflections about his experiences on death row so they could further inform this chapter. We draw from this reflective account to describe the context of life in prison on death row before drawing on our analysis of Jon's letters to describe his experiences of time within this context.[5] In all quotations any underlining or emphasis replicates the original.

DAILY LIFE ON DEATH ROW

At the time of Jon's reflective account in November 2016, there were 242 men on death row in Texas, all of whom were held in the Polunsky Unit, just outside Livingston. This is the lowest number of men on death row in Texas since the 1980s. Before 1923, counties in Texas were responsible for their own executions, but in 1923, the state of Texas authorized

---

[4] We are very grateful to the governor and staff of the prison in England that provided office space and a locked filing cabinet to facilitate analysis of the correspondence undertaken by one researcher currently serving a prison sentence and one visiting the prison to work collaboratively on this task within the prison environment.

[5] Where Jon's letters are referenced, they are dated. The reflective account was written November 23, 2016. When the reflective account is cited it is not dated.

the use of the electric chair and ordered that all executions be carried out by the state in Huntsville. In 1928, death row was located in the East Building of the Huntsville Unit, nicknamed "The Walls." Executions are still carried out here to this day. In 1965, death row was moved to the Ellis Unit and remained there until 1999–2000 when, with a growing death row population and a limited capacity and following an escape from death row in Ellis in 1998, it was relocated to the maximum security Polunsky Unit.

For Jon, this history meant that he knew two death rows: the Ellis Unit from 1979 to 2000 and Polunsky from 2000 to 2009. Geographical location was not the only difference between these two prisons. In Ellis, Jon worked in the jewelry and leather shops, he could watch films on a communal television, and he enjoyed much more free association time. He wrote,

> [Life in Ellis] showed that 90% of death row guys can live in a more open setting and be secure, safe and actually prosper, until their cases take their course. But the powers don't want that. They want to punish and harass guys, every day, along the way. Because they were embarrassed for a moment in 1998 [when the escape happened].

In Polunsky, men on death row are held in single cells and kept in nearly total isolation. They do not work, attend education programs, or worship communally.

Ruth met Jon in 2000, so all of the letters reviewed for this chapter were written while he was on death row in Polunsky. Within the Polunsky Unit, death row is housed in the infamous "12 Building." This building is made up of six "pods"—A through F. F-Pod is the segregation or punishment area, but all the cells in 12 Building are designed for "administrative segregation." All cells are built the same—5.6 meters (17.9 feet) square, with slit windows high up the wall and a concrete door with a "bean slot" for food, to cuff each man before he is removed from the cell, and to uncuff him after he is returned. Each pod is divided into six sections, again, A through F. There are two rows in each section and seven cells per row. This means that 84 men can be housed in each pod; a total death row capacity of 504 cells. In the center of these 84 cells is a "picket" area for staff. The picket area has a view to the recreation yard that joins the pod and the "day room" within the pod where prisoners exercise alone.

Jon described how all the men who have a date for their execution are housed in A-Pod: "I spent many years on A-Pod. A mixed blessing. I could say good-bye to friends, but I had to see guys leave crying, with no hope in their eyes, cursing, posturing, fighting or going meekly."

Across all the different pods there are three levels of administrative segregation. Level 1 prisoners receive the most "privileges" (e.g., visits, radios, hygiene products, reading materials), but these can be removed for noncompliance with the regime. F-Pod is the punishment section. Prisoners housed on F-Pod get reduced privileges. According to Jon,

> Three days of rec. [recreation], rather than five, or less [if they are] on "Level 3." Can only buy limited hygiene products . . . and limited correspondence items. Can't buy any food stuffs. And less visits, if one gets visits. And no special visits.[6] Even if one has a date your level determines how many visits you can get.

Recreation is normally 1 hour per day, and visits allowance is one per week, plus visits from ministers and lawyers. Privileges can also be restricted during a "lockdown," either unplanned in response to a security concern or planned due to the likelihood of short staff, such as at Thanksgiving.

Routines on death row rarely vary from one day to the next, save for slight alterations when someone is being taken away for execution: "The only routine to change when guys had dates was to stop traffic. No one moved until the man was in the van and gone. Whether he left from the cell, or from his visit." Timings on death row bear little resemblance to routines in life outside prison:

> Breakfast is usually 2:30–3:30 am. Lunch at 9:30–11 a.m. Supper about 3:30–4.30 p.m. . . . Food is starch filled. Lots of potatoes and

---

[6] Special visits are longer visits permitted once a month for 4 hours each time, on 2 consecutive days, for visitors who have traveled more than 300 miles.

corn, some sort of beans at every meal, lunch and supper. Pork or beef or ham casseroles prevail. Usually 2 veggies a meal. Usually chicken once a week. . . . Diet line [people with dietary requirements, often due to diabetes] is supposed to have ham steak or pork chops 4–5 times a month, but it is usually replaced with pork patties. . . . [Food is brought] in "7 tray" carriers. Usually 2 at a time. One officer brings the drink. You are supposed to stand away from the "bean hole," i.e., slot, as it is opened. Tray is put in there, officer steps back. You get tray, put down your cup, step back. Officer pours, steps back, you get cup and slot is closed. Some may pick this time to "jack the slot." Put your arms out and won't let it be closed until "Rank" [a more senior officer] is brought to talk to you. The officers cannot continue until that slot is closed. I never did this.

This kind of behavior results in a "case"[7] and being put on Level 2 or 3.

Showers are offered every day, but "start early, as they try to get you to refuse."[8] There are 12 showers per pod. Officers make a round, putting one person in each shower, then come back and take each person out, replacing them with someone else:

You are supposed to be stripped (they don't always do it, especially the women. The men are supposed to, but they know who may give them trouble and who won't. Some guys do bring bad treatment on themselves) handing your boxers and towel and soap stuffs to the officers. Put boxers back on. Kneel down with hands behind you—put them out of the slot [in the door] (many have trouble doing this, so shower and rec. less) to be cuffed. Stand. Door opens, officer is to hold your arms as you walk. Put you in shower, take cuffs off through slot.

This procedure is repeated for recreation and for visits, but a person is fully dressed to go to a visit and strip-searched on the way out and back. Men on death row wear white overalls with black letters stating "DR" on

[7] A *case* is an internal disciplinary procedure for an alleged infraction of the prison rules.

[8] Jon's letters describe how some staff chose to offer time out of cell for showers or recreation at unsociable hours very early in the morning in the hope more people would refuse or not respond because they are sleeping, and thus forfeit their opportunity for that day, thereby reducing the workload.

the back. They are permitted one pair of overalls at a time and one jacket in winter. Recreation is permitted for 1 hour per day. Many men on death row refuse the showers and the opportunity to recreate. Jon believes this is partly because of the psychologically and physically painful security routines required for participation. Jon, however, said, "I'd make myself always go to rec., and shower, even if I didn't want to." In adverse weather conditions recreation is offered in dayrooms inside the prison. Jon recalled a small procedural victory through his commitment to exercising these rights when staff had tried to thwart them:

> We were not supposed to go outside—even if you wanted to—if it was raining or below 36°F. One time, the officer was trying to get people to refuse. She would say: "Rec outside, or not at all." It was 28°F and <u>sleeting</u>. Me and Boxcar (I forget his name—God Bless him) suited up to go out [to separate yards]. Thermals, overalls, T-shirts and Jacket. We were going to jack the yard till a Seargent [sic] showed up. (She wouldn't call one). We got lucky. He showed up after 30 mins. I banged on the glass, got him to come out. He asked what the hell we were doing out there! Ruth—I could barely talk! We told him. He said he'd have her put us in dayrooms. . . . But! She left <u>us</u> out there <u>2.5</u> hours!! But, she put all the rest in the dayrooms. Even the ones she had refused.

Life on death row is remarkably solitary. Jon wrote, "I'd go days without very much contact at all." Despite the restrictive geography and regime of life on death row, Jon's reflective account details the lengths to which he and others went to communicate with each other, the limited possibilities for communications with staff, and the potential for communications with others beyond the prison, such as lawyers and visitors. In his reflective account, Jon recalled,

> One could "talk" to guys in other cells. Especially if your open sides faced each other. Holes were dug in backs of walls at times (until the phone fiasco of '08, and ANGLE IRON was put in the corners of every cell). I used to let Fleetwood listen to my radio—with double line headphones—by running the line thru the hole.

There was an ongoing battle between the prison administration's efforts to reduce possibilities for communication and the prisoners' determination to maintain it:

> For years one could throw lines under the doors—from section to section—to pass kites [messages] or mags [magazines]. . . . you could send items to each other like this also . . . [then] they put rubber plates on the bottom of all doors.

Such maneuvers served to keep people in touch with each other even if their cells were farther apart, but they also permitted a small level of industry and economy:

> I kept a library and let guys use books when they wanted. As long as they took care of them. Have to wrap them up to throw from one dayroom to the other, so the covers didn't tear. Then, <u>friends</u> could sell, or trade in, the ones I asked them to pick up! One of the things I did to keep busy, keep reading material, (I always told guys: "IF YOU INTEND TO THROW AWAY ANY BOOKS—GIVE THEM TO ME"), make a few $, and help others.

These were opportunities not just to keep in touch with and show some care for others but also to "hustle" to improve one's quality of life and, perhaps most important, to keep busy and pass the time. However much contact could be restricted, Jon described how it could not be eliminated other than by choice:

> Talking to neighbors through side slots [of doors] was easy. Harder to talk to someone further away, due to Echo Factor. You could yell at them to "Get out there," i.e. catch your line. Then pass whatever. You could talk to guys in the dayroom in front of you. At night, when quiet, you could play chess by calling out your move.

Despite the solitary nature of life on death row, friendships could, therefore, be established:

> When Fleetwood and I were neighbors, and one of us was in the dayroom, we'd play dominoes. Guy in the dayroom shuffles them

on the mat, pick up 9 and put them in the bars, so the person in the cell could see them. He'd [man in the cell] tell you which one to play.

Jon prioritized connections and would always take as long as he could in his visits with his lawyers and the students who interned with them, which is how Ruth met Jon. Despite this, Jon could see how this was not the case for everyone: "I enjoyed all day lawyer visits. Some guys heard what [their lawyer] had to say and went back. At times, people don't want to talk." Even for a socially oriented person, such as Jon, the difficulties of life on death row meant he did not want to be communicable at all times.

EXPERIENCING TIME ON DEATH ROW

In this section, we draw on the letters Jon wrote during his last 9 years on death row. The themes that emerge from Jon's correspondence about time have much in common with existing literature about experiences of time in prison, especially experiences of long-term imprisonment (Crewe et al., 2016; Hulley et al., 2016; Leigey & Ryder, 2015) and solitary confinement (O'Donnell, 2014). However, there are also differences, the most notable of which is that the distinctions that have been drawn in previous literature about changing experiences of time across different stages of long prison sentences are not reflected in Jon's account of time. What has, instead, resonated much more strongly with Jon's letters, is the three-fold distinction between chronological, ontological, and experiential time from the broader sociological literature about time, introduced earlier. We use this three-fold distinction to structure our analysis.

In the first section, we look at Jon's approach to chronological time. Following this, in the second section, we consider how Jon survived ontologically in time. Jon's death sentence meant that he did not have the luxury of being able to "cryogenically suspend" (Wahidin, 2006) his time in prison in the hope of a brighter future. He did not know whether he had a future. We describe instead how Jon used his time to forge and maintain connections with people outside and within the prison. In the final section, we look at how Jon's choice to remain connected with others in the prison and the outside world meant that he had to resist entirely submitting to an "emotional numbness" (Hulley et al., 2016) that would have reduced the pain of living with executions. We show how Jon simultaneously negotiated the incredibly traumatic and the mundane, and the conflation of the two, in the everyday routines of life on death row, where showers, recreation, dominoes, fantasy football, and trading commissary intersect with watching friends and associates walk, or be forcibly taken, to their execution.

ACTIONS—CREATING CHRONOLOGICAL TIME

Jon's letters are choreographed through references to, and documentation about, his legal case. Jon's future beyond his next court date was never certain, and so this was the calendar that mattered most to the organizing of his life:

> The judge ruled against me . . . I don't know exactly how much trouble I'm in. The outlook is not good. And I don't know how soon I will end up with a date [for execution]. The first one has to be at least 90 days away. It is possible I could get a date within a few weeks . . . I have to prepare for the worst. Cause even though 90 days seems a long time to someone waiting to get out of jail, it goes fast when a date is up coming. (June 8, 2005)

The appeal process and the lack of an imaginable future meant that, despite Jon's having spent more than 20 years in prison, many of the elements of constructive adaptation Crewe et al. (2016) found in the experiences of mid- and later-stage long-term prisoners were somewhat different for Jon. Practically, and psychologically, he strategically sought to resist adapting to life in prison:

> I have always felt freedom was close at hand. We would find the guy [who did it], or get a reversal on Batson [the issue of racial bias in jury selection], or [an accuser]'s statement would get a new trial, or [another witness] would tell the truth: SOMETHING! That's why I feel I wasted all these years. I would never buckle down and do anything long term. School, writing a book, etc. I felt that was giving up

and resigning myself to my fate. Maybe I was just fooling myself so I would not give up. (December 9, 2008)

Jon attributed his preference for life in the present to his need to stay focused on his case and hopeful for a reversal, but it is equally possible that the sentence of death did not permit him to move past the injustices of his case and engage in more long-term planning for an uncertain future. As recognized by O'Donnell (2014), this orientation to the present gave Jon psychological advantages over his environment. But unlike O'Donnell's findings, Jon's focus on the present did not preclude him from dwelling on regrets about the injustices of the past—both remorse for those caused by him and frustrated incredulity about his ongoing incarceration in the context of his continued innocence claim. Of course, Jon's capacity to stay connected with his past while living in the present might have been because righting these injustices was the key to securing his future.

In their study of long-term prisoners, Crewe and colleagues (2016) found that individuals further into their sentences had "come to accept their predicament" (p. 21), and consequently they focused "less on the past than the future, and their use of the present was constructive, rather than merely depletive" (p. 21). Such mid-term prisoners are said to demonstrate a form of *productive agency* "in which they sought to make the most of a situation that was not of their choosing, but from which they believed they could derive some personal value" (p. 21).

Jon demonstrated both productivity and agency in his resistance to routines that corresponded with the chronology of prison life. Unlike the long-term prisoners of Crewe et al. (2016), however, Jon's productive agency was not directed toward the future but grounded in the present. His efforts were directed at righting the wrongs of the past (his legal case) and at staying alive in a present that was external to the prison. Jon kept himself busy through repetitive actions, such as engaging in fantasy football leagues with other people both inside and outside the prison, making a small amount of money through hustling commissary goods for stamps, listening to radio shows, planning for visits, praying, and letter writing. However, he resisted allowing these activities to fall into a regular chronological routine that accorded with the prison's schedules.

His routines were regular enough to provide something of a rhythm to his life, although they were rarely equidistant. There were many points in his letters when he quoted the time of his writing a letter, and yet there were no patterns in what time of day this was completed or the activities that punctuated his letter writing:

> Hey! Guess who? Just wrote to Faith. And sent my Mom that beautiful birthday card that your Mom sent me . . . and wrote to Meredith . . . it's 8:50 p.m. now. Not complete dark yet. Went outside 2nd today. No sun, but shot baskets running. I bet I drank 3 gallons of water, and sweat out 4! (July 4, 2005)

> It's actually 2:45 AM of the 9th. I conked out at 8 PM and slept till midnight. Then wrote Linda. (February 8, 2006)

> I need to write Mary tonight. I'll probably stay up. I slept most of the morning. After we prayed—of course—and then showered. I wasted most of Sat. night with puzzles. Some reading. (July 1, 2006)

Standard chronological conceptions of time were diminished in relation to Jon's in-prison use of time. Our analysis concluded that, effectively, Jon's routine on death row was precisely to resist routine, which permitted him a sense of agency in a highly controlled environment. Jon confirmed this in a reflective account:

> I always tried not to fall into "routine." As much as I could. I might get up at breakfast—about 3 AM—and stay up writing. Then, rec. at 6:30–7 am for 2 hrs. Shower, await lunch at about 10:30 AM, go to sleep, get up for supper, stand at the window and watch the airport. Watch planes from Houston at dusk and early evening. Exercise a while. Clean up. Listen to the radio and dance half the night. Stay up till breakfast, then sleep till lunch. I guess my "routine" was not to have one.

In contrast to the routines of adaptation that Cohen and Taylor (1972) argued can help prisoners to buffer the anxieties of life in prison through making life predictable, Jon's routines were explicitly designed to resist the adaptive benefits of growing accustomed to life in a harsh and inhumane environment. This was so because, on death row, adapting means giving up: "I <u>have seen</u> people lose hope and almost dwindle in front of your eyes. And I never knew what to say" (October 19, 2005).

Jon's resilience rested on a present-oriented agency that was neither passive nor reactive but productively resisted the chronological challenges of the present to preserve hope in an insecure future. The cyclical nature of his "present" appeared to provide some psychological defense against the assault on his agency from his environment and its implications for the future.

MEANING—BEING IN ONTOLOGICAL TIME

Meisenhelder (1985) argued that our temporal identity depends on our capacity to imagine a future in which one has expanded as an individual. This sense of existing in and through time provides meaning to life and guards against a sense of futility. The death penalty requires people to live in a futureless world. This inescapable ontological assault is individual, and it is communal. On death row, people live under the threat of their own execution, and they routinely witness others being taken away for execution:

> Three more guys got dates. I only know Fleetwood. I sent him a kite (note) to ask to borrow 7 flags (stamps). He was in <u>52</u> cage (cell). My answer ☺ came back from 76. 'F' section is 71–84. I didn't even know he had a date. . . . I can't help but look over there and wonder how long till it's my turn. (April 7, 2005)

During the years in which Jon was on death row and corresponded with Ruth, there typically were at least two executions per month.[9] Jon lived on A-Pod for much of this time, so he had the distinctly mixed blessing of being able to "say goodbye" to fellow prisoners while having the reality of execution regularly reinforced. In Calkins's (1970) distinction

---

[9] There were an average of 24 executions per year in Texas from 2000 to 2009 (Texas Department of Criminal Justice, 2017).

between linear and cyclical time, she described how linear time is "predicated upon a well ordered past, present and future moving on a linear continuum divided into equal parts" (p. 489). In contrast, she argued that within a cyclical perspective of time, "the present may be engulfing, and the future, unpredictable" (p. 490). Although these two models seem to be mutually exclusive, for Jon they were continually interacting. Connections with other people are vital to flourishing socially (Smith, 2010) and psychologically (Seligman, 2011). Jon's correspondence showed how he prioritized connections with others to retain meaning in life in the present. These connections demanded some engagement with linear chronological time within and outside the prison, even while the present was "engulfing" and the future was "unpredictable."

Most notably, although Jon attempted to resist chronological time in the form that it is imposed within the prison setting, he submitted to it where it could provide a temporal connection to others outside of prison. For a period in the mid-2000s, for example, a radio station local to the prison set up a "shout out show," whereby friends and family of prisoners could call and leave both recorded and live messages. People in prison could listen to these messages if they had a radio:

> I yelled at Cash to tell him his mom was on the s.out show. "Tell me what she says" . . . [then] someone had called in I didn't want to hear. So I turned the radio off. It's right next to my head in the corner of the bunk. Then I dozed for maybe 30 seconds. Snapped awake and remembered the radio was off. "Oh! Shit!" turned it on . . . and heard "we have a call" and it was you!? Thanks!! It was good to hear your voice. (June 25, 2006)

> Thank you! For the call today. It was great, as always, to hear your voices and share a bit of your lives. (August 27, 2006)

Feeling a sense of togetherness in time, despite distance, can be existentially comforting—knowing there are people in the world thinking of you, to whom your life is important. Life on death row may limit the capacity to "expand" one's temporal identity, but with great effort, Jon succeeded in "expanding" his interpersonal identity. However, this simultaneously opened him up to the pain of an impotent existence in a temporal realm, where he could do little to help others and others were also largely unable to help him:

> I wasn't much support for Annette when we visited [to tell Jon that his stepmother, who raised him, had died]. I couldn't think . . . Miss Williams called the Chaplain. But he can't help me. I know how to pray. And I been crying alone for years. (September 29, 2005)

People serving shorter sentences or life sentences can turn their focus inward (Crewe et al., 2016) and suspend time outside (Wahidin, 2006). In contrast, for people on death row, there is no domain within which the kinds of relational connections that bring meaning to life can be formed without simultaneously exaggerating the pain of one's predicament.

Jon's letters show that he established good relationships with most people around him on death row and close relationships with a few people. This means that people on death row can, to a limited extent, "look after" each other in times of need:

> They are hot on us at the moment. Not only the whole cell phone thing, but Dorsey threatened to kill an officer before he dies. His date is soon. So, they put him in "B" section all alone. In a management cell they made up just for him. We are able to slide a line under these doors. Even between sections. Someone saw John with a line to Dorsey. So, they taped the bottom of those doors. And are watching us close. No one here would help Dorsey kill. But guys will help him with kites and stamps and food. Coffee. But we can't now. We can only pray for him. Lots of dates soon. (March 8, 2008)

Jon's letters also showed how prioritizing connections with people inside prison could mean that he would attempt to regulate his activities in relation to the temporal requirements of the regime when it meant he could interact with someone important to him:

> I traded my shower so I could go to C dayroom Friday. I took 4 books to loan, and bout 10 items to "exchange" (☺), dominoes to play Fleetwood, water bottle and 3 kites (Notes). I brought back 2 books and

a 2.5–3 foot high stack of mags. Won <u>2</u> more dominoes games than he did and made two deals to send some stuff the next day! ☺ Then had to 'BIRD BATH' in the cell! Ha! But no big deal, cause we don't rec on Sat. and we showered first. So it all works out. (May 25, 2008)

But forming connections with those around you on death row means the weight of one's mortality and powerlessness is felt acutely with every execution, even more so when it is the execution of a friend:

Today Donnie Miller moved in down-stairs. But he'll move by Monday or Tues to the "Date" section. His date is Feb 27th. Don is one of my real good friends that is left. (November 9, 2006)

Fleetwood—Michael Riley—has a date tonight. My last neighbor before I went to level 2. We did fantasy football all the time. . . . Can only pray. (May 19, 2009)

Jon relied on a sense of a spiritual connection with God to buffer his powerlessness in his temporal connections. He did so by asking God to intervene for good. This transcendence appeared to bring him more solace in his pleas for others than it did to help him deal with his own pains, frustrations, and his sense of injustice. Talking of his stepmother's illness, he wrote, "What do you pray for? No pain, or a long life? It's a good thing I believe in prayer! Cause I'm sure as hell helpless to do anything else. And I have plenty to pray about" (July 17, 2005).

When it came to his own predicament, although Jon expressed gratitude to God for his life, he did not look to his faith as a way to come to terms with his sentence. He expressed impatience in relation to its resolution:

No, I didn't exactly say "Thank you for putting me on death row." Sorry. But I did thank the Lord for all the blessings I have been given since here. And for keeping me safe all these years. And to please give me direction. And, please! Can it be soon?! Before I'm too feeble! (October 30, 2005)

I hope God has plans for me. And soon! This place is getting old. (October 16, 2006)

Jon's relationship with chronological time, therefore, appeared to be mediated through his ontological experience of time. He found meaning in an uncertain existence through his connections with other people. He mediated the difficulties of his powerlessness within these relationships through his sense of connection with God. In the final section, we consider the implications of this approach for how Jon experienced time on death row—how he felt through it and about it.

FEELING—EMOTIONS IN EXPERIENTIAL TIME

The research literature has suggested that the effects of adapting to a long time in prison include generating a social distance between people, heightening distrust of others, and experiencing increased difficulties in managing social interactions (Liem & Kunst, 2013). Hulley and colleagues (2016) suggested that these characteristics relate to an overall "emotional numbing." Although such numbing may function well as a coping mechanism by reducing the pains of imprisonment, it can also be damaging (Hulley et al., 2016, p. 788). Jon's correspondence paints a complex picture of how he negotiated his experiences of time in light of his determination to stay connected and close to other people while balancing his need to cope with the constant presence of death. Executions were often mentioned in Jon's letters without the emotional response one might expect. However, the extent of Jon's relational connections and the content of his letters show a man who remained emotionally connected to others.

There are many examples of Jon discussing traumatic or confusing events in a way that acknowledged that he felt these experiences. Still, his emotions were presented briefly and then swiftly receded from his writing. He often mentioned someone's impending execution date but then immediately returned to something more mundane, such as his poor choice of running backs in a game of fantasy football: "Fleetwood has a date for the 22nd. He almost won the fantasy [football] this week. I wish he would have. I didn't come close! Picked 2 good backs, decent kicker and the rest sucked. I'll do better this week" (September 15, 2005).

Such an apparently glib response could evidence social distance and emotional numbing, but it could also be a way to protect others with whom Jon is connected from the harsh emotional realities he is forced to navigate. There are points at which this was explicitly acknowledged in his letters. On June 14, 2008, when discussing the execution of "KC," Jon wrote in some detail about what happened when men were taken from the Polunksy Unit over to The Walls in Huntsville to be executed. He then explicitly reprimanded himself for sharing this detail and quickly reverted to a discussion of the mundane:

> You sit in that cell from about 1 p.m. till time. They give you the choice to "put on" a diaper, or they have 3 big trusties[10] (one of each race) that will put it on you. There is food and drink within reach if you want. And a telephone to use. Then they bring whatever last meal you asked for at about 4 p.m. Chaplains, they say, bring cigarettes if you want. Anyway—enough of that. I wasn't able to make cards for about 2 or 3 months. You may have noticed. (June 14, 2008)

The challenge appeared to be in staying emotionally numb enough to be able to survive on death row but also to be emotionally alive enough to form and maintain relational connections with others. This latter objective included not overtraumatizing people by proxy. There are times when Jon's letters showed that the toll of life on death row hampered his ability to reach out to others in correspondence:

> I hope you get this by the 18th. I should have mailed it yesterday. But I was emotionally drained. Hoping and praying all day that Shannon would get a stay. But we knew it was unlikely. So, he's gone. At 33 [years old]. (November 9, 2006)

However, Jon's commitment to correspondence demonstrated how emotional connection, as well as emotional numbing, functioned to buffer the existential challenges of life on death row and kept him in touch with the feelings of "normal" life:

> Ya'll have a festival to work this month? I hope you do well with it. . . .
> Are you getting discouraged with how things are going? I know you

---

[10] *Trusties* are prisoners who occupy positions of trust within the prison and are therefore able to do certain jobs within and often outside of the prison.

must be tired at times. I hope watching all of that good football has perked you up? (July 10, 2006)

Although much of his present was difficult to engage with and to share emotionally, his connections with others showed an emotional intelligence that thrived relationally. Despite the injustices Jon experienced on death row, he thought he had grown relationally in connection with others over that time in a way that he felt would make him a better person in any imagined future:

> Do I think I should have been free 20 or so years ago . . . "should" I have been? Yes. But was I <u>ready</u> to be? Probably not. . . . I knew Dad and other family meant a lot, but hadn't <u>felt</u> that loss, so didn't have the appreciation then that I do now for family and friends. I wanted to do some things then for others, but probably would have gotten out the same ol' greedy self-absorbed me. I like to think I would have learned. But I doubt I would have. (December 9, 2008)

And there is also evidence that, despite the challenges, he achieved a more empathetic presence on death row by mediating the multiple pains of others and their consequences:

> I can barely support myself, much less anyone else. I tried to talk Jo-Jo out of cutting an officer. No luck. But I did (until he moved) listen to some of his "poetry." Mostly to do with: "You ain't wrote me—I hope you remember when I'm gone." I told him to give them a chance. They have to deal with you being here also. (January 22, 2008)

LAST WORDS: RELATIONAL PROTECTION, PERMEABILITY, AND PRODUCTIVE DISCOMFORTS

Jon's experiences were unique, and his situation, as someone who has maintained his innocence over 4 decades on death row, is unusual even among death row prisoners in the United States. Nevertheless, there are powerful lessons in Jon's life for understanding human adaptations to extreme situations of routine trauma, loss, and isolation. These experiences also provide a singular opportunity to explore the varied dimensions of the construct of time that are, as Adam (1990) argued, too often taken for granted by those of us who live in less extraordinary circumstances. This chapter further demonstrates that academics can work collaboratively with people who are currently serving time in prison, in multiple jurisdictions, thereby expanding the growing movement of "convict criminology" (see, e.g., Earle, 2016; S. Richards & Ross, 2001). More broadly, this collaborative process and the findings it has produced suggest that there are ways to continue to be productive, connected, and emotionally alive that even a death sentence cannot kill.

In his recent work on "the public realm" Sennett (2016) described the differences between borders and boundaries in natural sciences. He extrapolated what these differences might mean for social interactions, understood within the context of time. He outlined how boundaries impose limits that result in "closure through inactivity," whereas borders are zones of "active exchange," meaning they are "more full of events in time" and also more "productive of evolutionary change" ("Borders and Boundaries," para. 2). He related these observations to the structure of plant cells, describing how in a healthy plant, a cell wall has to be resistant enough to provide structure, but it also incorporates a cell membrane that is both porous and resistant and provides for the flow of life-giving nourishment. If a cell becomes too tightly sealed, with too little interaction, it dies. Sennett used this analogy to consider how urban design can help to promote or diminish the kinds of social interactions that Smith (2010) argued are vital to the development and maintenance of personhood.

A similar dynamic is at play in Jon's emotional survival within one of the most boundaried contexts imaginable. His approach demonstrated the emotional rigidity required to buffer the trauma of continual executions but simultaneously exposed his fragility as he actively maximized his ability to retain such life-giving connections as are possible within the limited porosity of his situation. Time, then, is not only an overarching context within which and through which we feel but is also a component of the kinds of interactions that Sennett (2016) argued are life-giving. These interactions are all the more life-giving when they happen in "places made by and through participation . . . in a space made for other purposes" ("Context," para. 7). Jon's own reflections mirror this sentiment:

> Remember me telling you <u>lots</u> of us can talk at once? You would have loved the tenacity, stick-to-itness, exhibited in order to have about 12–14 [of us] able to talk with Carlos before he was taken. And it will happen again with Jonathan. Little victories. Heart-lifting, but heart breaking in the end. (January 13, 2007)

Choosing to live in a connected way is not easy. Sennett (2016) argued that such porousness is uncomfortable. But he believed that these discomforts are the hard choices we have to make when faced with the relative safety of "isolation and segregation," rather than "the risks entailed in interaction" ("Borders and Boundaries," para. 22). He argued that these interactions disrupt our "mutual neutrality," which can lead to a sense of both "difference" and "indifference" ("Difference and Indifference," para. 10). Jon's relational tenacity and generosity not only brought him life-giving connections but also nurtured a criminological sensibility in others beyond the boundaries that confined him.

In this chapter, Jon's willingness to expose his personal correspondence to scrutiny by relative strangers has troubled and, we hope, expanded some of the findings in the literature about the experiences of time in prison. But beyond this, Jon's relational openness has let us into his world and helpfully disoriented some of the assumptions about time we have brought to this work. We have found that collaborating in this way, although certainly logistically and ethically challenging, has helped to shape the questions we asked, how we asked them, and how we answered them. In so doing, it has made our criminological task feel inescapably personal and political. But probably more important than all of this, it has helped to disrupt our comfortable distance from some of the pains inherent in aspects of our contemporary "justice" system:

> They killed Fleetwood Tuesday. He was my neighbor and sometime Fantasy Football partner before I went to Level 2. I miss not "saying

Goodbye," but being able to. Know what I mean? Lots of guys are getting dates soon. Way too many. (May 22, 2009)

Way too many.

REFERENCES

Adam, B. (1990). *Time and social theory*. Cambridge, England: Polity Press.

Birks, M., & Mills, J. (2015). *Grounded theory: A practical guide*. Retrieved from https://researchonline.jcu.edu.au/37746/1/37746%20Birks%20and%20Mills%202015%20Front%20Pages.pdf

Calkins, K. (1970). Time: Perspectives, marking and styles of usage. *Social Problems, 17*, 487–501. http://dx.doi.org/10.2307/799681

Cohen, S., & Taylor, L. (1972). *Psychological survival: The experience of long-term imprisonment*. London, England: Penguin.

Cope, N. (2003). "It's no time or high time": Young offenders' experiences of time and drug use in prison. *Howard Journal, 42*, 158–175. http://dx.doi.org/10.1111/1468-2311.t01-1-00273

Crewe, B., Hulley, S., & Wright, S. (2016). Swimming with the tide: Adapting to long-term imprisonment. *Justice Quarterly, 34*, 1–25.

Earle, R. (2016). Race, ethnicity, multiculture and prison life. In Y. Jewkes, J. Bennett, & B. Crewe (Eds.), *Handbook on prisons* (2nd ed., pp. 568–585). Abingdon, England: Routledge.

Flanagan, T. J. (1981). Dealing with long-term confinement: Adaptive strategies and perspectives among long-term prisoners. *Criminal Justice and Behavior, 8*, 201–222. http://dx.doi.org/10.1177/009385488100800206

Grounds, A. T. (2005). Understanding the effects of wrongful imprisonment. *Crime and Justice, 32*, 1–58. http://dx.doi.org/10.1086/655352

Hulley, S., Crewe, B., & Wright, S. (2016). Re-examining the problems of long term imprisonment. *British Journal of Criminology, 56*, 769–792. http://dx.doi.org/10.1093/bjc/azv077

Johnson, R., & McGunigall-Smith, S. (2008). Life without parole, America's other death penalty: Notes on life under sentence of death by incarceration. *The Prison Journal, 88*, 328–346. http://dx.doi.org/10.1177/0032885508319256

Leigey, M. E., & Ryder, M. A. (2015). The pains of permanent imprisonment: Examining perceptions of confinement among older life without parole inmates. *International Journal of Offender Therapy and Comparative Criminology, 59*, 726–742. http://dx.doi.org/10.1177/0306624X13517868

Liem, M., & Kunst, M. (2013). Is there a recognizable post-incarceration syndrome among released "lifers"? *International Journal of Law and Psychiatry*, *36*, 333–337. http://dx.doi.org/10.1016/j.ijlp.2013.04.012

Meisenhelder, T. (1985). An essay on time and the phenomenology of imprisonment. *Deviant Behavior*, *6*, 39–56. http://dx.doi.org/10.1080/01639625.1985.9967658

O'Donnell, I. (2014). *Prisoners, solitude, and time*. Oxford, England: Oxford University Press. http://dx.doi.org/10.1093/acprof:oso/9780199684489.001.0001

Richards, B. (1978). Experience of long-term imprisonment: An exploratory investigation. *British Journal of Criminology*, *18*, 162–169. http://dx.doi.org/10.1093/oxfordjournals.bjc.a046888

Richards, S., & Ross, J. (2001). The new school of convict criminology. *Social Justice*, *28*, 177–190.

Schroeder, A. (1976). *Shaking it rough: A prison memoir*. Toronto, Canada: Doubleday.

Seligman, M. (2011). *Flourish: A new understanding of happiness and wellbeing— And how to achieve them*. London, England: Nicholas Brealey.

Sennett, R. (2016). *Quant: The public realm*. Retrieved from http://www.richardsennett.com/site/senn/templates/general2.aspx?pageid=16&cc=gb

Smith, C. (2010). *What is a person? Rethinking humanity, social life, and the moral good from the person up*. Chicago, IL: University of Chicago Press. http://dx.doi.org/10.7208/chicago/9780226765938.001.0001

Texas Department of Criminal Justice. (2017). *Death row information*. Retrieved from https://www.tdcj.state.tx.us/death_row/dr_executions_by_year.html

Vannier, M. (2016). Women serving life without the possibility of parole: The different meanings of death as punishment. *Howard Journal*, *55*, 328–344.

Wahidin, A. (2006). Time and the prison experience. *Sociological Research Online*, *11*. http://dx.doi.org/10.5153/sro.1245

Wahidin, A., & Tate, S. (2005). Prison (e)scapes and body tropes: Older women in the prison time machine. *Body & Society*, *11*, 59–79. http://dx.doi.org/10.1177/1357034X05052462

Zamble, E. (1992). Behavior and adaptation in long-term prison inmates: Descriptive longitudinal results. *Criminal Justice and Behavior*, *19*, 409–425. http://dx.doi.org/10.1177/0093854892019004005

STORIES OF SURVIVING DEATH ROW AND POSTEXONERATION TRAUMA

10

Once Numbered Among the Dead, Now I Live!

Joe D'Ambrosio with Rev. Neil Kookoothe

"It will be the sentence of the court that you die in the electric chair on June 1, 1989, at 6:00 a.m." With these words the Common Pleas Court of Cuyahoga County, Ohio, sentenced me to death for a crime I did not commit. These words would begin a 22-year journey that was intended to lead to a date with the executioner and a lethal cocktail of chemicals that would end my life. These words would create in me an existential crisis that would shape and form my life from this point forward. These words would provide the framework within which I would measure time and anticipate my death while at the same time providing the tenacious determination that would define my struggle for justice and freedom.

http://dx.doi.org/10.1037/0000084-011
Living on Death Row: The Psychology of Waiting to Die, H. Toch, J. R. Acker, and V. M. Bonventre (Editors)

THE CASE

In September 1988, 19-year-old Anthony Klann was found murdered and floating in Doan Creek in the University Circle area of Cleveland, Ohio. With no identification on his person, he was transported to the Cuyahoga County morgue as a John Doe. Days later, Paul "Stoney" Lewis called the morgue and inquired whether they had in their possession a body matching Klann's physical description and appearance. In that call, Lewis described not only the fatal neck and chest wounds sustained by Anthony but also defensive wounds and markings that had not been publicly reported or disclosed as part of any police investigation. He accurately described the appearance and the location of wounds that would have been known to the perpetrator alone.

Lewis not only identified the body but also assured the police that he could provide them with the identity and whereabouts of the killers. With Lewis in tow, the Cleveland Police were directed to my apartment on Coventry Boulevard in Cleveland. I was promptly arrested there for the murder of Anthony Klann.

I had known Anthony only marginally and for a total of only 3 weeks before my arrest. I was, however, with Anthony and several coworkers the night before his murder; we spent the night of Thursday, September 22, engaged in a bar crawl, downing beers at a couple of local watering holes. Lewis was also present off and on throughout the evening.

At one point during the evening, Anthony and a codefendant became embroiled in a heated exchange in the men's room of the bar that was enough to have us bounced out of the place and sent on our way. That drunken outburst was also the perfect foil to allow Lewis to point an accusatory finger at two others and me. The drunken outburst, he alleged, led directly to Anthony's murder. In fact, Anthony was seen drinking at the same watering holes a full 24 hours after the state said he was killed. Nevertheless, that drunken outburst and that accusatory finger started me on a 22-year odyssey that would strip me of everything I had previously known. It would change the way I lived and moved and my very being in the world. It would be the fight of my life as I confronted the power of the courts and a justice system that was anything but just.

With what seemed to be an airtight identification at the ready, the Cleveland police, the Cuyahoga County prosecutor, and the Cuyahoga County coroner set out to retrofit a narrative that would justify their theory of the case. They turned a blind eye to any other possible suspects or any other theories or motives that would explain the untimely death of Anthony Klann. Indeed, no further investigation was conducted after Lewis handed over the alleged perpetrators to the police. The case was solved within 48 hours of the discovery of Klann's body. The tough-on-crime police and prosecutor had their man, no doubt about it!

UNCOVERING THE TRUTH

Eleven years would pass before I was befriended by Fr. Neil, a Catholic priest and spiritual advisor who had become involved with many of the men on Ohio's death row. This was no ordinary spiritual advisor, to be sure. Besides being a Catholic priest, he was also a licensed attorney and a registered nurse. After concelebrating my mother's funeral mass in December 1998, he paid a visit to me at my cell to offer sympathy and counsel at my mother's passing. I thanked him for his counsel, but even more, I begged him to look into my case for me. I was about to start my federal appeals, the last legal recourse before the state of Ohio would execute me, and I had no one to advocate for me. No one listens to a dead man walking.

Initially reluctant because of time constraints, Fr. Neil agreed to read my trial transcript after I indicated I had the shortest capital trial in Ohio history. The entire proceedings lasted less than 3 days and were recorded in only one legal volume. Fr. Neil was utterly baffled by the fact that a man could be tried and sentenced to death and that the legal proceedings recording that event could be conducted in only 66 hours and memorialized in 462 double-spaced legal pages. This was the string that, once pulled, began to unravel and expose the state's misconduct that had resulted in my wrongful conviction. I was convinced that Fr. Neil, along with new federal appellate attorneys, would uncover the truth and that the truth would set me free.

On his first reading of the transcript, Fr. Neil discovered that the coroner had either lied or been mistaken when she testified that Klann had been able to scream for his life after his throat had been sliced and two large holes were opened in his trachea. He knew that this was a physical impossibility. After Anthony's airway was compromised, he would have been rendered unable to speak, let alone scream. From this point forward, Fr. Neil would ask himself one recurring question: "If this is wrong, what else could be wrong?" He would soon discover just how far wrong things could go.

Fr. Neil's search for the truth would eventually lead him to the records room of the Cuyahoga County Justice Center. He researched the criminal records of all of the major actors associated with this case. He discovered nothing new or surprising until he pulled the records for the deceased victim, Anthony Klann. Fr. Neil then discovered that shortly before his death, Anthony had witnessed the rape of a young blind man who had cerebral palsy. Anthony was the only witness called to testify in the rape case, and he appeared as a witness for both the state and the defense. Unfortunately for Anthony, the rapist was released from jail before the case could proceed to trial. The rapist was none other than Paul Lewis. Lewis had previously been convicted of rape and, if convicted again, he was looking at considerable time in prison. Solution: no witness, no trial. Anthony turned up dead, and the case was dropped. Lewis pointed the accusatory finger, and I was arrested, charged, and ultimately convicted.

Unfortunately for me, my case was proceeding to court at the same time as the Paul Lewis rape case. Although the same prosecutor was simultaneously in charge of both the rape case and the murder case, with all the same parties involved, he claims he never saw any confluence between the two cases. Thus, it was in February of 1989 that I, Joe D'Ambrosio, an honorably discharged sergeant from the United States Army with no criminal history, was tried and sentenced to death for a crime I did not commit.

Sentenced to death! It was not a sentence of 20 years to life or 30 years to life. It was not a sentence of life without the possibility of parole. It was a sentence of death!

A PROCESS OF DEHUMANIZATION

Life on death row is an oxymoron. Speaking of "life on death row" does a disservice to the men and women incarcerated on death rows across the country and around the world. Death row is not a place of life, but a place of death and only death. To be sure, the sentence of death begins immediately on its pronouncement. It only culminates years in the future, when a death warrant is read, a state-sanctioned homicide is perpetrated, and another corpse in a body bag is wheeled out of a sterile and theatrically staged execution chamber. The machinery of death begins its slow, unrelenting grind with a judge's pronouncement and the loud banging of a gavel.

Death row is a series of daily "little deaths" that are engineered to deconstruct, destroy, dehumanize, and denigrate the human person. This slow deconstruction of the person is necessary, of course, for all players in this macabre process. Over time, this dehumanizing provides the salve and the balm that will allow participants to rationalize their actions and preserve their psyches after they realize they have been participants, wittingly or unwittingly, in the taking of another person's life. They have, after all, lowered themselves to the level of the convicted murderer. An eye for an eye, a tooth for a tooth, a life for a life. Death begets death.

This process of dehumanization is necessary for the judges, prosecutors, defense attorneys, bailiffs, stenographers, clerks, and jurors, all of whom justify their involvement under the guise of following the law: "We are only doing our jobs; we must do what the law demands of us." With this salve, personal responsibility can be mitigated or abrogated altogether.

It begins early in the judicial process. The man in the orange jumpsuit sitting at the defense table conjures up images of unspeakable violence, loathsome guilt, and criminal character and intent. After all, "He wouldn't be wearing that prison uniform had he not done something wrong! He's not a man; he's an animal!" The parade of testimony, evidence, and character witnesses that follow will all be carefully orchestrated to prove a point or win the case, even if it means the truth be damned. The process, more often than not, is a game of chess rather than a search for truth and justice. The animal must be put down!

The morbid balm of dehumanization is also necessary for those who work in state departments of rehabilitation and correction. Everyone from clerical personnel to wardens, corrections officers, medical technicians, and executioners must somehow come to perceive the inmate as something less than human if they are to participate in the process of state-sanctioned homicide. Imagine if you can, the angst that must surely come with the certain knowledge that you are an accomplice in the premeditated taking of another's life. Now imagine that angst multiplied many times over if you are in a jurisdiction that executes with some frequency.

Moreover, in a pathological sense, this sick balm of dehumanization is necessary even for the convicted inmate. The man must be stripped of everything that has heretofore provided him with any sense of importance, self-worth, or dignity. It is much easier to go to your own execution if you perceive yourself to be the animal that others perceive you to be. The inhumane treatment that strips you of your humanity thus begins with the gavel and ends in the grave. Over the years, they strip from you everything that is human. Over the years, they strip from you everything of value. Over the years, they strip from you everything that speaks of life. In a very real sense, by the time they execute you, you are already dead.

The first thing they strip from you is your freedom. It is immediate, severe, intimidating, and frightening. Four guards who were in constant attendance for the court proceedings, watching me like a hawk, set upon me immediately on the pronouncement of my sentence of death. Until this point, other than being handcuffed during transportation from my cell to the court, I had complete freedom of movement of my arms and legs, my hands and my feet. Such unfettered freedom of movement would soon become both a distant memory and a deep, longing hope for the future.

With the judicial uttering of only a few words, I was bound and chained within seconds, as if I had become a dangerous pariah. The guards placed a belly chain around my waist with links 2½ inches long and 1½ inches wide. Next, my handcuffs were attached to the belly chain by a short, unforgiving chain. I then had virtually no movement of my hands or arms. The cuffs were tightened so severely that they restricted not only bodily movement but the flow of blood as well. It was not only humiliating but also painful. The ankle fetters came next, also connected one to another by a short length of restrictive chain. I was quick to learn the dead-man-walking shuffle, lest I lose my balance, stumble, and fall.

I entered the courtroom that fateful day as Joe D'Ambrosio. I exited, with all eyes on me, akin to something more reminiscent of Jacob Marley, from Charles Dickens's *A Christmas Carol*. What the onlookers saw was not a dignified man, but a murderous beast! Five years following my exoneration, many people still look at me and see not a man but a beast. Once presumed guilty, always guilty, in the minds of many.

Fully chained and shackled, always escorted by two guards: This would be my mode of transport for the next 20 years anytime I left my cell and the death row cellblock proper. This restricted range of motion and loss of freedom was not limited to bodily movement. I was about to discover that my geographical space would be similarly curtailed as well. The 4-hour drive from the county jail in Cleveland to death row was sheer hell. Chained for the duration as described earlier, and stuffed into the back of a sheriff's vehicle, I soon found myself having to urinate. I was informed that I would have to hold it until we arrived at the Southern Ohio Correctional Institution because there would be no stopping along the way. I was also informed that it would not be in my best interest to soil myself or urinate on the upholstery. With that subtle threat hanging over my head, the transport was nothing less than pure agony.

Despite my obvious discomfort, physical relief was not the first item on the guards' agenda following our arrival at the prison complex. My agenda and my distended bladder no longer mattered. First up was a bit of well-planned psychological torture. I was escorted up a short flight of stairs into a large space resembling a high school gymnasium. Standing around the perimeter of this space were two junior guards, or "gray shirts," a senior "white shirt" guard, and the two sheriff's deputies who had escorted me. All of them watched intently as I was summarily stripped of my orange jumpsuit, showered, and deloused.

Still naked and covered with delousing powder, and still needing to relieve myself, I was then escorted down a short hallway, with two cells to my left and windows to my right. I was informed that these were the holding cells where the condemned spent their last 24 hours before execution. Another door was opened. I was shoved into a sterile room, where I was introduced to the instrument of my pending demise: "Old Sparky," Ohio's well-worn electric chair, which at some date in the future would take the spark out of me. Naked you come into the world and naked you exit the world.

After this sobering introduction to the machinery of death, I was instructed to put on the uniform that would distinguish me both inside and outside of the prison as one of the condemned. It consisted of a white surgical scrub top and navy blue pants with a red stripe down the outside of the leg. They say clothes make the man, right? Even the clothes on your back contribute to the dehumanizing process. The Nazi concentration camps came readily to mind. After I was so attired, I was mercifully led to my cell where I was able to find the blessed relief of solitude and, at last, of an empty bladder.

My cell, another impediment to freedom, was a 6-by-9-foot cinder-block room. It had a solid metal door with a small vertical slit window (there were no windows to the outside) and a small food slot through which meal trays were passed back and forth. A silver metal combination sink/toilet was anchored to one side of the room. A thin concrete slab with an even thinner, worn mattress and a threadbare blanket was anchored to the other side. This was the totality of my belongings, symbolic of my despair on day one on death row.

This environment, or some semblance thereof, would be my home for the next 20 years and for the greater part of 23 out of 24 hours a day at the three correctional institutions that at one time or another would house Ohio's death row. To call it a recipe for sensory deprivation would be an understatement. It was home sweet home, and it was all mine, for a crime I did not commit.

Life on death row is all about the stripping away of the old self, the human self, and stigmatizing the convicted man or woman with a new identity. This institutional imprinting of a new identity seeks simultaneously to dehumanize the person and perpetuate a system of justice that tries to legitimize itself by creating a persona that the public finds more palatable for warehousing and executing a human being. It is reasonable and appropriate, one can argue, to incarcerate "the worst of the worst" or a Jack the Ripper, a Unabomber, a killer clown, or an anonymous inmate number than it is to do so to a Ted Kaczynski or a John Wayne Gacy or a Joe D'Ambrosio.

A man who is nothing more than a number is easy to catalog. A man who is identified only by number can simply be processed like any other number. Everyone is the same. No one is different. There is no reason to treat a number with respect and dignity. Give the man a name, however, and you are forced to relate to him in a whole new way. Give a man a name and you afford the man a dignity that is rightly his, a dignity that seeks to be understood. When a man has a name, he has a story. His story seeks to be told. And hearing the story opens up whole new vistas for humane treatment, rehabilitation, understanding, and restoration. The stories behind the names, however, would likely lead to institutional change and a penal system that is focused on restoration and rehabilitation, rather than on locking up and throwing away. A number has no story. A number has no hope, and a number has no life.

The taking of my name was perhaps one of the most painful challenges of my time on the row. I was no longer Joe D'Ambrosio. I was number A209351.

I was named after my father. I was the only male in my family; I had three sisters. My dad died when I was just 17 years old, but our common name created a bond and an expectation that transcends time, space, and death. The name Joe means "God adds or increases." The meaning was never lost on me. My dad had great expectations for me, and I did not want to disappoint him. He wanted me to become a man in every sense of the word, a man like himself who carried himself with honor and integrity. He wanted me to become a man whose word was his oath and a man of whom he could be proud. The clearing of my name and, by extension, his name and the D'Ambrosio name was a driving factor in my fight for a new trial, for justice, and ultimately, for exoneration.

My dad added much to my life and the life of the family. He instilled in me and all our family a hard-work ethic, an attitude that a job worth doing is worth doing well. He provided a good education, a loving home, and a life that, although at times was lean and hard, was always filled with love and laughter. These are good memories, to be sure. I wanted to do the same for my family. I wanted to pass the name down to a new generation to honor his posterity. After being incarcerated for 22 years on death row, it seems that children, grandchildren, and great-grandchildren are now beyond my reach. The D'Ambrosio name will die with me.

I followed my dad into the military and fought for the same values for which he fought. I rose to the rank of sergeant in just a few short years, believing in the honor, commitment, dignity, and courage that these United States hold so dear. I believe in the truth and loyalty professed by the men and women of the armed services, and I was willing to put my life on the line to defend these truths. Joe D'Ambrosio was a soldier in every sense of the word. Number A209351 was a failure and a disgrace; his story was better consigned to the dung heap of history rather than passed on to future generations.

Joe D'Ambrosio had a life as an auto mechanic and a wannabe disc jockey. Joe D'Ambrosio was always the life of the party and everyone's best friend. I enjoyed simply spending time with my buddies in rural North Royalton, Ohio—a country boy at heart. We went swimming and motorcycle riding. We shot pool and drank beer. We found fun in bowling alleys and auto repair garages. We found camaraderie everywhere we went and with everyone we met. Joe D'Ambrosio had the heart for the little guy and was always known to come to the defense of those who could not defend themselves. Number A209351 was none of these things. Number A209351 was simply a number; there was no history, no story worth sharing. Number A209351 was a failure and a disgrace.

On Ohio's death row I was incarcerated with other men, with other anonymous numbers. If the truth be told, I suspect I was one of the lucky ones. Although I had an inmate number assigned to me, I was spared the indignity of also being branded with a nickname that would serve to further associate me with an alleged crime or some other unsavory character defect. For instance, a man a few cells down from me was nicknamed "Hands." He was convicted of amputating his victim's hands so she could not be easily identified when her body was discovered. Another inmate was known as "Bulldog" for his propensity for violence toward anyone who crossed him or looked askance at him. He had many furious outbreaks on the row, and many lived in fear of him.

My name is Joe D'Ambrosio, but the state of Ohio renamed me A209351. The State of Ohio incarcerated me with other numbers and with men the likes of Hands and Bulldog. Imagine what that does to the human psyche. Imagine what that does to reshape and remold you into someone else's image. You are no longer your own man. They try to make you into someone else, and you die a bit more each day.

Being incarcerated for 22 years on Ohio's death row, I was also deprived of my right to free association and community. Although some of this loss was immediate, the stripping away of my family and friends, coworkers, and acquaintances was a slow, gradual, and unrelenting process that took place over the decades.

Following sentencing, I was immediately transferred from the Cuyahoga County Justice Center in Cleveland to the Southern Ohio Correctional Institution in Lucasville, Ohio, a distance of some 225 miles, 3½ hours travel time by car. As I said, my father died when I was 17, and my family had limited means and resources. They had neither the time nor the money to allow them to take an entire day off work to visit me for a short couple of hours before turning around and going home again.

If time, distance, and finances were not enough to discourage visitation, the state provided additional incentive to isolate me from friends and family by limiting the days and times I was allowed to have visitors. In its largesse, the state allowed up to two visits per month, limited to only 3 hours at a time. In addition, anyone wishing to visit me had to be on my preapproved "visitors list," which was limited to 15 people who had to have known me before my incarceration. Each was also required to be approved through heavy vetting by the prison.

You might think that the telephone or other social media would serve to foster important relationships and communication. But you would be wrong. All calls from the prison were required to be placed collect and were limited to 15 minutes in time. Another collect call had to be placed if more conversation was needed. The cost of these calls was exorbitant and more often than not was prohibitive. If cost was not enough, all calls coming from the prison were monitored or recorded, and an intermittent warning was interwoven throughout the call. This recording and the announced warning served to intimidate the parties and limited the topics discussed to mostly mundane and inconsequential matters. It was impossible to develop deep, human, and intimate relationships. All social interaction was limited to a superficial level.

In many respects, when I was exonerated at the age of 48, I was still operating and interacting with the world on the level of a 26-year-old. I felt like Rip Van Winkle. Friends and family had moved on, growing and changing with the times, but I was in a time warp. To be honest, 5 years out, I am still learning how to manage in a world that often seems filled with opportunity, wonder, and excitement, yet is oddly foreign as well.

Family and friends were supportive and well meaning, to be sure, but over time, the circumstances of my conviction and sentencing were just too much for them to cope with. The "out of sight, out of mind" phenomenon creeps in. Before you know it, visits stop and phone calls are not accepted. Relationships, even familial ones, seem to shrivel up and die. My mother and my sister Joann both died while I was on the row, and my two living sisters and I have no relationship to speak of. I have found family and community with a few faithful friends, including the folks who believed in me and advocated for me along the way, my church community, and with new friends who meet me and are willing to put their faith and trust in me.

Managing relationships while on the row is also a treacherous terrain. The "neighborhood" consists of some 200 men who find themselves in circumstances similar to your own. Yet you dare not inquire too deeply into the nature of those circumstances. Many of the guys play their cards quite close to the vest and resent it when boundaries are crossed and personal space is invaded. The problem lies in the fact that you often never know where the boundaries are or when a line has been crossed. The boundaries often change from day to day or are dependent on a man's mood at any given time. Because many of the guys have some type of mental illness or are educationally deficient or lacking in social skills, relationships behind the wall are often shallow and superficial. Simple bantering and glib shenanigans rule the day.

You do develop friendships and relationships while in prison, but these relationships are qualitatively different from those formed on the outside. I believe that only someone who has done time would be able to understand the nature of these relationships. An ever-present undercurrent of suspicion seems to underlie every interaction behind the walls. Who can be trusted and who cannot? Who is known to be a snitch and who is not? Who is stable and who is not? Who has violent tendencies and who does not? Do they want something from me and, if so, what? Travelling the terrain is often like running an obstacle course.

This is all complicated even further by the fact that on the row we were, for the most part, on lockdown for 23 out of 24 hours per day. During the hour we were assigned for recreation, no more than five guys were permitted to be out of their cells and in the rec cage (yes, cage) at any one time. To facilitate this, you are permitted to recreate only with men who are housed in the same pod as you and on the same range. Thus, you recreate with the same four guys day in and day out. This limited social interaction does little to foster quality human growth and development. In fact, growth is truncated and stagnation is the norm.

Rather than try to navigate this terrain, I chose an alternate path during my incarceration. I developed a few close relationships with some of the guys in the cells immediately surrounding mine. For the most part, these were men who were incarcerated around the same time I was or, like me, were from the Cleveland vicinity. These connections at least provided some common ground from which we could build a somewhat stable acquaintance.

I chose to spend my free time within the confines of my cell. Because I had no other advocate until well into my period of incarceration, I was determined to act as my own advocate. I analyzed my case over and over. When I was finished analyzing, I analyzed it all again. I did my best to learn the law in all of its intricacies. I acted as my own lawyer on many occasions, filing motions and briefs when my assigned attorneys failed to do so or when they wrote me off and simply would not listen to my concerns and suggestions. I knew my case better than anyone, and if I was to be afforded another opportunity before the courts, I wanted to be prepared. I would not allow ineffective assistance of counsel and a wrongful conviction and sentence to happen a second time.

I came to know the law so well that many encouraged me to seek employment as a paralegal following my exoneration. My appellate attorneys were amazed at my understanding of difficult legal concepts, and I became an integral part of the legal team contributing to successful arguments before both state and federal courts.

When visitation did occur on the row, it was also dehumanizing. I was allowed no physical contact with any of my visitors, not even so much as a handshake. After corrections officers had escorted my visitors to await my arrival, I was led, as if on exhibit, into the small cinderblock cubicle that served as the visitation room. Communication took place via an old, often malfunctioning, telephone handset. We were only able to see one another through a small wire-enmeshed glass window. This arrangement had unfortunate effects on both my visitors and me.

It had the effect of making me feel like a modern-day leper, an untouchable. My nightmare circumstances and my shame were on display not only to family and friends but also to other visitors who happened to catch a glimpse of my Jacob Marley–like appearance as I was paraded to my assigned cubicle. Innocent or not, the embarrassment and humiliation were beyond description. I often wondered what thoughts ran through the minds of the many visitors who saw me. What crime did they imagine I had committed? What kind of monster did they think I was? Did it ever cross their minds that I, or anyone else incarcerated, might truly be innocent? If the truth be told, there comes the point when not having visitors is sometimes a blessed relief.

My visitors were subjected to an intense entry process before they were escorted to the death row visiting center. Nothing was allowed beyond the entry building except a car key. Anything else brought in either had to be returned to their locked car or locked away in a safe provided for them in the prison entry building before they were allowed to visit. A corrections officer was present on their side of the visiting room at all times to monitor inappropriate conversation or behavior. What was considered inappropriate varied according to the whims of the guard on duty. Visitors could be and were turned away after traveling several hours and hundreds of miles because of inappropriate dress. Shorts that were too short, sleeveless blouses and bare shoulders, clothing that was considered too tight or too revealing ended up being an embarrassment to them and a reason to deny them visitation privileges. Such intimidation led to fewer and less frequent visits over time. Who could blame anyone for not wanting to subject themselves to such a regimen?

The lack of human touch and any sort of human intimacy takes its toll as well. The desire to be touched and to touch is a human one. To know that someone cares and understands, and is there for you, can be expressed by a simple yet profound touch. Without that touch, I was left to guess whether I had any real loved ones in my life or only death row voyeurs and pen pals.

A hierarchical class system is well established on the row. Several hierarchical systems would be more accurate. "Survival of the fittest" describes one such pecking order: The strong dominate the weak, the muscle-bound intimidate the little guys, and the more aggressive men lord over the more mild mannered. There is a place for everyone, and everyone knows his place. It actually works out well once the boundaries are set. Although occasional skirmishes and violent outbreaks occur, they are fairly few and far between and certainly nothing like what is portrayed in the media.

Financial well-being established another hierarchy. Every inmate was given a nominal sum of money each month to purchase basic necessities from the commissary, such as toilet paper, toothpaste, deodorant, soap, and stamps. Contrary to popular belief, these things are not simply given to the inmate. They must be purchased. Even visits to the prison doctor were billed at $3.00 per occurrence. Beyond this monthly state pay, you could earn additional funds if you were willing to take on other menial positions. At various times, I was assigned to be the porter for the pod, the range barber, or the kitchen and dietary aide. These tasks are not fulfilling, but you will do almost anything when you are in need.

A man enjoys even higher status if he is lucky enough to have family support or find a pen pal who will occasionally make a deposit into his commissary account. I was one of the fortunate ones, at least during the latter half of my incarceration. Through the generosity of newly found friends and advocates, I was able to purchase a small television for my cell and a typewriter to aid with my legal work. In addition, various friends would provide me with a sundry box or a food box once or twice a year. You cannot begin to know how much of a difference this makes on the row. I could buy cigarettes or coffee to barter with other inmates for goods and services, and at times I had the opportunity to share my bounty with some of the less fortunate guys. It was not always a dog-eat-dog existence. That being said, if you have little to barter with, then little is your return and the more difficult is your day-to-day reality on the row.

RETURN TO LIFE

I lost much over my 22 years on the row. I did not know the full extent of my loss until after my exoneration and my reacclimation to life on the outside. I had been a mechanic while serving in the army, and I had hoped to return to that career on my release. When I got out and had the opportunity to pop the hood on Fr. Neil's car and inspect the engine, I was lost and confused. I immediately realized I had no knowledge and no proficiency that would enable me to diagnose, let alone repair, such a complicated piece of machinery. Too much had changed in the engines of late model cars; I did not even recognize much of what was under the hood and knew that I would no longer be employable in the auto industry. Kiss that career goodbye!

In fact, I could kiss any job goodbye. No one was going to hire me after 22 years of incarceration, wrongful or otherwise. What does a 50-year-old man with no experience, no education, and no skills have to offer an employer? A job search under such conditions is impossible. In addition, I was conducting my search in the midst of the greatest economic downturn since the great depression. The market was flooded with men and women who were far more employable than I was. I jokingly told anyone who was willing to listen that I had worked for the state of Ohio for the last 22 years. No one was buying it. If not for Fr. Neil hiring me at his parish, I would most likely still be unemployed.

I was never one for book learning, so a return to the classroom was not an option. I simply was not interested. I just wanted to get on with my life. Put a project or a task in front of me and show me how to do it just once, and I was good to go. But there were no apprenticeships or internships available for a man of my age and circumstances. I now have a full-time position with full benefits in facilities engineering in Cleveland. I am content, at least for the time being. Even so, I feel that the justice system stripped me of both an education and a career.

Perhaps the most challenging area for me has been the dating game. For a time, I was relating to women as I would have when I was 26. Laughably, that did not work then, and it certainly does not work now. It is difficult for me to manage these relationships. When I find someone I am interested in dating, I have to determine the appropriate time to inform her of my past. Do I tell her when I ask her out? Do I tell her during our first date? How long do I wait? Chances are she will do a Google search on my name, only to discover the whole sordid story and think that I am lying to her or that she has gotten involved with the monster the Internet portrays me to be. If I do find a woman who is interested in going out with me, I still have to contend with her family. Dads and brothers are often not as forgiving as the women might be. It is all so very complicated.

I have my own baggage, to be sure, but women of my age come with theirs as well. Most have already had one or two marriages and all the accompanying complications. Children, if there are any, present a whole other set of concerns. I have pretty much come to the conclusion that I will remain single. I feel that the state of Ohio and the justice system stripped me of a wife, children, and family. In a very real sense then, they stripped me of my future.

In her March 5, 2010, opinion and order setting me free, Judge Joan Synenberg of the Cuyahoga County Court of Common Pleas said, "Although perhaps not swift in this case, justice did prevail." I disagree. Justice does not keep an innocent and wrongfully convicted man locked up for 22 years. Yes, the right outcome was eventually obtained, but it certainly was not justice.

Many people remark that, after all this, I nevertheless am not an angry or bitter man. I am not a bitter man. Bitterness will get me nowhere. To go through life with a bitter or angry attitude would only allow the prosecutor and the justice system to have the last word. I will not allow that to happen. I, Joe D'Ambrosio, am the victor in this struggle, not the state of Ohio.

In *The Shawshank Redemption* (Glotzer, Lester, Marvin, & Darabont, 1994), Tim Robbins's wrongfully convicted character, Andy Dufresne, comments, "Get busy living or get busy dying." Andy Defresne's words of wisdom have become a mantra for me. What do I have to be bitter about? I am alive. I am free. I have been wrongfully stripped of so much, and this scar will be with me for life. Now, however, I choose to live, and so I am going about the business of again clothing myself with dignity and justice.

REFERENCE

Glotzer, L. (Producer), Lester, D. V. (Producer), Marvin, N. (Producer), & Darabont, F. (Director). (1994). *The Shawshank redemption* [Motion picture]. United States: Castlerock Entertainment.

11

"Dreaming That I'm Swimming in the Beautiful Caribbean Sea": One Man's Story on Surviving Death Row

Charles S. Lanier

I f you were to ask someone on the street, or even a neighbor, "What do you think it's like to live on death row, condemned to die?" many people probably would tell you, "It's nothing I really spend much time thinking about." In many respects, contemplating life on death row is like thinking about our own eventual demise—death itself. We know it is "out there," but it is so far away, so comfortably distant, that it escapes our day-to-day consciousness. Yes, we should pay attention, but it is safer, perhaps, to ignore its inconvenient presence.

And yet, some have stepped away from the crowd and studied death row—the management of a death row population (Hudson, 1999; Lombardi, Sluder, & Wallace, 1996), the psychological distress under which men and women condemned to die must live (Bluestone & McGahee,

Special thanks go to Juan Roberto Meléndez-Colón and Judi Caruso for their help in the preparation of this chapter. I appreciate your insights and the time you spent with me in getting this story told correctly.

http://dx.doi.org/10.1037/0000084-012

1962; Johnson, 1989), the lives of executioners and death team members (Johnson, 1998), and the overall conditions under which the condemned exist (Jackson & Christian, 1980; Johnson, 1989, 2016; Johnson & Davies, 2014).

Even the courts have been called on to focus their energies on the conditions of death row. The condemned living on various death rows around the country have asked the courts to address the oppressive and denigrating conditions under which they live while waiting to die— and courts have responded. In a case challenging conditions for death-sentenced prisoners at the Mississippi State Penitentiary in Parchman, Plaintiff Willie Russell claimed,

> Prisoners housed on Death Row are knowingly and deliberately sub-jected to profound isolation, lack of exercise, stench and filth, mal-functioning plumbing, high temperatures, uncontrolled mosquito and insect infestations, a lack of sufficient mental health care, and exposure to psychotic inmates in adjoining cells. (*Gates v. Cook*, 2004, p. 327)

In some cases, like *Gates*, persuasive evidence was presented to the courts, and they recognized that living under such austere and inhumane conditions was a violation of the Eighth Amendment prohibition against cruel and unusual punishment. At other times, the courts have reinforced the position discussed in *Rhodes v. Chapman* (1981), when the United States Supreme Court held that "the Constitution does not mandate comfortable prisons" (p. 349). For instance, in a suit focused on "high temperatures" on death row at the Union Correctional Institution in Raiford, Florida, the 11th Circuit Court of Appeals agreed with the district court that "slight discomfort [should] be expected in a residential setting in Florida in a building that is not air-conditioned" (*Chandler v. Crosby*, 2004, p. 1298).

People who have lived on death row for years have provided many personal narratives—some are stories of continued survival (Flores, 2007; Masters, 2009; Moore, 2005) whereas others are not (Cahill, 2009; Chessman, 1954; Rossi, 2004; Williams, 2007). All these tales are interest-ing and even inspiring, but at the same time, they are sad and troubling stories of life and death. What follows in this chapter is neither a wide-ranging examination of death row and the conditions under which death rows operate, nor any other scholarly introspection into the frightening journey undertaken by condemned travelers on their way to the ultimate penal sanction. Rather, it is a conversation with one man—a survivor of Florida's death row.

JUAN ROBERTO MELÉNDEZ-COLÓN

His name is Juan Roberto Meléndez-Colón. On September 17, 1984, Juan was sentenced to die in Florida's electric chair for the murder of Delbert Baker. He would pass the next 17 years, 8 months, and 1 day on death row, waiting patiently for his innocence to be established. His patience was matched by the determination of the state of Florida as its officials waited for an opportunity to kill him. In December 2001, Juan's patience was rewarded when Florida Circuit Court Judge Barbara Fleischer overturned his capital murder conviction, which led to the charges against him being dismissed.

Juan had experienced life behind prison walls before his trip to death row at Raiford. A decade before he was convicted of capital murder, he had been arrested for armed robbery in Florida and served a 6-year term of imprisonment.

Charlie (Dr. Lanier): When you got arrested for this crime, that was in what year?

Juan: I mean, I was arrested on May—on a Monday, May the second, 1984.

Charlie: 1984. OK. Had you ever been arrested before or put in jail before?

Juan: Yes, I was arrested before.

Charlie: Was it something serious or just, you know, like a 30-day jail sentence?

Juan: No. It was a, it was a felony, armed robbery.

Charlie: So, you spent time in prison before.

Juan: Yes. Yes, I had spent time in prison before.

Charlie: How much time?

Juan: I was sentenced in 1975. I don't remember the day when I was sentenced, but I was sentenced to 10 years in prison for armed robbery, and I did 6 years and 9 months and that was—that will be all of it. That was how the system was at that time. You do such amount of time and you do not get out on parole. You do not get out on paper.

Charlie: All right. So, you had no paper after that time. Now, where were you, like in Raiford or something like that?

Juan: You said while I'm in prison?

Charlie: Yes, when you were in prison you did the 6 years, where was that at?

Juan: I was in Florida State Prison and, where everybody goes, about 2,000 prisoners in there. So, I was . . .

Charlie: What was the name?

Juan: [Inaudible], it is like Sing Sing. It is where everybody goes to be assigned. From there, they ship you to another institutions and other prisons and stuff like that.

Charlie: But it was maximum security.

Juan: Yes.

Charlie: Yes. OK.

Juan: Yes, you better believe it—gun towers and everything.

Later in the interview, Juan credited not being a novice to the world inside prison walls as helping him survive his experience on death row:

Charlie: Because one of the interesting questions is, is when you went into death row, you had a little bit of experience with prison. You didn't just like walk off the street straight to prison, right?

Juan: Yes. Yes, and it helped me survive.

Charlie: Right.

Juan: So, that will give you an idea . . .

Charlie: Right.

Juan: What the environment is. I feel—and this is a good question because in my days now, when I was inside and right now, I still feel the same way. I feel sorry for them went inside the first time and never had a taste of the prison because it's different. So, United States prison and you go to death row, you—some kind of way you can adapt yourself or whatever. You can handle yourself better. So, I feel very sorry for the ones that went straight into [death row].

Regardless of his prior experience with the Florida prison system, Juan was both angry and scared by the time he arrived on death row. His anger was spawned from what he believed was an unfair trial by the citizens of Polk County—a locale where "they used to burn crosses in the KKK in their parades."

Charlie: You said they were long days in the county jail, right? Is that right?

Juan: Yes.

Charlie: Yes, long days. So, you get sentenced on September 17th, 1984, and they took you right to prison, right to death row?

Juan: Yes.

Charlie: What are you thinking? I mean, you had some experience with prison—right?—and the stress and trying to deal with it and trying to cope. And all of a sudden now, you're in the county jail, you blow trial and, boom, you're on your way to death row. Brand new experience. So, what are you thinking then? I'm assuming you took a bus over there?

Juan: Yes. Everything changed when they sentence you to death—they will put shackles in your legs, a chain in your waist, handcuffs in your wrist, and they—and the whole environment changed. My feeling was I was scared. I will not lie to you. I was very scared, but I was very angry because I feel that the reason that I went in, they found me guilty was because they didn't believe my witnesses and didn't believe me because of my race and because where I'm coming from, who I am. And that's what I was more angry about. I even say it when they interview me and say, "Well, the only reason they found me guilty because they didn't believe my witnesses because my witnesses were all Black, from the African-American race." But I told them right then and there and then I will be back, in the name of Jesus I will be back and it's all in black and white. It's in the papers because I'm an innocent man, and you people are wrong.

Juan expounded on his fear of being sent to death row, and it turns out his fear was less about what awaited him "inside" than what transpired at his trial "outside." For Juan, the real fear was the present—the distrust and obvious hatred toward him among the citizen jurors of Polk County.

Charlie: You were scared of the sentence or you were scared of the conditions?

Juan: I wasn't scared of the sentence. And I'll tell you what scared me because I thought it's going to be a process, you know? In my naive mind, in my naive ways, and what I will think about the system is that when you go to—when they find the real—the killer in another trial, they want to know who really did it.

So, I think I think oh, I'll go through this process, and I know I didn't do it, and later they might get the killer or whatever. So, that's what I had in my mind. That's how naive and stupid I was. So, I just followed, and they think that I know English. I don't know English. This is the type of English I know at that time: I would say five words in English; believe me, three of them would have been cuss words. So, that's not English. So, I'm thinking that I know English and that I know everything.

And then, I got very scared, and I realized I was in some trouble when they showed the crime scene to the jurors. It was, in my case, the victim's throat was slashed. He was shot three times. There's blood everywhere. So, they're showing these pictures to the jurors in color and big—I mean about 12 inches and square, big pictures. The only thing they had was the frame. They're showing all these pictures in colors to the jurors. And when they saw the pictures, they looked straight at me.

Charlie: So, when you . . .

Juan: I saw that hate, and I saw in the eyes, and I felt if they had opportunity right then and there to kill me, they would have done it. That's how I felt. That's when I got real scared. That's how I felt.

Another hurdle for Juan in his new environment was his inability to speak English. This was compounded by his fear that he would be executed shortly. Condemned prisoner Timothy Palmes was electrocuted on November 8, 1984—shortly after Juan arrived on death row. In Juan's mind, he was going to be taking his seat in Florida's electric chair in the near future. In fact, three additional men were taken off the row and executed over the next 6 months. The executions—of James Raulerson (January 30, 1985), Johnny Witt (March 6, 1985), and Marvin Francois (May 29, 1985)—occurred frequently enough to keep Juan on edge and worried about his pending demise:

Charlie: When you go to death row at first, you didn't have good English skills. So, how did you interact with the guards?

Juan: I feel dumb, but whatever good that I learn about English, the worst of the worst—the ones the prosecutors called monsters—taught me how to read, how to write, and how to speak English.

Charlie: But when you first went in, how did you negotiate, if the guard is telling you, "Do this. Do that." You know, whatever he's telling you to do, how did you deal with that? Did they have all Spanish . . .

Juan: Amigo, all I can tell you is what happened. When I first went in, I'm scared, OK? So, I go in there. And this happened just like I'm telling you. I go in there on a Tuesday. Not that Thursday, the following Thursday, they killed the 10th person in the state of Florida. So, what do you think is going on in my mind? They are killing people here every week. How long is it going to be before they kill me? So, that's in my mind. So, I learned how to box. I learned all the exercise you can defend yourself or something. Well, I'm not going to that chair. Electricity—I've been scared of electricity all my life.

So, anyway, as they get to the 10th person, I decided to come up with a plan. I took all the sheets from my bunk, I cut them all in pieces and I took the pieces of the sheet and I made a little rope with it and I tied the little rope and I tied it to the cell door bars. So, the cell door bars slide a, a certain way. So, when they push the button in the control room it stays all tied up, the cell door is not going to open. They'd have to cut the ropes off. So, I'm thinking, "Well, by the time they come and get me, I can get a good warm-up, and when they come over here, and I can fight them."

This is what's going through my mind. I'm lost in there. So, now, I've got the bars all tied up, and I'm doing exercises, feeling real good, and I'm trying to make muscles coming out of my eyebrows to intimidate the guards because I'm scared. But anyway, here comes the correction officer, African American person, and when he see the doors all tied up, he gets angry. And then, he starts cursing. I don't know too much English, but I know how to curse.

So, in a very bad way, I reminded him of his mother, father, all the way down. So, the correction officer and [I] were just cursing each other out and the rest of the condemned men, they got involved with it. And to my surprise, they went against me. They say that I was wrong, that all I do is get up in the morning and get in the cell door bars and nag and curse and cry about my innocence. Then, they told me that I do not know how to read. I do not know how to write. I do not know how to speak English. And then, they told me the most beautiful thing I could hear at that time: They told me they would teach me. And just like I've told you before, the worst of the worst, the ones the prosecutors call monsters, they taught me how to read, taught me how to write, taught me how to speak English. And believe me, my amigo, if they would never have taught me, I would never survive.

Juan did surmount his not-so-unfounded fear about dying on death row—he did survive, and eventually, he was freed. Establishing his innocence was important to him but so was his concern that the real murderer of Delbert Baker was roaming free to commit further acts of violence.

Charlie: When you first went on the row, you mentioned something about 10 days later they executed somebody. Did I get that right?

Juan: Yes. That's what I was talking about, and that's what I was thinking when—I was thinking they was executing in there every week because when I went to that one in Florida, Florida was the number one executing people, was number one before Texas.

Charlie: So, you're thinking at that time—so, I think you made a comment that you didn't know the process. So, I'm just trying to get your mind-set. When you first get in there and you see somebody executed after a week or so, you're thinking . . .

Juan: That's what I'm telling you. That's what I'm . . .

Charlie: It'd be me tomorrow, right?

Juan: That's right, amigo. That's what—exactly, you got it right. That's exactly what's in my mind.

Charlie: OK.

Juan: So, I've been thinking they're killing people here every week. How long it's going to be before they get me?

Charlie: So, one of the things when you—you'd said a number of times you were scared when you went to death row. It's not so much, "I'm scared that somebody is going to get me—you know, that I'm afraid of jail." You're scared is, it all revolves around the fact that this threat of death was hanging over your head.

Juan: Exactly. And not only that, amigo, and believe me and I thought about this a lot, here I am doing all this damn time for a crime I did not commit and what do you think the real killer is doing?

Charlie: Yes. He could be doing anything.

Juan: He's doing more killing.

Again, his fear of being pulled out of his cell and executed in short order remained, as did his anger.

Juan: Potentially, all violent crimes, and here I am, doing this time for—so, there's a lot of things going through my head now. I'm very angry.

Charlie: And this is right—again, sort of right when you first get to death row. This is what's on your mind.

Juan: Yes.

Charlie: But you're angry about this guy being out there. You're innocent.

Juan: Yes. And I'm angry with the system that want to kill me for something I did not do.

Charlie: And that you could be executed any day.

Juan: Yes.

Charlie: You're not thinking 3 years down the line. You're thinking . . .

Juan: No. No. And especially in that time, mi amigo, don't forget that Florida was the first one when they reinstated the death penalty, Florida was the first one they executed in 1979. So, Florida was hot when I came in with the first nonvoluntary execution.

SUICIDE AND PSYCHOLOGICAL TRAUMA

One aspect of life on death row that seems particularly troubling to most people who live there is making friends with a person who eventually might be executed. The loss of a friend, or even just another death row acquaintance, is bad enough, but it is also a reminder that your own death at the hands of the state may be just a little closer with each passing execution. Although Juan got over the belief that he was going to be executed fairly quickly once he arrived on death row, he nonetheless had friends who were killed along the way.

Juan: And the hardest thing for me in there was so you understand is when they execute one of them. He's from—in a cell, and I'm in another cell next to him. He's a person that I know for 10, 15 years, maybe more. He cries on my shoulder. He shared with me his most intimate thoughts and I shared mine with him.

I learned to love him and one day they snatched him out of there, and I know what's going to happen. They're going to kill him, and I cannot stop it. In that time, it was the electric chair. So, they got to generate the electricity because it's 2,010 volts; they got to go through his body to get him killed, and I can hear the buzzing sound. And, amigo, I'm not lying to you, right today, it's still in my mind, and I cannot stop it. And I know precisely the time when they burn the life out of him because the lights keep going on and off, and I cannot stop it.

And the worst thing of all, some of them are innocent like Jesse Tafero, Benny Demps, Leo Jones, Pedro Medina, and my homeboy from Puerto Rico, Angel Nieves-Diaz, who on a legal plea bargain they offered him 5 years. He did not take it simply because he did not commit the crime. It cost him his life. And all I can say is, "I'll see you soon." And for me, that was the hardest thing inside.

Confronting the trauma generated by the death of a family member or close friend is a challenge under the best of circumstances. However, given the circumstances of living on death row, the anger and powerlessness one feels can manifest itself in thoughts of suicide, just ending it all. Juan was no different from many others on death row in wanting his life to end by his own hand rather than sitting and waiting for his death sentence to be carried out by the state of Florida.

Juan: Here I am. I wanted to kill myself, OK? I'm tired of it. I want out of there. All that was going on in my head is to hang myself. I will tell you how they do it. They got what is called a runner. A runner is an inmate in population. He's not sentenced to death, and so they do the work in the death row facility place because the guards, they don't do nothing. All they do is watch you, and some of them give you a hard time when they can.

So, the runner is the one that supplies us with the toothbrush, the toothpaste, the mop, and the broom. But he can also supply you with a tool that you can take your life with, and he knows it. All you have to do is give him four stamps or rolling paper, and he will give you this tool.

Charlie: And people know this, right? People know that this guy can give you . . .

Juan: Yes. The guards know it, amigo.

Charlie: OK.

Juan: It's a plastic garbage bag.

Charlie: That's right.

Juan: So, it's real simple. When the guard isn't looking, he will swing that bag in the cell so you can make a rope then put a noose in it. You put the noose in your neck. So, you tie the other part in the cell door bars, then you throw yourself down, and then you're dead but you're free. That's what the demons used to tell me: "Why? Why do you have to go through all of this? You are a Puerto Rican, a real macho man. Don't give them the satisfaction, just do it yourself. You say you didn't do it. Do you think they're going to believe you? They're going to kill you anyway. So, grab that bag." And that's what stayed in my mind.

So, now, I want to take this trip. You see I'm tired of it. I want out of there. I'm depressed. So, I tell the runner, "Give me. Give me that garbage bag." So, when the guard is not looking, he swings the bag inside my cell. I took that bag and twisted it all up and I made a rope. Then I put a noose in it. Then, I look at my bunk and I look at the rope and I say to myself, "I better lay down and think about this a little bit more."

So, I lay down. And when I lay down, I fell in a deep, deep, deep sleep, and I start dreaming that I was a little kid again, doing the things I used to do when I was a little kid, the things that made me happy, the things that made me smile. You see I was born in Brooklyn, New York, but I was raised on the island of Puerto Rico. They took me back when I was just a little kid.

So, when I get up in the morning and look to the east side, there's a wonderful mountain. And if I walk 6 minutes toward the south, I find myself in the most beautiful beach in the world, at least to me. So, here I am, dreaming that I'm swimming in the beautiful Caribbean Sea—a little kid again. The water is warm. The sky is so bright. The sun is so warm. It's a beautiful day. The sky is so blue.

Then, I get to see something that I never saw before: four dolphins coming my way, and they passed me, and they turn around, and a pair got on one side, and a pair got on another side. And they started flipping and jumping like dolphins do. So, I was having a ball in there, mi amigo—so happy. Then, I look to the shore and there's a beautiful lady waving, smiling, throwing kisses at me, and she seems so happy. And I know why she's happy. She's happy because I'm happy. That's my beautiful mother.

Then I wake up. When I wake up, the bunk smells like a beach. Then, I took that rope that I was going to take my life with, and I walked straight to the toilet with it. I looked at the toilet, looked at the rope, and I said real loud, "I don't want to die," and I flushed it. But the true fact is, mi amigo, it was lots and lots and lots of beautiful dreams. Every time I got depressed, every time I wanted out of there, every time suicide thoughts came to my mind, our creator God sent me a beautiful dream. And I was wise enough to grab all of them dreams as a sign of hope that one day I would be out of there, that I would be free.

Like God was telling me, "Hey, I know you didn't do it. But, I control the time; you get out when I say you get out. You just got to trust me." And when I analyze everything, I come to one conclusion: It took 17 years, 8 months and 1 day to also change the man. So, when you see, hear, all of this, that's what saved me: dreams. And I was wise enough to have that hope that better days will come, thinking positive.

And Juan gained his positive outlook by way of his family and eventually through his renewed belief in God. Several decades ago, Robert Johnson (1989) wrote about the people who inhabit death row:

> The stress suffered by condemned prisoners is manifested in feelings of powerlessness, fear, and emotional emptiness. Deterioration is a constant and formidable enemy of the condemned. . . . Without support and assistance, many prisoners will eventually succumb to the pressures of death row confinement. (p. 122)

Juan luckily had the support of family and friends on death row, and that knowledge sustained him through the years of his imprisonment.

Juan: But my family suffered a lot, especially my mama and five aunts. I don't know how this generation is in these days, but in my days when I was growing up, if my aunts caught me doing something wrong, believe me, amigo, there is going to be a good ass whooping. And then, I got to get on my knees to pray to God that she don't tell mama. Because when she tell mama, there's going to be another good ass whooping. But, when I was hungry, they always feed me. When I needed clothes, they always bought them for me, and on death row, they never forgot me. They wrote me lots and lots of letters, sent me a lot of photos of the ones that were born, you know, and I saw all of them grow up through pictures. They really love to keep the family together.

Charlie: This was your mother and aunts?

Juan: Yes. That's my aunt and mama. No, now, I will tell you about my mama. I believe she suffered more than anybody. She also wrote me lots and lots of letters that gave me so much hope and helped me keep the will to live. There's one letter that I always keep with me, and when I'm down and sad and weak, I read it, and it always boosts me up, and it goes like this. She wrote and said, "Son, I just built an altar, and that altar, I put the statue of the Virgin of the Guadalupe in it, and I cut roses, and I put them in it. And I pray three rosaries a day, hoping, searching, looking for a miracle. And the miracle will come, son, because I know that you are innocent, and God knows that you are innocent."

For some, one of the more surprising revelations of Juan's stay on death row was the guidance and instruction he received from his fellow prisoners. Fellow inhabitants of death row also inspired Juan with a will to conquer his time on the row and make it back to the world outside. It was his peers on death row that taught him English during his stay there. And when his anger reached its peak, they counseled him to behave in a more productive manner—even if some of them lost their own way during the passage of time.

Charlie: So, you're there in the early stages, the first week, 2 weeks. You're very angry. You're scared, and we know why—you're pissed off being there. And at some point—I don't know if you're saying things or shouting things—but at some point, other people sort of get on your case a little bit and say you got to get with it, you know? Is that about that right?

Juan: Yes. Yes, because I was acting very irrational. I was thinking something like a revolution in there, mi amigo, and acting like a fool, and they told me, "No, you got to use your head. You beat them with papers just like they did to you" and, "Don't use violence. That's what they want you to do." And so they calmed me down.

Charlie: These have to be other Spanish-speaking prisoners, right?

Juan: No. No. No, mi amigo, they were some dudes. They were speaking the English that I don't understand.

Charlie: OK. So, they're talking to you, and they're telling you, "You got to calm down," but they're also telling you you got to learn English, right?

Juan: Exactly.

Charlie: And this was early on. This wasn't 10 years into your bid, right? This was early on.

Juan: Early on. And then throughout the years, I'm looking at them, and some of them went crazy. Some of them committed suicide, and some of them did not worry and educated themselves and became mentors.

Beyond the anger and fear that accompanied him to the condemned housing unit, Juan also battled boredom during his stay on death row. Life on the row was difficult for the men housed there, and its effects ravaged many of the people sitting in cells, waiting for their date with the executioner. As another death row prisoner, this one from Louisiana, noted in his memoirs,

> On death row, we had to build our day-to-day existence in a vacuum. The existence was senseless; we were just waiting to die. For a long time, indeed, I didn't care whether I lived or died. I had little reason to live. (Rideau, 2010, p. 45)

To wage this war against the ennui that plagued his life on death row, Juan watched television, read books, went to the yard.

Charlie: So, let me ask you this. You're in there for a couple of weeks. You're acting out. I'm just saying a couple of weeks. It could be a couple of months. I don't know. But after a bit of time, they say you got to change the way you're doing things. What did you do during that period? Did you just exercise in your cell? Did you have books? You had rec—you must have gone out for rec.

Juan: We do a lot of reading. We have a TV, but the TV—all you have to do is watch it for 1 year, and then you don't have to watch it for the next 15 years because it's the same damn thing. It's same one channel to the other one. You got four channels and one channel with the same thing. So, anyway, we got that. We get books we can read. You cannot send a book. The book has to come straight from the publisher.

Charlie: Right.

Juan: And things like that. We get the newspaper. We're aware of some of the news and stuff like that.

Charlie: The yard.

Juan: We got the yard. We go to the yard 4 hours a week—2 hours on a Monday, 2 hours on a Wednesday if it's not raining. All they got to do is see a little cloud in the sky: "Inclement weather today; no yard," and there's not one single drop of rain falling.

But the ones who worried about things were the ones that got old before their time. And so, people in there with black hair, in a year or 2, their whole hair was white, walking like zombies. So, a lot of things that—I didn't want to end up like that, so I followed the mentors, the ones that were trying to educate me. And in the end, I learned to let hate and anger go. Don't let it dominate you. I learned to—when you get depressed, try the best you can to get out of that stage. I used to use a towel, wet a towel, and clean the cell. I get tired, really tired. I lay down in the bunk, and I read.

Juan recalled an incident that happened in the yard when they were let out for recreation—an event that would land him in segregation and facing greater boredom and more challenges than normal. This event stemmed from the death of one of his friends, who was stricken when they were out in the yard. This man was all but ignored by the correctional and medical staff and as a result died before he could be removed from the yard.

Juan: Yes, amigo. I've seen two people kill two people in the yard.

Charlie: So, you went out with a number of other people.

Juan: Yes, other people. I've seen—I remember one time going out to the yard seeing all the ones. Like I told you, we go 4 hours a week: 2 hours on a Monday, 2 hours on a Wednesday if it's not raining. And this Monday, we all went, all the ones that taught me how to read, how to write, and how to speak English. But very particular, this African American person, this Black man. I call them brothers. They all taught me how to read and how to write and how to speak English. But this one, he was pushy: "You need to learn this. You need to learn that." And believe me, my friend, I loved him dear for that.

So, the brothers, the African Americans, they like to play basketball, and some others play volleyball in the yard. I did weights because I like to burn steam and go back to the cell and rest a little bit better. So, this Monday, we all went. There was not that cloud in the sky. So, they take us out the yard. The process they got to go through. That's why they don't want to take us out.

So, they take us out to the yard. And I'm lifting weights, and the other ones are playing basketball. And my friend, my brother—this African American person that I'm telling you about—he was playing basketball.

So, but all of a sudden he falls down, and we all stop what we were doing and ran across to him. When I got close to him, I noticed that white foam was coming out of his mouth and nose.

So, I assume this got to be a stroke, a heart attack. So, we tell the guards in the gate, "We have a man down that needs medical assistance." So, they take their time with a walkie-talkie, and they call the clinic and here comes the so-called nurse. It's a big tall White man with great big belly. So, they let him go inside the gate and tell us in the yard to put up our back to the fence, and from the gun towers, they point machine guns at us.

You better not move. They will shoot you. So, now my friend's on the ground and the so-called nurse inside the yard, this tall White man with his big great belly. And I noticed that he did not have a medical bag, but he had something—he had about a half a pound of chewing tobacco in his mouth, and you can see this black stuff is running to the side of his mouth and every once in a while, he spits. He's in the yard now, and there's the brother on the ground.

So, now, we tell him, "He's not breathing. He needs air." So, he tell us, "I have to go to the clinic and get an oxygen tank." So, he walks really— and he spits. So, he walks real slow back to the clinic. Come back real slow back to the yard and then he take the oxygen tank and put it in my friend's mouth. And then, the nurse gets up, and we tell him he's still not breathing. He needs air.

Then, the nurse said, "I have to go back to the clinic and get another oxygen tank. This one here is not working," and he spits. So, I tell him, "You don't have to. You can do CPR, mouth-to-mouth." But, amigo, telling one of them to do CPR, mouth-to-mouth to a brother on the ground, you're wasting your time. So, the nurse looks up. Then the nurse looks down. Then, he made a statement using these two racist words, "The M and the N, and now I'm not going to put my mouth in there," and he spits.

And I said, "You don't have to. I'll do it. You just do the counting," and he agreed. I'm so glad he agreed because I'm trying to save my friend's life. So, I went down there, and I take my T-shirt off, and I wipe the white foam my friend got on his mouth and nose. And the so-called nurse, he start counting: one, two, three, and I blow air. One, two, three, and I blow air again. One, two, three, and I blow air, and my friend opened his eyes. I'm so glad he opened his eyes. I see a sign of hope. He's going to live.

But all of a sudden, his eyes rolled back, and he made a frown with his face. Then, he breathed real hard, and air came out. I think that was his soul that left him because he died right in my arms. So, now I'm angry, and I want to do something to this so-called nurse that let my friend die in the yard like a dog. Just as I was about to do something to the nurse, the rest of the condemned men snatched me out of there, threw me in the corner, and they say, "Puerto Rican Johnny don't get to no more trouble that you already are in."

When Juan complained about the lack of treatment his friend received, he was sanctioned and taken to segregation:

Juan: I still go to the confinement, to the hole, for 90 days for disrespecting a member of the staff, whatever that means, but I learned a lesson. I learned that I had to look and search and trust something more powerful than the system. And believe me, the ones that did not grab something spiritual either went crazy or committed suicide.

Some of them become Muslims, and they taught others how to read, how to write, how to speak English, how to respect. Some of them become Buddhists. I don't know what they worship, but they taught others how to love, how to have compassion, and how to forgive. Some of them become Christians. That's what I did. I went back to my roots and tried to remember everything my mama told me about Jesus Christ, the Holy Ghost, and Virgin Mary. She's Catholic to the bones.

And this is my personal opinion. I believe that we are all serving the same God with different names. Then all we have to do is make good choices in life, do good deeds, and you have no problem going to heaven. And this friend of mine, who the State of Florida let him die in the yard like a dog, 1 month after his death, he won new trial. By letting him die in there like a dog, the state of Florida denied my friend the right to prove his innocence.

And, yet, Juan's trip to "the hole" had a salutary effect. Maintaining a positive outlook, and having hope, are integral to surviving a stay on death row.

Charlie: When you talked a minute ago about spiritual—some people have to get spiritual, you know, something in order to survive. Was that like a turning point for you? You went back and said, "I got back from my Christian roots after this."

Juan: Well, I had to turn to the Bible. I had to go back to my roots, everything my mother taught me about Jesus Christ, the Virgin Mary, and the Holy Ghost.

Charlie: With that specific point, was that like a very significant point for you in terms of . . .

Juan: A turning point.

Charlie: Yes, a turning point.

Juan: Right. Yes. Yes. Yes.

Charlie: But is that sort of saying it promoted you to go back and say, you know—I mean, that's got to be a pretty—and you had 90 days to think about it, right? When this happened, you had 90 days in the hole.

Juan: Yes. Yes.

Charlie: And that gives you time to think about this because when you . . .

Juan: I see what you're talking about now. Yes. I had a lot of times to think about it.

Charlie: That's what I'm trying to say. This incident is fresh in your mind. When you get set up for 90 days, does it—is this where it sort of crystallized, and you sort of got your faith back or . . .

Juan: Yes. Yes. It's all about thinking positive, mi amigo. That's how you survive.

Charlie: You saw people that thought negatively, right?

Juan: Yes. They went crazy, and they committed suicide, most—a lot of them.

Admittedly, it was a struggle to preserve and maintain his innocence over time. Juan recalled drawing on his dream to keep hope alive and to stave off thoughts of taking his own life. He related, "Every time I got depressed, every time I want out of there, every time suicide thoughts came to my mind, God sent me the beautiful dream," the dream in which Juan is swimming in the beautiful Caribbean Sea and four dolphins are coming his way. He also drew on the strength he received from his family.

Charlie: So, 10 years in. So, you had hope up until that 10 years, and then you sort of began to falter—is that it?

Juan: Yes, getting better and better and realizing that everything that happened to me was out of my power. I have no power to resolve the problem. So, I have to hope in something—a miracle.

Charlie: And part of the hope came from your mother, your aunt. You had other people that supported you along the way.

Juan: Yes. Yes. And people from the free world that wrote me letters and made me feel that I was not by myself in this matter.

On January 3, 2002, Juan Roberto Meléndez-Colón was released from prison after existing on death row for almost two decades, and he finally got the chance to put Union Correctional Institution at Raiford in the rearview mirror. An abiding sense of hope, a sincere spiritual faith, and the loving support of family and friends all served to help Juan survive almost 18 years under sentence of death in Florida—a state boasting the fourth highest number of executions since the court reauthorized capital punishment in *Gregg v. Georgia* in 1976.

In addition to establishing his own innocence, one of Juan's concerns focused on what "the real killer is doing." As his various appeals were denied and the time for his execution drew ever closer, he finally found out. In a search of his old case files, members of his current defense team located a taped confession made by a man named Vernon James. Although he had passed away, the defense located witnesses who knew that James had confessed to the murder before he died. After almost 20 years, the September 13, 1983, murder of Delbert Baker was solved, and Juan Roberto Meléndez-Colón was freed.

In *Rhodes v. Chapman* (1981), the court held that "the Constitution does not mandate comfortable prisons" (p. 349) but that the conditions of confinement "must not involve the wanton and unnecessary infliction of pain, nor may they be grossly disproportionate to the severity of the crime warranting imprisonment" (p. 347). Death row housing that violates this screed thus appears to violate the Constitution's Eighth Amendment protection against cruel and unusual punishments.

In fact, this issue has been brought to the court's attention—so far unsuccessfully—on several occasions. For instance, some inhabitants of death row have claimed that years of being warehoused while awaiting execution is a violation of the Constitution's prohibition of cruel and unusual punishment (e.g., *Elledge v. Florida*, 1998; *Knight v. Florida*, 1999; *Valle v. Florida*, 2011).

Moreover, in a Memorandum regarding the denial of certiorari in a Texas death penalty case, Justice Stevens reflected,

> Often, a denial of certiorari on a novel issue will permit the state and federal courts to "serve as laboratories in which the issue receives further study before it is addressed by this Court." *McCray v. New York*, 461 U.S., at 963. Petitioner's claim, with its legal complexity and its potential for far reaching consequences, seems an ideal example of one which would benefit from such further study. (*Lackey v. Texas*, 1995, p. 1047)

Yet, in reflecting on the notion that some men and women should face decades of isolation in solitary confinement awaiting execution in "laboratories in which the issue receives further study," I wonder about the humanity of the justice's calculation. How much misery and psychological damage must people condemned to die experience before the state either releases them or puts them to death? Perhaps the attention brought to this issue by men like Juan who have been exonerated and removed from death row before they were executed may inspire the justices to finally focus on the conditions under which the condemned are compelled to await their fate.

Juan is but one of a number of Americans who have been unjustly convicted and sentenced to die. In fact, according to the Death Penalty Information Center (2017), since 1973, 157 people have been exonerated and freed from death row. His willingness to expend his energy on informing his fellow citizens about the inequity of a death penalty system that compels convicted murderers (whether guilty as charged or wholly innocent) to spend the years of their imprisonment in a dehumanizing fashion is commendable.

Hopefully, the exhortations of Juan and his fellow exonerees (see, e.g., Witness to Innocence, https://www.witnesstoinnocence.org/exonerees) who have returned home will continue to shed light on the life of condemned prisoners. This is "his story," and although not generalizable to all death rows, it nonetheless remains instructive. Juan raises troubling issues that we recognize from a wide range of scholarly sources and popular literature. What is missing, though, is the will of the nation's legislatures and courts to confront these matters in a responsible and humane fashion.

REFERENCES

Bluestone, H., & McGahee, C. L. (1962). Reaction to extreme stress: Impending death by execution. *The American Journal of Psychiatry, 119,* 393–396. http://dx.doi.org/10.1176/ajp.119.5.393

Cahill, T. (2009). *A saint on death row: The story of Dominique Green.* New York, NY: Doubleday.

Chandler v. Crosby, 379 F.3d 1278 (11th Cir. 2004).

Chessman, C. W. (1954). *Cell 2455, death row: A condemned man's own story.* New York, NY: Prentice-Hall.

Death Penalty Information Center. (2017). *Innocence and the death penalty.* Retrieved from http://www.deathpenaltyinfo.org/innocence-and-death-penalty

Elledge v. Florida, 525 U.S. 944 (1998).

Flores, C. D. (2007). *Warrior within: Inside report on Texas death row.* Benton Harbor, MI: Patterson Printing.

Gates v. Cook, 376 F.3d 323 (5th Cir. 2004).

Gregg v. Georgia, 428 U.S. 153 (1976).

Hudson, D. (1999). *Managing death-sentenced inmates: A survey of practices* (2nd ed.). Lanham, MD: American Correctional Association.

Jackson, B., & Christian, D. (1980). *Death row: A devastating report on life inside the Texas death house*. Boston, MA: Beacon Press.

Johnson, R. (1989). *Condemned to die: Life under sentence of death*. Prospect Heights, IL: Waveland Press.

Johnson, R. (1998). *Death work: A study of the modern execution process*. Belmont, CA: Wadsworth.

Johnson, R. (2016). Solitary confinement until death by state-sponsored homicide: An eighth amendment assessment of the modern execution process. *Washington and Lee Law Review, 73*, 1213–1242.

Johnson, R., & Davies, H. (2014). Life under sentence of death: Historical and contemporary perspectives. In J. R. Acker, R. M. Bohm, & C. S. Lanier (Eds.), *America's experiment with capital punishment: Reflections on the past, present, and future of the ultimate penal sanction* (pp. 661–685). Durham, NC: Carolina Academic Press.

Knight v. Florida, 528 U.S. 990 (1999).

Lackey v. Texas, 514 U.S. 1045 (1995).

Lombardi, G., Sluder, R. D., & Wallace, D. (1996, March). *The management of death-sentenced inmates: Issues, realities, and innovative strategies*. Paper presented at the meeting of the Academy of Criminal Justice Sciences, Las Vegas, NV.

Masters, J. J. (2009). *That bird has my wings: The autobiography of an innocent man on death row*. New York, NY: HarperCollins.

Moore, B. N. (2005). *I shall not die: Seventy-two hours on death watch*. Bloomington, IN: AuthorHouse.

Rhodes v. Chapman, 452 U.S. 337 (1981).

Rideau, W. (2010). *In the place of justice: A story of punishment and deliverance*. New York, NY: Alfred A. Knopf.

Rossi, R. M. (2004). *Waiting to die: Life on death row*. London, England: Vision.

Valle v. Florida, 564 U.S. 1067 (2011).

Williams, S. T. (2007). *Blue rage, black redemption: A memoir*. New York, NY: Simon & Schuster/Touchstone Books.

12

Continuing Trauma and Aftermath for Exonerated Death Row Survivors

Saundra D. Westervelt and Kimberly J. Cook

Death row exonerees are factually innocent men and women who have been wrongly convicted of capital crimes, sent to death row, and later exonerated.[1] Our research documents the aftermath challenges faced by these exonerated death row survivors (Baumgartner, Westervelt, & Cook, 2014; Cook, Westervelt, & Maruna, 2014; Westervelt & Cook, 2010, 2012b, 2013). On release, death row exonerees confront the continuing trauma of having lived on death row. They confront the crippling stigma of having been condemned to death and significant challenges in rebuilding their identities free from that stigma. They encounter new relationships with families who matured without them and who, in some cases, abandoned them, thinking they would never return. They also experience the physical, emotional, and psychological damage created by living in isolation, despair, and neglect. Confronting

---

[1] See the Death Penalty Information Center's (2017b) list for the criteria used for inclusion.

http://dx.doi.org/10.1037/0000084-013
Living on Death Row: The Psychology of Waiting to Die, H. Toch, J. R. Acker, and V. M. Bonventre (Editors)

these challenges is made more difficult without systemic support or assistance. They are "kicked to the curb," as described by death row exoneree Sabrina Butler, left mostly to their own limited resources and networks to figure it out. She recalled, "They didn't give me jack! They just took the handcuffs off me, and sent me out the door" (Westervelt & Cook, 2012b, p. 60). It is from these voices that we learn about the aftermath of living on death row.

What is the impact of being condemned for crimes you did not commit? To be told you are so heinous and unworthy that you will be executed, eliminated from humanity? To hear your mother's cries and children's sobs as you are taken away ostensibly forever? What is the impact of living in a box, a cage, for years on end, in virtual isolation, with little human contact, almost none of which is positive, caring, loving? What is the impact of watching those around you taken to their deaths, smelling the moment of their extermination, wondering whether you will be next?

We gained insight into answers to these questions through extended discussions with 18 death row survivors, who are among the few uniquely qualified to shed light on the trauma associated with living on death row. Interviewing or even talking with individuals living on death row is exceedingly challenging, made difficult by the layers of security separating death row inhabitants from the general public, from loved ones, and even from each other. Even fewer individuals can explain the struggle of managing the trauma of surviving death row. Most people on "the row" never experience freedom again. They are either executed or, because of significant errors in their original cases, resentenced to a penalty less than death, such as life imprisonment (Liebman, Fagan, & West, 2000). Few death row occupants are released because of evidence of their factual innocence, and those who are released go through grueling years of legal challenges to obtain their freedom. According to the Death Penalty Information Center (2017a), as of August 2017, 159 former death row prisoners have been released on the basis of substantial evidence of their factual innocence. We call these individuals *death row exonerees* and *death row survivors* interchangeably.

OUR STUDY

We conducted life-history interviews with 18 death row exonerees from across the United States between 2003 and 2007, resulting in over 3,500 pages of typed transcript. (See Table 12.1 for information about our participants.) Exonerees were chosen from the Death Penalty Information Center's (DPIC; 2017b) list of individuals exonerated from capital crimes because of substantial evidence of their factual innocence. When we began our study, 110 individuals were on that list; the list now includes 159 exonerees. When we began, only two lists of exonerees of any kind existed: the DPIC list and the Innocence Project's (https://www. innocenceproject.org/cases/) list of DNA exonerees (which in August 2017 included 351 DNA exonerations). When we began our study in 2003, the National Registry of Exonerations (NRE; https://www.law. umich.edu/special/exoneration/Pages/detaillist.aspx) had not yet been launched. By August 2017, the NRE had documented 2,081 exonerations from wrongful convictions in the United States since 1989. We chose to work from the DPIC list because it was inclusive of all exonerees who had originally been convicted of capital crimes, regardless of mechanism of exoneration and because "death is different" (Bedau, 1987). We believed death row exonerees had experienced complex trauma over and above those convicted of noncapital crimes because of their experience of being condemned to death and, in some cases, being close to execution.

Exonerees were chosen for participation according to the amount of time incarcerated and on death row, the state in which the conviction occurred, time since exoneration, race or ethnicity, and gender. (For a detailed explanation of the methods used in this study, which is beyond the scope of the discussion here, see Westervelt & Cook, 2007, 2012b.) Our research required travel to each exoneree because, at that time, exonerees did not have regular gathering events, as they do now, such as at the annual Innocence Network meetings (http://innocencenetwork.org/ networkconference/) or the annual gathering of exonerated death row survivors sponsored by Witness to Innocence (https://www. witnesstoinnocence.org/).

Table 12.1

Biographical Details of Participants

Name	Sex	Race	Age at conviction	State where tried	Years in prison[a]	Years on death row[b]	Year of exoneration	DNA?	Actual offender(s) identified?[c]	Compensation received?[d]
Beeman	M	W	23	OH	3	2.5	1979	no	yes	no
Bloodsworth	M	W	24	MD	8	1.5	1993	yes	yes	yes
Brown	M	B	24	FL	13	13	1987	no	no	no
Butler	F	B	19	MS	5.5	2.5	1995	no	no	yes
Cobb	M	B	37	IL	7	4	1987	no	yes	yes
Fain	M	W	35	ID	18	17.5	2001	yes	no	no
Gauger	M	W	41	IL	3	0	1996	no	yes	no
Gell	M	W	23	NC	6	4.5	2004	no	yes	yes
Howard	M	B	23	OH	26	1	2003	no	no	yes
James	M	B	23	OH	26	1	2003	no	no	yes
Keaton	M	B	19	FL	2	1	1973	no	yes	no

Krone	M	W	35	AZ	9.5	2.5	2002	yes	yes	yes
McMillian	M	B	47	AL	5	5	1993	no	no	yes
Meléndez-Colón	M	L	33	FL	17.5	17.5	2002	no	yes	no
Rivera	M	L	25	NC	2	1.5	1999	no	yes	no
Taylor[e]	M	B	29	IL	13	10	2003	no	no	yes
Tibbs	M	B	35	FL	2	1.5	1982	no	no	no
Wilhoit	M	W	32	OK	4	4	1993	no	no	no

Note. From *Life After Death Row: Exonerees' Search for Community and Identity* (pp. 31–32), by S. D. Westervelt and K. J. Cook, 2012, New Brunswick, NJ: Rutgers University Press. Copyright 2012 by Saundra D. Westervelt and Kimberly J. Cook. Reprinted with permission.

[a]This category includes only the years in prison for this wrongful conviction and does not include any prior years of incarceration on other charges. In addition, several participants were not released from prison immediately after exoneration as they completed sentences on other, unrelated charges. That time is not included here. This category also does not include any time they spent in jail or prison awaiting trial, which in some instances was 2 to 3 additional years. Numbers (for years in prison and years on death row) are not exact and may have been rounded slightly up or down by 1 to 3 months. [b]The number of years spent on death row may not equal the years spent in prison. Several exonerees received retrials after appellate review and were reconvicted on the same charges, but were sentenced to life in prison rather than death. At that point, they were moved from death row into the general population of prison until their eventual exonerations. [c]This category includes cases in which the actual perpetrator of the crime for which the exoneree was wrongfully convicted either has been tried and convicted for that crime or has been publicly acknowledged in some way as the actual offender, even if not convicted. [d]Of those receiving compensation, only three—Bloodsworth, Butler, and Cobb—were provided compensation via compensation statutes in their states. The others were compensated as a result of litigation pursued against local, county, and/or state officials and agencies. [e]This exoneree prefers to remain anonymous. We have assigned this pseudonym to him.

The focus of our initial study was on the aftermath of wrongful convictions, which had received the least attention of issues around wrongful convictions at the time. What happens to exonerees after exoneration and release? How do they reintegrate into their families and communities? What obstacles do they encounter to reintegration? How do they cope? At that time, we did not specifically intend to examine the enduring trauma experienced by those who had lived on death row. For context, we asked our participants about their time on death row, about their harrowing experiences of being sentenced to die for a crime they did not commit, and how they coped with the turmoil those experiences created. From these discussions, the continuing trauma of a life lived under sentence of death emerged as a significant theme. Our participants made it clear that the effects of life on death row did not stop when the prison door opened to their freedom. Although we had conceptualized life after death row as distinct from life on death row, they demonstrated that the two are inextricably linked. Here, we more explicitly examine this link—how the experience of life on the row colored the life they attempted to rebuild after they left it behind and how new traumas postexoneration added insult to injury.

Emerging from our research, we now work with exonerated death row survivors and others affected by wrongful convictions in a variety of ways, in the tradition of public sociology (Burawoy, 2004). We remain in contact with our original research participants as much as possible and now consider many of them close friends. In fact, we often celebrate life's milestones with them (e.g., marriage, arrival of a grandchild, publication of a book or movie about their case). Saundra Westervelt recently concluded a 5-year tenure on the board of directors for the nonprofit organization Witness to Innocence, whose mission is "to abolish the death penalty" and "to support death row survivors and their loved ones as they confront the challenges of life after exoneration" (Witness to Innocence, 2017, para. 1). Kim Cook serves on the board of directors of Healing Justice (http://www.healingjusticeproject.org/), whose mission is to provide support, reconciliation, and recovery in cases involving exonerations. We have both participated in Innocence Network conferences and Witness to Innocence annual gatherings, where exonerated men and women come together to provide peer support for each other. Occasionally, lawyers and other advocates contact us for advice on how to prepare for a client's or a client's family member's release after a wrongful incarceration. In addition, our social media presence helps to maintain and expand our contact with others who experience wrongful convictions. Exonerees are the "owners," and we have become the "wise," to use a concept from Goffman's (1963) study of stigma.

THE SUSTAINED CATASTROPHE OF A WRONGFUL CAPITAL CONVICTION

We have previously written that a wrongful capital conviction is a "sustained catastrophe" similar in scope and traumatic impact to being a prisoner of war or victim of a life-threatening disease or physical abuse (Westervelt & Cook, 2008, 2012b). Unlike a natural disaster, when the original traumatizing event lasts for a relatively short time, a wrongful capital conviction and incarceration is a traumatic experience that is sustained over a long period. Our participants were incarcerated for periods ranging from 2 to 26 years, averaging 9.5 years (Westervelt & Cook, 2012b, p. 30). The catastrophe begins with the arrest of an innocent person; continues through the pretrial detention, trial, and conviction; and extends seemingly endlessly and toward death every day the innocent person is incarcerated on death row. Snatched from their lives and held hostage by the state, death row survivors see the similarities of their experiences to those of other survivors of catastrophes and human atrocities (Westervelt & Cook, 2008, 2012b). Catastrophes alter people's understanding of themselves, their communities, and their place in the world around them. As described by Cohen and Taylor (1972),

> Sometimes the blow is sudden and physical: a motor car accident, being caught in a flood or hurricane. Sometimes it is long lasting: suffering a prolonged illness, fighting through a war, being evacuated to a strange area, or being cut off from loved ones. Such experiences have disturbing consequences: we talk of people "going grey overnight," "being scarred for life," "becoming stunted" or "crippled" or even "never being the same

again." These experiences are literally or metaphorically shattering: they break the web of meaning we have built up around ourselves and at the same time show how fragile this web is. (pp. 42–43)

Generally speaking, when the moment of trauma ends, trauma survivors struggle to recover from their traumatic experiences, and many experience posttraumatic stress disorder (PTSD; Herman, 1997). According to the National Institute of Mental Health (NIMH; 2017), "People who have PTSD may feel stressed or frightened even when they are not in danger" (para. 2). Some factors that can increase the risk of PTSD include feeling "horror, helplessness, or extreme fear . . . [and] dealing with extra stress after the event, such as loss of a loved one, pain and injury, or loss of a job or home" ("Risk Factors," para. 1). Sociologically, scholars have revealed that traumatic life experiences diminish a person's social well-being, producing negative effects on one's sense of self and close relationships (Herman, 1997). The study of PTSD is a moving target (Bair & Long, 2014); it is beyond the scope of this chapter to offer a thorough review. For our purposes, documenting the experiences of exonerated death row survivors reveals that the sustained traumatic conditions to which they are subject continue well beyond their exonerations.

Focusing on the aftermath (Westervelt & Cook, 2012a) of a wrongful conviction, our initial assumption was that the sustained catastrophe of a wrongful capital conviction and traumatizing event ends when the death row survivor is exonerated and released from prison, at which point the rebuilding and management of the aftermath of the original disaster begins. However, our data and our ongoing contact with exonerated death row survivors informed us that the sustained catastrophe, in fact, extends into the postexoneration period, becoming a continuing trauma. At exoneration and release, death row survivors transition into a new stage of the catastrophe that remains contaminated by their death row experience, when the original trauma of the wrongful capital conviction is compounded by systematic inattention, stigma, and lack of recognition of the trauma they have endured (Westervelt & Cook, 2010, 2012b). The social and psychological consequences of life on death row are given added dimension by the continuation of the abuse after release, just in different forms—for example, continued insistence on their guilt by system officials, exclusion from resources that could assist them with reintegration, inattention to their needs, and failure even to recognize the injustice they have experienced or the depth of the injury (Westervelt & Cook, 2010, 2012b). Thus, the aftermath experiences exacerbate the original sustained catastrophe of their wrongful capital conviction as they grapple with the impact of a life shaped by death row within an unfriendly and often unwelcoming environment. Consequently, we prefer to call this *continuing-traumatic stress*, rather than posttraumatic stress.

FACING DOWN DEATH

"Expertise" comes in many forms, although our academic worlds tend to view scholars as the experts in various fields. It also is true that our exonerees' harrowing experiences of wrongful capital convictions, incarceration, and survival create an expertise with a different set of credentials. (Westervelt & Cook, 2012b, p. 125)

We focus here on our experts, the death row survivors we know, as they share their experiences of life on death row. It is important to look at the trauma experienced while living on death row to understand the long-term impact of living under sentence of death. These issues have been explored in more depth in earlier chapters of this volume. We examine the themes that emerged from our death row survivors' time on death row.

The trauma for condemned prisoners likely began when they first learned they would be charged with a capital crime and that they might be sentenced to death for a crime they did not commit. However, the trauma intensified when they were actually convicted and sentenced to die. Hearing that they might be killed was sobering, to say the least. It shook them to the core of their being. Whatever future they had envisioned evaporated at that moment. Fear engulfed them as they contemplated their new life and potential death. As Alan Gell recalled,

I remember [being] carried to death row. . . . You know, I had the same perception that a lot of people in society had. You know. I remember riding on the road thinking, "Oh my God. I'm innocent.

And they're guilty. And these are like the worst of the worst. And I'm fixing to have Charles Manson and Hannibal Lecter and just, you know, evil, evil monsters surrounding me. . . . Am I gonna survive that? Never mind what the state's gonna do to me, I mean, what are they gonna do to me?"[2]

Perry Cobb's moment of realization went like this:

It's a little hard to describe . . . in words how you really feel when [you hear you are sentenced to death]. See, two things was happening to me at the same time. This is the first time I ever experienced fear. . . . But now, it's for everything. It's for my life. . . . I guess it's like a mother giving birth and the child dies at birth. I don't know. I really don't know. But I do know that it's a pain that no artist can draw if a person's able to give it to him in words. I don't believe that they can put it on a, a canvas . . . you talking about self. And . . . you know, I thought about my children. I really thought about them. I wanted to see my children real bad. I thought, when would I have a chance to see them . . . your mother, your dad and grandparents, sisters, and especially your children. You'll never be able to see them, do anything. . . . It's like a, a dry, rotten weed in the wind. It's gone. It's a dusting, and you'll never see 'em again. . . . It's really hard to give you that. I can't give it to you. . . . That moment was my whole life. That was my life.

This trauma is exacerbated by the cries they hear from those around them in the courtroom—from children, parents, and other loved ones. As Alfred Rivera recalled,

My cries from my family are what caused me to become emotional and sob uncontrollably. I thought about the uphill battle that awaited me to prove my innocence. I also thought about my son and his mom and how this would affect their lives.

Living with the knowledge that they might be killed at any moment was a burden that contaminated the atmosphere on death row, creating

---

[2] Direct quotes are from our research interviews with each participant, some of which also appear in prior publications. These quotes have been edited as little as possible to preserve dialect and promote readability.

a heaviness of fear and despair. Alfred Rivera offered his description of death row:

> Life on death row is stressful as one should imagine. Dealing with the possibility of being executed is a heavy burden that causes psychological trauma and emotional damage. I remember one guy on death row jump[ed] over a rail about two stories up trying to cause his death. I remember a guy who did not want to continue litigation of his appeals because he was tired of continually having to live in the condition of a sitting duck. I remember a guy who would not touch his legal material or read anything about his case because he believed the chips were already stacked against him. These are some of the realities of death row and the psychological effects that death row has on one's psyche. The hardest thing on death row for me was visits from loved ones. I couldn't stand to see them leave me and me not be able to embrace them. It was hard for me because everyone knew this wasn't my place and I should not have been there. It's hard on death row knowing that the day your appeals are exhausted you're doomed to execution. It's hard on death row becoming intimate friends with a guy and then seeing him be led out to await his death the next 48 hours. It's hard to look at a guy and see how he may be executed for something he may not have done. There's nothing easy psychologically/mentally about death row. It's pure pain and suffering.

Living with the uncertainty of whether they would be killed drove them to the brink of madness. Several of our participants contemplated giving up by committing suicide or relinquishing their rights to appeal. Juan Meléndez-Colón said, "After ten years, you don't care if they kill you, you live or you die. You're tired." Meléndez-Colón came close to suicide during his nearly 18 years on Florida's death row and at times found himself talking to and playing with the insects in his cell to stay sane.

Other participants came close to their actual executions, coming within hours of being killed. Florida death row exoneree Shabaka Brown described his outburst against the guards who took him from his cell to measure him for his burial suit, without even bothering to explain what they were doing. The inhumanity and mundaneness of the routine were shocking to him, and it led him to fight against his captors, leaving him without his two front teeth. Brown received a stay of execution about 15 hours before his scheduled death in Florida's electric chair.

The most poignant description of a participant's confrontation with death came from our only female death row exoneree, Sabrina Butler. Butler received an execution date during sentencing, yet no one on her legal team explained that the date was immediately stayed pending appeal. Consequently, as that date came closer, Butler grew more agitated as she imagined herself being taken to the death chamber, in handcuffs with a ball and chain strapped to her feet. She became desperate as the day arrived and she waited for the guards to take her to her death:

> When that day came I was the scaredest person in the world. That is a feelin' that I wouldn't wish on my worst enemy. I stood there at the little old door . . . the slot in it. . . . And I thought, by me watchin' TV, and stuff, that they was gonna come and get you, and you was gonna have this ball and chain on. And these people gonna be walkin' beside you. You goin' down this long hall. . . . And I was scared to death, and the girl [next to me] kept tellin' me, "Sabrina, they're not gonna do nothin'. . . ." You know, I was standin' there cryin'. I kept telling her, "Yeah, they gonna kill me. They gonna kill me. Somebody call my mama, or somethin' and tell 'em that, you know, I love 'em." . . . That whole day, I just sat in my room. I couldn't sleep. I couldn't eat. That is the most humiliating, scary thing that any person could ever go through. I was scared to death because I thought that they was gonna kill me for somethin' that I didn't do.

Later, a guard came by, and she asked why she was not being taken. Only then did she learn that she was never scheduled for death that day. The guard recommended she call her attorney.

The atmosphere of death for those on death row is made thicker by the executions going on around them. Our participants watched many fellow inmates taken to their deaths. As friend and recent death row exoneree, Anthony Ray Hinton, indicated, 54 prisoners were executed around him during his 30 years on Alabama's death row (Pelley, 2016). Our participants knew when executions were imminent. When the method was electrocution, they could hear the machinery being tested. In some cases, the lights would dim or flicker. They often knew the moment of death by the smell in the air.

Although the public views those on death row as subhuman monsters, death row inmates have gotten to know each other as human beings. In some cases, they have become close friends. Watching another human being, especially a close friend, being taken to his or her death takes an emotional toll unlike any other. Juan Meléndez-Colón described this trauma most clearly:

> That was one of the hardest parts of being there was when they kill somebody. You got to recognize this, you livin' in a cell. You got a man next door to you for nine years . . . ten years. You become attached without even knowing it. You know. And he tells you things, and you tell him things. And you tell him things that you won't even tell your own family because nobody understands but you and him. So he leans in your shoulder and you leans to his shoulder. And now they come, they snatch him, they kill him. Then you think, "I'll probably be next." So that was the part that probably . . . was the hardest part for me in there, when they kill people.

Scott Taylor summed it up this way when describing death row:

> The thing about . . . death row was, uh, the common thing was death. I mean, the whole intention of you being there is . . . to be killed. . . . That was a common thing. I mean, if a guy didn't get executed, either, these guys are dying of heart attacks, guys are dying [because their] brain exploded, guy died of AIDS. Guys had heart attacks, and everything else. I mean, that there were natural deaths, executions or someone kill themself.

Although our participants did indeed face down death during their time on death row, what was the impact of this in the aftermath? What does it do to someone to live every day in an environment saturated with fear and the reality of impending death?

AFTERMATH OF LIVING ON "THE ROW"

"We all got damaged, one more than another one. But, we all got damaged....
It hurts all the time—everyone hurts from it," said Juan Meléndez-Colón.
What is the damage exacted by these years on death row? What must death
row survivors confront when they return to their families and communities
to rebuild the lives interrupted, and almost taken, by their wrongful capital convictions? Here we try to illuminate aspects of their postexoneration
experiences that stem from their time on death row, as opposed to their
struggles to reintegrate after prison or to continue to establish the wrong-
fulness of their convictions. Although we try here to focus on the trauma
resulting from their death row experiences, our participants certainly have
not experienced these aspects of their aftermath separately. It is all part of
the continuing trauma of their wrongful capital convictions.

Disrupting the Psychological Self

Death row survivors confront enormous psychological damage caused
by their wrongful capital convictions and time on death row. The confinement, isolation, and heavy atmosphere of death create psychological
problems not easily left at the prison door on the day of release. A common form of continuing psychological trauma death row survivors often
discuss is their feeling of survivor guilt. Even though they are innocent of
the crimes that put them on death row and they fought for their innocence
from the beginning, they still ask, "Why me?" "Why was I released?" "Why
was I not executed?" Having watched so many others taken to their deaths,
they left death row knowing that others they knew would be executed.
They also left believing that other innocent individuals still languished
on death row, and it was difficult for them to enjoy their freedom knowing they were leaving others behind. The guilt they carry now, even many
years after release, haunts them and prevents them from remaining in
contact with those they once knew on the row and tempers the joy over
their freedom. Gary Gauger summed it up best:

> You just feel badly that these guys had to go [to their deaths] and you
> didn't, you know? There's no other way to say it. You just feel badly.

... There's a lot of people in jail that don't deserve to be there. You feel guilty about it. You just, "Why was I spared and they weren't?" Especially if you don't do everything you possibly can to make things better. Then you feel guilty about it, but it burns you out. It's very hard on you emotionally. . . . I thought I would write prisoners I knew, that were still behind bars, and I cannot bring myself to write them. I cannot bring myself to read their letters. I had a really good friend who's stuck there for life. Should have been getting treatment in a mental institution. But he's stuck in a max joint instead. Can't afford a lawyer. . . . I can't bring myself to read his letters. I can't write people. . . . And I don't know why. I feel very guilty about it. But I just . . . I know what they're going through. I know what they're into. And I feel like all I can say is, "Yeah. That's too bad. Sucks don't it?" I just don't feel I have anything for 'em. I have nothing to give 'em. And I know that any kind of a letter's gold in prison. I really should give 'em that. I don't. And it's probably very selfish.

Yet another consequence of life on death row is that death row survivors confront multiple symptoms associated with PTSD. As sociologists, we of course cannot diagnose them as having PTSD. But we can note the frequency with which they discuss struggling with psychological and emotional problems that are earmarks of this disorder: distrust, fear, detachment, depression, disorientation, anger, disruptive dreams of their time on death row.[3] This should not be surprising given the literature that clearly indicates the experience of PTSD by those who have been incarcerated, tortured, abused, and held captive (see Westervelt & Cook, 2012b, pp. 169–170, for more information). Noncapital exonerees have made similar occasional references to having PTSD symptoms such as flashbacks and panic attacks (Westervelt & Cook, 2012a).

Our survivors provided valuable insights into their experiences with this emotional trauma. For example, Dave Keaton, often referred to as #1 by his fellow death row survivors because he is the first death row exoneree

---

[3] In fact, the tendency to distrust people became a critically important consideration for our research methodology when inviting exonerees to participate in our research (see Westervelt & Cook, 2007, 2012b).

of the modern era (see DPIC, 2017b), struggled to explain his frequent bouts of depression:

> I used to get in these deep depressions. . . . Nothing, . . . nothing, nothing would be satisfying to me. . . . Mostly I was just sick because I didn't really sit down. I didn't want to walk. I didn't want to eat. . . . And there was nothing that, everything was just, man, it was just a bore. A total, total bore. Now, there was, there was, nothing, nothing, nothing. . . . It was, I mean it was total emptiness; it was total.

Like others facing depression, Dave used alcohol and drugs to manage these episodes of depression, not an uncommon coping strategy for many of our participants.

Gary Gauger resonated with such episodes of "nothingness" when describing a depression that was brought on by a deposition he gave in a lawsuit against the state, prompting a flashback to his interrogation:

> I can only describe the symptoms as, particularly in severe episodes, as it feels like what I would imagine having a stroke. I don't lose physical mobility, but I get very confused. It's very frustrating. I can't articulate even simple ideas. You know, people ask you simple questions, and I can't answer back. After my deposition, I had a flashback of being in the interrogation room during the deposition, and for the next week it was very similar to what it was like the week after my arrest. Where, um, very confused. I couldn't drive my truck. I couldn't carry on simple conversations. I couldn't explain how I felt about anything. It's like having a stroke.

He continued to describe his depression, saying,

> Good days. Bad days. Days are days. They're all the same. They're all different. I don't know. My depression, it comes and goes so unexpectedly. And sometimes it'll go for weeks, and I don't even know it until it lifts, and then I go, "Wow! That was a rough one." You know you've been out of it almost. It's like you've been sloggin' through the swamp in the fog for three weeks. . . . And when you're depressed, it's like you've always been depressed, you'll always be depressed, there's no hope for ya.

These periods of depression are compounded by feelings of detachment and disorientation and of anger as well. Death row survivors often discussed how they felt separate from those around them, apart from them, and not truly connected or interacting with them. Perry Cobb explained it as follows:

> I can't say that [my feelings] were dead. I said that [they] had just fled.…
> I didn't have no feelings. I didn't like. I didn't love. I didn't hate. I didn't
> dislike. I was just, I see you and that was it.

That said, the one feeling survivors did often have and were forced to learn to manage is anger. They referenced how others in their networks believed they had anger "issues" that had to be addressed and that could explode without warning. They felt anger over any number of wrongs they had experienced—anger over their wrongful convictions, anger over their treatment by prison officials while on death row, anger over the lack of resources available to them after release, anger over the system officials who put them on death row (in their view), anger over the friends who abandoned them, anger over time and loved ones lost. In a few cases, they searched for help with their anger from professionals, but this was not common. More often, they unloaded their anger on the loved ones around them or attempted to numb it with alcohol and drugs.

Finally, survivors struggled with an array of fears from having lived in such close confinement and isolation on death row. This problem comes in a variety of forms. For example, they may have gotten lost in buildings and large spaces, felt claustrophobic in small confined spaces, and become anxious sitting in a corner where they could not see the door. They did not like the feeling of "chaos" that comes from large crowded spaces, such as a mall or street fair. This discomfort may be chronic. Although it is most intense in the initial period after release, it can linger for many years. During some of our interviews, we had to rearrange the interview space to ensure that the death row exoneree was comfortable in that setting. When interviewing Juan Meléndez-Colón in his hometown in Puerto Rico, we watched him rearrange the chairs in restaurants we visited. He also got up repeatedly to walk around after a few minutes of discussion.

These symptoms of PTSD are compounded by the invisibility sur-vivors encounter after release. Unlike veterans returning from war who are recognized as having PTSD and offered some services (though not enough), the needs of death row survivors are invisible to the govern-ment and to the communities to which they return (Cook et al., 2014; Westervelt & Cook, 2010, 2012b). Exonerees are excluded from services provided to parolees, they must fight for an expungement of their felony records, and they typically do not receive compensation of any kind, much less official recognition of their innocence. Their invisibility then fuels the depression, detachment, and anger already at play and makes a bad situ-ation worse. Rather than receiving assistance to manage their mounting emotional and psychological needs, they must count on their own limited resources to address the trauma that pervades their lives.

Disrupting the Social Self

"Inmate" is a master status unlike most others; it overpowers other statuses and is exceedingly difficult to discard (Hughes, 1945; see also Goffman, 1963). "Death row inmate" compounds the stigma and dam-age (Westervelt & Cook, 2012b). In general, people fear those who have been in prison (Petersilia, 2003) and even more so those who have been wrongfully convicted (Clow & Leach, 2015), which is a testament to the enduring quality of the erroneous determination of guilt. In Goffman's (1963, p. 70) terms, prisoners have been discredited as a result of "ill fame" (see also Clear, Rose, & Ryder, 2001; Elliott, Ziegler, Altman, & Scott, 1982; Harding, 2003; Hirschfield & Piquero, 2010; Winnick & Bodkin, 2008).

> People's interactions with ex-prisoners are negotiated through the prism of the stigma they carry, causing people to treat them with disdain and suspicion. As a result of their discrediting stigma, ex-inmates are perceived as dishonest, immoral, and, in some cases, even less than human. (Westervelt & Cook, 2012b, p. 173)

Fear of those who have been incarcerated, particularly if they have been consigned to death row, likely stems from stereotypes of those who com-mit crimes worthy of incarceration. In the case of death row, most people believe that those sentenced to death have committed heinous and violent crimes resulting in someone else's death. In addition, because of extensive media exposure (O'Sullivan, 2001; Rafter, 2000), the general public may have impressions of the brutal and violent nature of the prison environment, exacerbating the public fear of returning death row prisoners. When wrongly convicted death row inmates are released from prison, they may face additional trauma by being rejected by the communities in which they hope to live. In some cases, public officials continue to assert exonerees' guilt, even as they are released from prison because of overwhelming evidence of their factual innocence. Thus, regardless of our participants' claims of innocence, they are most often viewed as returning death row inmates—people to be feared, isolated, and rejected. Kirk Bloodsworth described his experience with community rejection:

> But when I got down here [to my hometown in Maryland], I was a pariah to the community and to everybody around. Everybody thought . . . "You got out on a technicality." I said, "Technicality? DNA's a technicality?" . . . This was a reoccurring theme, everyday almost.

Bloodsworth also described incidents when people he had known since childhood avoided him in public places. In the local grocery store, someone complained to the store manager and asked for Kirk to be removed from the premises.

Mississippi exoneree Sabrina Butler lamented her unfair stigmatization in her hometown, where her case was high profile:

> I'm all on TV. And I'm this person . . . this heinous murderer that stomped my baby. . . . They have just destroyed my life! And nobody has said, "Hey! We're sorry." And I'm angry. I am very angry because I can't get back what they took from me! I can't get that back. And that's the part that makes me mad. It makes me mad because I got children, and my kids hear this. "OK. Well, you know your mama ain't no good, you know, your mama killed your brother."

Here, Butler also explained how the stigma affected her family; her children were often bullied in school for having a mother on death row.

319

Greg Wilhoit expressed less concern for his own situation than that of his loving and committed parents who experienced this "stigma by association":

> In my case, it was Guy and Ida May Wilhoit. They lost their identity pretty much. Everywhere they went they were like the mother or the father of an individual so vile and so reprehensible that not only had he forfeited his right to live in society, he forfeited his right to live all together. Try livin' with that.

Given this unrelenting stigma, our participants have fought to reconstruct their identities as responsible, innocent members of the community. Often, they felt compelled during our interview to claim their innocence repeatedly, to assert their reputability as worthy, normal people. We see this as an attempt to reestablish their reputations in the face of a stigma that has pursued them and shaped how others see and treat them. Alabama death row survivor Walter McMillian is most emblematic of this battle with stigma.[4] Throughout the interview, he articulated how no one who knew him could ever think he was capable of such a heinous crime. The following exchange illustrates his insistence on his reputability:

> I ain't had a soul . . . nobody . . . I mean, black or white, even spoke to me no kind of way like that because everybody know, *everybody* know I didn't do it. I mean it just, it ain't some, "You mighta coulda did it." It's impossible for me to done it, you know.

And later:

> I ain't seen nobody yet, act no kinda way, you know, like they mad at me, or got nothin' against me about sayin' how they believe I had somethin' to do with the child getting' killed . . . killed the child, somethin' like that . . . black or white. I mean, I talk with all kinda white people, all kinda black people. And everybody know it. They know the truth.

---

[4] Walter's story also is described in rich detail by his attorney, Bryan Stevenson (2015), in *Just Mercy: A Story of Justice and Redemption*. We are grateful to Bryan Stevenson and his team at the Equal Justice Initiative for helping us to include Walter in our research.

And again later:

> That's right. . . . Like I say, everybody's treatin' me just as good, or
> better. So I am blessed. . . . See, if it had of been possible that I did it,
> you know, that would make a difference to, you see. But everybody
> know it *impossible.*

Scott Taylor made it clear:

> I want people to believe me. You know. . . . I didn't do it. You know.
> I'm free and I still plead, "Look, I didn't do it." . . . I still feel like I have
> to convince people that I didn't do it. . . . Before people hear me, you
> know, I'm being judged. You know. When they mention the case, are
> they saying, "Man, maybe he did do it?"

In this way, confronting the continuing trauma of having to defend their innocence, our participants are battling double stigmas of having been incarcerated and having lived on death row. They want people to believe they are not violent, brutal people deserving of death. They want to rebuild their identities and reputations around innocence.

Time on death row disrupts the survivors' identity and ruptures their family and other social relationships. This, of course, is a common consequence of incarceration in general (Haney, 2003), and our participants said this disruption was intensified when they were condemned to death row. Prison makes it difficult to maintain ties with those on the outside—for example, visits and phone calls are not made at will, contact visits are limited, and mail is subject to surveillance (Johnson, 1998; Petersilia, 2003). As Goffman (1961) noted, the point of a total institution is, in part, to isolate the inmate to ensure disconnection from preexisting statuses and relationships. Death row intensifies the isolation because visitors are not allowed contact with inmates and access is even more restricted (Westervelt & Cook, 2012b). Death row is typically located in only one or two maximum-security institutions in a state, and the death row institution may be far from where the person was originally convicted. Visitors may have to travel many hours to reach the prison. Maintaining familial and friend relationships becomes exceedingly difficult, and rebuilding those relationships after release is even more strained.

Among our participants, almost everyone lost someone while on death row. In several cases, they were told of a parent or grandparent's death often weeks after the actual death had occurred. One participant, Shabaka Brown, learned of his brother's death after the prison would not allow him to donate his kidney, even though he had been identified as his brother's only viable match. Several survivors were divorced while on death row or soon after release. Several exonerees lost custody of their children. Sabrina Butler battled for 4 years to regain custody of her older son after her release. In other cases, exonerees' children were adults by the time of their release. Everyone lost valuable time with children and loved ones, time at holidays and birthdays and family events, time spent building relationships and sharing in each other's lives. In those years, the family adapted without expectation of their loved one's return, expecting instead to see them executed (Sharp, 2005; Vandiver, 1989). Most of our participants discussed the difficulty of rebuilding those relationships when they returned and, in some cases, grieving the losses of those who had died in their absence. Their relationships most certainly are never the same, and sadly some could not be saved.[5]

Securing employment is another area where the aftermath of death row disrupts the social self. Most exonerated death row survivors receive no assistance with record expungement. The felony capital conviction that remains on their records severely limits their access to stable employment. Exonerated death row survivors have reported that they have a difficult time finding employment. Their job skills were obsolete, their resumes had big gaps, and they had a difficult time maintaining a schedule. Particularly traumatic for them was "the box" on employment applications asking about criminal background. Because their wrongful convictions had not been expunged, prospective employers often discovered that they had been convicted of capital murder. Without meaningful assistance to acquire new skills and clear their names, they reported feeling extremely frustrated, angry, and helpless in their efforts to be financially solvent (Westervelt & Cook, 2012b, pp. 65–69).

---

[5] This is a complex aspect of continuing trauma after release; please refer to Westervelt and Cook (2012b) for a more detailed exploration of these issues.

Finally, death row disrupts the physical health of those who live there. Health care in prison is not good (Fleury-Steiner, 2015; Johnson, 1998). Our participants reported receiving the lowest priority, perhaps because they are expected to one day be killed. As Juan Meléndez-Colón bluntly stated, "See, they not gonna give you the best medicine. You condemned to death. Why give you the best medicine when they probably kill you tomorrow?"

Our participants discussed the many ailments that were caused or exacerbated by their confinement, lack of access to basic medical care and nutrition, and stress. These maladies included arthritis, asthma, dental issues, diabetes, digestive problems, eyesight problems, heart problems, hepatitis, high blood pressure, and skin rashes. Their health problems were structured by the lack of quality care they received while on the inside and then were exacerbated by their continuing lack of access to health care after release. Given that all our participants were released before the passage of the Affordable Care Act, the extent of their access to health care was almost solely dependent on their employment benefits or their spouse's employment (if married). Thus, most of our participants struggled with medical and dental issues at some point after release. In some cases, family members or advocacy organizations were able to provide resources to tend to pressing needs. However, in many cases, needs went unmet.

Now, almost 10 years after our final interview for the original study, we have been able to see the continuing impact that our participants' time on death row has had on their overall well-being. Sadly, of the 18 original participants in our study, five died either directly or in part from health issues resulting from their time on death row and in prison.[6] Clearly, the disruption of the social and physical self is a consequence of their wrongful capital convictions and time on death row and a source of continuing trauma that they must negotiate and manage on a daily basis. This disruption is magnified by the state's failure, in many cases, to fully recognize their innocence and provide basic assistance in rebuilding their identities, skills, and families.

---

[6]Tim Howard (Ohio), Dave Keaton (Florida), Walter McMillian (Alabama), Delbert Tibbs (Florida), and Greg Wilhoit (Oklahoma) have all passed away.

CREATING BETTER OUTCOMES

After exoneration and release, death row survivors confront a web of difficult and confusing obstacles to starting over: finding a place to live; reconnecting with family; acquiring new job skills; finding a job; accessing physical, dental, and mental health care; buying clothes; getting an official ID of some kind—and the list goes on (Westervelt & Cook, 2012b). Whether assistance is available to them (and how much) is structured by the support group around them, the advocates and/or organizations responsible for their exoneration, the state in which they live, and even the nature of the exoneration itself. Some receive meaningful assistance from the moment they leave prison, whereas some are left mostly on their own.

In some cases, the Innocence Project that worked with the exoneree provides social work services, at least initially. For example, the Innocence Project in New York retains caseworkers who help exonerees get back on their feet and work closely with them for 2 years. A few organizations have emerged to provide at least some assistance to death row exonerees. Of note are Witness to Innocence and Healing Justice. Witness to Innocence is the nation's only organization by and for death row survivors. It is an abolitionist organization that provides outlets for death row exonerees to tell their stories and to come together for camaraderie and emotional support. Witness to Innocence employs a staff social worker to help death row exonerees with any pressing and emergent needs. Healing Justice was established more recently by Jennifer Thompson, advocate and victim in a highly publicized wrongful conviction case in North Carolina (see Thompson-Cannino, Cotton, & Torneo, 2010). Healing Justice works with exonerees to locate services in the areas in which they live. Healing Justice also brings together exonerees and original crime victims in wrongful conviction cases for weekend retreats to promote healing and understanding. Finally, we recognize the tireless work of advocate and attorney Jon Eldan. Jon has been working with exonerees for many years to help them negotiate the complexities of Medicaid and the Affordable Care Act to access health care. He has established After Innocence (http://www.after-innocence.org/), a nonprofit organization dedicated to assisting exonerees with reentry services.

Although the resources provided by these organizations are life altering for many death row exonerees, what is missing is a coordinated response to the aftermath problem by government and nonprofit agencies. No matter how well-meaning and persistent, the nonprofit organizations that currently bear the burden of reentry assistance for survivors always will have limits to their scope and resources. The public agencies responsible for wrongly incarcerating survivors must begin to take more seriously their responsibilities toward helping exonerees rebuild, beginning with the recognition of the harms the state has created (Westervelt & Cook, 2010). In the final years of the Obama Administration, the federal government began to show interest in developing strategies to directly assist exonerees or to work with states to provide assistance.[7] For example, the federal government included exonerees in the language for the reauthorization of the Second Chance Act (2007), which provides resources to local and state agencies working on inmate reentry and lowering recidivism. However, this bill is stalled in committee (Second Chance Reauthorization Act, 2017).

State governments also have to step up to the plate by actively assisting exonerees with expungement of their records, expenses now mostly borne by the exonerees or their advocates (Shlosberg, Mandery, West, & Callaghan, 2014). State governments should seriously examine the compensation statutes they have in place to remove obstacles to meaningful, comprehensive, and immediate assistance. Those 18 states with no compensation statute should examine statutes in other states that have proven to be effective and institute a new compensation policy immediately (see the Innocence Project; Norris, 2012).

In short, the state that is responsible for the wrongful capital conviction should take ownership of its role in ameliorating the damage caused to death row survivors and their families.

---

[7] This is based on personal knowledge of the authors who were directly involved in meetings with the federal government through their work with Witness to Innocence and Healing Justice.

CONCLUSION

Our research documents that the trauma of a wrongful capital conviction and incarceration does not stop when death row exonerees are released from prison. The disruptions of the social and psychological selves initiated by their time on death row continue into their postrelease lives and are, in some ways, exacerbated by the stigma, invisibility, and rejection they so often confront. It is clear to us that for this population the concept of posttraumatic stress might be better conceived as continuing traumatic stress.

Although many may believe that the social and psychological trauma of life on death row ends at the moment of release, death row survivors tell a much different story. Freedom is certainly better than incarceration, but the aftermath of living on death row is lifelong, generating continuing trauma from which there may never be full recovery. The sustained catastrophe of their wrongful capital convictions continues after their release as they confront the aftermath without the benefit of open recognition of the harm done to them or the needs they then have (Westervelt & Cook, 2010). In spite of their efforts to rebuild their lives and families, the experience of life after death row is characterized by displacement, struggle, and continued isolation. In spite of their efforts to recreate a place in the world they left, many are never able to find a place in which they completely fit. As Juan Meléndez-Colón said,

> We're in another world now. And the world, it's not people. It's not because people do not understand you. It's more that you do not understand people. This is they world, not yours. You got to put yourself back in *they* world.

As we have said elsewhere about death row survivors, life after death row is best understood as

> being dislodged and displaced, thrown into a state of anomie with little to no assistance with reconstructing or refinding connection and community. At the core of the exoneree experience is their expulsion from their place in this world: Where do they fit in? Where do they now belong? . . . From the mundane everyday tasks of pumping

gas and grocery shopping to the emotionally draining difficulties of managing loss, guilt, and depression, they confront new battles around every turn. Sent into the fray with no preparation and little or no assistance, they struggle to build a new life and find a new home. Although some have more success than others in building that life, the process for all of them is painful and challenging. (Westervelt & Cook, 2012b, p. 104)

This is the aftermath of the sustained catastrophe and continuing traumas of a wrongful capital conviction and life lived on death row.

REFERENCES

Bair, J. P., & Long, K. M. (2014). Critical issues in the evolving diagnosis of PTSD. In S. J. Morewitz & M. L. Goldstein (Eds.), *Handbook of forensic sociology and psychology* (pp. 201–214). New York, NY: Springer Science and Business Media. http://dx.doi.org/10.1007/978-1-4614-7178-3_14

Baumgartner, F. R., Westervelt, S. D., & Cook, K. J. (2014). Public policy responses to wrongful conviction. In A. D. Redlich, J. R. Acker, R. J. Norris, & C. L. Bonventre (Eds.), *Examining wrongful convictions: Stepping back, moving forward* (pp. 251–266). Durham, NC: Carolina Academic Press.

Bedau, H. A. (1987). *Death is different: Studies in the morality, law, and politics of capital punishment.* Boston, MA: Northeastern University Press.

Burawoy, M. (2004). Public sociologies: Contradictions, dilemmas, and possibilities. *Social Forces, 82,* 1603–1618. http://dx.doi.org/10.1353/sof.2004.0064

Clear, T., Rose, D., & Ryder, J. (2001). Incarceration and the community: The problem of removing and returning offenders. *Crime and Delinquency, 47,* 335–351. http://dx.doi.org/10.1177/0011128701047003003

Clow, K., & Leach, A. (2015). After innocence: Perceptions of individuals who have been wrongfully convicted. *Legal and Criminological Psychology, 20,* 147–164. http://dx.doi.org/10.1111/lcrp.12018

Cohen, S., & Taylor, L. (1972). *Psychological survival.* New York, NY: Pantheon.

Cook, K. J., Westervelt, S. D., & Maruna, S. (2014). The problem of fit: Parolees, exonerees, and prisoner reentry. In A. D. Redlich, J. R. Acker, R. J. Norris, & C. L. Bonventre (Eds.), *Examining wrongful convictions: Stepping back, moving forward* (pp. 237–250). Durham, NC: Carolina Academic Press.

Death Penalty Information Center. (2017a). *Innocence and the death penalty.* Retrieved from http://www.deathpenaltyinfo.org/innocence-and-death-penalty

Death Penalty Information Center. (2017b). *Innocence: List of those freed from death row*. Retrieved from http://www.deathpenaltyinfo.org/innocence-list-those-freed-death-row

Elliott, G., Ziegler, H., Altman, B., & Scott, D. (1982). Understanding stigma: Dimensions of deviance and coping. *Deviant Behavior, 3*, 275–300. http://dx.doi.org/10.1080/01639625.1982.9967590

Fleury-Steiner, B. (2015). Effects of life imprisonment and the crisis of prisoner health. *Criminology & Public Policy, 14*(2), 407–416. http://dx.doi.org/10.1111/1745-9133.12132

Goffman, E. (1961). *Asylums*. New York, NY: First Anchor Books.

Goffman, E. (1963). *Stigma*. New York, NY: Simon & Schuster.

Haney, C. (2003). The psychological impact of incarceration: Implications for postprison adjustment. In J. Travis & M. Waul (Eds.), *Prisoners once removed* (pp. 33–66). Washington, DC: Urban Institute Press.

Harding, D. (2003). Jean Valjean's dilemma: The management of ex-convict identity in the search for employment. *Deviant Behavior, 24*, 571–595. http://dx.doi.org/10.1080/713840275

Herman, J. (1997). *Trauma and recovery*. New York, NY: Basic Books.

Hirschfield, P., & Piquero, A. (2010). Normalization and legitimation: Modeling stigmatizing attitudes towards ex-offenders. *Criminology, 48*, 27–55. http://dx.doi.org/10.1111/j.1745-9125.2010.00179.x

Hughes, E. (1945). Dilemmas and contradictions of status. *American Journal of Sociology, 50*, 353–359. http://dx.doi.org/10.1086/219652

Johnson, R. (1998). *Death work*. Belmont, CA: Wadsworth.

Liebman, J., Fagan, J., & West, V. (2000). *A broken system: Error rates in capital cases, 1973–1995*. Retrieved from https://www.fedcrimlaw.com/members/DeathPenalty/ErrorRates-DeathPenalty.pdf

National Institute of Mental Health. (2017). *Post-traumatic stress disorder*. Retrieved from https://www.nimh.nih.gov/health/topics/post-traumatic-stress-disorder-ptsd/index.shtml

Norris, R. (2012). Assessing compensation statutes for the wrongly convicted. *Criminal Justice Policy Review, 23*, 352–374. http://dx.doi.org/10.1177/0887403411409916

O'Sullivan, S. (2001). Representations of prison in the nineties Hollywood cinema: From *Con Air* to *The Shawshank Redemption*. *Howard Journal, 40*, 317–334. http://dx.doi.org/10.1111/1468-2311.00212

Pelley, S. (2016, January 10). *Life after death row*. Retrieved from http://www.cbsnews.com/news/60-minutes-life-after-death-row-exoneration/

Petersilia, J. (2003). *When prisoners come home*. New York, NY: Oxford University Press.

Rafter, N. (2000). *Shots in the mirror: Crime film and society*. New York, NY: Oxford University Press.

Second Chance Act. (2007). 34 U.S.C. § 60501 *et seq.*

Second Chance Reauthorization Act. (2017). H.R. 2899, 115th Cong., 1st Sess. Retrieved from https://www.congress.gov/115/bills/hr2899/BILLS-115hr 2899ih.pdf

Sharp, S. (2005). *Hidden victims*. New Brunswick, NJ: Rutgers University Press.

Shlosberg, A., Mandery, E., West, V., & Callaghan, B. (2014). Expungement and post-exoneration offending. *The Journal of Criminal Law & Criminology, 104*, 353–388.

Stevenson, B. (2015). *Just mercy: A story of justice and redemption*. New York, NY: Spiegel & Grau.

Thompson-Cannino, J., Cotton, R., & Torneo, E. (2010). *Picking cotton*. New York, NY: St. Martin's Press.

Vandiver, M. (1989). Coping with death: Families of the terminally ill, homicide victims, and condemned prisoners. In M. Radelet (Ed.), *Facing the death penalty* (pp. 123–138). Philadelphia, PA: Temple University Press.

Westervelt, S. D., & Cook, K. J. (2007). Feminist research methods in theory and action: Learning from death row exonerees. In S. Miller (Ed.), *Criminal justice research & practice: Diverse voices from the field* (pp. 21–38). Boston, MA: University Press of New England.

Westervelt, S. D., & Cook, K. J. (2008). Coping with innocence after death row. *Contexts, 7*, 32–37.

Westervelt, S. D., & Cook, K. J. (2010). Framing innocents: The wrongly convicted as victims of state harm. *Crime, Law, and Social Change, 53*, 259–275. http:// dx.doi.org/10.1007/s10611-009-9231-z

Westervelt, S. D., & Cook, K. J. (Eds.). (2012a). *Albany Law Review: Revealing the impact and aftermath of miscarriages of justice, 75*, 1223–1630.

Westervelt, S. D., & Cook, K. J. (2012b). *Life after death row: Exonerees' search for community and identity*. New Brunswick, NJ: Rutgers University Press.

Westervelt, S. D., & Cook, K. J. (2013). Life after exoneration: Examining the aftermath of a wrongful capital conviction. In C. R. Huff & M. Killias (Eds.), *Wrongful conviction and miscarriages of justice: Causes and remedies in North America and European criminal justice systems* (pp. 261–281). New York, NY: Routledge.

Winnick, T., & Bodkin, M. (2008). Anticipated stigma and stigma management among those to be labeled 'Ex-Con'. *Deviant Behavior, 29*, 295–333. http:// dx.doi.org/10.1080/01639620701588081

Witness to Innocence. (2017). *Our mission*. Retrieved from https://www.witness toinnocence.org/

Appendix
Rethinking Death Row:
Variations in the Housing
of Individuals Sentenced to Death

The Arthur Liman Public Interest Program,
Yale Law School

In 2015, nearly 3,000 death-sentenced prisoners were incarcerated in state and federal facilities in the United States. Most were housed in some form of isolation. A growing body of research documents the harms of long-term isolation on prisoners' mental and physical health and correlates isolation with increased violence in prison. Further, prison administrators report the challenges and costs of staffing isolation units. Proposals for reducing the use of isolating conditions in prison have been put forth by the executive branch of the federal government, by state correctional leaders, and by the legislative branches of the federal and state governments. Detention of juveniles in solitary has been a specific source of concern. In 2016, both the Colorado legislature and the Los Angeles County Board of Supervisors enacted provisions banning the use of isolation for juveniles, defined in Colorado as individuals under the age of 21

Adapted from "Rethinking Death Row: Variations in the Housing of Individuals Sentenced to Death," by The Arthur Liman Public Interest Program, Yale Law School, 2016. Copyright 2016 by The Arthur Liman Public Interest Program, Yale Law School. Footnotes and Appendix omitted. The complete report is available at https://law.yale.edu/system/files/documents/pdf/Liman/deathrow_reportfinal.pdf

and in Los Angeles as individuals younger than 18. Lawsuits have success-fully challenged isolating conditions—resulting in consent decrees to limit the use of isolation either for all prisoners or for subpopulations, such as the seriously mentally ill and juveniles. Reports and articles document the harms of such isolating confinement and analyze its legal parameters.

These concerns raise questions—in terms of both practices and as a matter of law—about the use of long-term isolation for a specific set of prisoners, those serving capital sentences and often housed on what is col-loquially known as "death row." A few prior reports have surveyed condi-tions; for example, in 2013, the American Civil Liberties Union (ACLU) detailed the severity of isolation experienced by death-sentenced prison-ers and criticized the practice of imposing long-term isolation as an auto-matic consequence of death sentences.

Lawsuits challenging the practice have also been filed. In 2012, Alfred Prieto, a death-row prisoner in Virginia, argued that automatic segrega-tion violated his constitutional right to an individualized decision about the need for placement in isolation. A trial-level judge agreed, but on appeal, the Fourth Circuit reversed. The court held (over a dissent) that because all death-sentenced prisoners in Virginia were subjected to the same treatment, Mr. Prieto's isolation was not "atypical," and therefore he had no liberty interest protected by the Due Process Clause in avoiding such confinement. Although U.S. Supreme Court review was sought, after Mr. Prieto was executed, his petition for certiorari was dismissed as moot.

More generally, members of the U.S. Supreme Court have questioned the constitutionality of profound isolation. In June 2015, Justice Kennedy raised the issue when concurring in the reversal of a grant of habeas cor-pus relief obtained by Hector Ayala, who had been sentenced to death. Justice Kennedy wrote that, in all likelihood, Mr. Ayala would have spent "the great majority of his more than 25 years in custody in 'administra-tive segregation' or, as it is better known, solitary confinement." Justice Kennedy explained that, if following "the usual pattern," the prisoner had likely been held "in a windowless cell no larger than a typical parking spot for 23 hours a day; and in the one hour when he leaves it, he likely is allowed little or no opportunity for conversation or interaction with anyone." Justice Kennedy drew attention to the "human toll wrought by extended terms of isolation" and called for change through more "public inquiry," through judicial discussion of the harms, and in an appropriate case, through decisions by judges about "whether workable alternative systems for long-term confinement exist and, if so, whether a correctional system should be required to adopt them."

The isolation of prisoners is also the subject of case law in many jurisdictions and of international concern. The European Court of Human Rights has concluded that the Convention on Human Rights imposes limits on isolating conditions, and research in Great Britain detailed the injuries of what it termed "deep custody." International standards also address isolation. In 2015, the United Nations Commission on Crime Prevention and Criminal Justice met to revise its standards for the treatment of prisoners. The results are the Standard Minimum Rules for the Treatment of Prisoners (known as the "Nelson Mandela Rules"), which were adopted by the U.N. General Assembly in 2015.

These rules define "solitary confinement" to be "confinement of prisoners for 22 hours or more a day without meaningful human contact"; "prolonged solitary confinement" is "solitary confinement for a time period in excess of 15 consecutive days." The Mandela Rules state that "in no circumstances may restrictions or disciplinary sanctions amount to torture or other cruel, inhuman or degrading treatment or punishment." The Mandela Rules provide specific "practices, in particular" that "shall be prohibited"; included are "indefinite solitary confinement" and "prolonged solitary confinement." Moreover, the Rules state that "solitary confinement shall be used only in exceptional cases as a last resort, for as short a time as possible and subject to independent review, and only pursuant to the authorization by a competent authority" and "shall not be imposed by virtue of a prisoner's sentence." In addition, "solitary confinement should be prohibited in the case of prisoners with mental or physical disabilities when their conditions would be exacerbated by such measures" as well as for "women and children."

This Liman Report contributes to this discussion by providing an analysis of the statutory, administrative, and procedural rules governing the housing of death-sentenced prisoners in the United States, by summarizing past research on conditions for death-sentenced prisoners, and by offering a detailed account from correctional administrators in three states who have chosen to use their discretion not to put individuals sentenced to death in isolation. Part I provides both an overview of the legal parameters governing the housing of death-sentenced individuals in the 35 jurisdictions that had such prisoners in 2015 and a review of prior research on housing conditions of death-sentenced individuals. After examining statutes, administrative codes, and available department of correction policies in those jurisdictions, we learned that correctional officials have substantial discretion to decide how to house death-sentenced prisoners.

Part II summarizes interviews conducted in the spring of 2015 with correctional administrators in three jurisdictions—North Carolina, Missouri, and Colorado—that permitted death-sentenced prisoners some degree of direct contact with each other or the general prison population. Specifically, as of 2015,

- North Carolina housed 156 death-sentenced prisoners, separated them from the general population, but afforded them similar access to resources and programs as other prisoners. Death-sentenced prisoners were able to spend 16 hours each day in a common room and were permitted to exercise and dine in groups.
- Missouri housed 28 death-sentenced prisoners, integrated them into the general population of a maximum-security prison. Death-sentenced prisoners shared cells with other prisoners and had all the same privileges and opportunities as those who had not been sentenced to death.
- Colorado, which confined three death-sentenced prisoners, placed them in a designated unit together with other prisoners classified as in need of increased supervision. All prisoners housed in the unit had access to a common room in small groups for at least four hours each day; death-sentenced individuals had most of the opportunities available to other prisoners in the unit.

A central finding of this report is that prison officials have many options when determining the housing of individuals sentenced to death.

Our hope is that this report will provide models for lessening the isolation of death-sentenced individuals and invite innovations in the housing arrangements for all prisoners.

I. A NATIONWIDE LOOK AT DISCRETION IN "DEATH ROW" HOUSING

As of 2015, 35 jurisdictions (34 states and the federal government) housed death-sentenced prisoners. These 35 jurisdictions varied widely in the number of death-sentenced prisoners in custody. As of the fall of 2015, California had the largest number—745. Both Wyoming and New Hampshire each housed one person sentenced to death.

We searched the statutes and administrative codes of these jurisdictions to identify materials governing death-sentenced prisoners. Such provisions may be found in a jurisdiction's criminal laws, capital sentencing provisions, or rules governing the execution of death sentences. We also reviewed case law discussing housing for death-sentenced prisoners.

We sought to learn about whether laws addressed single-celling; hours in cell; participation in groups for meals, recreation, and programming; contact with other death-sentenced prisoners, the general population, visitors, or prison staff; access to books, television, or other media; and opportunities, if any, for periodic reviews of and changes in housing. As we detail below, many of these topics were not the subject of statutes, regulations, and administrative policies.

We also researched policies adopted by state and federal corrections departments to govern the housing of death-sentenced prisoners. We consulted the publicly available policy and procedure manuals for each jurisdiction's department of corrections and supplemented our findings with secondary sources, such as law review articles and newspaper reports.

Further, we sought to learn about prior resources on the housing of people serving capital sentences. Below, we summarize four surveys that included information on housing practices for death-sentenced prisoners: a 2013 survey by the ACLU, a 2014 survey by the Association of State Correctional Administrators (ASCA) and the Liman Program at Yale Law School, a 2013 survey by ASCA, and a 2008 survey that was prepared by Professor Sandra Babcock for the Death Penalty Information Center. The surveys all reported high degrees of isolation for death-sentenced prisoners.

To preview what follows, this review of statutes and regulations documents that most jurisdictions do not require isolation of death-sentenced prisoners and leave correctional officials substantial discretion to determine housing conditions. Many correctional departments' policies impose isolation; the four surveys further document how profoundly isolating the conditions have been for many prisoners. In contrast, in a few jurisdictions, correctional officials have published policies describing the placement of death-sentenced prisoners in less restrictive housing conditions.

A. Laws Governing Isolation of Death-Sentenced Prisoners

1. Placement in Isolation or Segregation

In 19 of the 35 jurisdictions with death-sentenced prisoners, statutes and regulations specifically address death-sentenced prisoner housing. Seventeen states do so by statute, and four of those 17 also address housing in regulations. Two (Florida and Ohio) do so by regulation.

In three states—Idaho, Pennsylvania, and Wyoming—statutes require but do not define *solitary confinement* for death-sentenced prisoners. Idaho's statute states, "Whenever a person is under death warrant, execution of which has not been stayed, the warden of the prison in which the person is incarcerated shall keep the condemned person in solitary confinement until execution." Pennsylvania's statute provides, "Upon receipt of the warrant, the secretary shall, until infliction of the death penalty or until lawful discharge from custody, keep the inmate in solitary confinement." The Wyoming statute states that a death-sentenced prisoner shall be kept "in solitary confinement until execution of the death penalty."

Three state statutes—Washington, Texas and Florida—reference single cells. Washington's statute provides that a death-sentenced prisoner "shall be confined in the segregation unit, where the defendant may be confined with other prisoners not under sentence of death, but prisoners under sentence of death shall be assigned to single-person cells." Texas's governing statute calls for prisoners confined in "death row segregation" to be held "in single occupancy cells." Florida's administrative regulations require "single-cell special housing . . . of an inmate who, upon conviction or adjudication of guilt of a capital felony, has been sentenced to death."

Florida, South Dakota, and Texas call for death-sentenced prisoners to be segregated from the general prison population, although not necessarily from each other. The governing regulation in Florida provides, "Death row housing shall be separate from general population housing." South Dakota's statute directs that death-sentenced individuals "shall be segregated from other inmates at the penitentiary." In a general provision not limited to death-sentenced prisoners, Texas states that institutions "may not house inmates with different custody classifications in the same cellblock or dormitory unless the structure of the cellblock or dormitory allows the physical separation of the different classifications of inmates."

Administrative regulations in Oregon and Ohio reference "death row." Oregon regulations state, "It is the policy of the Department of Corrections to assign inmates with a sentence of death to the Death Row Housing Unit or to a Death Row status cell." Ohio's regulations provide both that prisoners sentenced to death "may be assigned to an area of the institution . . . which area shall be known as 'death row'" (and that "absent significant extenuating circumstances, no inmate shall be assigned to or housed in death row unless that inmate has been sentenced to death"), as well as that correctional officials

> may assign or reassign an inmate who has been sentenced to death
> to a security classification or special management status other than
> that which is normally used for such inmates, based on the security
> or medical and mental health requirements for the inmate.

Connecticut has legislation crafted in 2012 when the state legislature abolished the death penalty. In lieu of the death penalty, the statute created a new category, "murder with special circumstances," and specified certain conditions of confinement for individuals convicted under the statute. The Connecticut statute states that the Commissioner of Correction place "special circumstances" inmates in administrative segregation until reclassification.

In Alabama, California, Colorado, and New Hampshire, statutes name specific institutions at which death-sentenced individuals are to be housed. Alabama directs death-sentenced prisoners to the "William C. Holman unit of the prison system at Atmore"; California references San Quentin State Prison Colorado directs prisoners to the "correctional facilities at Canon City" after a death warrant is delivered; and New Hampshire names the "state prison at Concord."

In a few jurisdictions, statutes expressly state that corrections officials have discretion when making decisions on housing death-sentenced prisoners. For example, Louisiana's statute directs the Department of Public Safety and Corrections "to incarcerate the offender in a manner affording maximum protection to the general public, the employees of the department, and the security of the institution."

In sum, most jurisdictions do not have statutes mandating segregation, isolation, or other particulars related to the housing conditions provided to death-sentenced prisoners.

2. Visiting and Time Out of Cell

Some jurisdictions discuss visiting and out-of-cell time for death-sentenced prisoners. Colorado, Idaho, South Dakota, and Wyoming all state that a death-sentenced prisoner should be permitted visits with his lawyer, spiritual adviser, and family. Under Colorado's statute, prison "rules shall provide, at a minimum, for the inmate's attendants, counsel, and physician, a spiritual adviser selected by the inmate, and members of the inmate's family" to have "access" to the inmate. Idaho permits "access" to "the attorney of record, attending physicians, a spiritual adviser of the condemned's choosing, and members of the immediate family of the condemned." South Dakota, which requires segregation of death-sentenced prisoners, mandates that

> no other person may be allowed access to the defendant without
> an order of the trial court except penitentiary staff, Department of
> Corrections staff, the defendant's counsel, members of the clergy

if requested by the defendant, and members of the defendant's family.

Wyoming authorizes access by "physician and lawyers [and] . . . relatives and spiritual advisers of the prisoner."

The laws of Alabama, Indiana, and Pennsylvania address visiting and describe categories of individuals who may do so. Under Alabama's statute,

> while so confined, all persons outside the said prison shall be denied access to [a death-sentenced prisoner], except his physician and lawyer . . . , and the relatives, friends and spiritual advisors of the condemned person, who shall be admitted to see and converse with him at all proper times, under such reasonable rules and regulations as may be made by the Board of Corrections.

In Indiana, the death-sentenced prisoner's "(1) attorney; (2) physician; (3) relatives; (4) friends; and (5) spiritual advisor may visit the convicted person while the convicted person is confined." If a death warrant has been issued, Pennsylvania requires that death-sentenced prisoners be housed in solitary confinement and that, other than correctional staff, "no person shall be allowed to have access to the inmate without an order of the sentencing court," other than "counsel of record or other attorney requested by the inmate" and "a spiritual adviser selected by the inmate or the members of the immediate family of the inmate."

Most jurisdictions' laws do not address in-cell conditions or the number of hours that death-sentenced prisoners must spend in cell each day. A few—including Florida, Ohio, and Oregon—discuss out-of-cell time and certain other conditions. For example, Florida's regulations provide for a minimum of 6 hours per week of outdoor exercise. Ohio's regulations specify "five hours of recreation per week."

B. Policies Governing Isolation of Death-Sentenced Prisoners

Eighteen states had published policies addressing death-sentenced prisoners. Further, in jurisdictions where we could locate no official policy, we supplemented our knowledge by reviewing the Department of Corrections' websites or handbooks, as well as secondary sources such as reports in periodicals and law review articles.

Policies varied widely in terms of specificity and topics. For example, Ohio's policies do not require automatic assignment of death-sentenced prisoners to the highest security classification, which carries the most restrictive housing conditions. In Idaho, death-sentenced prisoners are initially placed in restrictive housing (also known as administrative segregation), and corrections officials must then conduct a hearing to determine if the prisoner can be moved to the less restrictive "close-restrictive custody." If remaining in segregation, the death-sentenced prisoner's placement must be reviewed "at least once a year" to decide if a shift to close-restrictive custody is appropriate. In contrast, as of the fall of 2015, in Virginia, death-sentenced prisoners were required under Department of Corrections' policy to be held in single-person cells and confined for 23 hours per day. According to news reports, when the Prieto litigation was pending, policy shifts occurred to allow death-sentenced prisoners some access to each other and to visitors.

C. Prior Research Regarding Death-Sentenced Prisoner Housing

This report is not the first to consider death-sentenced prisoner housing, which has been the subject of research focused specifically on the topic, as well as on solitary confinement more generally. Four such surveys, based on different information sources, are detailed below. The reports consistently portray corrections officials as housing death-sentenced prisoners in very restrictive and isolating conditions. In addition, some commentators have also raised questions about the necessity and the legality of isolation on death row.

In 2013, the ACLU published a report, *A Death Before Dying: Solitary Confinement on Death Row*, which was drawn from a survey of "advocates for death row prisoners and others knowledgeable about death row conditions." Based on responses about housing conditions in 26 states, the Report concluded that 93% of those states held death-sentenced prisoners in their cells for 22 hours or more per day. The cells ranged in size from 36 to 100 square feet; most were "the size of an average bathroom." Meals and medication often came through slots in the cell door, and death-sentenced prisoners were allotted an hour or less of exercise a day, alone in a small pen.

As the ACLU survey put it: "Many prisoners will go years without access to fresh air or sunshine." Policies on visits were highly restrictive. In most of these states, death-sentenced prisoners were not permitted to have physical contact with their visitors and, in some, prisoners were required to remain in arm and leg restraints during visits. In general, the ACLU found that prisoners were forced to live in a state of "extreme social isolation" and "enforced idleness" as the "overwhelming majority of states" did not provide access to work opportunities, educational programming, or vocational training.

In 2014, ASCA joined with the Liman Program to gather information on the numbers of people in isolation and the conditions in "administrative segregation," one form of restrictive housing. The resulting report, *Time-in-Cell*, was based on survey responses from 46 jurisdictions. Thirty-four of those jurisdictions—housing about 73% of the more than 1.5 million people incarcerated in U.S. prisons—provided data on all the people in restricted housing, whether termed *administrative segregation*, *disciplinary segregation*, or *protective custody*. In that subset, more than 66,000 prisoners were in restricted housing. Given that number, ASCA and Liman estimated that some 80,000 to 100,000 people were, in 2014, in restrictive housing settings in prisons. *Time-in-Cell* focused on conditions in administrative segregation across the country, demographic information regarding these prisoners, the length of prisoners' stay in administrative segregation, their weekly time in-cell, conditions within these cells, and segregated prisoners' access to recreation, programming, visits, and social contact. One subset of the survey's questions, answered by some of the responding jurisdictions, addressed the housing conditions of death-sentenced prisoners. Twenty-eight jurisdictions reported that death-sentenced prisoners were housed in administrative segregation or some other form of separation from the general population.

A third source of information comes from a 2013 ASCA survey, asking correctional directors about housing policies; officials in 29 states responded, providing jurisdiction-specific information. Two states, Maryland (which has since abolished the death penalty) and Missouri, reported holding death-sentenced individuals in the general population. Correctional departments in the other 27 jurisdictions all indicated that death-sentenced prisoners were held in some form of "segregated" or "other" housing. Of these 27 jurisdictions, 14 reported that segregated death-sentenced prisoners could engage in some form of congregate activity. In addition, 11 states indicated that death-sentenced individuals were permitted some movement without restraints. Twenty-five jurisdictions reportedly provided programming for death-sentenced prisoners.

Another survey, for the Death Penalty Information Center, conducted in 2008 by Professor Sandra Babcock working with a group of her students, compiled a state-by-state comparison of 31 jurisdictions based on interviews with capital defense attorneys and through materials published by various departments of corrections. This research identified 20 jurisdictions that held death-sentenced prisoners in cells for 22 hours or more per day. Eleven permitted death-sentenced prisoners to participate in group recreation, and nine provided some educational opportunities, occupational training, or work opportunities. Ten jurisdictions allowed contact visits with the prisoner's family, and 17 permitted contact visits with the prisoner's lawyer.

As noted, other commentators have also raised concerns about death-row housing. For example, in 2005, Andrea Lyon and Mark Cunningham reviewed analysis of the "mainstreaming" of death-sentenced prisoners in Missouri and argued that evidence of the success of that practice raised questions about the constitutionality of imposing profound isolation. More recently, Marah Stith McLeod also relied on the Missouri data as well as on other literature to argue that prison administrators ought not to have the discretion to impose the isolation of death row; given the severity of conditions on most death-rows, she argued that the democratic processes of legislatures ought to decide whether that form of punishment is necessary and just.

II. HOUSING ARRANGEMENTS
FOR DEATH-SENTENCED PRISONERS
IN NORTH CAROLINA, MISSOURI, AND COLORADO

We identified at least six states—California, Colorado, Missouri, Montana, North Carolina, and Ohio—that did not impose confinement of 20 hours or more in cells each day for death-sentenced prisoners. To learn more about the policies and their implementation, we chose North Carolina, Missouri, and Colorado, three states that varied in the size of their death-sentenced prisoner populations and in the degree of these prisoners' integration with the general prison population. We then reviewed their statutes, administrative regulations, and prison policies, as well as scholarly research, surveys, and media reports, and we interviewed administrators from each state's corrections department. Like many states, neither North Carolina nor Missouri has a specific statute or regulation governing the housing of death-sentenced prisoners. As noted, Colorado's statute leaves correctional administrators significant discretion by providing for incarceration at the correctional facilities at Canon City and for visiting by the prisoner's "attendants, counsel, . . . physician, a spiritual adviser . . . and members of the inmate's family."

Below, we begin with North Carolina, the state with the largest death-sentenced prisoner population—156 people—of the three. We interviewed Kenneth Lassiter, deputy director of operations for the North Carolina Department of Public Safety (NCDPS); he served as the warden at Central Prison, the facility holding male prisoners sentenced to death. In April of 2015, at the time of the interview, North Carolina's death-sentenced housing arrangement had been in place for over a decade.

We then turn to Missouri and the materials provided by George Lombardi, director of the Missouri Department of Corrections (MDOC), who was the director of adult institutions in 1989, when MDOC changed its policies on death-sentenced prisoners. Director Lombardi also coauthored a report on the transition. As noted, others have also done research on the Missouri "mainstreaming" practices; we had the benefit of a study by Mark D. Cunningham, Thomas J. Reidy, and Jonathan R. Sorensen, who compared the rate between 1991 to 2002 of violent misconduct by integrated death-sentenced prisoners to that of non–death-sentenced prisoners, as well as a follow-up study published in 2016 and reviewing 25 years of data.

To learn about Colorado, we interviewed Rick Raemisch, executive director, and Kellie Wasko, deputy executive director, of the Colorado Department of Corrections. Director Raemisch, who was appointed in 2013, instituted a series of changes in the housing of death-sentenced prisoners and for the general prisoner population.

As is detailed below, in each state, correctional officials praised their own systems, each of which enabled death-sentenced individuals to live with other prisoners. In each interview, the directors explained the reasons for and the process of transition and why they understood the reforms to be a success in terms of improving the lives of those in prison, lowering rates of violence, and reducing the challenges faced by staff.

A. North Carolina

North Carolina has one of the largest death-sentenced populations in the country, with 156 death-sentenced prisoners as of 2015. Since 1984, the state has executed 43 people. As of the spring of 2016, the last execution was in 2006.

According to Deputy Director Lassiter, North Carolina's death row policies have been in place for more than a decade. Deputy Director Lassiter recalled having looked into the history of death row during his time as warden of Central Prison; he reported finding no information suggesting that the prisoners had previously been held in a greater degree of isolation.

Deputy Director Lassiter explained that, as of 2015, the NCDPS housed 153 male and three female death-sentenced prisoners. The men were incarcerated in Central Prison and the women at the North Carolina Correctional Institution for Women, both in Raleigh. Men sentenced to death were placed in what was known as Unit III of Central Prison. Though they were housed separately from the general population, they were afforded roughly the same privileges as other serious offenders held in Central Prison.

Deputy Director Lassiter described Unit III as including eight cell pods. In each pod, 24 single cells opened onto a central dayroom. Each cell measured approximately 11 by 7 feet and was equipped with a bed, a sink, a toilet, a small writing table, a narrow window, and a radio. The dayrooms were outfitted with a television, several stainless steel tables, and showers. Death row prisoners could spend time and watch television in the dayroom together from 7 a.m. until 11 p.m.

Death-sentenced prisoners ate their meals as a group in a common dining hall at a different time than other prisoners. Individuals sentenced to death were permitted at least 1 hour per day to exercise in groups and to shower. Deputy Director Lassiter estimated that, depending on which unit activities were scheduled, the prisoners typically spent more than 1 hour a day in their recreation yard. Death-sentenced prisoners were also permitted to work jobs within Unit III, including as a barber, janitor, recreation clerk, and in the library, canteen, or clothes house.

North Carolina permitted two noncontact visitors each week. Access to religious services was within the unit. The religious services consisted of a 1-hour Christian worship service every Sunday, a 1-hour Islamic worship service every Friday, and a 90-minute Bible study class every Tuesday morning. Programming, such as working towards a GED, was not regularly available to death-sentenced prisoners, but Director Lassiter indicated that case managers would try to find volunteers to fulfill individual requests. In the case of a disciplinary infraction, a death-sentenced prisoner would be sent to what was called Unit I, the restricted housing unit, where he would eat meals, exercise, and shower apart from other prisoners.

Deputy Director Lassiter also explained that if an execution date were set, both male and female death-sentenced prisoners would be moved 3 to 7 days prior to the scheduled execution to the "death watch" area of Central Prison. The single cells in the death-watch area each had a bed, lavatory, commode, and writing table. The prisoner, who spent the entire day in the cell except 15 minutes for a shower, had no contact with other prisoners. Visits from attorneys, religious advisers, psychologists, and family were permitted; contact visits were at the warden's discretion.

Housing policies for death-sentenced prisoners had not been a subject of significant political debate. One brief flurry took place after a death-sentenced prisoner wrote a letter in 2012 to a newspaper and claimed that he enjoyed a luxurious life on death row. In response, legislators introduced a bill that would have banned television on death row. Deputy Director Lassiter, then the warden of Central Prison, testified that television served the department as a management tool. Although the bill came out of committee, it was not enacted.

Deputy Director Lassiter expressed unequivocal support for NCDPS's death row policies. He explained that prisoner-on-officer violence was nearly nonexistent on death row, and prisoner-on-prisoner violence was extremely rare. Death row had fewer disciplinary infractions, fewer fights, and fewer assaults than any of the other units at Central Prison. According to Lassiter, death row prisoners who subsequently had their death sentences commuted had better behavioral records in the general population than other prisoners.

Deputy Director Lassiter explained that "giving inmates an opportunity to create social connections with other inmates and providing some sense of normalcy is an important part of why our policies are successful." He acknowledged that some corrections officials believed that death-sentenced prisoners were inherently more dangerous, but said that North Carolina had a "totally opposite mentality." "Our inmates police themselves within their own community," he continued, "Part of the reason that works is that they are not isolated 23 hours each day." The mental health consequences of isolating death row prisoners were, from his point of view, likely to lead to more problems with violence and discipline than isolation solved.

Deputy Director Lassiter also believed that the relatively safe conditions on North Carolina's death row were in part because most of the prisoners no longer viewed death row as the place where they were going to die. "The majority of inmates sentenced to death ultimately don't end up being executed. The list of people removed from death row is a lot longer than the list of executions," he explained. Accordingly, death row prisoners had a strong incentive to behave well. Moreover, he noted that many death row prisoners were of a different profile than other prisoners at Central Prison. They were generally not habitual offenders but tended to have been convicted of a single, serious crime. Deputy Director Lassiter speculated that this difference in background helped explain the success of North Carolina's policies.

Deputy Director Lassiter noted that when he was the warden of Central Prison, he dined on a regular basis with the death row prisoners on Unit III, in part because they were his "favorite prisoners to interact with." He added that death row prisoners tended to be "extremely remorseful and take responsibility for what they have done and wish they could go back and change it. Generally, prisoners with a death sentence have a totally different view of life than another inmate." When asked whether he had ever considered changing North Carolina's approach to housing death-sentenced prisoners, Deputy Director Lassiter responded emphatically: "Our system is proven to work, and we have no desire to tweak it."

B. Missouri

As of January 2016, Missouri had 28 death-sentenced prisoners, all of whom were housed at the Potosi Correctional Center (PCC) in Mineral Point. Since 1989 and as of the spring of 2016, the state had executed 86 people. The state's last execution occurred in May 2016.

The housing system for death-sentenced prisoners in Missouri was designed in response to protest and litigation challenging the use of isolation and poor conditions. Before 1989, death-sentenced prisoners in Missouri were housed in a separate belowground unit at the now-closed Missouri State Penitentiary (MSP). Death-sentenced prisoners did not leave the housing unit for services, programming, or recreation; the limited program opportunities available were brought to the unit. Prisoners were allowed to exercise an hour each day in a separate area and were kept in 6- by 10-foot cells for the other 23 hours of the day. Director George Lombardi characterized conditions on death row in MSP as "marginal."

In August 1985, a class of death-sentenced prisoners at the Missouri State Penitentiary filed a lawsuit pursuant to 42 U.S.C. §1983. The prisoners alleged that the defendants, administrators in the MDOC, had violated their First, Sixth, Eighth, and Fourteenth Amendment rights. According to Director Lombardi, opposing this lawsuit seemed "futile."

On May 22, 1986, the parties initially entered into a consent decree intended to eliminate conditions that "may" have denied death-sentenced prisoners their constitutional rights. The consent decree included provisions to protect prisoners' access to legal mail, religious services, telephones, medical and mental health services, visitation, and recreation. The decree provided for specialized training for corrections staff, including administrative segregation training for custody staff and mental health care training for caseworkers. The consent decree also described a multi-tiered classification system for death-sentenced prisoners, with different custody or security levels, in which death-sentenced prisoners with good behavior could receive greater privileges. MDOC was also permitted, with court approval, to transfer death-sentenced prisoners to a new location. In 1989, with court approval, the MDOC moved all death-sentenced prisoners to PCC, a recently opened maximum security prison.

When death-sentenced prisoners were first moved to PCC, they were housed in a separate unit, with death-sentenced prisoners classified as minimum custody in one wing, and all other death-sentenced prisoners in another wing. Director Lombardi described PCC as better and cleaner than MSP but noted that staff still had to arrange for services to be brought separately to death-sentenced prisoners. Following the transfer, death-sentenced prisoners filed a motion for contempt to challenge conditions at PCC and their segregation from other prisoners.

While the renewed challenge was pending, administrators and staff in the MDOC began to consider better ways to manage death-sentenced prisoners and to provide them with a similar level of services as provided to the general population. The process of bringing meals and medical services to death-sentenced prisoners, as well as locking down the prison whenever these prisoners left their cells, was cumbersome. Director Lombardi stated that the idea that capital offenders were inherently more dangerous than other long-term prisoners did not make sense to corrections staff. The conversation developed into a discussion of the feasibility of integrating death-sentenced prisoners into the general population at PCC.

The full integration of PCC took place incrementally. Prison officials started calling death-sentenced prisoners "capital punishment inmates" and began to escort minimum custody death-sentenced prisoners to the dining room to eat with the general population. Death-sentenced prisoners were then given permission to visit the law library and to work in the laundry. For the first time, these individuals were classified using the Adult Internal Management System (AIMS). Prisoners were able to play softball together and did so without incident. By January of 1991, all individuals with capital sentences were mainstreamed into the general population. At the time, corrections staff "expressed surprise at the ease with which the transition occurred."

The transition was completed before the district court ruled on the plaintiffs' motion for contempt, and the defendants moved thereafter to vacate the consent decree. The District Court of the Eastern District of Missouri (to which jurisdiction had been transferred following the transfer of the prisoners to PCC) found that the defendants had complied with the requirements of the consent decree and that no unconstitutional conditions existed. The court vacated the decree and terminated its continuing jurisdiction over the matter. The prisoners appealed, but the Eighth Circuit affirmed the lower court decision.

As of the winter of 2015, all of Missouri's death-sentenced prisoners were housed at PCC. PCC houses death-sentenced prisoners, life-sentenced prisoners, and parole-eligible prisoners. As of 2015, the procedure for receiving and housing prisoners was that death-sentenced prisoners were transferred directly from courts and jails to PCC, a maximum security facility (Custody Level 5); non-death-sentenced prisoners were first sent to one of three diagnostic centers in the state to determine their custody level before being assigned to a facility. Once death-sentenced prisoners arrived at PCC, they were treated no differently than other prisoners in the institution.

Upon arrival at PCC, all prisoners were initially assigned to one of the administrative segregation units during their reception and orientation and could then be moved to a double cell in the transitional administrative segregation unit. PCC then used its AIMS classification system to categorize all prisoners into one of 13 housing units.

Prisoners could be promoted from the transitional unit to one of two "baseline" general population units, where they ate meals with the rest of the prisoners and could attend religious and educational services. If approved, prisoners could advance to one of the two general population units, where they had access to recreation and programming in large groups and could purchase a television and radio. Prisoners who were conduct-violation free for a certain period of time could be moved to the "honor dorm," where they were "out of their cells most of the day." Death-sentenced individuals could be double-celled with other general population prisoners, regardless of sentence.

Like the rest of the prison population, death-sentenced prisoners could be assigned to the protective custody unit, where they ate and participated in recreation as a group. Prisoners could be placed in the special needs unit, where they exercised and attended mental health programming separately but took meals with the general population. Correctional administrators assigned some death-sentenced prisoners who were not special needs to this unit for the purpose of ensuring a permanent single cell. Prisoners who had "difficulty in adjusting to institutional life" were placed in the partial treatment unit.

Death-sentenced prisoners had the same privileges and could access the same services afforded to all prisoners in their housing unit. For example, death-sentenced prisoners in the general population were allowed 8 hours of recreation each day and permitted to do crafts for 6 of those hours. PCC offered Narcotics Anonymous and Alcoholics Anonymous programs and vocational education programs. Prisoners at PCC could also participate in a dog adoption program that enabled prisoners to train dogs that had been held in shelters and could be adopted by people in the community. Death-sentenced prisoners could apply for jobs, access the commissary, enjoy equal access to visitation and phones, and visit the law library. Visitation hours were 3 days a week for 8 hours each day.

Unique to death-sentenced prisoners was their housing prior to execution: After an execution date was set, a death-sentenced prisoner was moved into protective custody. The prisoner was subsequently taken to a segregated holding cell 2 to 3 days prior to the scheduled execution.

Director Lombardi stated that mainstreaming death-sentenced prisoners eliminated the burdensome costs of maintaining separate death row facilities. PCC no longer had to assign staff to escort death-sentenced prisoners around the facility. There was no longer a need to arrange for death-sentenced prisoners to have access to health care and medications, psychological counseling, and the law library. Commissary hours, visitation days, and medical services access were expanded after the transition because separate time windows for death-sentenced prisoners were no longer required. Jobs in the laundry also became available for administrative segregation prisoners when death-sentenced prisoners gained access to all employment. Director Lombardi thought that the MDOC would incur less in legal expenses arising from prisoners' litigation about death row conditions.

Director Lombardi noted that in the prison as a whole, disciplinary infractions and violence had decreased after the integration of death-sentenced prisoners. He stated that while there was some initial skepticism, staff encountered no problems with the gradual process of integration and that he had generally found no difference between death-sentenced prisoners and other long-term prisoners. Additionally, Director Lombardi believed that because death-sentenced prisoners were no longer subject to automatic long-term administrative segregation, there were fewer mental health problems following integration.

Director Lombardi stated that it seemed that death-sentenced prisoners at PCC have slightly lower rates of assaultive behavior than other prisoners. Director Lombardi credited the incentive structure: Just like any other prisoner, a death-sentenced prisoner could be sent to administrative segregation for harming someone but could earn the highest level of privileges available with a good disciplinary record. Furthermore, most prisoners facing execution were still engaged in appeals or collateral attacks on their convictions, motivating them to avoid sanctions. Lombardi believed that such a system, in conjunction with services such as counseling and the dog adoption program, motivated death-sentenced prisoners to behave well.

Lombardi considered the integration of death-sentenced prisoners into the general population a success. He stated that integration is "so ingrained in the system now that it's no big deal. We don't even think about it." According to him, "We did the right thing, and it's proven time and again that it is the right thing."

C. Colorado

As of 2015, the Colorado Department of Corrections (CDOC) had a total of three death-sentenced prisoners, all male, who were housed at Sterling Correctional Facility in Sterling, Colorado, which was overseen by Warden James Falk. As of 2016, the last execution in Colorado was in 1997.

The question of solitary confinement has been an issue for the Colorado prison system for several years. Relatively few individuals were sentenced to death, but a significant number of other prisoners were held in isolation until 2011 when Tom Clements became the director of corrections. Under his leadership, Colorado reduced that population from more than 1,400 to about 700. After Director Clements was murdered by a former prisoner in 2013, Rick Raemisch, who had been the head of the Wisconsin Department of Corrections, was appointed; he continued Director Clements's efforts to lower the number of individuals in isolation.

Until 2014, Colorado housed death-sentenced prisoners in administrative segregation at Sterling Correctional Facility; no separate facility was provided for those with death sentences. At the time, administrative segregation was the most secure custody level in the CDOC. Prisoners were locked in their cells 23 hours a day, with 1 hour out for exercise and showering. Prisoners could not leave their cells unless they were in full restraints and escorted by at least two correctional officers. Meals, pharmaceutical, educational, and library services were delivered to the cells. Prisoners were permitted to have a television and 2.5 hours of noncontact visitation time per week.

Colorado reformed its housing policies for death-sentenced prisoners in 2014 as part of its more general effort to reduce reliance on administrative segregation. According to Director Raemisch, a long period of isolation is psychologically damaging and has the effect of "taking someone who has committed a very violent act and possibly making them more violent." Director Raemisch noted during our interview that, prior to reform

> Colorado had failed in its mission. . . . Its mission is not to run a more efficient institution, which is what segregation is for. Running an efficient institution is a noble goal, but the mission really is to protect the community. You don't do that by sending someone out worse than they came in.

By March 2014, CDOC had decreased the population held in solitary confinement to 577 and, as of the spring of 2016, to some 160 prisoners.

CDOC extended its reform efforts to death-sentenced prisoners. On March 4, 2014, Deputy Executive Director Kellie Wasko sent an e-mail to all CDOC employees announcing the planned introduction of a policy eliminating administrative segregation for death-sentenced prisoners. Director Raemisch noted that part of the impetus for this change was the long period that death-sentenced prisoners would likely spend living in Colorado prisons. While death-sentenced prisoners might never reenter the larger community, Director Raemisch viewed reform of those prisoners' conditions as an issue for the well-being of the prison community and its safety.

As a first reform, CDOC permitted the three male death-sentenced prisoners to be with each other; this change evolved into the current policy under which death-sentenced prisoners are housed with non-death-sentenced prisoners in a "close custody management control unit" (MCU), first housed at Sterling Correctional Facility in Sterling, Colorado, and, by 2016, at the Colorado State Penitentiary (CSP).

The discussion about reforming housing for death-sentenced prisoners originated in the upper level of CDOC, and administrators then sought feedback on the reforms from corrections officers. Director Raemisch called his staff's handling of segregation reform "amazing." He noted that they had achieved "a complete change in culture" in a short amount of time. Deputy Executive Director Wasko said that the biggest part of training staff on these reforms was to point out that death-sentenced prisoners were functionally the same as many others in the prison; staff were "already walking around with that type of offender [convicted of serious crimes of violence]. The only difference is the sentence. Several hundred inmates have life without possibility of parole."

As of the spring of 2015, death-sentenced prisoners were classified as "close custody" prisoners. Within the "close custody" classification, prisoners were placed into various status designations based on their management needs. Death-sentenced prisoners were designated to and housed in a close custody MCU. Prisoners in the MCU each had their own cell, measuring about 7 by 13 feet. Each MCU had about 16 prisoners, and both death-sentenced and non-death-sentenced prisoners could be housed together within the same MCU. Death-sentenced prisoners generally had the same living conditions and privileges as other close custody prisoners in the MCU. According to Wasko, "They are not identified as death-sentenced offenders. You couldn't pick them out. They are treated like all other prisoners in the management control unit."

As of 2015, MCU prisoners were permitted to leave their cells for a minimum of 4 hours a day, 7 days a week; prisoners spent 2 hours in the morning and 2 hours in the afternoon in groups of about eight prisoners, some of which was spent together in a dayroom. During such times, corrections officers, who were not physically in the dayroom, maintained visual contact at all times. Prisoners were permitted 4 hours of indoor or outdoor recreation per week.

In terms of the backdrop before the reforms under Director Raemisch, the Colorado prison system had also faced litigation (as had Missouri) about conditions for death-sentenced prisoners. In 2009, three individuals claimed that they had been subjected to cruel and unusual punishment because they were denied the opportunity for outdoor exercise for an extended period of time. The case was settled by the joint request of the parties under an agreement in which Colorado moved death-sentenced prisoners to Sterling so they could have access to outdoor recreation. At the time, Sterling Correctional Facility did not have outdoor areas for groups; recreation was available on an individual basis. As noted above, death-sentenced individuals were part of the MCU, and those prisoners were later moved to another facility, the Colorado State Penitentiary (CSP). That prison was the subject of another case, brought by a non-death-sentenced prisoner about its lack of outdoor recreational space. As of the spring of 2016, Colorado was building an outdoor recreation area for CSP; the expected completion date is in December 2016.

Returning to the rules for the MCU prisoners in general, Colorado permits six noncontact visits a month, each lasting 2 hours. After 30 days, MCU prisoners become eligible for no more than two contact visits (of no more than 90 minutes) per month. In addition to legal telephone calls, death-sentenced and other MCU prisoners could make eight 20-minute telephone calls per month.

MCU prisoners received meals in their cells. They were eligible for in-unit work opportunities. They were also eligible for in-cell programming through a television or self-service kiosk. While MCU prisoners were given access to religious guidance and publications from the prison Chaplain's Office, they were not authorized to attend group religious services or group programming. Director Raemisch expected that CDOC MCUs will continue to evolve and that more programming, such as cognitive behavioral therapy and anger management, will be added.

These reforms have encountered some political resistance. In 2014, in *The Complete Colorado*, an online political blog, a CDOC employee, a district attorney, and a relative of a victim of a Colorado death row prisoner all expressed opposition to the proposed reforms. Bob Beauprez, the 2014 Republican candidate for governor, also opposed the change and referenced it in advertisements criticizing the incumbent, John Hickenlooper, who was thereafter reelected, and the reforms continued.

Director Raemisch views the revised policies on housing of death-sentenced prisoners and the larger project of reforming segregation in Colorado as a success. In his view, the changes have had a positive effect on the demeanor and personalities of prisoners. Director Raemisch and his top administrative staff "believe that in the long run, this policy will lead to a safer facility. . . . All the evidence is pointing in that direction." Director Raemisch reported that prisoner-on-prisoner violence had stayed the same since the segregation reforms began and that prisoner-on-staff assaults were at their lowest since 2006.

When asked about the popular perception of death-sentenced prisoners as more dangerous because they have nothing left to lose, Director Raemisch explained that the CDOC "believes just the opposite." They "have no evidence to show that [death-sentenced prisoners] are more violent in the facility." Director Raemisch's sense was that, while "there may be a few inmates who are very dangerous," those inmates can be managed accordingly; their presence does not mean that isolation reform cannot be done safely. He and his administrative staff "all believe that people can change."

III. LOOKING FORWARD

This review of the laws and policies governing death-sentenced individuals makes plain that many correctional systems have a range of options when deciding on the conditions of confinement for death-sentenced prisoners. The correctional leaders in North Carolina, Missouri, and Colorado report the success of their systems. In addition, as discussed below, empirical work has been done on the Missouri system and in Colorado studies of the impact of reforms of solitary confinement are underway.

Specifically, the assessment by Director Lombardi that death-sentenced prisoners in Missouri were not more likely to commit disciplinary infractions than their fellow prisoners was confirmed in an analysis by Mark Cunningham, Thomas Reidy, and Jon Sorensen. The researchers reviewed incidents of violent misconduct by prisoners at PCC between 1991 and 2002, a period after the integration of death-sentenced prisoners.

That study compared the rate of misconduct by prisoners sentenced to death with that of prisoners sentenced to life without parole or to shorter prison terms. The researchers found that death-sentenced prisoners committed violent misconduct at roughly the same low rate as prisoners sentenced to life without parole. Both groups were also significantly less likely than parole-eligible prisoners to commit violent misconduct: Their rate was "about one-fifth of the rate of violent misconduct among parole eligible inmates." In addition, from 1991 to 2002, there were no homicides or attempted homicides committed by the death-sentenced prisoners. The authors concluded that the "practice of integrating death-sentenced inmates in the general population of a maximum-security prison is strongly supported by these findings" and that the findings undermined "conventional assumptions that death-sentenced inmates require super-maximum security protocols." The authors concluded that this demonstrated death-sentenced prisoners could be integrated safely into the general prison population.

In 2016, the authors published a follow-up report that relied on 25 years of data on the Missouri "mainstreaming" policy. The researchers evaluated 85 prisoners with capital sentences who were housed in the general population and 702 prisoners serving life-without-parole sentences, as well as 3,000 prisoners serving term sentences. The study concluded that those prisoners with capital sentences had "equivalent or lower rates of violent misconduct" than did either of the other sets of prisoners. In addition, the study found that "rates of violence among Missouri [death-sentenced] inmates were markedly lower after being mainstreamed than they had been under the prior era of heightened security conditions on 'death row.'" The researchers argued that the "failure of assumptions of high violence risk undergirding death row has important public policy and correctional implications." As the title *Wasted Resources and Gratuitous Suffering: The Failure of a Security Rationale for Death Row* reflected, the authors viewed their data as supporting a national change in policies to reduce the isolation of individuals serving capital sentences.

In sum, the mix of empirical work and reports of experiences of North Carolina, Missouri, and Colorado demonstrates that less restrictive, less isolating housing policies on death row have, in the judgment of correctional officials, contributed to the safety and security of prisoners and correctional staff alike.

Index

About the Editors

Hans Toch, PhD, is distinguished professor emeritus at the University of Albany at the State University of New York, where he is affiliated with the School of Criminal Justice. He obtained his PhD in social psychology at Princeton University, has taught at Michigan State University and at Harvard University, and in 1996, served as the Walker-Ames Professor at the University of Washington. Dr. Toch is a fellow of both the American Psychological Association and the American Society of Criminology. In 1996, he acted as president of the American Association of Correctional Psychology. He is a recipient of the Hadley Cantril Memorial Award (for *Men in Crisis*), the August Vollmer Award of the American Society of Criminology for outstanding contributions to applied criminology, the Prix deGreff from the International Society of Criminology for Distinction in Clinical Criminology, and the Research Award of the International Corrections and Prison Association. Dr. Toch's research interests range from mental health problems and the psychology of violence to issues of organizational reform and planned change. His books include *The Social Psychology of Social Movements* (1965, 2013), *Reforming Human Services: Change Through Participation* (with J. D. Grant, 1982), *Violent Men* (1992), *Living in Prison* (1992), *Mosaic of Despair* (1992), *The Disturbed Violent Offender* (with Kenneth Adams, 1994), *Police Violence* (with William Geller, 1996), *Corrections: A Humanistic Approach* (1997), *Crime and Punishment* (with Robert Johnson, 2000), *Acting Out* (with Kenneth Adams, 2002), *Stress in*

Policing (2002), *Police as Problem Solvers* (2005), *Cop Watch: Spectators, Social Media, and Police Reform* (2012), *Organizational Change Through Individual Empowerment: Applying Social Psychology in Prisons and Policing* (2014), and *Violent Men, 25th Anniversary Edition* (2017).

James R. Acker, JD, PhD, is a Distinguished Teaching Professor at the School of Criminal Justice, University at Albany. He earned his JD at Duke Law School and his PhD at the University at Albany. He is the author of *Questioning Capital Punishment: Law, Policy, and Practice* (2014), and coeditor of *America's Experiment With Capital Punishment: Reflections on the Past, Present, and Future of the Ultimate Penal Sanction* (3rd ed., 2014). He has written numerous scholarly articles addressing the death penalty, wrongful convictions, criminal law, and related subjects.

Vincent Martin Bonventre, JD, PhD, is the Justice Robert H. Jackson Distinguished Professor of Law at Albany Law School. He received his PhD in government, specializing in public law, at the University of Virginia; a JD from Brooklyn Law School; and a BS from Union College. He was a law clerk to Judges Matthew J. Jasen and Stewart F. Hancock, Jr., of the New York Court of Appeals. Between those clerkships, he was selected by Chief Justice Warren Burger to serve as a United States Supreme Court Judicial Fellow. He teaches, comments, advises, and has authored numerous works on courts, judges, and various areas of public law. Those areas include the judicial process, the Supreme Court and state high courts, criminal law, and civil liberties.

ML   9/2018